Praise for this edition of *Philosophy in Practice*

"If the first edition of Adam Morton's *Philosophy in Practice* wasn't the best introductory textbook on the market, this second edition surely is. Morton's approach to teaching takes into account what we have learned about learning and critical thinking over the past twenty years, and the text emphasizes *doing* philosophy as an integral part of learning it. The exceptionally useful *Online Teacher's Manual* goes to great lengths to guide pedagogy and maximize the efficacy of this innovative textbook. If you want an introductory textbook which makes it possible to teach philosophy as a verb to undergraduates, one that makes possible real conversation with beginners, this is it."

MICHAEL SILBERSTEIN, Elizabethtown College

"I find it hard to imagine that one could get very far into this engaging book without wanting to think through, for oneself, the core issues of philosophy. Fortunately, Adam Morton has also provided the basic resources one would need to deal responsibly with those great issues."

GARETH B. MATTHEWS, University of Massachusetts–Amherst,
author of *Socratic Perplexity and the Nature of Philosophy*

"This highly imaginative introduction to philosophy not only presents key ideas and arguments in an accessible and engaging way; it is an immensely valuable resource for activities in class that help students to see that they can themselves think philosophically."

ALAN MILLAR, University of Stirling

Praise for the First Edition

"This book is doubly unique. It engages students directly in the activity of philosophizing, leading them into the heart of important problems through stimulating exercises. And, it provides students with a unified account of a variety of philosophical issues."

ZEV TRACHTENBERG, University of Oklahoma

"The engaging enthusiasm of the author, and his delight in problems, puzzles, and arguments, crackles from page to page."

TIMES LITERARY SUPPLEMENT

Philosophy in Practice

An Introduction
to the Main Questions

Second Edition

Adam Morton

Blackwell
Publishing

BLACKWELL PUBLISHING
350 Main Street, Malden, MA 02148-5020, USA
9600 Garsington Road, Oxford OX4 2DQ, UK
550 Swanston Street, Carlton, Victoria 3053, Australia

First edition published 1996
Second edition published 2004 by Blackwell Publishing Ltd

Library of Congress Cataloging-in-Publication Data

Morton, Adam.
  Philosophy in practice : an introduction to the main questions / Adam
Morton. — 2nd ed.
      p. cm.
  Includes bibliographical references and index.
  ISBN 1-4051-1617-X (alk. paper) — ISBN 1-4051-1618-8 (pbk. : alk. paper)
  1. Philosophy — Introductions. I. Title.

  BD21.M67   2003
  100 — dc21

                                                          2003012193

ISBN-13: 978-1-4051-1617-6   — ISBN-13: 978-1-4051-1618-3

A catalogue record for this title is available from the British Library.

Set in 10/13 pt Photina
by Graphicraft Ltd, Hong Kong

Contents

Contents

Thanks

My ideas about how to teach philosophy have developed over many years. Teaching at Princeton, Ottawa, and Illinois at Chicago, I became convinced that beginning philosophy students need a less passive way of learning, so that the cognitive skills that are at the heart of philosophy can gradually develop. I began writing what I called "ear training" and "talking technique" exercises for my classes. But then at Bristol, Paula Boddington's brilliant teaching style opened up new possibilities for me. Much of this book is a development of the Boddington method.

Susanna Braund, Ross Cogan, Gill Heath, Rex Hollowell, Peter Howard, Hirsch Joshi, and Kevin Magill gave me valuable and sometimes devastating comments on drafts of this text. My first-year students at Bristol and Zev Trachtenberg's students at Oklahoma provided detailed and heartfelt criticism, and suffered teaching disasters with good humor. Zev's detailed comments on two different drafts were invaluable. Comments from teachers and students who have used the first edition were also tremendously helpful to me in preparing the second edition. Alan Millar's comments were particularly thorough and to the point. Special thanks to Bill Watterson whose intervention made possible the use of the cartoons.

The selections from Colin Turnbull's *The Mountain People* in chapter 4 are quoted by permission of Simon & Schuster and Random House.

This book is for Edith.

Note to Teachers

There is an instructor's guide for this book, giving advice on course-planning and on using individual sections in class. I strongly recommend consulting it before planning a course, and considering its advice on individual sections. It is available on the web at www.blackwellpublishing.com/pip.

The Contract

THERE IS NO POINT STUDYING PHILOSOPHY UNLESS YOU ARE PREPARED TO THINK FOR YOURSELF. You may be interested in philosophical issues like the relation of mind to body, the difference between right and wrong, and the meaning of life. You will not understand philosophical theories of these things unless you have yourself struggled with the questions. You may be interested in what the great philosophers – Plato, Aristotle, Descartes, Kant, Wittgenstein – have said. You will not understand what they have said unless you have thought some of their thoughts for yourself. You may just be wanting to get good grades in a philosophy course. Then the sad fact is that people with brilliant minds and amazing memories sometimes do not get the top grades in philosophy courses, because they have not tried to think for themselves.

Perhaps you want just to learn what philosophers have said and to understand the main philosophical theories, and don't want to do some real thinking. You don't want to find that some of your deepest beliefs may be challenged; you don't want to become puzzled by questions you are not given the answers to; you don't want to take the risk that at the end you may feel you know less than you did before. Then STOP. Don't read this book. Don't take a philosophy course. Study something else.

Perhaps you have firm religious convictions and you want philosophy to prove to you that they are the only beliefs that an intelligent person could have. Or perhaps you believe that science has the answers to all questions, and you want philosophy to prove that anyone with less than total faith in science is a fool. Then STOP. Don't read this book. Don't take a philosophy course. Study something else.

This book should help you to think for yourself. It should help you to see the difference between good thinking and bad. Good thinking is sharp, creative, and careful. It aims at finding out the truth rather than winning arguments or impressing people. Bad thinking is unimaginative and sloppy. Sometimes it is boring and sometimes it is flashy. It aims at impressing people. It hates to admit it might be wrong. My promise is that if you work through this book, ideally guided by a philosophy teacher and with discussion with other students in a group, you will at the end be a clearer, more careful, and more creative thinker. And you will appreciate the efforts and problems of philosophers who have tried to be clear, careful, and creative about the most difficult problems human beings can think about.

(If you are reading this book without a teacher, then you will have to be your own teacher. You may want to consult the website referred to in the note to teachers a couple of pages back.)

So, if you have got this far and did not stop at the STOP signs above, it is time to begin thinking for yourself. (1) to (6) below defend six claims. Each one makes a case for a belief. Think about each of them. Your reaction may be to reject the claim as ridiculous, even after reading the defense of it. After you have found your own reactions to all of them, see which of the four reactions (a) to (d) is nearest to what you think.

(1) Different people use the same words for colors, though they sometimes disagree, for example, whether something is blue or green. But each person's experience of colors is quite different from each other person's. For one thing, many associations are different: the colors of one person's mother's clothes and one person's toys are likely to be different from those of another. Also, the colors you see depend on the whole structure of your brain, and the detailed structure of different people's brains is different. So it is very likely that the experience one person has when they see a color is completely different from the experience someone else has when they see the same color.

(2) Christians believe that when people die their souls live on in heaven or hell. But this becomes very confusing when we look at a person's whole life and wonder which part of it is continued in heaven. Suppose that someone is a good, kind, nice-tempered person and then has a car accident and spends the last year of their life with a changed personality. For the last year this person is short-tempered, untruthful, and violent. Is it the earlier or the later personality that has an afterlife? One answer might be that both do. If God can give a person one afterlife then he can give them many. So it is possible that after our deaths our lives continue not from where they stopped but from all our living moments.

(3) Scientific theories change all the time. Once, scientists believed that all matter was made of tiny atoms; then in the nineteenth century they decided that matter was a continuous fluid-like substance; then in the twentieth century they went back to thinking that matter was made up of atoms. So in the future scientists could believe almost anything. The science of the next century might go back to thinking that the earth is flat and the sun goes round it.

(4) We value justice: we think that an unfair society ought to be changed. And we also value democracy: we think that people ought to have a lot of influence over who makes laws for them and what those laws say. But justice and democracy will always conflict. For people are full of jealousies and resentments of other people, and their kind instincts usually apply only to people close to them. So people will use their democratic power to

further their own interests and oppose the interests of others. The only way to get justice is to have impartial, wise rulers who give people what is right, not what the people think they want.

(5) Most of what we believe is unscientific rubbish. We are surrounded by folk remedies for diseases, folklore about what makes a happy life, and popular psychology about how to deal with our troubles. We believe in moral codes that we pick up unquestioningly from our parents. But there is very little evidence that any of these things are true. Most of the beliefs and morality of our time may seem to later ages to be superstitious nonsense.

(6) We value the earth and the life that it supports. But one of the main problems for the earth is the human race. There are so many humans that they exclude other species, and industrial societies cause ecological disasters. Humans are intelligent enough to love the earth and to see the harm they are doing to it. So one duty that humans can understand is the duty to reduce the damage to the planet. This will mean an earth with far fewer humans on it. It may mean that the earth would be best with no humans at all.

You may find some of these ridiculous. Probably some of them are ridiculous. You may also be surprised to find that different people find different ones ridiculous. And when you have finished this book you may have changed your mind about which ones are ridiculous. To see how different people react to them, classify each of them as one of the following.

(a) *Ridiculous*: this does not even make sense. No one could really believe it; (b) *Impossible*: although someone might believe this, there is no way it could be right; (c) *On the way to truth*: although I do not believe this the way it is stated here, I think there could be good reasons for believing something a bit like it; (d) *True*: I agree with this.

Write down your reactions in the table.

	Ridiculous	Impossible	On the way to truth	True
(1)				
(2)				
(3)				
(4)				
(5)				
(6)				

Now see whether other people have reacted in the same way. Try to find the people whose reactions are most different from yours.

The reactions to (3) and (5) are worth comparing. How do people who classify (3) as (c) or (d) classify (5)? (And the other way round. And how do people who classify (5) as (a) or (b) classify (3)?) Do people who react differently to (3) and (5) also have different reactions to some of the other claims? Which ones?

The reactions to (2) and (6) are also worth comparing. How do people who classify (2) as (a) or (b) classify (6)? Do people who react differently to (2) and (6) also have different reactions to some of the other claims? Which ones?

The contrast between (3) and (5) is different from the contrast between (2) and (6). Different reactions to (3) and (5) are very likely to be the results of differences of belief. So people who have different reactions to them should try to find out what beliefs each has that the other does not. Different reactions to (2) and (6) are more likely to be the results of differences of ways of thinking. So people who have different reactions to them should try to find out how they think differently, how they trust or are suspicious of different ways of thinking through problems.

You should save your reactions to the six claims. At the end of the book you may want to reconsider them. But reading this book, or studying philosophy, is not going to tell you whether they are true or false. This is important. People often think that when they study philosophy they will find some argument by some philosopher that will tell them what reality is really like or why the universe exists, or suddenly make sense of their lives. This may happen. Some people find Plato such a philosopher, some Lucretius, some Hume, and some Wittgenstein. But that is not the main point. The main point is to find out how to think about these and other important questions. Thinking about them may tell you that they have no answers, or that there are much more important questions to ask. But as your thinking becomes stronger and more confident you will hold on to your powers to think and discuss more than to the answers they give you. You may remain uncertain about the deep questions of life and the universe, but you will be more certain that you can think clearly, argue persuasively, and see through other people's bad reasoning.

Part I The Lure of Certainty

Here is an outline of the sequence of topics in Part I. At the beginning of each chapter this thread of prose will reappear in a way that shows the connection of the chapter with the whole of Part I.

Philosophers evaluate patterns of thinking. In particular, they have often tried to find patterns of thinking that will give certainty about the world and about morals. Philosophical doubt is a way of finding out which beliefs are not certain; and logical arguments are a way of going from one belief to another belief that is just as certain. Many philosophers have doubted beliefs that others have thought certain – for example, the existence of God – and other philosophers have tried to find logical arguments to support these beliefs.

Rationalist philosophers are optimistic that we can get certainty about the world or about morals by using logical arguments and similar kinds of reasoning. They consider extreme forms of doubt in order to prove how certain their beliefs are.

Can our beliefs about right and wrong ever be made completely certain? Some philosophers, rationalists about morals, try to determine with logical arguments what we must think right or wrong. But if the moral beliefs of a particular society can be shown to be right then the moral beliefs of other societies must be wrong. Moral relativists think that the moral beliefs of all societies are equally right and so they disagree with moral rationalism.

Can we have certain beliefs about the world around us? Many of our beliefs about the physical world cannot be supported just with logical arguments. Our evidence for them depends not on deduction but on induction. But thinking about induction suggests that very few beliefs about the physical world can be completely certain.

Thus it is unlikely that either our beliefs about morals or our beliefs about the world around us can ever be completely certain. Some philosophers think that this shows that reason is powerless. But reason is not powerless, since some uncertain beliefs are more reasonable than others. Once we see this we can begin to understand how we can live without certainty.

Aims of Part I

By the end of Part I you should be able to

◆ *understand the concepts of belief, certainty, reason for belief, logical argument, skepticism, moral relativism, moral rationalism, scientific rationalism, inductive reasoning, deductive reasoning;*
◆ *understand why philosophers have often wanted to find reasons that make scientific and moral conclusions certain;*
◆ *understand why later philosophers have concluded that certainty about many important matters cannot be obtained;*
◆ *understand why not being able to get certainty does not make skepticism or moral relativism inevitable.*

1 Certainty and Doubt

Introduction

PHILOSOPHERS EVALUATE PATTERNS OF THINKING. In particular, they have often tried to find patterns of thinking which will give certainty about the world and about morals. Philosophical doubt is a way of finding out what beliefs are not certain, and logical arguments are a way of going from one belief to another belief that is just as certain. Many philosophers have doubted beliefs which others have thought certain – for example, the existence of God – and other philosophers have tried to find logical arguments to support these beliefs.

Rationalist philosophers are optimistic that we can get certainty about the world or about morals by using logical arguments and similar kinds of reasoning. They consider extreme forms of doubt in order to prove how certain their beliefs are.

Can our beliefs about right and wrong ever be made completely certain?...

Chapter Objectives

By the end of this chapter you should be able to answer the following questions.

◆ *What is philosophical doubt?*
◆ *Why does the closed belief trap suggest the certainty assumption?*
◆ *What is the difference between skepticism and dogmatism?*
◆ *Why is a moral skeptic not always a cynic?*
◆ *What is Socrates' argument for skepticism?*

Definitions

The following words used in this chapter are defined in the list of definitions at the end of the book:

certainty assumption   metaphysics   skepticism
dogmatism   philosophical doubt

1.1 Patterns of Thought

Philosophy is thinking about thinking. (It is many other things too, as we shall see. But most of them connect with thinking about thinking.) We think about many things: what the world is like, what other people are thinking and feeling, what we should do. And when we think we follow patterns of thought. For example, you might be thinking what to do in a given situation. Then you might consider a list of options and try to discover the likely consequences for other people if you follow each one of those options. And then you might think whether one has the right to inflict those consequences on those people. That is a pattern of moral thinking. Another pattern of moral thinking might be to consult with more experienced or wiser people, and to do what they recommend.

Or – to take a very different example – you might be thinking what the weather will be like this season. (What sort of crop should you plant, and when should you plant it?) Then you might consult the Farmer's Almanac, which gives predictions for the year's weather on the basis of the weather in previous years and the behavior of animals. Or you might read many books on climate and weather, and many books on different plant species and on farming techniques, in order to try to make your own scientifically based prediction.

> Philosophical questions take a pattern of thinking and ask how it works and how well it works.

In each case one can ask: what are the advantages and disadvantages of thinking in this way? If people think out moral problems in terms of consequences and rights, are they going to lead happy and harmonious social lives? Are they going to do the actions which, in some absolute sense, are "the" right actions? (Is there any such sense?) If people think about the weather on the basis of the Farmer's Almanac are they going to get true predictions? Are they going to get useful predictions? These are philosophical questions, because they take a pattern of thought and ask how it works and how well it works.

You have to know what your purpose is before you can discuss the advantages and disadvantages of a way of thinking. Is the aim to discover truth? To lead a good life? To make everyone happy? To survive? Different ways of thinking may be good or bad for these different purposes. Philosophy is slightly obsessed with the aim of discovering truth. And that is an aim worthy of respect; it dignifies the human species. But it is worth remembering that we can ask hard questions about how discovering truth relates to other human purposes – and that the first concern of most animals and many humans is not to arrive at the truth but just to survive.

Two kinds of thinking are particularly important. One is the careful reasoning from evidence that is found in science. (Not that science does not use imagination and intuition as well.) Or, more generally, this kind of thinking is any logical thinking that is not based on fantasy or thoughtless obedience to authority, and that tries to establish in a step-by-step way what the world is like.

We can ask the same questions about this kind of thinking. When will it give true answers? How much of the truth about the world can it tell us? Are there disadvantages to thinking this way? (If someone concluded that science will give us false or incomplete answers then they might think that there is some other way of thinking that supplies more answers. Religion, perhaps. So then they might think that religious thinking has some advantages.) This would be a disadvantage of one kind of thinking, a limit to its powers, but not a disadvantage of another. So we are more likely to get some sensible conclusions if we ask about the advantages and disadvantages, or powers and limits, of particular kinds of thinking rather than of thinking in general.

The other important kind of thinking is the kind we use when we want above all to act as we ought to, to fulfill our obligations and to treat other people as they ought to be treated. This is moral thinking. It is particularly difficult when we have to make important decisions, where it is not obvious what the right thing to do is. Moral and political dilemmas face individuals and whole societies all the time. We think our way through these problems in a variety of ways. Several are discussed later in the book. Again, we can ask how well they work. We can pick some aim of decision-making – happiness, social harmony, or whatever – and ask whether people thinking through their decisions in some particular way will achieve this aim. And here another deep and important question arises. What are the right aims to choose? Does it make sense to ask what are the right decisions?

So philosophers pay most attention to two kinds of thinking – scientific, and moral/political. And there are reasons for thinking about these two kinds of thinking together, seeing how they combine and how they are different. One reason is that they can undermine or contradict one another. For example, scientific reasoning might show that human beings evolved from animals or that human psychology is based on desires for food, power, and sex. And this might destroy the foundations of the traditional moral codes that we rely on to solve social problems. Or an attractive way of making political decisions – for example, by democratic voting – might con-

A basic philosophical topic is the interaction of scientific thinking and moral or political thinking.

tradict a mathematical or psychological theory that says that this method will not work. (See the voting paradox in Box 2.) Conflicts are always possible between the ways we think out how things are, and the ways we think out how they ought to be. Boxes 1 and 2 describe two such conflicts. The only way to resolve them is to think about each pattern of thought and what can be expected of it.

Box 1 How Psychology Could Conflict with Ethics

We praise people when they do good things and blame them when they do bad things. But there are exceptions. When someone does something good by accident we do not praise, and when someone does something bad by accident we do not blame. If person A runs out in front of person B's car and is injured, we do not blame B if there was no way of knowing what A was going to do.

In the past hundred years we have learned how people are shaped by their early childhood. Some psychologists believe that by the age of four, basic facts about your personality are fixed in ways that you cannot easily change. Suppose that your early childhood determines you to react with anger to people in authority. Then it is as difficult for you not to lose your temper when a superior at work criticizes you as it would be for a driver to know that someone was about to run in front of her car. Suppose that you assault your boss when she tells you your work is terrible. Should you be blamed for what you have done? You could not have helped it.

Psychological theories of this kind may be false. Or they may be true. But suppose such a theory was true. Would this show that we ought not to blame people for what they do? Would it make us think that there was little difference between drivers involved in accidents they could not anticipate, and people who assault others? Finding out how we would change our beliefs about right and wrong, praise and blame, if we came to think that people have no choice over their actions is a typical philosophical problem. It is philosophical because it involves comparing very different ways of thinking, and seeing how they are related. (Free action is discussed in Chapter 14, Sections 4 to 7.)

Box 2 A Voting Paradox

We have three people, and they have to choose between three candidates for dog catcher.

Alice's preferences are: 1st choice Mark, 2nd choice Luke, 3rd choice John.
Bella's preferences are: 1st choice Luke, 2nd choice John, 3rd choice Mark.
Carol's preferences are: 1st choice John, 2nd choice Mark, 3rd choice Luke.

So a majority – Alice and Carol – prefer Mark to Luke. And a majority – Alice and Bella – prefer Luke to John. So it might seem that the top candidate should be Mark, then second Luke, and third John. But wait a moment: a majority – Bella and Carol – prefer John to Mark. So what seemed like the bottom candidate is preferred to the top candidate.

Suppose they first vote between Mark and Luke, and then between the winner and John. Luke will be eliminated; John will beat Mark and get the job. Suppose that they first vote between Luke and John, and then between the winner and Mark. John will be eliminated; Mark will beat Luke and get the job. So who wins depends on the order in which the votes are taken.

Does this show something wrong with democratic voting?

1.2 How Conventional Are Your Beliefs?

Most people believe most of the 14 claims on the list below. (Most people you are likely to know, that is.) So you very likely believe most of them. But it is unlikely that you believe all of them. To see whether you have a very ordinary or a rather unusual set of beliefs, ask yourself whether you agree or disagree with them.

In each case you should score your reactions 1–5 as follows: (1) strongly agree, (2) tend to agree, (3) no opinion or don't know or can't decide, (4) tend to disagree, and (5) strongly disagree. (You may think some of them are too vague or unclear to have an opinion about. In that case score 3.)

(a) There is no intelligent life on the other planets of our solar system.
(b) Germs, viruses, and other tiny living things cause many diseases.
(c) People who act kindly to others are usually happier than those who act cruelly.
(d) This universe is the only one there is.
(e) It is wrong to inflict pain on other animals for no good reason.
(f) Humans may kill animals in order to eat them.
(g) A human life is not complete if it does not include some religious or spiritual aspect.
(h) There really are chairs and trees around us, but numbers and geometrical shapes are simply things we invented to help us think.
(i) Children do not have the same rights as adults to make important decisions for themselves.
(j) The earth is a very small and not very central part of the whole physical universe.
(k) The lives of all people are equally valuable.
(l) Most of what is written in science textbooks is true.
(m) We can be completely sure that the chairs and trees around us really exist, but the electrons and quasars discussed in physics may turn out to be illusions.
(n) People who commit crimes of violence should be punished, whether or not this makes them less likely to commit more crimes.

Now add up the numbers corresponding to your reactions to the fourteen claims, and use your score to compare yourself with three intellectual personality types.

Type A people have beliefs that are very similar to those around them. They may have grown up among people who are very certain in their views, and who have never questioned their beliefs. Or they may have reflected deeply and decided that the views of their society are in fact right. A type A person might score 30 or less on these questions. (A score of 20 or less suggests that a person agrees with most people more than most people do!)

Type B people have normally conventional beliefs. They do not disagree much with what most people around them think, but they have been exposed to some influences from beyond their immediate upbringing and they take some of these influences seriously. A type B person might score between 31 and 42 on these questions.

Type C people have slightly unconventional beliefs. Because of influences on them, or their experiences, or because of their own thinking, they suspect that some important beliefs of the people around them might be wrong. A type C person might score between 43 and 54 on these questions.

Type D people have radically unconventional beliefs. They may have thought very deeply in a way that makes them think differently from most people. Or they may be in rebellion against their upbringing. A type D person might score between 55 and 70 on these questions. (A score of 60 or more suggests that a person may disagree with others so much that it is sometimes hard to communicate with them.)

Do you recognize yourself in any of these types? If so, does your score on the questions agree? If not, why? Would different questions have revealed something that these questions miss?

A more subtle diagnosis

If your score suggests you are type A or type B, look again at your answers to (a), (d), (j), and (l). If the score for these adds up to 6 or less it might be fair to describe you as a scientific dogmatist. You think that contemporary science is the best and last word on the way things are. Then look again at your answers to (c), (g), (i), and (k). If the score for these adds up to 6 or less it might be fair to describe you as a moral or religious dogmatist. You think that the beliefs you were raised with about what is valuable are not to be doubted.

If your score suggests you are a type C or type D, look again at your answers to (a), (b), (d), and (j). If the score for these adds up to 20 or more then it might be fair to describe you as having an alternative belief system. Your beliefs may come from some source or authority different from those of most people. If on the other hand your score suggests you have slightly or radically unconventional beliefs and your score for (a), (b), (d), and (j) does not add up to 20 or more, then it might be fair to describe you as an individual thinker. You make up your own mind about what to believe.

Note: This was a very short and simple questionnaire. It could easily give a wrong description of your beliefs. If you think the description is wrong, find three beliefs that you would agree with but that someone who truly fitted the description would not agree with.

Studying philosophy is not going to tell you which of the 14 beliefs listed above are true. What it can do is to show you how to think out disagreements about things like these. And it can help you to discover the deeper causes of disagreements about things like these.

Type A and B people should consider whether it is really so likely that so many of the beliefs that people happen to hold at this moment in time are true. Thinking about the reasons why some philosophers are skeptical about knowledge and about morals should help with this.

People with an alternative belief system should consider whether the reasons they have for their beliefs would really stand up to some hard questioning. Thinking about why philosophers usually find a way out of really profound skepticism should help with this.

Individual thinkers should consider whether their own powers of thinking are really enough. Can you really think everything out for yourself? Thinking about the reasons many philosophers have for thinking of human reason as a feeble and fallible tool should help you with this.

And whatever your position or personality, you will want to be able to defend your beliefs. Defending your beliefs may involve finding a few that are weaker than the rest and that have to be sacrificed for the good of the whole. To do this you need to develop your powers of argument, and you need to know what attacks on your beliefs to expect.

If you are reading this in a classroom context you might pause to find out the answers to the following questions:

◆ What is the average score for your whole class or group on the questions?
◆ Which intellectual personality type – A, B, C, D – do the greatest number of people fall into?
◆ How many are surprised at the number of people of different types from themselves?
◆ What reasons do people with conventional beliefs give for people having unconventional beliefs?
◆ What reasons do people with unconventional beliefs give for people having conventional beliefs?

Note: Although most people now believe most of the 14 claims listed above, many people do not believe some of them. And most people in some cultures in the past have disagreed with many of them. Moreover, philosophers have given thought-provoking reasons why we should not believe some of them.

Each of (a), (b), (c), (d), (f), (j), and (k) would have been strongly disagreed with by most people in some culture in the past. And for each of (d), (e), (g), (h), (i), (j), (k), (l), and (m) there is some great philosopher who has argued that it is false.

1.3 Conviction, Opinion, Doubt, and Belief

Separate the following claims into (a) convictions (that is, things that you are absolutely sure are true); (b) opinions (that is, things you think are true, though you are not absolutely sure); (c) conjectures (that is, things that you think might be true); and (d) doubts (that is, things that you think are probably not true). You can record your answers by putting (a) to (d) in the second column of the list below.

Claim	Score (a)–(d) here	Score (i)–(v) here
(1) Washington is the capital of the USA		
(2) Each human being has a destiny that they must follow		
(3) $38 + 12 = 40$		
(4) Murder is wrong		
(5) There is a God		
(6) Dinosaurs once lived on the earth		
(7) Everything in the Bible is true		
(8) People should never tell lies		
(9) People are born again in other bodies after their deaths		
(10) Water is a compound of hydrogen and oxygen		
(11) The moon is a satellite of the earth		
(12) Greed and selfishness usually lead to a happy life		
(13) Democratic government is the only way of having a fair society		

Check whether other people (for example, others in your classroom or discussion group) classify these into convictions, opinions, conjectures, and doubts in the same way that you do. Do not discuss your disagreements directly, but see if you can trace them to deeper disagreements about the value of different patterns of thought. Some of these patterns of thought are listed as (i) to (vi) below:

(i)   reliance on religious authority;
(ii) reliance on textbook science;
(iii) believing what most other people believe;
(iv) reasoning from evidence by the scientific method;
(v)   generalizing from your own experience;
(vi) trusting your own intuitive convictions.

Are there other patterns that may be partially responsible for your disagreements?

Choose four claims from the list of 13 above that you and others classify differently. Now go back to the list, and in the third column write the number

of the pattern of thought (from (i) to (vi)) that is most relevant to the disagreement. Discuss with others before you make your choice.

If several groups have carried out this exercise they may find that each group has identified different patterns of thought. Why is this?

Are there items on the list that you classify as both conjectures and doubts? Is this because you are pulled one way by one pattern of thought and another by a different one? Which ones?

Philosophers use the word "belief" in a slightly special way, so that conjectures and doubts are not beliefs, and opinions and convictions are beliefs. A belief is, roughly speaking, anything you will say "yes" to if asked if it is true. So, using the word "belief" in the way philosophers do, which of (1) to (13) do you believe?

1.4 Trusting Textbooks

Consider the pattern of thinking summed up by this rule: believe *only* what you can find in school textbooks of physics and chemistry. Suppose that you do not doubt the truth of anything in these books. What problems might still arise about this rule?

Here are some problems that might arise. Which ones are the most serious problems?

(a) Perhaps these "bibles" cannot be used without information derived from other sources.
(b) Perhaps there are important questions that they will not give answers to.
(c) Perhaps some claims in some textbooks contradict some claims in other textbooks.
(d) Perhaps the rule "believe only what you can find in school textbooks of physics and chemistry" is not itself found in any such textbook.
(e) Perhaps just from reading the textbooks you cannot know what they mean. (Perhaps they need interpretation.)
(f) Perhaps there are alternative interpretations of the textbooks.

Here are some situations where these problems might arise.

(1) You want to know what kinds of food will be tasty.
(2) You want to know what color the statue on your aunt's mantelpiece will turn if you drop it in a vat of sulphuric acid.
(3) You want to know if you should make your career in corporation law or in famine relief.
(4) You want to know how many gallons of fuel your car will use in an hour, but your textbooks describe everything in liters and meters.

(5) You want to know why some people have more energy than others.

(6) You find a book about what substances are found in various foods, without a title or preface identifying it as a chemistry or physics book, and you want to know if you should believe what it says.

Which of the problems (a)–(f) are likely to arise in which of the situations (1)–(6)? For example, problem (2) is likely to arise in situation (a), because the textbook is not going to tell you what the chemical composition of the statue is. (Some problems may occur in more than one situation, and in some situations more than one problem may occur.)

There are many questions that you can ask about a pattern of thinking besides "Does it give true conclusions?" Some such questions are: "Can people actually think in this way?" "How much understanding will thinking in this way give?" "What effects will thinking in this way have on people's lives (what is the cost)?" "Is there a better way of solving whatever problems the thinking deals with?" There are many others.

1.5 Certainty: the Closed-belief Trap

Patterns of thinking are ways of changing our beliefs or desires. Astronomers think about the stars they see in the sky and come up with beliefs about the universe; political thinkers consider the problems of their societies and come up with suggestions about desirable ways out of them. How do we know that the beliefs we come up with are true, and that the desires we come up with are for anything worthwhile? We could look for evidence. But that could be wrong too. The stars we think we see in the sky could be illusions; and we could be wrong about the nature of our social problems and the consequences of our proposed solutions. We are always judging beliefs and desires against other beliefs and desires.

Are the things people normally believe just a delusional system that everyone shares? To show that they are not, philosophers often try to show that some of our beliefs are absolutely certain.

"So what?" you may say. How else could it be? But this situation is responsible for a worry that lies behind many philosophical projects. The worry is that our beliefs and desires may form a closed self-sustaining system, like an incurable delusion or a closed-off ideology. Let me describe this worry in more detail.

Suppose someone has paranoid delusions. She thinks that everyone is plotting against her and trying to cause her harm. You try to explain to her that this conviction is ruining her life, and urge her to get some treatment. But of course she just thinks you are saying this for some purpose of your own, which will result in harm for her. Whatever you say will be twisted by her to fit her delusions.

Next consider a group of people with a group ideology. They have some strange beliefs, perhaps that aliens are going to save them from a flood that will devastate the earth. Every piece of evidence that is presented to them can be either interpreted as supporting this belief, or rejected as an attempt to deceive them. Their beliefs give the group cohesion, and support strong emotions of solidarity and suspicion. The combination of the structure of the belief and the structure of the group means that it is extremely hard to persuade members of the group to have the slightest doubt about their shared ideology.

In both these cases a whole system of beliefs is immunized against refutation. It has ways of adapting or ignoring any evidence or argument used against it. So if it contains false beliefs, they will never be discovered by someone still in the grip of the system. Someone remaining in the grip of the system will have the comfort of thinking that they are right and everyone else is wrong, while in fact their beliefs are full of errors. But someone who escapes from the grip of the system will feel a sudden rush of liberation, as if their eyes had suddenly been opened.

The deep philosophical worry is this: we don't think we are caught in any such closed-belief trap. Our eyes feel open. But then that is just what we would think if we were caught in a self-sustaining delusion. How can we be sure that our normal system of beliefs, including beliefs about the world around us, beliefs about right and wrong, beliefs about our political ideals, and many others, do not form such a system? If we were really fundamentally wrong about the universe, and about right and wrong, would we ever find out? (To think more about this, work through Section 1.7.)

There is no doubt that we do usually interpret evidence, new beliefs, in terms of the beliefs we already have. So, for example, if you seem to see a purple and green striped elephant suddenly appear and dance on its trunk around the room and then disappear, you are likely to dismiss this as an illusion or a hallucination. (Why? Because without even knowing it you have the belief that there are no purple and green striped elephants, and that people who seem to see what does not exist are suffering from illusions or hallucinations. If you had been raised in a different culture you might have thought that you were really seeing a particularly vivid manifestation of the elephant god.)

And if you are deciding what you should do in a difficult situation you rely on the values you absorbed from your society as a child. And the emotions you feel in response to a situation are affected by the models and ideals presented to you by your culture. What is the difference between this and a group delusion? (To think more about this, work through Section 1.6.)

Many philosophers have wanted to show that some beliefs and values are not just self-sustaining delusions. (Sometimes they have wanted to defend the beliefs and values of their time and place, sometimes some beliefs and values that they have invented for the purpose.) In doing this they have often made an assumption, which I shall call the *certainty assumption*. It is that the way to show that beliefs are not illusions of this kind is to show that they are *certain*, that we can be absolutely sure they are not false. We can show that there is no way they could be false. If we can convince ourselves that a belief is certain in this way – better still, if we can show that it is part of a system of beliefs all of which are certain – then we know that in believing it we are not falling into a delusional trap.

The certainty assumption is very demanding. It is extremely hard to know that something you believe couldn't possibly be false. And it is important to see that the assumption is not in any way forced on us. We don't have to make it. Still, philosophers have put a lot of effort into showing that their chosen beliefs are certain: beliefs about the world, beliefs about mathematics, beliefs about political systems, or beliefs about how we should act. And it is clear what the appeal of the assumption is, why it is so tempting. For *if* we could show that a central core of our beliefs were absolutely certain then we could conclude that we were not doomed to remain in some delusional system.

The certainty assumption has an emotional as well as an intellectual appeal. For many people grow up with a very definite set of religious and moral beliefs, which structure their lives. Without them they would be lost. If you have grown up in such an atmosphere of certainty then you will not trust beliefs that are not certain. Ideally, you want to show that your own religious and moral beliefs are certain. As a second best, you might want some other set of beliefs that is just as comfortingly sure. Then you would not be lost.

Part I of this book starts with seeing what happens when we make the certainty assumption. Then we will see some reasons why it is dubious; why certainty is very rare in both science and morals. The questions we are asking here concern the sources of conviction and of doubt – what general systematic things can we say about what makes a belief certain and what makes it doubtful? Eventually we will be able to see how to discuss belief and delusion without making the certainty assumption.

1.6 Cheat: a Story about Deception

Last week, three of us were playing cards late at night. We were Hilary, Robin, and Sammy – I'm not yet going to tell you which one I was. We were playing Cheat, which is a game that little children often play, but if you are really smart and subtle like me you can find a special smart and subtle interest in it.

Cheat works like this. You deal out the deck among all the players. Then one player starts by putting down a card, face down, and says what it is. Then each player in turn has to put up to four cards, face down, on the growing pile. The cards have to be all the same and in sequence with what the previous player put down: so if the last cards were sevens you have to put down eights or sixes. Or at any rate you have to *say* that you have put down eights or sixes. The aim is to get rid of all your cards before anyone else does. So if you have only one eight, or no eights at all, you might put down four cards and say they were eights. Anyone who thinks you are lying can challenge you by saying

Box 3 Quixotic Doubt

Vivid examples of the false-belief trap are found in several works of literature. Cervantes' Don Quixote, a classic of Spanish literature, is a good example. It concerns Don Quixote, a Spanish nobleman living after the age of chivalry, who has immersed himself in the mystique of knights on horseback doing brave deeds and rescuing innocent maidens. He lives in a social world where these ideas are not recognized, but he insists on traveling around acting like a chivalrous knight. He is accompanied by his servant, Sancho Panza, who is a sensible and down-to-earth person. On many occasions Quixote interprets what is happening in terms of the completely inappropriate concepts of chivalry. He sees windmills as giants and charges at them. When the sails of the windmills turn and strike him he takes this as confirming his belief, as the "giants" have moved their giant arms. He sees a flock of sheep as the dust made by two armies going into battle and rides off to join the losing side, and when the shepherds try to stop him from riding into their sheep he takes this as more evidence that he is in a battle. He sees a man walking along with a basin over his head to protect himself from the rain, and interprets this as an enemy in an enormous helmet. When the peculiar size and shape of the helmet is pointed out to him he makes up an elaborate story about the kind of foreigner who would have such a helmet. When Sancho suggests that the helmet looks a lot like a basin he replies that a helmet that looks like a basin must be repaired, so he must take it and get it restored into proper helmet shape.

Many stories have fools in them, who believe ridiculous things. But Don Quixote is no fool. His strange beliefs come from his thinking too much, and too elaborately. He can reinterpret any evidence to suit him. He does so because he is the prisoner of some beliefs, the ideas of chivalry, that shape all his thinking. As the book develops, the sensible Sancho is caught up in his master's delusions, and very often his common sense is not enough to protect him from the power of Quixote's imagination. Cervantes wants the reader not only to laugh at Don Quixote and Sancho Panza, but also to have a sense of troubling recognition: are all of us not like them?

"Cheat!" If you were lying you have to pick up the whole pile. But if you were telling the truth the person who challenged you has to pick it up. I'm sure people all over the world play versions of this game, whatever names they call it.

Well, we were in the middle of a game, and I was doing quite well. I was down to four cards in my hand, when the person to my right put down four cards and said "four threes." I was pretty sure four threes had already been played and were sitting there in the pile. So I cried out "Cheat!" And, what do you know, I was wrong – they were four honest threes. So I had to pick up about twenty cards. This made me think why it was hard to know whether the other person was telling the truth. The problem is that you know what cards are in your hand, but you don't know which of the other players has which of the other cards. And you don't know what is in the deck. If you have two threes and the other person says they are putting down three threes you know they are lying, but if they say they are putting down two threes you just don't know.

So I decided to be very careful. The pile was starting again from nothing now, so I memorized all the cards people were putting down. I'm really organized in my head, so I can do that. And I didn't accuse anyone of lying unless I knew that the cards in the pile and the cards in my hand made what they said impossible.

Then the most amazing thing happened. The person to my right – same sneaky person – put down three cards and said "three jacks." Well, that very person had put down three jacks the time before. And it sure wasn't a six-jack deck. So I called out "Cheat!" But when the cards were turned over they were three jacks. Since I had to pick up the pile I searched through it to see what had happened for the last twelve moves. (They got a bit impatient about this, but it was my house and my beer and my cards.) What I discovered was that my sneaky neighbor had been lying even when she could have told the truth. Not the play before but the one before that, she had had to put down jacks or nines, and had three jacks in her hand, but she had put down two nines and a five and said they were three jacks. Why? Just so that next time round she could put down three jacks and sucker me into calling her a liar. It was when she was telling the truth that she was fooling me.

From that point onward I played as sneakily as I could, trying to get even. I never told the truth at all. And they kept calling "Cheat" on me. I figured out why. Since I was lying all the time they knew I was lying all the time, even when they couldn't prove it directly. So I got sneakier yet, and decided to lie every third move. But just as I was getting into this, Hilary played her last card and the game ended. I had the most cards in my hand so I had to write all three term papers due the next morning. It only took me an hour.

While I was writing the term papers (a philosophy course – I can handle that stuff with half my mind, or maybe a quarter), we talked about how to play Cheat. I had already figured out Sammy's strategy. She would lie when she could tell the truth, so that when she was telling the truth you would think she was lying. I thought that was pretty tricky, but Hilary's strategy was even trickier. She told the truth nearly all the time, so whenever you challenged her you were wrong and had to pick up the pile. Then when she didn't have the right card she would coolly put down another card and call it what someone else had put down about twelve moves before, and no one would dare challenge her. They'd always figure it was the other person who had been lying. They'd even think that perhaps they had been lying when they hadn't.

Next morning I went to class – a 9 a.m. class – to deliver the essays. But it had been cancelled! I could have waited until next week to write the papers. And there on the blackboard was a message from Hilary and Sammy, saying

"Hi. Hope you like our little trick." And they had written it the previous evening. The cheats.

This made me think. If they could fool me they could fool anybody. Just about. And maybe more people were fooling me. Especially if they used Sammy's trick: lying when you don't have to, just to set up suspicions about what is actually the truth. And maybe some people were using Hilary's strategy, telling the truth until something crucial comes along, and then lying. And suppose my parents and all the people around me had been doing this all my life?

These thoughts really upset me. I began to doubt everything everyone said to me. I began to sleep badly. I stopped reading newspapers because I didn't trust them. So I went to the student counselling service and had an interview with a counsellor. He persuaded me that there was no point doubting everything because you just go crazy that way. I found this quite comforting, and the counsellor said he'd tell me more next time but we had to stop now because he had to go see an urgent case – a suicidal student. I walked back to my room, but on the way I saw the counsellor going into a restaurant with Sammy.

For all of the next day I decided to be the only person who always told the truth. But then I thought, "if everyone is lying to me then most of what I believe is false." And even the people who are talking straight to me are passing on information from others, who might be lying. So when I try to tell the truth I am just passing on more lies. It would be more honest to lie all the time. So that's what I do now. In fact this story never happened; it's a lie too. And though you think you know my name is Robin, and Hilary and Sammy are girls, and that Sammy was sitting to my right at the game, that's a lie too. Or maybe it isn't.

1.7 Tree-worshipers and Flat-earthers

Tree-worshipers

Consider the tree-worshipers. They are an ancient and very civilized culture whose beliefs are (probably) quite different from yours. Their system of beliefs is centered on a faith in the power of trees. The wind blows because trees wave their branches and fan it along; winter comes because trees drop their leaves and thus allow heat to flow out of the earth along their twigs; people can think and feel, though in a way that is crude compared to the thoughts and emotions of trees, because the structure of their nerves resembles the root-system of a tree. (So they describe their emotions in terms of, for example, feeling parched, feeling buds forming, wanting pollination, and so on.) The history of the universe is best understood in terms of a primal acorn growing in cosmic dust until it becomes a branching tree-structure of galaxies. Whenever you ask them "why?", the "because," for the tree-worshipers, involves some reference to what trees can do.

Imagine that you are a modern scientifically minded person, and that you find yourself living among the tree-worshipers. You want to persuade them that their views are wrong. For example, you might point out that winter and summer also occur in some deserts where there are no trees. Or you might propose an experiment in which trees are cut down in order to see whether the wind becomes less strong.

Think of three more such points you could make which might show them weaknesses in their view of the world. State each in one or two sentences. State them right here.

(1) _____

_____

(2) _____

_____

(3) _____

_____

But the tree-worshipers could have answers to these points. For example, they could reply to the objection that summer and winter happen in deserts by saying that in winter the heat in the earth beneath desert regions is drained through the leafless trees of nearby tree-rich regions and by the wind. That is one reason why trees make wind: they want to blow air over deserts and the sea to cool them down. And typically there are stronger winds in winter. And they could refuse even to consider any experiment involving cutting down trees, on the grounds of the harm caused to these sacred creatures.

What answers might they make to your three points? Actually state answers they could give. Write down one-sentence answers they might make to your (1), (2), (3) above. Write them below. And below each, write a reply you might make to their answer.

reply to (1)   _____

response to reply _____

reply to (2)   _____

response to reply _____

reply to (3)   _____

response to reply _____

(An alternative method is for each person to write (1), (2), (3), then pass them to another person for replies, and then to a third for responses to the replies.)

This could be the beginning of a discussion between you or some other representative of our culture and the tree-worshipers. It would have to be a very long discussion. At the end – supposing that they are intelligent and reasonable – what do you think you will have persuaded them? Will their views have changed? In the direction of being more like yours or more unlike yours?

Flat-earthers

Think of the reasons we have for believing that the earth is roughly spherical. (Actually write down several – six, perhaps. For example, if you fly a plane due west for long enough you eventually end up where you started.) Now imagine a convinced and intelligent flat-earther – that is, someone who believes that the earth is a flat disk rather than a sphere. Find a reply that the flat-earther can make to each of your reasons for thinking that the earth is spherical. Make the replies interesting enough so that they actually might make a spherical-earther hesitate. (Examples: Has anyone actually flown a plane absolutely due west all the way around the earth? Why should we believe that following a compass needle always leads you in a straight line rather than in a circle?)

Did you find your imaginary flat-earther challenging any of the following scientific beliefs?

Scientific beliefs	Advantages
(a) Light travels in straight lines, rather than in circles or other curves.	
(b) The sun follows a regular straight or uniformly curved path through the sky.	
(c) What look like the same stars and constellations seen from different parts of the earth really are the same stars and constellations.	
(d) Compasses do generally point to the north, and when they do not we can correct for the fact.	

Suppose that someone were to deny all of these scientific beliefs. They might then be able to defend the claim that the earth is not even roughly spherical. But there would be a price to pay. Items (i) to (v) below are some advantages of our standard scientific beliefs that might be lost by someone who denied (a) to (d). In the right column above, mark which of the advantages (i) to (v) could be lost if that belief were denied.

(i)   We can predict what stars will be in what positions at different points on the earth.
(ii) We can explain how telescopes, microscopes, and eyes work.
(iii) We can predict eclipses and other changes in the heavens.
(iv) We can navigate by the stars.
(v)   We can explain the world around the earth using the same principles we use for explaining what happens on earth.

1.8 Revising History: 1984

In his novel *Nineteen Eighty-Four* George Orwell describes a horrifying total-itarian state in which the government controls every aspect of people's lives and thoughts. Here the central character, Winston, is puzzling over the discrepancy between his own apparent memories and official history.

> *At this moment, for example, in 1984 (if it was 1984), Oceania was at war with Eurasia and in alliance with Eastasia. In no public or private utterance was it ever admitted that the three powers had at any time been grouped along different lines. Actu-ally, as Winston well knew, it was only four years since Oceania had been at war with Eastasia and in alliance with Eurasia. But that was merely a piece of furtive knowledge which he happened to possess because his memory was not satisfactorily under control. Officially the change of partners had never happened. Oceania was at war with Eurasia; therefore Oceania had always been at war with Eurasia. . . .*

> *The frightening thing . . . was that it might all be true. If the Party could thrust its hand into the past and say of this or that event, it never happened – that, surely, was more terrifying than mere torture and death?*

> *The Party said that Oceania had never been in alliance with Eurasia. He, Winston Smith, knew that Oceania had been in alliance with Eurasia as short a time as four years ago. But where did that knowledge exist? Only in his own consciousness, which in any case must soon be annihilated. And if all others accepted the lie . . . then the lie passed into history and became truth. . . . It was quite simple. All that was needed was an unend-ing series of victories over your own memory.*

Does Winston think that the party's version of history, or his, is actually true? There is support in the text for each possibility. *Underline* sentences in the text above that suggest that he thinks the party's version of history is true. *Ring* any sentences that suggest he thinks that his remembered version is true.

It is more interesting, and more frightening, to consider how he might think of his own memories as false. What, according to this selection, allows him to think this?

Could there be a society in which people allowed the state to correct their memories? Could the control be so complete that a single person had no way of being sure that he or she was not simply suffering from delusions? Are there ways in which our society might be thought to be like this?

1.9 Doubt

If you can *show* that it is certain that something is true then you can refute anyone who doubts it. So a good technique for probing how much delusion or error there could be in some beliefs – the results of a way of thinking – is to see how you could try to refute someone who doubted them. To do this you need people who doubt. They can be real people, or imaginary people invented for the sake of a philosophical experiment.

These doubters are skeptics. Their attitude is *skepticism*. There are real skeptics, people who doubt whether science gives the truth about the universe, or whether orthodox medicine actually cures diseases, or whether God exists, or whether democracy is a good system of government. In philosophy we also consider doubt about things which no real person doubts. For example, we need to consider skepticism about whether there really is a physical world around us (whether your body and the earth you stand on really exist) or about the existence of other minds (whether the people around you really do have thoughts and feelings much like yours). Perhaps it is not psychologically possible for a person to doubt the existence of the physical world or the minds of other people. But still, we can consider a skeptical attitude to these things, and how it might be defended or attacked.

As a result, the range of things that can be doubted, the range of topics where we can consider the pros and cons of a skeptical attitude, is very wide. And one dimension to this range is whether the skepticism is about a fairly small, perhaps practical, matter; or whether it is about something extremely fundamental, perhaps so fundamental that it is hard to imagine someone failing to have the belief. For example, a practical skepticism about science might involve doubting whether conventional science-based medicine really does know the causes of, or have cures for, life-threatening diseases: whether, for example, chemotherapy is actually effective against leukemia. A more abstract skepticism about science might doubt whether the methods used to conduct scientific experiments and create scientific theories are suitable for understanding some things. (For example, science might be unsuitable for studying the human mind, or human society, or such possibilities as telepathy.) And a very abstract "metaphysical" skepticism about science might argue that science is fundamentally mistaken because it assumes that the physical world is real when in fact it is an illusion.

There is a similar range of skeptical attitudes to moral matters. At the straightforward end of the range, someone might doubt that some ordinary beliefs about morality are right. For example, they might doubt that it is in fact wrong to tell lies, or that patriotism is a virtue. And at a middle level, someone might doubt a fairly fundamental value of their culture: for example, someone might doubt that an ordered society in which people live productive contented lives is better than an anarchic one in which people can act without constraint. And then at the "metaphysical" end of the range, there may be an extreme moral cynic who says "all these fools are deluding themselves that there is a difference between right and wrong."

(I called the extreme positions "metaphysical." "Metaphysics" and "metaphysical" do not have very clear meanings, but they usually mean "concerned with our really basic beliefs about reality, those which it would be very hard to doubt, or for that matter to find evidence for".)

In everyday life, if one person says something and another describes herself as skeptical, she means that she doubts that what the first person said is true. ("My car can accelerate to 100 mph in five seconds." "I'm just a bit skeptical about that.") Skepticism in philosophy usually differs from this in two ways.

The first is the kind of things that are doubted. In philosophy it is usually most profitable to consider how one might doubt things that are commonly believed and fairly difficult to doubt. (For example, the kinds of skepticism about science and about morals discussed in the last section.) The reason why it is more profitable to consider doubt about these things is that philosophy examines the value of various ways of thinking. So in philosophy we focus on the beliefs that come out of particular commonly used patterns of thought, and consider how one might doubt them.

But there is another characteristic of philosophical doubt. Outside philosophy "I doubt it" often just means "I think it's false." Someone says to you "Although I borrowed your car yesterday and returned it eight hours and 500 miles later I am not responsible for all those scratches and dents," and you say "I doubt you." Here you are saying that you think that what the person said was false. But sometimes people are more subtle, or perhaps more careful, in what their doubt amounts to. If someone asks you if you think there is life elsewhere in the universe, and you say "I'm inclined to doubt it," you may well just mean "I don't know that there is life elsewhere" rather than "I believe that there is no life elsewhere." (Note that one might then say "I'm skeptical about that.")

When philosophers talk of doubting something they usually mean something even more abstract. They usually mean that they do not believe that the reasons or evidence for the claim justify it according to the very high standards that come from some philosophical theory. So, for example, philosophical skepticism about whether people have thoughts and feelings does not usually express the thought "perhaps people don't have thoughts and feelings" (let alone the thought "it is false that people have thoughts and feelings"). Instead, it will normally express the thought "the reasons we normally give for attributing thoughts and feelings to people might be good enough for everyday life, but they aren't good enough for philosophy."

(But there is a position, eliminative materialism, that does come near to denying that people have thoughts and feelings. It is discussed in Part III of this book, in Chapter 12, Section 11.)

So there are three kinds of doubt: *vulgar doubt* just means thinking that something is false; *careful doubt* means not thinking that it is true; and *philosophical doubt* means thinking that the reasons for believing something do not meet really high standards.

1.10 Doubting What Someone Says

Here is a series of mini-discussions. In each of them the second person is expressing doubt about what the first person is saying. After the mini-discussions there is a table, in which you should mark the cases where the doubt is likely to be vulgar doubt, careful doubt, or philosophical doubt, respectively. (In some cases it may be more than one of them.)

The definitions again: *vulgar doubt* just means thinking that something is false; *careful doubt* means not thinking that it is true; and *philosophical doubt* means thinking that the reasons for believing something are not convincing. Now here are the mini-discussions:

(1) Adam: The CIA murdered my cat. I saw two men in trench coats hanging around my yard, and talking into cellular phones, then I found my dear puss dead.
Boris: I really doubt that.

(2) Alice: My grandmother was dying from leukemia and she visited a faith healer. He put his hands on her head and said a prayer and she was cured.
Bertha: Perhaps she just went into spontaneous remission, and the episode with the healer was just a coincidence.

(3) Alphonso: We now know that the universe is billions of years old. With modern telescopes we can see galaxies that are so far away that it must have taken billions of years for their light to get to us.
Brigitta: How do you know that these galaxies really exist? Perhaps nothing we see through telescopes is the way it looks. Perhaps something we just don't understand makes these images appear in them.

(4) Andrea: There are many simple mathematical problems that have never been solved. For example, we still don't know if the series of pairs of prime numbers separated by just one other number – like 2 and 3, 5 and 7, 17 and 19 – goes on for ever, or whether there is a greatest such pair.
Brunhilde: You're assuming that these questions have answers waiting for us to discover them. Perhaps in fact we invent rather than discover these

things. So perhaps the greatest pair of these primes doesn't exist until someone finds a proof that makes mathematicians happy.

(5) Arturo: It is important that everyone in society has equal access to education. Otherwise some people have their prospects in life unfairly restricted.
Beatrice: I'm not convinced. Who will dig the ditches and drive the taxis when everyone has a Ph.D.?

(6) Asphodelia: George treated me really badly. He said he would be here at noon, and now I've been waiting three hours in the rain.
Bruno: Don't judge him so harshly. Perhaps his car wouldn't start.

(7) Albert: I've just read in the paper about a man who murdered 12 people because he didn't like the magazines they were reading. How can anyone be so bad?
Belinda: I think I remember reading he belonged to some weird religion. Perhaps they're right: after all, some of those magazines give me pretty evil thoughts – mostly lust for material possessions. Who knows, maybe murder isn't so wrong on the ultimate scale of things after all?

(8) Acacia: I think Carol must subconsciously hate me. She says she's my friend, but she's always telling my other friends malicious things about me, and she always seems to turn the conversation so that what I say sounds ridiculous.
Barry: I'm not convinced you can explain anything with all this subconscious stuff. Who knows why she's always causing you grief.

Mini-discussion	Vulgar doubt	Careful doubt	Philosophical doubt
(1) Adam and Boris			
(2) Alice and Bertha			
(3) Alphonso and Brigitta			
(4) Andrea and Brunhilde			
(5) Arturo and Beatrice			
(6) Asphodelia and Bruno			
(7) Albert and Belinda			
(8) Acacia and Barry			

Which cases (if any) of vulgar or careful doubt are also cases of philosophical doubt? Which cases (if any) of vulgar or careful doubt are *not* cases of philosophical doubt? Which cases of philosophical doubt are *not* cases of careful or vulgar doubt?

In which cases where what the person expresses is philosophical doubt might it be reasonable also to express careful or vulgar doubt? (That is, when would it not be crazy or stupid or completely weird to have a vulgar or careful doubt?) In which cases where what the person expresses is vulgar or careful doubt might it be reasonable also to express philosophical doubt about the question?

You should find that there is an ordering in strength of the three kinds of doubt. When it is reasonable to have a vulgar doubt about something then it is usually reasonable to have the other kinds of doubt. And when it is reasonable to have a careful doubt it is usually also reasonable to have a philosophical doubt. But not the other way round. So the range of topics about which there can be philosophical doubt (sometimes as well as the other kinds) is very wide.

1.11 How Skeptical Are You?

Issues of skepticism are quite troubling to many people. Some people are rather *dogmatic* in their opinions. That is, they have very definite beliefs and they cannot see how any intelligent or well-informed person could disagree with them. Others are rather *skeptical* in their opinions. That is, they are inclined to think that the truth, if there is such a thing, is very hard to know, and so we should not give too much authority to what anyone says. Dogmatic people see skeptics as spreading dangerous uncertainty, and skeptics see dogmatists as living in an illusory world of false certainty. Each fears the other. Dogmatic opinions are often very conventional, that is, they are at the A or B end of the scale that you assessed in Section 1.2. But this is not always the case. Someone with very firmly held but unusual opinions – for example people like those described in Section 1.2 as having alternative belief systems – can also be dogmatic. In particular, people who hold antireligious views often hold them just as dogmatically as those of deep but narrow religious faith.

Most people's opinions lie between dogmatism and skepticism. To see where between these extremes your opinions lie, record your reactions to the claims listed below. Score your answers 1–4 as follows: 1 (no opinion, or don't know, or don't think there is an answer), 2 (tend to agree or tend to disagree), 3 (agree or disagree), 4 (strongly agree or strongly disagree).

(a) There is a God.
(b) Belief in anything supernatural is completely mistaken.
(c) We survive death, in some form or other.
(d) Doctors really know the causes of diseases.

(e) Science and medicine are completely irrelevant to the really important things in life.

(f) If you treat other people well then you will gain from it yourself.

(g) There is an objective difference between right and wrong.

(h) Morals are just made up by societies to make people behave in convenient ways.

(i) Another culture whose beliefs about the relations between men and women are different from yours is just wrong about them.

(j) When cosmologists make theories about the big bang they are discovering the truth about the origin of the universe.

(k) If a psychologist persuades someone that they have a subconscious hatred of their mother, though the person had never felt any conscious hostility to her, then the psychologist has probably discovered a hidden feeling that the person had all along.

(l) When different religions differ about what is necessary for salvation some of them are right and some are wrong.

First, add up your scores for (a), (b), (c), (l). Call this total R (for religion). Then add up your scores for (d), (e), (j), (k). Call this total S (for science). Finally, add up your scores for (f), (g), (h), (i). Call this third total M (for morals).

If your R score is 4–6, you are extremely skeptical about religious matters; if R is 6–8, you tend to skepticism about religion; if R is 10–12, you tend to be dogmatic, that is unskeptical, about religion; and if R is 12–16, you are extremely dogmatic about religion. (*Note*: this scheme includes dogmatic atheists among those who are not skeptical about religion.)

If your S score is 4–6, you are extremely skeptical about scientific matters; if S is 6–8, you tend to skepticism about science; if S is 10–12, you tend to be dogmatic, that is unskeptical, about science; and if S is 12–16, you are extremely dogmatic about science.

If your M score is 4–6, you are extremely skeptical about moral matters; if M is 6–8, you tend to skepticism about morals; if M is 10–12, you tend to be dogmatic, that is unskeptical, about morals; and if M is 12–16, you are extremely dogmatic about morals.

Now look for correlations with the scores of others taking the questionnaire. Are those who are skeptical about religion generally skeptical or dogmatic about science? Are those who are dogmatic about science generally skeptical or dogmatic about morals? Why might this be?

Note that this classification of attitudes as skeptical or dogmatic is pretty superficial. Later we will see much more subtle classifications. But note also that these attitudes are not just fixed aspects of people's characters. It is central to the enterprise of philosophy to understand that skepticism and dogmatism are things we can think and argue about. After some reflection and discussion – after doing some philosophy – someone may become more or less skeptical.

Biases

The questionnaire reveals some definite biases. Suppose that instead it had asked for your reactions to claims such as "Mice are smaller than elephants," "Whales are fish," "$2 + 3 = 5$," and "Wood is a metal." Almost everyone would score these 4, "strongly agree or strongly disagree," and so almost everyone would come out as very dogmatic and unskeptical. So the selection of questions reflects biases about the topics where we really might gain by more thinking or considering more evidence. These biases could be wrong, but they would be generally shared by contemporary philosophers.

1.12 Moral Skepticism

Beliefs about right and wrong are among the beliefs that can be doubted. We can be dogmatic or skeptical about moral beliefs. And if we are skeptical we can have vulgar, careful, or philosophical doubt about them. If someone says "I think I should go to the party tonight," and someone replies "I doubt that; you promised that you would stay home and write a letter to your grandmother," then this is vulgar doubt. The first and second person share moral beliefs but disagree about what to do in this particular case. Then there is a careful doubt about whether we should consider something wrong. Thus people can debate about whether capital punishment, or smoking marijuana, or insider trading are wrong. These are very different cases, but with all of them people are likely to agree that there are some moral principles but disagree about what they are. And then there is philosophical doubt applied to right and wrong, in which someone seriously questions whether any moral principles can be right.

There are some moral beliefs that most of us just cannot make ourselves doubt. For example, consider your attitude to a group of soldiers who kill thousands of innocent noncombatants. (Perhaps they wipe out the inhabitants of a peaceful village, just for fun.) Imagine that you see television footage of harmless old people and children being hunted down and butchered: would you be able to suppress a reaction of horror, outrage, and moral condemnation?

That is not to say that philosophical doubt is impossible here. Although most of us cannot help believing that it is wrong to murder innocent people, we are capable of looking for the reasons for our belief in the wrongness of murders, and then of asking hard questions about the nature of those reasons.

What kinds of doubt we can have for different moral beliefs tends to be related to what the beliefs are about. For our thoughts about right and wrong concern most of our lives, so we have moral beliefs about all the very different kinds of things we do. Here is one simple classification of them. We can have moral beliefs about four general topics.

Personal relations   We praise and condemn people for the way they run their emotional and family lives, and the way they treat their friends. Societies have rules about sex.

> Some moral rules seem to be arbitrary conventions. But there are actions which it is almost impossible not to feel are deeply wrong.

Economic life   Stealing is usually condemned, and business people have to be able to trust one another.

Life, death, pain   There are things that we hesitate to do to one another. In particular, killing and causing pain are usually taken to be wrong.

The environment   People assume a responsibility for the world around them. This gives them a concern with the welfare of other species, the appearance of cities and landscape, and the future state of the whole planet.

People often have rather different attitudes to moral beliefs about these four areas. Many people consider moral principles about personal relations to be somewhat arbitrary devices. They think that societies invent rules about family life and about sex whose purpose is just to make social life run smoothly. (Other people give a much more profound significance to some of these moral rules, for example, those concerning marriage or sexuality.) The situation is rather the same for beliefs about the morality of economic life. It is not too hard to think of many of them as arbitrary conventions. Doubting them, in this case, can consist in imagining how different conventions might be adopted in a different society. Most people, though, take the moral prohibition against stealing as a pretty serious matter.

On the other hand, skepticism about beliefs concerning life and death and the infliction of pain is much more difficult. Is torture wrong just because society will run more smoothly if we forbid it? It might be that society would run more smoothly if we were allowed, say, to torture criminal suspects to extract the truth from them. The repugnance most people feel to torture, murder, or rape feels as if it has a deeper origin, expressed in the intuition that there are things one just cannot do to another human being.

Beliefs about the environment are different from both beliefs about life and death and beliefs about personal relations. Many people think that our societies ought to have more, and more definite, principles about these matters. Yet we find the topic puzzling: why should we care about rare species of slug?

1.13 When is a Skeptic a Cynic?

A moral skeptic does not have to be a cynic. That is, a moral skeptic does not have to be someone who treats others as if no moral principles applied to his or her behavior. For philosophical skepticism about moral beliefs involves questioning the reasons for those beliefs, and you can do this while still having them. You can ask why torture is wrong, and you can even think that none of the reasons that you can find as to why it might be wrong are very good ones – and yet remain convinced that torture *is* wrong.

Below there are descriptions of six situations in which a person expresses doubts about a moral belief. The people could be described in the following ways:

cynical: the person doubts that the moral belief expresses anything that truly limits his or her actions;

questioning: the person doubts that the moral belief is true, though other moral beliefs might be;

pathological: the person just does not understand what "ought," "should," and "right" mean;

philosophical: the person wants to find out what the reasons for the belief are, whether or not it is true.

(a) Arthur is arguing with some friends about capital punishment. One friend expresses the view that people who commit crimes ought to be punished, whether or not this deters others from committing those crimes. Arthur says "I'm not so sure that there is any point to punishment for its own sake at all. Why when one person has suffered is the situation improved if another person also suffers?"

(b) Betty is a cannibal. She was abandoned as a child and has lived for years in the woods by herself. Every now and then she ambushes a hiker and eats him. She is captured and in the few words that she remembers she protests that she wants to go back to the woods. When police and social workers explain that she cannot go back to eating people she just stares back in puzzlement.

(c) Carina owns dozens of luxury apartments which she rents to rich people. She has found a way of deducting her own living expenses from the rent she gets, so that although she lives a very luxurious life she declares almost no income to the tax authorities. A friend protests that this is cheating, and she replies, "Those rules are for little boring people; if you have the imagination to find a way around the rules you deserve to get away with it."

(d) Daniel is studying anthropology, and has just learned about the variety of ways in which families and the relations between the sexes are organized in different cultures. He is faithful to his girlfriend but realizes that such a monogamous attitude would be seen as weird in many places. He asks "Why do I feel so strongly that promiscuity is wrong? I'm sure there must be some way in which the way we live is best."

(e) Eduardo is six years old. Another child pushes him off the slide at the playground. He runs after the child and punches him. Eduardo's mother tells him off for hitting a smaller child who has not attacked him. "But he started it," says Eduardo, "that's a bad kid."

(f) Felicia is proud of her intelligence and independence of mind. She thinks that most people are stuck in ways of life that they have fallen into just because they cannot imagine anything different. So she goes around setting up situations in which people have to make awkward choices. She flirts with her friends' boyfriends to shake up her friends' relationships. She invites people to brunch when she knows they are planning to go to church. She notices every little white lie and questions to make the liar either admit to it or retreat into an even bigger falsehood. When the havoc she is causing is pointed out to her she says "No one should live without examining their motives, even if it is uncomfortable for them."

Which of these six people deserves which of these four labels? Some may deserve more than one of them. What moral beliefs are doubted by each of the people, and why?

What would Felicia say about Betty? In what ways are Betty and Eduardo similar? In what ways are Felicia and Carina different? Which of these people would you prefer to associate with in your own life? Are they the same as the ones that do not doubt your own convictions? Which of these people ought to be prevented from acting on their beliefs or lack of beliefs? Are they the same as the ones that do not doubt your own convictions?

1.14 Socratic Skepticism

Moral skeptics are often taken to be cynics. Doubt is equated with disbelief. The most famous victim of this was the ancient Greek philosopher Socrates, who lived from about 470 to 399 BC. In fact Socrates had a strong faith in an objective right and wrong. But his insistence that neither he nor any of his contemporaries had clear ideas about such things as virtue and justice, and his insistence on arguing for this conviction in public, were among the reasons why he was put to death.

Socrates' moral skepticism shows one way in which a philosopher can adopt a skeptical attitude to basic moral beliefs, including those which it is very hard to doubt. His method depends on the fact that when we express our moral beliefs we use words like "right," "wrong," "virtue," "justice," "fair," "unfair." But using a word is not the same as understanding it, nor the same as being able to explain what it means. Socrates argued that we usually do not know what these moral words mean. So, according to Socrates, we are not capable of defending our beliefs about, for example, justice, since we do not know what justice is.

Socrates' way of arguing usually went like this: he would first demand to be given a clear and general definition of the moral ideas in question ("virtue," "justice," or whatever). Other people would then propose definitions and he would attack these definitions, showing that they did not really define the concept in question. He would then conclude that we do not really know what virtue or justice is. (This strategy is clearest in the dialogue *Meno*, discussed below.)

At the heart of his skeptical arguments was an important realization. We may label it *Socrates' discovery*: often we cannot define ideas that are essential to beliefs we feel certain about. This discovery lies behind arguments such as the following:

Socratic skeptical argument: first version

We cannot define virtue.
Therefore we do not know what virtue is.
Therefore we do not know which acts are virtuous.

(The argument uses the word "virtue," because that is the one discussed in Plato's *Meno*. But "rights," "justice," or many other moral, or non-moral, terms would do as well.)

How convincing is this? It is not at all obvious that you don't know what virtue is just because you cannot define it. (Do you know what a saxophone sounds like? Can you define what a saxophone sounds like?) But taken as an explanation of a kind of skeptical position it is more convincing. Suppose that our ideas about right and wrong, justice and injustice, were radically mistaken. In order to see that they were mistaken we would have to see what right and wrong, justice and injustice really were. It would not be enough just to have convictions that we express by using the words "right," "wrong," "just," "unjust." But we could never do this, Socrates would argue, if we could not even define the terms. So we can rephrase the argument as follows:

Socratic skeptical argument: second version

We cannot define virtue.
If we were mistaken about virtue we could never realize it unless we could define virtue.
Therefore we do not know that we are not mistaken about which acts are virtuous.

It is clearer from this version of the argument that it expresses philosophical skepticism rather than moral cynicism. But the way Socrates expressed himself is more like the first version than the second version. That makes it less surprising that he was put to death.

The philosopher Plato was a pupil of Socrates. He immortalized his teacher in a series of dialogues in which Socrates appears as a wise and ever-questioning seeker after truth. (A dialogue is discussion in which two or more people consider each other's views.) A typical early dialogue is the *Meno*. In it Socrates is discussing with a younger man, Meno, whether virtue can be taught. ("Virtue" means for them roughly "the capacity to do the right thing in public life." The concept is similar to that of being excellent or admirable. Some of Socrates' contemporaries claimed to be able to teach it.) Socrates persuades Meno that first they must know what virtue is. Meno proposes several definitions, which Socrates shoots down, usually by showing that they don't define virtue but only some special kind of virtue. Socrates claims that we do have real definitions of mathematical ideas, and gives a famous theory, involving the soul's existence before birth, to show how this could be. But we don't have anything like this kind of knowledge in ethics. Therefore, Socrates concludes, people who happen to be good and wise leaders aren't really act- ing from knowledge. Instead they have an intuitive knack that gives them true opinions in many particular cases.

(This is only one of the lines of argument found in the *Meno*. The dialogue is rich with ideas. Besides the themes that virtue cannot be defined or taught, Plato also argues for four other ideas that have proved very influential in later philosophy. One idea is that anyone, whatever their background or intelligence, can understand mathematics if they think carefully and intelligently about it. Another is that we understand abstract concepts like those found in math- ematics or ethics because we met them in a spiritual existence before birth. A third is that no one ever does a wrong action knowingly: evil is always the result of mistaking what is actually bad for what is good. And the fourth is that knowing something is more than simply having a correct belief about it. Some of Plato's ideas are discussed further in Chapter 4, Section 4)

Here is one passage from the *Meno*, where Socrates has persuaded Meno to give a definition of virtue. Dots (. . .) indicate where some of the text has been left out.

Socrates: . . . Do you claim that virtue is the power of acquiring good things?

Meno: Yes

Socrates: And by "good" do you mean such things as health and wealth?

Meno: I include acquiring both money and high government positions. . . .

Socrates: . . . Don't you want to add "just and righteous" to the word "acquisition" in your definition? Would you call it virtue even if wealth or power are unjustly acquired?

Meno: Certainly not.

Socrates: So, when acquiring wealth or power is virtuous, justice or self- control or piety . . . must be part of the story. Otherwise, although it is a means to good things, it will not be virtue.

Meno: No, how could you have virtue without these?

Socrates: In fact if you are poor because you didn't get money unjustly then your poverty is actually virtuous.

Meno: It would seem so.

Socrates: Then to have such goods is no more virtue than to lack them.

Which of the following is the best description of the main conclusion of this passage, the point that Socrates is most trying to make?

- ◆ Virtue is not simply getting wealth and power.
- ◆ Meno's definition of virtue as the power of getting good things is wrong.
- ◆ Unjustly acquired wealth is not a good thing.
- ◆ It is as virtuous to be poor as to be rich.

Suppose Plato was right that virtue cannot be defined. Would it follow that we do not know what virtue is? Consider the following arguments. In what ways are they similar to or different from the Socratic skeptical argument?

Romeo cannot define the sound of a saxophone.
Therefore he does not know what a saxophone sounds like.

Juliet cannot define love.
Therefore she does not know what love is.

(For more about premises, conclusions, and arguments see Chapter 2, Sections 3 to 6, and Chapter 5, Sections 4 to 6.)

Conclusions of This Chapter

- ◆ *To understand patterns of thinking we have to consider how we might doubt our beliefs.*
- ◆ *To doubt a belief is not to be sure that it is wrong.*
- ◆ *Skepticism about moral beliefs does not hare to mean being cynical about life or human relations.*
- ◆ *Sometimes when we see how we might doubt our beliefs we learn that we do not really understand what it is that we believe.*

Further Reading

Books or book chapters that can take you further into the issues discussed in this chapter are listed below. The easier ones are listed first, on each topic. *More difficult* reading is marked with an asterisk (*).

The publication or other details are the most well-known or most suitable editions of the work. You may find that your library or bookstore has other editions; these will probably be fine.

Reasons for belief

Chapter 1 of Martin Hollis, *Invitation to Philosophy*. Blackwell, 1985.
Chapter 1 of Willard Quine and Joseph Ullian, *The Web of Belief*. Random House, 1978.
Chapter 1 of Adam Morton, *A Guide through the Theory of Knowledge*, third edition. Blackwell, 2002.

Plato and Socrates

Plato, *Meno*, in *Collected Dialogues of Plato*, edited by Edith Hamilton and Huntington Cairns. Pantheon Books, 1961.
*Gregory Vlastos (ed.), *The Philosophy of Socrates*. Macmillan, 1972.
Plato, "Innate Knowledge" (selection from *Meno*) in John Cottingham (ed.), *Western Philosophy: An Anthology*. Blackwell, 1996.

Electronic resources

Routledge Encyclopedia of Philosophy (available online at many universities): articles on Doubt, Plato, Socrates.
Stanford Encyclopedia of Philosophy (http://plato.stanford.edu/): *Skepticism, moral*.

Meno: It would seem so.
Socrates: Then to have such goods is no more virtue than to lack them.

Which of the following is the best description of the main conclusion of this passage, the point that Socrates is most trying to make?

◆ Virtue is not simply getting wealth and power.
◆ Meno's definition of virtue as the power of getting good things is wrong.
◆ Unjustly acquired wealth is not a good thing.
◆ It is as virtuous to be poor as to be rich.

Suppose Plato was right that virtue cannot be defined. Would it follow that we do not know what virtue is? Consider the following arguments. In what ways are they similar to or different from the Socratic skeptical argument?

> **Romeo cannot define the sound of a saxophone.**
> **Therefore he does not know what a saxophone sounds like.**

> **Juliet cannot define love.**
> **Therefore she does not know what love is.**

(For more about premises, conclusions, and arguments see Chapter 2, Sections 3 to 6, and Chapter 5, Sections 4 to 6.)

Conclusions of This Chapter

> ◆ *To understand patterns of thinking we have to consider how we might doubt our beliefs.*
> ◆ *To doubt a belief is not to be sure that it is wrong.*
> ◆ *Skepticism about moral beliefs does not hare to mean being cynical about life or human relations.*
> ◆ *Sometimes when we see how we might doubt our beliefs we learn that we do not really understand what it is that we believe.*

Further Reading

Books or book chapters that can take you further into the issues discussed in this chapter are listed below. The easier ones are listed first, on each topic. *More difficult* reading is marked with an asterisk (*).

The publication or other details are the most well-known or most suitable editions of the work. You may find that your library or bookstore has other editions; these will probably be fine.

Reasons for belief

Chapter 1 of Martin Hollis, *Invitation to Philosophy*. Blackwell, 1985.

Chapter 1 of Willard Quine and Joseph Ullian, *The Web of Belief*. Random House, 1978.

Chapter 1 of Adam Morton, *A Guide through the Theory of Knowledge*, third edition. Blackwell, 2002.

Plato and Socrates

Plato, *Meno*, in *Collected Dialogues of Plato*, edited by Edith Hamilton and Huntington Cairns. Pantheon Books, 1961.

*Gregory Vlastos (ed.), *The Philosophy of Socrates*. Macmillan, 1972.

Plato, "Innate Knowledge" (selection from *Meno*) in John Cottingham (ed.), *Western Philosophy: An Anthology*. Blackwell, 1996.

Electronic resources

Routledge Encyclopedia of Philosophy (available online at many universities): articles on Doubt, Plato, Socrates.

Stanford Encyclopedia of Philosophy (http://plato.stanford.edu/): *Skepticism, moral.*

2 Sources of Conviction

Introduction

PHILOSOPHERS EVALUATE PATTERNS OF THINKING. In particular, they have often tried to find patterns of thinking which will give certainty about the world and about morals. Philosophical doubt is a way of finding out what beliefs are not certain, and logical arguments are a way of going from one belief to another belief that is just as certain. Many philosophers have doubted beliefs which others have thought certain – for example, the existence of God – and other philosophers have tried to Find logical arguments to support these beliefs.

Rationalist philosophers are optimistic that we can get certainty about the world or about morals by using logical arguments and similar kinds of reasoning. They consider extreme forms of doubt in order to prove how certain their beliefs are ...

Chapter Objectives

By the end of this chapter you should be able to answer the following questions.

◆ *Why is skepticism used to undermine authority?*
◆ *What is a logical argument?*
◆ *What arguments can be used to show that there is a God?*
◆ *Why do modern philosophers now think that neither authority nor reason alone can be a source of knowledge?*

Definitions

The following words used in this chapter are defined in the list of definitions at the end of the book:

argument	*logic*	*reason*
authority for belief	*paradox*	*traditionalism*
faith	*proof*	

2.1 Authority

You have questions and you want answers. And you want your answers to be as certain as possible. The questions are of many kinds: what is the explanation of some physical events, what political system should your country adopt, what is your friend likely to do next, what can happen to the stock market, or whatever? And because there is no obvious best way of getting the answers you want, you might consider different ways of getting them.

Any general way of getting answers to questions will be a way of thinking, the sort of thing philosophy aims to evaluate. But considering a way of thinking as a strategy for acquiring knowledge focuses attention on some particular qualities this strategy may have, or may lack. You want it to give you true answers. But even if it gives you some true answers the method may be so flawed – it may be based on guesswork or prejudice – that you couldn't say that what it gives is at all certain or reliable. Or it may give you a mixture of true and false answers, and then you must ask what the proportion of true to false is likely to be, and whether there is any way of telling them apart.

Very often we trust that a way of thinking will give us reliable true beliefs because it draws on a source of knowledge. It is as if it rests on some very solid ground. For example, we usually treat our senses, such as our eyes and ears and touch, as reliable sources of knowledge. If we see something, we normally assume that it is real. But there are limits to what we can learn just from our senses, so we often look for other trustworthy sources. Two such sources that make frequent appearances in philosophy are *authority* and *reason*. We use authority as a source when we appeal to some collection of beliefs which we think we can trust. They could be the traditional beliefs of a culture, or the contents of some book, or the opinions of some wise person. We use reason as a source when we trust our own capacities to think and argue. Authority and reason have often been seen as rivals, especially when "authority" has meant religious faith and "reason" has meant science and philosophy.

First, consider authority. There are many possible authorities. One is simply the standard opinions of your culture – "what everybody knows." Another is sacred books, such as the Bible. Another is the opinions of people with special qualities: experts, wise people, prophets. (Parents are authorities for most children's beliefs.) Science can be an authority, if it is taken as a collection of textbooks rather than as a method of making and testing theories. Experts who know the standard scientific theories and explanations come up with opinions that many people accept without question. People believe what their doctors tell them; scientific textbooks are treated as bibles.

Some philosophies give authority a large place. They are usually versions of *traditionalism*, the view that it is reasonable to accept the traditional beliefs of your society as true. Traditionalism is often expressed as a three-stage process. You start with beliefs that people generally feel confident about.

(Especially intelligent or wise people, of course.) You then consider any new information available to you, and you try to integrate it into this background of traditional belief as smoothly as possible. (You may have to modify some traditional view – for example saying that it doesn't hold in some special cases – or you may have to reject some new data, perhaps labeling it as an illusion. But both of these are to be kept at a minimum.) Lastly, armed with modified traditional beliefs and cleaned-up new information you try to deduce answers to the questions that concern you.

> An authority for beliefs provides a stock of shared beliefs, which people can use as a basis for resolving disputes or making new discoveries.

One important feature of traditionalism is that it allows a common ground between people. That is, when people disagree about something they can usually find a way of continuing a constructive discussion if there is some authority that they both accept as a source of beliefs. The most basic way this can happen is when we treat our senses as authorities. Suppose that two people disagree about whether, say, there are any orange and black striped cats, but both agree that our eyes give accurate information about the world around us. Then they can resolve their disagreement if one can show the other an orange and black striped cat and say "see, here's one." (The philosophy of empiricism, discussed in Part II, Chapter 9, is based on this.)

But this won't always settle a dispute. Suppose no orange and black striped cat can be found, or suppose that one person produces an orange and black striped animal and the other says "that isn't a cat." Then some more extensive agreement may be needed to allow the discussion to continue. Perhaps they can both take commonsense beliefs as an authority ("it looks like a cat and its parents were cats, so it's a cat"). Or perhaps they can both take contemporary science as an authority ("the laws of cat genetics say this combination of colors ought to be possible"). The important point here is that an authority for beliefs does not usually solve people's disputes by just giving them an answer. More often, it provides the common ground from which they can go on to find some way of agreeing.

The ancient Greek philosopher Aristotle suggested something like traditionalism as an all-purpose strategy. And a number of moral thinkers have suggested something like it as a way of answering moral questions. Moreover, some scientific ways of thinking seem to fit the traditionalist pattern.

But the important question is not whether some intelligent people have been traditionalists. (That would be to justify authority by appeal to authority.) The important question is whether in fact there is any authority that we can trust as a reliable source of true beliefs. Is there any person or book or tradition that we can use to say "this is certainly true, because the authority tells us so"?

The greatest enemy of traditionalism is the skeptical attitude. Skeptics will object to any authority: "How do we know that it is not part of a closed-belief trap?" That is, what assurance do we have that the authority is not giving a pattern of answers that disguises the fact that much of what it says is false?

(See Chapter 1, Section 5 on the closed-belief trap.) The force of the worry is easiest to see when the authority is the beliefs of a culture or a religious tradition. Suppose that some of the beliefs of a culture are seriously false. Then if the test of whether something is to be believed is whether it is consistent with traditional belief, these serious falsehoods may never be abandoned. (Suppose, for example, that one traditional belief is that all diseases are caused by evil spirits, and another is that everything seen through a microscope is an illusion. Then microbes seen through a microscope will never be considered real, and thus never count as causes of disease.)

Or suppose that a holy book tells people that some form of behavior is wrong. Perhaps it tells you that it is a great sin for you to eat in the presence of your mother-in-law. (A ridiculous example is best here, to keep the discussion away from any particular moral code.) It will also probably say that God or some other more-than-human power has inspired the book. So if we question the moral advice the answers we get will lead eventually to a circle: it is a sin to eat in the presence of your mother-in-law because the holy book says so, and the holy book is right because it was inspired by God, and we know that it was inspired by God because it says so in the holy book.

Do not conclude from this that there are no scientific or moral authorities. That does not follow at all from worries about closed-belief traps. The conclusion to draw is that it is very hard for a traditionalist to persuade a skeptic that the source of traditional beliefs really has the authority it claims, that it really is a source of true beliefs. The traditionalist may be right, but the skeptic will not be persuaded.

Below there are four mini-dialogues. In each one the first person makes a claim that is challenged by the second person. Several of the speakers appeal to authority for what they say. And several are skeptical of the claims of other speakers.

Which speakers are appealing to authority? What authorities is each one appealing to? When is the purpose of a speaker's skepticism simply to doubt what the other speaker says; and when is the purpose to support an appeal to a different authority?

Mathieu: I think my cat can do arithmetic. If two cars and three motorcycles go past the house she wags her tail five times.
Miriam: Don't be silly. Everyone knows cats are stupid.

Marc: I expect my children to be intelligent, good-looking, and well adjusted, like me. You see, my wife is almost as intelligent, good-looking, and sensible as I am, so our children will doubtless inherit all our qualities.
Naomi: Why are you so sure that children have to resemble their parents? Perhaps when children are like their parents it is because they have been raised the same way and had the same experiences. Or perhaps it is just

chance. Anyway, don't be surprised when your offspring turn out to be stupid, ugly, and mixed up. Or bright and rebellious.

Luc: My guru says that love is only possible between people with the same color soul. My soul is purple. He taught me that, and it has helped me understand many things about my life. But my girlfriend has a dark green soul. Even I can see that. And that is a very bad combination. So we will have to split up.
Leah: Have there been any experiments to test this theory of color and love? I mean, real experiments where the experimenter can't fix the results. I read in a psychology book that when people are too similar they find friendship rather than love. Perhaps you and your girlfriend should have some proper personality tests.

Jean: I have just read a book about human evolution, which explains to me why men go bald. It seems that millions of years ago babies used to hang on to their mothers' hair. And since men didn't take care of babies until the 1970s men had no need for long hair. I had been really worried about going bald in a few years' time, but now I see that it is all according to nature's plan.
Judith: I'd treat any theory about what happened millions of years ago with a lot of suspicion. Really, for all we know, anything could have happened back then. And I think a lot of bald men look really sexy.

2.2 Faith

A special kind of authority shapes the beliefs of many people. It is religious faith. For many people, also, this plays no role in determining what they believe, so that there is often a very deep divide between people, not only about what they believe but also about the reasons they accept for justifying belief. Each side thinks the other is missing something important. The purpose of this section is not to settle the issue, but to get clearer about what the important things might be that you might miss either by having or failing to have religious faith.

"Faith" can mean many things, so let us start with a definition. Faith for our purposes now is a trusting attitude to some very special source of information about basic aspects of life, typically a source associated with revelation by God, that is not subject to correction by evidence or rational argument. Suppose, for example, that it is a part of a person's faith that she should be charitable to others even at great cost to herself, because that is how God wants people to live. Suppose that someone gives her reasons why it is not a good idea for her to act in this way. "It just makes you poor, and these people you're giving it to, they just fritter it away on luxuries." If it is really a matter of faith, she will not try to rebut these reasons, but will just say "It doesn't matter what evidence you produce: my faith goes deeper than evidence so I'll stick with what

I believe right." So the idea is that faith is a kind of trust that is an alternative to giving reasons, not a kind of reason-giving or a competitor.

Here are three attitudes one could have to faith, as just described.

(a) *Dismissive.* The description doesn't really make much sense. It allows someone to have fairly weak reasons for belief and to ignore their weakness by saying that they are trusting rather than reasoning.

(b) *Acceptance for religion.* Religious beliefs have a special role in our lives that makes it inappropriate to ask for reasons for them. Sometimes a person is lucky enough to live among others whose faith she can share: that is a very special gift that she shouldn't ask too many questions about.

(c) *General acceptance.* You can't question everything. There are many things that you just have to take for granted: that other people are generally good, and generally telling the truth, that what people you respect believe is true, that scientific authorities know what they are saying. If you don't accept these things you'll find you're just lost.

If representatives of these three positions were trying to convince one another, there are many points they would make. Some are:

(i) Some of the things it seems sensible to trust may turn out to contradict one another, and then you have to do some hard thinking.

(ii) It may be socially inappropriate to question a belief although in fact it is false.

(iii) A person may be unable to give convincing reasons for a belief although it is true.

(iv) If your belief is true and given by some trustworthy source it should survive hard questioning.

(v) A person may be unable to give convincing reasons for a belief although it comes from a trustworthy source.

(vi) Sometimes when you live among others you pick up their beliefs unquestioningly, although there are serious problems with those beliefs.

(vii) Different people can take different things for granted. Then when they disagree they have to find some way of thinking through their differences.

Which of the points (i)–(vii) is relevant to which of the attitudes (a), (b), (c)?

2.3 Reason

Reason is the capacity to think. Human beings have just enough thinking power to solve many practical problems and to organize their societies. They can also take part in complicated discussions, trying to change one another's beliefs.

And they can understand mathematical proofs and scientific theories. These are rather different kinds of thinking. Philosophy began with a rather naive picture of humans as having a single power of thinking, which might work with or conflict with authorities such as traditional beliefs and what was written in books. As philosophy has developed it has become less naive, distinguishing different kinds of reasoning. For the moment, simply take reason to be the capacity to find reasons for beliefs, not by appeal to any authority but by the power of thinking.

Some of the most convincing reasons are found in mathematics. Mathematicians make proofs, which are particularly strong arguments that make conclusive cases for their conclusions. Here is a simple mathematical proof. Take any two even numbers, and consider what you get when you add them together. Each even number will be two times some other number (that is what makes it even). So the sum of the two even numbers will be two times the sum of those other numbers (that is, $2n + 2m = 2(n + m)$). So this sum will itself be even. So we can conclude that the sum of two even numbers is always even.

That was a very simple proof of a very simple fact. But the important thing about it is that it makes a completely convincing case for its conclusion. When you understand it, you *know* that the sum of two even numbers is always even. And you know that you can be completely sure of it. As sure as you can be of anything. Mathematics is full of proofs that are just as convincing as this. (Many of them are longer and harder, of course. But they usually break down into steps that are not much more complex than this.)

Since the beginning of philosophy, philosophers have been impressed by the capacity of mathematical proof to make things certain. (In the early days of philosophy, mathematics was mostly geometry – the proofs were of facts about triangles and other geometrical shapes. Since then, mathematics and philosophy have developed together, and some of the great philosophers have also been mathematicians.) Mathematics proves facts about such things as numbers and geometrical shapes. Could we also have proofs of facts about science, religion, and ethics?

The view that some basic facts can be proved beyond doubt is called *rationalism*. Rationalism has a great faith in the power of reason; it takes reason to be the main source of certain belief. There is rationalism about science, about religion, and about morals. These are different: it is quite possible to think that, for example, reason alone can show us the right system of morals though we cannot prove what the truth about any scientific matter is.

Rationalism about any topic holds that reason can guide us to the truth about that topic. A really strong rationalism holds that reason all by itself can discover the truth. All the truth: science, religion, morals, anything we can know. But it is very hard to believe that, for example, we can do science just by thinking and arguing, without having to perform experiments or collect data. (And even if we could prove the existence of God by reason alone, it does not follow that we can construct a whole religion just by the power of proof and argument.) One thing that needs to be considered here is the relation between reason and *evidence*. Evidence includes all kinds of information that we get by experience, using our senses. So it includes the results of observations and experiments in science, and the things that people learn every day by perceiving the world around them.

Can rationalism succeed? Can the power of reason show us how to find out the truth about the world, or religion, or morals? The first step toward seeing what reason can do must be to think a bit more deeply about proof and argument. The next section discusses argument; the section after that discusses proof, looking in particular at proofs of the existence of God.

2.4 Arguments

There are many ways of persuading someone of something you believe. Suppose you are having a disagreement with someone about cows. "Cows have horns," you say. "No," your friend replies, "bulls have horns, but cows don't." One thing you may then do is to take him by the arm and show him a cow with horns. Another is to repeat your claim with such conviction and sincerity that he accepts you as an authority on cows and changes his opinion. Neither of these is guaranteed to work. (People are stubborn.)

Another way is by *argument*. This does not mean quarreling. It means reasoning with him, saying things to him that make him share your belief. You might try saying: "Horns are for defence against predators, and cows need horns to defend themselves and their calves, just as bulls do, so it would be surprising if only bulls have horns." Or: "Remember that river where we had a picnic on an island, last September? It was called the 'Cow's horn river.' Do you think the name was a joke?"

The things you are saying to persuade him are arguments. They start with assumptions that you hope he will accept: that horns are for defense; and that you had a picnic on the Cow's Horn River. And they go on to a conclusion, that cows have horns, which you are trying to get him to accept. So the basic plan of an argument is to find assumptions that the other person accepts and that will then lead on, step by step, to the conclusion you want them to accept. This will not work if you disagree about so many things that you cannot find assumptions that you both share. Nor will it work if the other person does not accept the way in which you draw conclusions from the assumptions.

An argument leads step by step from some assumptions to a conclusion.

(So an effective argument requires some common ground between the person making the argument and the person whose beliefs the argument is meant to change.)

Philosophers have a standard way of writing out an argument, with the assumptions, called premises, at the top, and beneath them the steps of the argument leading down to the conclusion, with a "therefore" or a "so" before it. For example:

If George comes to the party and Alice is still there, there will be trouble.
George is coming at 10.
Alice will not leave till 11.
Therefore there will be trouble.

or

Martha is in New York or San Francisco or Tokyo.
If she is in New York she will have gone to the Empire State Building.
If she is in Tokyo she will have gone to the Imperial Palace.
She did not go to the Empire State Building.
She did not go to the Imperial Palace.
Therefore she is in San Francisco.

Call this way of writing out an argument *skeleton form* (because usually it represents just the frame, on which a person trying to argue for a position will have added many other details). Writing arguments out like this is meant to make the shape of the argument clearer: what the premises are and how the conclusion is supposed to follow from them. In simple cases, like the first of the two arguments above, this way of writing them out is enough to make the pattern clear. But in more complicated cases like the second one this may not be enough. Then a more complicated presentation may help; call it *tree form*, as in the example in Figure 2.1.

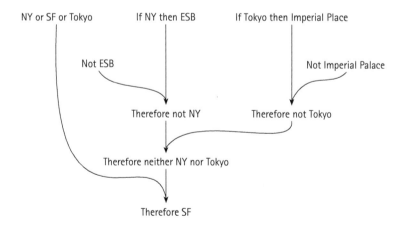

Figure 2.1

In real life people do not present arguments like this. They speak to each other in much less formal ways and somehow get across what they are assuming and what they are trying to show. So often in philosophy we take an argument presented very informally and we rewrite it, to make clearer what is going on. In doing this the order of some parts may have to be changed and some parts may have to be left out or, sometimes, added. So someone may argue as follows:

> Generations of conformists and nonconformists will always alternate. I mean, first you have some conservative people with very fixed opinions, who bring up their children very rigidly. Like my grandparents for example. Then their children, children of people of that generation, will inevitably rebel against them, as children always do, and turn into radical nonconformist types, trying out alternative beliefs and alternative lifestyles. Of course they will raise their children in a loose, permissive style. But children want authority and so this will just make tension between them and their children. So when these children rebel against their parents they will become conservatives again. Then it will all have gone round in a circle.

Philosophers would take this argument and rewrite it in skeleton form, as follows.

Children always rebel against their parents.
When children rebel against their parents they adopt the opposite attitudes.
The opposite attitude to conformity is nonconformity.
Therefore the children of conformist parents will be nonconformist.
Therefore the grandchildren of conformist parents will be conformist.
Therefore the great-grandchildren of conformist parents will be nonconformist.
Therefore conformist and nonconformist generations will alternate.

This example brings out several important points. First, notice how the order in which things are stated has got changed between the informal statement and the skeleton form version. The conclusion, which is stated at the end in the skeleton form, is stated at the beginning in the informal statement. This is quite common. For example, in newspaper editorials the conclusion, the thing that the editorial is trying to get you to accept, is very often not stated at the end. More often it is stated first of all.

Notice also how some assumptions that were not stated in the informal statement have been stated explicitly in the skeleton version. These are usually assumptions that the person making the argument would have considered too obvious to state, for example, that the opposite of conformity is nonconformity. (But sometimes when you state something that is considered "too obvious to state" you find that it is not obviously true at all.) And a number of things that were in the informal statement (like the attitude of the speaker's own grandparents) have been left out of the skeleton argument because they are irrelevant to its force as an argument.

The most important thing to notice about the example is that the argument is not completely convincing. There are two problems with the argument, two ways in which it might not convince someone. It is important that they are different. The first problem is that the premises are not obviously true. Children sometimes do not rebel, and when they rebel they do not always adopt opposing attitudes. The second problem is that even if the premises were true, it is not clear that the conclusion would follow from them. The premises could be true even if the conclusion was false. For suppose that at one time there are both conformists and nonconformists, and that their children are nonconformists and conformists respectively. Suppose some of these people marry. How will they raise their children and what attitudes will these children have? They could be part of a pattern that makes the conclusion false even though the premises are true.

Ideally, an argument should have true premises that lead in a clear and completely persuasive way to the conclusion. That is called a *sound* argument. Then it will show anyone who accepts the premises that the conclusion is also true. But this ideal is often hard to meet. If the premises are not true the argument can still be *valid*. That is, it can still show that if the premises were true the conclusion would be true. (So all sound arguments are valid, but some valid arguments are not sound.) The above argument about conformists and nonconformists is neither sound nor valid. (But see Section 2.7 below.) The part of philosophy that studies valid argument is *logic*. One central concept of logic, that of a deductively valid argument, is discussed in Chapter 5, Sections 4, 5, and 6.

2.5 Eight Short Arguments

For each of the arguments below, first find the main conclusion. (Think carefully about this. What is the argument trying to make you believe?) Then write the argument out in skeleton form, as described in the previous section, beginning with premises and going step by step to the conclusion. Remember that a skeleton form will often leave out some things mentioned in the informal statement of an argument, and you will sometimes have to supply things that have been left unstated.

(a) Even small children have human rights. For all human beings have rights. And while children are not the same as adults, they are human.
(b) For every activity there is appropriate clothing. Welders' eyes must be protected by goggles, and motorcyclists need windproof outer garments. And you would not go swimming in a winter coat. Eating is an activity like any other, and it too has its appropriate clothing. So to eat properly you have to change into the right clothes.

(c) Men are more creative than women. Just think of Bach, Beethoven, Plato, Einstein – all men. There just aren't any women among the great composers and mathematicians and scientists. It seems that it is always the men who come up with the novel ideas.

(d) When patients with cancer of the colon are operated on, sometimes it is discovered that the cancer has spread from the original site. These patients have a very high mortality rate. Those whose cancers have not spread and who survive the operation have a mortality rate roughly the same as the general population. Early diagnosis would reduce the mortality from this particular cancer. Then operations could be performed before the cancer had spread.

(e) If boys are allowed to wear earrings to school, parents will think that the school has no standards and will cease to support the school. For parents associate academic standards with proper dress. Girls on the other hand can wear earrings since there is a tradition of females wearing them. There is no tradition of males wearing earrings: they should be forbidden to do so at school.

(f) Acheulean stone tools are made from large flakes struck from boulders. Such tools are found where early humans and the australopithecines were both present. It seems that humans were the main toolmakers, though. Stone tools are not directly associated with the australopithecines that lived before the emergence of humans, and stone tool manufacture continued to flourish after the australopithecines became extinct. Furthermore, when hominid fossils (human or australopithecine) and stone tools are both present at the same site, at least some of the hominids tend to be human.

(g) It could be that everything I seem to perceive is really an illusion. For my senses quite often deceive me. For example, I sometimes look at a straight stick half in and half out of water, and I think it is bent. It is very hard to tell how common such illusions are. Some of them are very subtle and hard to detect.

(h) Sometimes there is no objection to the use of drugs by professional athletes. One purpose of professional sport is to provide an exciting competitive spectacle for the audience. In some circumstances the use of drugs by athletes, to increase their strength or stamina or even to increase their competitive spirit, will lead to a more exciting and competitive spectacle. And since professionals take part in sports willingly they freely assume the risks involved.

Which of these arguments are more persuasive, and which are less persuasive? (You can't answer this until you have determined what they are arguments for – that is, found their conclusions.) Rank them on a scale of 0 to 10, with 0 representing a completely unpersuasive argument and 10 representing a completely persuasive one. Find out if others agree with your rankings.

If they do not, then find out why. Try to separate out disagreements about whether the premises of an argument are true from disagreements about whether the argument succeeds in showing that the conclusion follows from the premises.

State, very roughly and informally, why the less persuasive arguments do not convince you of their conclusions. Then try to find similar reasons why someone might fail to be convinced by one of the arguments you do find convincing. Choose an argument you gave a score of 8 or more to, and state the strongest criticism you can of it.

Now write out arguments (b), (d), and (f) in tree form, as described in the previous section.

2.6 Puzzling Arguments

Sometimes an argument can lead from pretty obvious assumptions to pretty surprising conclusions. Here are three examples. Each of them leads to a conclusion you probably would not accept if it was just stated out of context. Yet the argument seems to lead you in a few easy steps towards accepting them. (Read them slowly and think about the ways in which they do or do not convince you.)

Cheap horses are rare.
Rare things are expensive.
Therefore cheap horses are expensive.

San Francisco is to the west of London.
Moscow is to the west of San Francisco.
So Moscow is further to the west of London than San Francisco is.
So Moscow is to the west of London.

Groucho has a brother, Harpo.
Harpo has a brother, Groucho.
The brother of a brother is a brother.
Therefore Groucho is his own brother.

These arguments are definitely not convincing. One reason that you are probably not convinced by them is that the conclusions are so implausible. So something must be wrong with the arguments. The puzzle comes in trying to see what this can be. The premises of the arguments look right, the argument itself seems reasonable, and yet the conclusion seems crazy.

Here are two ways you might react to the arguments after thinking about them:

♦ The premises might be false, even though they seem at first to be true. Perhaps it is not really true that all rare things are expensive; perhaps it is not true that Moscow is to the West of San Francisco; perhaps it is not true that the brother of a brother is a brother.

♦ The conclusions might be true even though at first they seem false. Perhaps cheap horses are expensive; perhaps Moscow is to the west of London; perhaps Groucho is his own brother.

These are not the only ways you could react to the arguments. You could also say that the premises are true and the conclusion is false and there is something wrong with the pattern of argument itself. (That is, in the terminology of Section 2.4 above, the argument might not be valid.) But if you had to choose between the two reactions above, which seems right for each of the three arguments?

2.7 Arguments within Arguments

Very often an argument contains smaller arguments. This will happen when an argument goes from its premises to its conclusion in several steps. Each of these steps will be a smaller argument within the full argument. Each will be a subargument. For example:

> **If George can love anyone he can love Louise.**
> **George can love his dog.**
> **Therefore George can love someone.**
> **Therefore George can love Louise.**

Here the second premise, "George can love his dog," leads to the first conclusion, "George can love someone." So the subargument is:

> **George can love his dog.**
> **Therefore George can love someone.**

The way the subargument fits into the whole argument is clearer if we write it out in tree form.

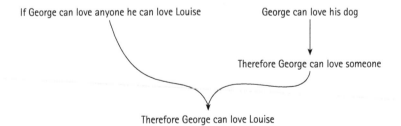

Figure 2.2

The argument that was used as an example in Section 2.4 above has several subarguments.

> **Children always rebel against their parents.**
> **When children rebel against their parents they adopt the opposite attitudes.**
> **The opposite attitude to conformity is nonconformity.**
> **Therefore the children of conformist parents will be nonconformist.**
> **Therefore the grandchildren of conformist parents will be conformist.**
> **Therefore the great-grandchildren of conformist parents will be nonconformist.**
> **Therefore conformist and nonconformist generations will alternate.**

The subarguments can be seen more clearly if the argument is presented in tree form.

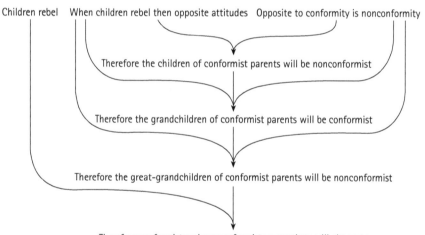

Figure 2.3

Find three subarguments. Write them out in skeleton form.

The whole argument is not valid. But the three subarguments are valid. (Remember that validity means that the conclusion would be true *if* the premises were true. If, moreover, the premises are true the argument is sound.) Are any of the subarguments sound?

2.8 Proofs of God

Philosophers and theologians have often thought up proofs of the existence of God. These are arguments which are meant to persuade anyone who doubts God's existence that they are wrong. Whether or not any of these proofs do show what they are meant to, many of them raise deep questions about time and space, causation and explanation, good and evil. And thinking about them raises important points about logic.

In order to put these arguments in context, here is a dialogue, a discussion between two imaginary students, in which some of the standard arguments about God emerge.

Andrea [*a biology student*]: I'm taking a fascinating course this semester, on the chemical origins of life. We're studying how the chemicals present in the world billions of years ago could have led to life. That's what the prof. says, anyway. He's not easy to understand, but if I can make sense of him in two months' time I'll know why we're here.

Brian [*a philosophy student*]: No you won't. You'll know how one scientist proposes to replace a mystery with another mystery. Your prof. may persuade you that we are here now because of chemicals billions of years ago. But why were they there? Why those particular chemicals at that particular time, and why did they happen to combine to form life?

Andrea: Well, what do you expect? You can't explain everything. If I say that a window broke because someone threw a rock at it you'll probably say I should tell you why they threw it. But maybe I just don't know.

Brian: If I knew why the rock was thrown it would sure make a lot more sense to me than if I thought maybe it was just a random act. I'd have someone to blame. It's just the same with the origin of life. If I can see some purpose behind it then I'll feel I really know why it happened.

Andrea: You're going to be disappointed, then. All we know yet is that the causes go back and back. We can get a bit beyond the chemistry of the early earth, though it gets rather vague. We can go back to the Big Bang, if you want to be really speculative, but you don't find purposes.

Brian: You do, you do, if only you'll raise your nose out of the chemicals for a moment. Think. There has to be some purpose. For otherwise everything is the effect of some cause which is the effect of some other cause which is the effect of some other cause. And so on backwards for ever. Nothing is ever explained. But we do know why things happen. And that's because we know that in the end there's a purpose. God made the world in the first place and laid down the laws of nature, the rules which it follows from then on.

Andrea: Sure, that sounds nice, but how do you know there is any such God?

Brian: Weren't you listening? I just proved there is a God. If there weren't a God then the chain of causes and effects would go back forever and we wouldn't ever know why anything happens. But we do know why things happen. I know you're talking to me now because you want me to buy you a beer. So there has to be a God.

Andrea: Isn't your God just another of this endless series of causes? Why did he make this very universe, and not some other one? Why did he make a universe in which I need you to buy me beers?

Brian: We don't know why God made this very universe. But we know we can't know this: God's mind is more complex than ours. So we have to stop there; it's not an arbitrary break. When we explain the universe in terms of God we are moving from one kind of cause to a very different one. So it isn't just the same series going on.

Andrea: I suppose I think that the random combinations that made the first life may have been so unlikely that we couldn't ever see why they had to happen either. Perhaps chaos is my God.

Brian: Sounds like you've proved the existence of lawyers. Let's have that beer.

The two people in this dialogue tried to persuade each other of their views. To do this each used a variety of arguments, and in addition some of what each one says is meant not as direct argument but as objections to the other person's arguments. Which one makes the better case? In order to get an intelligent opinion on this you need to know what each person's arguments really are. One technique that philosophers use to do this is to extract simple arguments in skeleton form from the actual details of what people say, in order to have a clearer view of what the argument says and the ways in which it may be convincing or unconvincing. (Modern philosophers do this to the argumentation found in the works of older philosophers. They get skeleton arguments out of the works of Plato, Descartes, or Hegel and then evaluate them.) Here are some skeleton arguments that may or may not be found in the dialogue above.

(1) Every event has a cause.
So there is something that causes all events.
So there is a God.

(2) We only understand why an event occurred when we see the reason why it happened.
To see why something happened we need to see a purpose behind it.
We do understand why things happen.
Therefore there is a purpose behind the universe.
Therefore there is a God.

(3) We do not understand why something happens just by citing a preceding cause of it.
Therefore giving causes earlier and earlier in time does not explain why anything happens.
Therefore we can only understand why anything happens by relating it to a cause outside time.
God, if he exists, is outside time.
Therefore there is a God.

(4) We do not understand why something happens just by citing a preceding cause of it.
Therefore giving causes earlier and earlier in time does not explain why anything happens.
Therefore we only understand why anything happens if we have an explanation of the very first moments in time.
Therefore there is a God.

(5) The causes of any event must be as mysterious as that event.
God's motives are mysterious.
Therefore God's motives are the causes of all events.
Therefore there is a God.

Of these five arguments, three can be found in the dialogue. That is, a case can be made for taking each of these three skeleton arguments as an outline of the way in which some person in the dialogue is trying to convince the other. Two of them cannot be found in the dialogue. They may be interesting arguments; they may even be right; but they are not what either person in the dialogue is saying.

Which are the three arguments that can be found in the dialogue? For each of the three arguments, find the parts of the dialogue that suggest it.

Which of the arguments (1) to (5) are the most convincing? Which are the least convincing? Suppose that you do not believe in a God: what objections would you make to each of the arguments? Suppose that you do believe in a God: which arguments would you choose as expressing part of the reason for your belief?

Suppose that you do not find one of these arguments convincing. Perhaps you do not find any of them convincing. How can you find ways of resisting them? Ideally, you do not just want to express the fact that you are not convinced; you also want to have some impact on the other person's views. You want to shake their confidence that their opinion is right, or at any rate that their opinion is easy to defend. One way of doing this can be seen early in the dialogue:

Brian: . . . Your prof. may persuade you that we are here now because of chemicals billions of years ago. But why were they there? Why those particular chemicals at that particular time, and why did they happen to combine to form life?
Andrea: Well, what do you expect? You can't explain everything. If I say that a window broke because someone threw a rock at it you'll probably say I should tell you why they threw it. But maybe I just don't know.

Let us take Brian to be arguing as follows:

Chemical explanations of the origin of life say that life was caused by the combination of chemicals billions of years ago.
These explanations do not explain why these chemicals were there.
Therefore these explanations do not really explain the origin of life.

In reply to this, Andrea is saying that if this argument were correct then the following argument would also be valid:

My explanation of the fact that the window is broken is that this rock was thrown through it.
This explanation does not explain why someone threw the rock through the window.
Therefore this explanation does not really explain why the window is broken.

Andrea takes this to be an obviously ridiculous argument. But it seems completely parallel to Brian's argument. So something must be wrong with Brian's argument.

This technique for attacking an argument consists in giving a *counterexample* to the argument: a parallel case in which premises analogous to those of the argument to be refuted lead to an obviously false conclusion. (Counterexamples to arguments are discussed in Chapter 5, Section 6.)

Some of the above arguments (1) to (5) for the existence of God are susceptible to attack by counterexample. Find counterexamples to argument (2). Note that there are two "therefores" in the argument. So you could apply a counterexample either to the argument leading to the first conclusion or to its extension to the second conclusion.

Suppose you think that the general idea of argument (2) is correct. How might you react to the counterexamples? (Argument (1) is also susceptible to counterexamples. They are harder to state, but they raise some interesting issues.)

Proofs of the existence of God often raise important issues that are not essentially about God. In the dialogue between Brian and Andrea each of the speakers seems to be relying on many unstated assumptions. Here is a partial list. Which ones seem to be implicitly assumed at which points in the dialogue?

(a) There must be a first point in time.
(b) The cause of an event must precede it.
(c) When we explain why something happens we give a cause of it.
(d) Sometimes simply giving a cause does not explain why something happened.
(e) A good explanation tells you more than just that the event occurred.
(f) Natural events occur in conformity with regular laws of nature.
(g) A random event cannot be explained.

Which of these are true?

> ### Box 4 The Ontological Argument
>
> The arguments for the existence of God discussed in this section have required assumptions that we can only know to be true by observing the world, and seeing the patterns of cause and effect, order and disorder, in it. Some philosophers have thought that God's existence does not depend on the world he created, and so in order to prove that God exists we should not have to use any facts about the world. The most famous proof along these lines is the ontological argument, discovered by Anselm of Canterbury, who lived from 1033 to 1109. One version of the argument runs:
>
> > God is God.
> > If God were not perfect he would not be God.
> > Therefore God is perfect.
> > If God did not exist he would be less perfect than if he existed.
> > Therefore God exists.
>
> Some later philosophers have accepted versions of this argument. Others have rejected it. (Descartes accepted it, St Thomas Aquinas rejected it, Kant rejected it.) It seems to many that the argument captures a deep feature of religious belief. It also seems to many that there is something wrong with the argument. If you do not find the argument convincing, try saying where it goes wrong.

2.9 Paradoxes

Sometimes an argument seems to show something that goes completely against what we believe. Such an argument is called a paradox. Here are two paradoxes.

Zeno's paradox. Suppose that the world's 100-meter champion is running from a starting line toward the finishing tape. Before he can get to the finish he will have to get halfway there. And before he can get halfway there he will have to get one-quarter way there. And before he can get one-quarter way there he will have to get one-eighth way. And before one-eighth, one-sixteenth. And so on. In order to run the short distance of 100 meters the champion will have to do infinitely many things. But doing infinitely many things will need infinitely much time. Therefore, despite appearances to the contrary, he will never get to the finishing tape.

The surprise exam. A logic professor says to her class: "You are going to have an exam next week. But it is going to be a surprise. It will be on a day when you do not expect it." All the students in the class wonder when the exam is going to be. They feel worried. But one clever student says: "Since it is going to be a surprise it cannot be on Friday, because if there was no exam before then we would know that there was only one day left. So it cannot be on Thursday either, as by Wednesday we would know that since it cannot be on Friday it would have to be on Thursday, and this would not be a surprise. For just the same reason it cannot be on Wednesday. Nor on Tuesday. Nor on Monday. So relax, there can be no surprise exam."

With a good paradox everyone agrees that the conclusion is false. The world champion can run 100 meters in a very finite time; the professor can give a surprise exam. But, if it is a good paradox, everyone will not agree what is wrong with the argument. These are good paradoxes, in that people have very different reactions to them.

Paradoxes can be seen as making reason contradict common sense or perception. Find one commonsense belief that is contradicted by each paradox, and one belief given by perception that is contradicted by each paradox.

Each paradox makes several assumptions. If you do not want to believe the conclusion you should consider disagreeing with one of the premises. Which of the following premises would be the easiest to give up?

For Zeno's paradox:

(a) Before the runner can get to the finish he will have to get halfway there.
(b) And so on. (That is, for all n, in order to get to the finish the runner will have to get $1/2n$ of the way there.)
(c) Doing infinitely many things will need infinitely much time.

For the surprise exam:

(a) If there is no exam by Thursday we know it will be Friday.
(b) If there is no exam by Wednesday we know it will be Thursday.
(c) If we know the exam is going to be on Thursday or Friday we know it is going to be on Thursday.
(d) If we know the exam is going to be on a given day then it cannot be a surprise on that day.

2.10 What to Trust on the Internet

You may think that it is nearly always obvious what the good sources of belief are. Comparing notes with others should show you that different people base their beliefs on very different grounds. But in case that is not enough, this section discusses a case where everyone agrees that it is very hard to know what sources to trust, and different people adopt very different strategies to cope with the resulting uncertainty.

Many of us get a lot of our information from the internet. We log on to news sites for current news and background articles; we look up information about entertainment and the weather. We find out facts about diseases and their treatments. We get opinions on controversies that interest us. We find stories, poems, movies, rants. Very often we believe what we find: we treat online newspapers like paper ones; we trust online weather forecasts as much as those on television. But there are many reasons for being much more cautious than we usually are. Anyone can put a document on the web, and when you access it you usually have no way of knowing who put it there, who is responsible for the site on which the document is found, or what commercial or political interests lie behind it. It is very easy to start a completely unfounded rumor by means of the internet. Why do we get such a lot of information from something so inherently fallible?

When getting information from a web page it is a good idea to be aware of the following:

(1) The identity of the authors and what organizations they are associated with.
(2) The credentials of the authors: if the information is medical, legal, or scientific, whether they have any professional qualifications.
(3) How up-to-date the information is: when the page was last modified, when the data was last checked.
(4) What the sources of information are, what references or links there are to standard authorities, databases, or experts.
(5) Whether there is advertising on the page and, if so, whether this is likely to affect the content of the page; whether the source of funding for the page is given.
(6) How much of the content of the page is presented simply as the authors' opinion: whether there are links to places where experimental and other evidence may be found.
(7) Whether contact information is given which could allow you to check up on the authors' qualifications, their sources and evidence, and their affiliations and funding.

How often do you find any of these? Which of them are most essential? What worries about the trustworthiness of the information will be raised by the absence of each of them?

Reflecting on these questions should make you more wary of trusting what you read on the internet. But perhaps it leads to reflections that can make you wary of other sources of information too. Which of considerations (1)–(7) above, or analogs of them, might suggest worries about: scientific textbooks, the things parents teach their children, the Bible, newspapers? Which of these worries are serious reasons for doubting the information found in these sources?

2.11 Transforming the Question

Philosophers used to debate whether reason or authority should play the main role in forming our beliefs. It is not hard now to see that this is an empty question. Early in the chapter we saw that an appeal to authority does not usually solve people's disputes by just giving them an answer. More often, it provides the common ground from which they can go on to find some way of agreeing. But in going on from a common ground people will need their powers of argument, in order both to persuade each other of what they believe and to keep a link with the common ground that makes argument possible. And they will need to find and evaluate new evidence in order to determine which belief has a better chance of being true. But both the power to argue and the power to evaluate evidence are parts of our power to reason. They are both part of that loosely linked ability that makes humans special, the power to think for oneself.

Reason cannot operate all by itself either. Arguments need premises, and the premises have to come from somewhere. One source of premises is an authority accepted both by the person making the argument and the people the argument is meant to convince. Another source is the evidence provided by our senses. Whichever is involved, something besides reason is needed. Pure intelligence will not give you the truth unless you have something to apply your intelligence to.

(Mathematical proofs, and some arguments like the Ontological Argument described in Box 4, can seem to get to a conclusion without needing any premises. Can they really? These are hard and controversial issues. Philosophers are still very puzzled about the nature of proofs in mathematics. But nearly all contemporary philosophers are convinced that most arguments that lead to knowledge about the world need premises that have to come from somewhere besides pure thinking.)

So the question we should be asking is not "Which is more important, reason or authority?" but "How can reason, authority, and evidence be combined to give us reliable knowledge?" (Perhaps sometimes reason and evidence alone can do the job, without help from authority. That would be a comfort to philosophers worried about the closed-belief trap.) To put the question this way is to think like a modern philosopher who does not see reason as a single human capacity, which might be able to give knowledge all by itself.

Conclusions of This Chapter

◆ *One way in which we can think out what is right is by using logical arguments.*
◆ *Logical arguments will not all by themselves settle all the important questions of philosophy.*
◆ *When people disagree about something they can very often find something else that they agree about, and then use their powers of logical argument to find an answer they can both accept.*
◆ *Questions such as the existence of God are very hard to answer just by logical reasoning, but when we try to evaluate arguments for and against the existence of God we find ourselves asking other important questions about what the universe is like and how we can understand it.*

Further Reading

On arguments

Chapter 1 of Martin Hollis, *Invitation to Philosophy*. Blackwell, 1985.
Chapters 3 and 4 of Willard Quine and Joseph Ullian, *The Web of Belief*. Random House, 1978.
Alec Fisher, *The Logic of Real Arguments*. Cambridge University Press, 1988.
Trudy Govier, *A Practical Study of Argument*, second edition. Wadsworth, 1988.
Merilee Salmon, *Introduction to Logic and Critical Thinking*. Harcourt Brace Jovanovich, 1984.
Chapters 7 and 8 of Robert M. Martin, *There Are Two Errors in the the Title of this Book*. Broadview, 1992.

On the existence of God

Chapter 1 of Nigel Warburton, *Philosophy, the Basics*. Routledge, 1992.
Chapter 7 of Richard Taylor, *Metaphysics*. Prentice-Hall, 1963.
Chapter 2 of Robert M. Martin, *There Are Two Errors in the the Title of this Book*. Broadview, 1992.
Robin LePoidevin, *Arguing for Atheism*. Routledge, 1996.
Kai Neilson, *An Introduction to the Philosophy of Religion*. Macmillan, 1982.
David Hume, *Dialogues on Natural Religion*. Anchor Books, 1990.
Selections from Anselm, Aquinas, Descartes, and Hume in Part V of John Cottingham (ed.), *Western Philosophy: An Anthology*. Blackwell 1996.

Electronic resources

Routledge Encyclopedia of Philosophy (available online at many universities): articles on Faith; God, arguments for the existence of; Necessary being; Reasons for belief.
Stanford Encyclopedia of Philosophy (http://plato.stanford.edu/): God, arguments for the existence of; *Logic, informal; Ontological arguments; Religion, epistemology of; Zeno's paradoxes* (italicized items are available as this book goes to press; the others should be available soon).

3 Rationalism

Introduction

Many philosophers have doubted beliefs that others have thought certain – for example, the existence of God – and other philosophers have tried to find logical arguments to support these beliefs.

Rationalist philosophers are optimistic that we can get certainty about the world or about morals by using logical arguments and similar kinds of reasoning. They consider extreme forms of doubt in order to prove how certain their beliefs are.

Can our beliefs about right and wrong ever be made completely certain? Some philosophers, rationalists about morals, try to find logical arguments for their moral beliefs. But if the moral beliefs of a particular society can be shown to be right then the moral beliefs of other societies must be wrong....

Chapter Objectives

By the end of this chapter you should be able to answer the following questions.

◆ *How is rationalism different from traditionalism?*
◆ *Why did Descartes use doubt in order to achieve certain knowledge?*
◆ *What is the evil spirit hypothesis?*
◆ *What is Descartes' proof that he exists?*
◆ *How can someone find reasons for doubting that they exist?*

Definitions

The following words used in this chapter are defined in the list of definitions at the end of the book:

Cartesian doubt	*ground clearing*	*skepticism*
demon possibility	*individualism*	*traditionalism*
empiricism	*Pyrrhonism*	
fideism	*relativism*	

3.1 Optimism about Reason

The conclusion of the previous chapter was that neither authority, reason, nor evidence alone can be a source of knowledge. They have to be combined. Combined in what proportions? Rationalism is the view that reason is the largest component. By thinking and arguing, making proofs and considering arguments, we can go a long way toward discovering the truth about important matters in science, religion, and morals. The previous chapter mentioned rationalism about mathematics, where it is at its strongest, and then discussed rationalism about religion, in the special case of the claim that we can prove that God exists. This chapter discusses rationalism about science.

Rationalism can be contrasted with *traditionalism* and with *empiricism*. According to traditionalism some authority, in particular the traditions or beliefs of some culture, can be the largest component in our search for knowledge. And according to empiricism, evidence gained by use of our senses can be the largest component. (Empiricism is discussed in Chapter 9.)

There are two basic features of rationalism that make it an approach to getting and evaluating beliefs that is very different from that of traditionalism. The first is that rationalism requires a *ground clearing step*. That is, it requires us to use in our reasoning only beliefs that reason itself can guarantee to be true. First you clear your mind of all the possibly misleading junk that clutters it, and then you bring in new, well-organized, properly functioning beliefs. (Empiricism also requires such a step. Traditionalism does not.)

> Rationalism and empiricism require *ground clearing*: first you clear your mind of all the possibly misleading junk that clutters it, and then you bring in new beliefs.

The other important feature of rationalism is that it is *individualistic*. That is, it aims to describe ways in which one person, all alone, could with enough time and patience build up a body of beliefs. One-person science never actually happens, of course, and one-person ethics seems a slightly crazy enterprise. But if you really want to have knowledge, according to rationalism, then after clearing the ground you must bring in only what you can prove logically, or that which fits the evidence that is part of *your* experience. This is in many ways an appealing ideal. And like many appealing ideals, it is obviously quite impractical.

Individualism and the ground clearing feature both stem from *optimism*. For the suggestion is that you can answer important questions by ignoring what people have thought in the past, or what wise people think today, and that you can get answers all by yourself. To think this is to have either a very high estimate of the powers of the individual human mind, or a very low estimate of the difficulties of the questions we want answers to. Indeed, both rationalism and empiricism are associated with the optimism of the early years of modern science. After centuries of slow progress, scientists (or "natural philosophers," as they would have called themselves) after the time of Galileo, found that they were getting answers to questions – for example, about the structure of the solar system or the reasons for the tides – which had previously been quite unanswerable. Moreover, these answers seemed to be very different from what traditional beliefs would have suggested. So it was not too unreasonable to hope that a few intelligent scientists could ignore the accumulated wisdom of humankind and think their way to the basic principles of nature. Things have not proved as easy as they hoped. And in fact the enormous optimism of rationalism gave way to the somewhat lesser optimism of empiricism. But optimism about the power of the human intellect is still a central part of the scientific attitude.

Optimism can spread from scientific to moral and political matters. If by clearing our minds of the clutter of traditional beliefs we can solve scientific problems then might we not also be able to solve problems about how to organize our lives and our societies? Below is an eloquent expression of rationalistic optimism by Mary Wollstonecraft, in her A *Vindication of the Rights of Women* of 1791.

> Men, in general, seem to employ their reason to justify prejudices, which they have imbibed, they can scarcely trace how, rather than root them out. The mind must be strong that resolutely forms its own principles; for a kind of intellectual cowardice prevails which makes many men shrink from the task, or do it by halves. Yet the imperfect conclusions thus drawn, are frequently very plausible, because they are built on partial experience, on just, though narrow, views.

> Going back to first principles, vice skulks, with all its native deformity, from close investigation; but a set of shallow reasoners are always exclaiming that these arguments prove too much, and that a measure rotten at the core may be expedient. Thus expediency is continually contrasted with simple principles, till truth is lost in a mist of words, virtue, in forms, and knowledge rendered a founding nothing, by the specious prejudices that assume its name.

Wollstonecraft is saying that it takes courage to avoid beliefs that seem right only because they are traditional, and to avoid social customs that seem moral only because they are easy for us to adopt. Instead, she thinks, a strong mind must "root out" prejudices, however plausible.

3.2 Individualism

Imagine an extremely intelligent 14-year-old. She has tremendous capacities of imagination, memory, and thought, but has been brought up in a rural community isolated from any of the developments in science or society in the past 200 years. Her community believes that girls' brains are smaller than boys' brains, so there is no point in educating girls, and that the only way for girls to achieve happiness is to marry young and have many children.

Because she is very intelligent she can see mistakes in the reasoning of people around her, and she realizes that some of the community's beliefs must be wrong. But of course she does not have any alternative system of beliefs to turn to.

What is the best way for her to get a fair evaluation of what is true, what is not true, and what may or may not be true, in the beliefs of her community, *while remaining within it?* Here are some things she could do.

(i) Search for evidence for each of the important beliefs of her community, ceasing to hold any belief if she finds strong evidence against it.

(ii) Search for evidence for each of the important beliefs of her community, not holding the belief until she finds strong evidence for it.

(iii) Consider each of the important beliefs of her community, then challenge a wise person of the community to a public debate about them.

(iv) Consider each of the important beliefs of her community and think privately about it.

(v) Write a book in which she gives reasons for doubting some commonly held beliefs.

Rank these five actions on two scales. First give each of them a score from 1 (least likely) to 5 (most likely) in terms of whether the action will enable her to draw an accurate conclusion about the truth of something believed by her community. Then give each of them a score from 1 (least likely) to 5 (most likely) in terms of whether the action will make it very difficult for her to remain a member of the community.

Do your rankings suggest any relation between discovering truth and remaining in the community? Do they suggest any conclusions about the prospects for one person discovering that a whole community's beliefs are wrong?

If she escapes the beliefs of her community she may move toward beliefs like those of modern people in Western countries. (This is not at all inevitable, though. Perhaps she is intelligent enough to see just where some of our central beliefs are wrong.) But some modern beliefs may be much harder for her to come to believe, all by herself, than others. Consider the following:

(a) modern physics;

(b) modern ideas about society (for example, about what the market can and cannot accomplish, or about what government control can and cannot accomplish);

(c) modern attitudes to women.

In each case consider two things: (1) whether she could come to understand the modern beliefs, whether the concepts in them could make sense to her; and (2) whether she could find reasons to hold the modern beliefs, thinking about these topics in her situation.

You will probably conclude that in each of (a), (b), and (c) she might be able to understand and find reasons for some beliefs but not others. State in each case: beliefs that she might be able to acquire, beliefs she might understand but would never believe, and beliefs that she would never understand.

3.3 Galileo's Rationalism

Galileo Galilei (1564–1642), born in Pisa in Italy, was the first great scientist to have the general intellectual character of modern physicists: his way of study-ing nature combined mathematics, practical mechanics, and experimental data. During his long life he laid the foundations for Newton's mechanics (which is the core of the physics used today) by introducing concepts such as that of accel-eration. He was the first to use a telescope to observe stars and planets, and he argued strongly for Copernicus' suggestion that the earth revolves about the sun. It was especially this last that got him into trouble with the Church. He was tried by the Inquisition and sentenced to life imprisonment, though he was allowed to live in his own house.

Galileo's importance comes from his rationalism. He argued for a way of think-ing about physical processes that describes them in mathematical terms in such a way that the processes are largely explained once the right theorems are proved. This contrasts with the more commonsense way of thinking that had previ-ously been standard in physics, which came mostly from the writings of the ancient Greek philosopher Aristotle.

In arguing against Aristotle's physics Galileo often appealed to simple experiments. (Some of them are simple but mechanically ingenious, setting a model for later physicists to follow.) But he also used some very abstract non-experimental arguments. Here are two.

Aristotle's physics held that all objects fall down toward the center of the earth and that heavier objects fall faster than lighter ones. Galileo argued that on the contrary (i) heavier objects do not inherently fall faster than lighter ones, and (ii) when an object falls it begins stationary and then accelerates, acquir-ing more speed as time passes.

To argue for (i) Galileo imagined a light object and a heavy one which may be connected by a thread. If the thread does not connect them, then accord-ing to Aristotle's physics, they will fall at different speeds. But as soon as the thread is tied they become one object, heavier than either of the two original objects. Will they thus fall faster than either object would fall alone? Or will they fall a little less fast than the heavier one would fall, being dragged back by the lighter one? Aristotle's physics suggests both answers. It suggests that the tied objects will fall faster than either one alone would, because together they make an object that is heavier than either one. And it also suggests that the tied objects will fall at a speed a little less than the heavier one – because we can consider each object independently, give it a tendency to fall at a speed proportional to its weight, and then think how the two will interact. The fact that Aristotle's theory suggests both answers, though only one can be right (and Galileo thinks neither is right), suggests that it is an incoherent theory that does not make enough sense to be applied to the real world.

Galileo was a scientific rationalist. He wanted to clear the way for mathematical physics by abstract argument.

To argue for (ii) Galileo considered what would happen, according to Aristotle's theory, at the first moment a very heavy object begins to fall. It seems that it will suddenly lurch from having no downward speed to having a very great one. But this seems absurd. Surely it makes more sense to suppose that falling objects accelerate downward, beginning with no downward speed and gradually increasing it.

These arguments have had a great impact on philosophy as well as on physics. (In Galileo's time physics was part of philosophy.) They suggest that we can at least eliminate impossible scientific theories by abstract reasoning, before we make any observations or do any experiments. Perhaps we can reduce the number of candidates for our theory of the world down to a very small number, and then make a few well-aimed experiments to decide which of this small number is the true one. (Or perhaps rational argument could settle the general form of our theory, leaving the values of a few parameters to be settled by experiment.)

Galileo's arguments also suggest that in order to get a good theory of the world, we may have to use some rather abstract concepts. For example, Galileo's physics uses the idea of acceleration, which is not easy to understand in commonsense terms. ("Acceleration is how fast your speed is getting faster." Try explaining that to an 8-year-old.) In fact it is hard to be very clear about acceleration without using quite a lot of mathematics. So as a preparation for interpreting any observations and experiments we plan to make, we will have to do some hard and abstract thinking to discover the right concepts to describe and explain them with. (Theories and observations both have to be expressed in words. What are the right words?)

(Galileo also suggested that some apparently obvious features of things, for example, their colors, are not important features of them from the point of view of physics. There is a sense, he suggested, in which objects don't really have these features. This point is taken up in Chapter 14, Sections 1 to 3.)

3.4 Impossible Theories

Some theories do not need to be refuted by evidence or better theories, because when you think about them you realize that they couldn't possibly be true. Galileo claimed that Aristotle's physics was such a theory. Here are some other mini-theories that disintegrate when brought into the light.

(1) All the children in Lake Wobegon are above average.

(2) Every statement is false.

(3) There is a fence along the east side of Elm Street. It has a post in front of each house, from number 1 at the south end to number 58 at the north end, and there is a chain hanging between each pair of these posts. There are flower pots suspended from these chains and every one of these 58 pots has a different kind of flower in it.

(4) It is very hard to be sure that anyone exists except yourself. So the easiest thing to believe is that in fact no one except yourself exists. In fact, it is true: I am the only person who exists. Everyone else is an illusion or a robot pretending to be a person. I have tried to persuade other people of this obvious fact, but they all resist it.

(5) There is an island in the Pacific Ocean called Russellia. The people who live on this island are divided into a number of tribes. Everyone belongs to a tribe. Each tribe elects a judge to settle disputes between its members. The judge does not have to belong to the tribe. Many judges do not belong to the tribe they are judge of. But if someone becomes the judge of any tribe except his or her own, he or she has to leave his or her tribe and join a special tribe, the Outsiders, which consists just of the judges who are not members of the tribe they judge.

The problems of these mini-theories can be described. If someone did not see why the theory couldn't possibly be true you would have to describe its problems to them. Which of the following descriptions, (a) to (e), captures the problems of which theory in the above list?

(a) The theory would have to apply to itself, but when it does it shows that it is not true.

(b) One part of the theory denies what another part asserts.

(c) The theory ignores a simple arithmetical fact.

(d) If the theory is true then something exists that, according to the theory, does not exist.

(e) The theory says of a class of things what could only be true of a subclass of it.

Sometimes an impossible theory can be made possible by changing it slightly. So for example "Every statement is false" can be made possible by changing it to "Every statement made by a professor is false." That change makes the theory much weaker, and also makes it very unlikely to be true (since professors sometimes say things like "2 + 2 = 4" or "It's raining today") even if you can no longer see its falsity just by thinking about it. An interesting modification keeps the strength of the theory while giving it a good chance of being true. So "Every statement is false" could be modified to say "All our complicated theories about the universe are false" or "Just about everything interesting to say about anything is false." Both of these might well be true.

Find modifications of the other mini-theories that make them possible. If you can, find modifications that also make them interesting and plausible.

3.5 Descartes' Optimism: Certainty from Doubt

The philosopher, scientist, and mathematician René Descartes (1596–1650) argued for a very optimistic attitude toward the power of the human intellect to understand the physical world. (In this he was influenced by the mild rationalism of Galileo, discussed in Section 3.3, who thought that abstract thought is a necessary preparation for understanding physics and astronomy.) If we think carefully and clearly then, according to Descartes, we can get a complete and certain understanding of the world. This amounts to a strong rationalism, because it claims that fundamental facts about the world can be discovered just by thinking.

> Descartes' exercise was one of suspension of belief. He meant to put aside temporarily all beliefs he could not be sure were true.

But Descartes adds a novel twist of his own. For Descartes, certainty is based on doubt. That is, if reason is to have a chance to show what certain beliefs it can give us, we must not burden it with the prejudices that have accumulated through careless thinking and reliance on authority. So Descartes thought, and argued in works such as his *Meditations on First Philosophy*, we ought to clear our minds of all our previous beliefs, until we know which ones are not mere prejudices. In some sense, we must doubt everything we believe. At the beginning of the *Meditations* he wrote:

> *Some time ago I noticed . . . that I should for once in my life seriously undertake to unmake all the opinions that I have picked up since my birth, and begin from new right from the foundations, if I wanted to establish something solid and lasting in the sciences.*

> *. . . It will not be necessary . . . to prove that all my former opinions are false, . . . but since reason has already persuaded me that I should prevent myself from believing things which are not entirely certain and indubitable, just as much as those which appear obviously false, the slightest cause for doubt that I find will be enough to make me reject any one of them. To do this it is not necessary to examine each single belief, which would be an endless task. But because destroying the foundations necessarily brings down the whole of the rest of the structure, I will first attack the principles on which all my former opinions rested.*

Descartes' program was therefore to try to go through all his beliefs, putting aside any that could be doubted. He would then be left with the absolutely safe ones. It is important to see that he was *not* proposing to *disbelieve* the beliefs that were put aside. The exercise was one of suspension of belief rather than disbelief. He compared it to taking all the apples out of a barrel and putting back only those that one has made sure are not rotten. Some apples will be obviously sound and go straight back in the barrel. Some will wait to be tested, and of these some will eventually go back in the barrel. Some will be obviously rotten and will be thrown away. And others will remain in an "undecided" category. Descartes' hope was that when he applied this method to beliefs rather than apples, very few would remain for ever in the "uncertain" category. Eventually all beliefs would be found to be belief-worthy or disbelief-worthy. The ones that were worthy of belief would be ones he could not doubt; they would be indubitable. Since they would be beyond doubt he could be certain that they were true.

(Here is another way of describing what he was doing. He wanted to see which of his beliefs he could be said to *know*. Knowledge is more demanding than belief; the standards are higher. Descartes would not count anything as knowledge unless it was completely certain.)

Each person has so many beliefs that it would take for ever to go through them all. So Descartes wanted a way of testing many beliefs at once. He had the idea of finding tests that would apply to large numbers of beliefs all at once. (Like using a transparent scoop to take a lot of apples out of the barrel, so you can then see at a glance if any of them are rotten.) The idea was to find really deep and general doubts, which would give reason for thinking that many beliefs are false. If a whole class of beliefs can be shown to survive such a powerful doubt, then we can be fairly sure that they are true. And the deeper the doubt, the more sure we can be that the doubts that survive it are true.

Descartes begins with fairly mild doubts, which are familiar from other skeptical arguments. He remarks that "I have sometimes experienced that my senses were tricking me, and it is prudent never to trust completely anything that has once tricked you." And then he goes on to wonder whether he might be dreaming, so that his beliefs "that I open my eyes, that I move my head, that I stretch out my hands, and all things like that, are nothing but false illusions, and perhaps my hands, indeed my whole body, are not the way I see them."

It is easy to think of many variations on the idea that your experience might be a dream. There is the possibility that you are in a virtual reality setup, so that when you move your limbs you are not interacting with a real physical world around you but with a computer program that produces input to sensors connected to your eyes in response to what you do. There is the possibility that everyone around you is conspiring to tell you a false story about the world you live in. And there is the philosopher's favorite, the possibility that you are a "brain in a vat": a human brain disconnected from its body and kept alive in a vat of nutrient fluid, while hooked up to a computer by its input and output nerves so that it is given experience just as it would be by an external world. But of course there is no world around the brain, or at any rate not one at all like the experience the computer gives it.

Some of these doubts are getting very deep. If what they suggest were true then many of your beliefs would be false. But Descartes points out that some beliefs would survive even these doubts. "Whether I am awake or asleep, two plus three will always be five, and a square will never have more than four sides." But suppose that there was a very powerful spirit, some sort of demon, who could not only feed his mind with illusory experiences, as if he were hallucinating, but who also could lead him to reason badly. Then his belief that $2 + 3 = 5$ could be a delusion, since the spirit was causing him to make mistakes in arithmetic. If there were such a spirit, Descartes could be sure of practically none of his beliefs.

There are many variations on the idea of such a deceiving spirit. There is the possibility that you are so deeply insane that you cannot reason. There is the possibility that the human mind is inherently flawed so that even its simplest thoughts do not correspond to anything real. Call any such possibility a *demon possibility*. A demon possibility is a possible situation such that if it were actually happening a very large number of your ordinary beliefs would not be knowledge. Say that a demon possibility "undermines" ordinary beliefs. So, for example, if you are actually dreaming then your belief that you have a left leg is undermined. For you could have lost your leg but be dreaming that you still have it. And if you are a brain in a vat then your belief that you have any body at all besides your brain is undermined. Some demon possibilities are deeper than others; they undermine more beliefs. Descartes' own demon possibility, the spirit who can make him mistaken about arithmetic, is a very very deep demon.

Descartes brought into philosophy skeptical arguments based on demon possibilities. These arguments are really quite different from many earlier skeptical arguments. To see the contrast, consider one very simple skeptical argument that many philosophers before Descartes could have used.

Basic skeptical argument

Informal statement   For just about any one of our beliefs we can think of circumstances in which it would be false. For example, I believe that I am the child of my mother and my father. But it is possible that I was adopted; it is very hard for me to be absolutely sure that I was not. I believe that Abraham Lincoln was president of the USA during the civil war. But it is possible that the history books are wrong. Since I am not a historian I cannot check whether the books are right, so there is for me this small element of doubt about Lincoln. And so on for just about all my beliefs – all, in fact, if I just try hard enough to find the right grounds for doubt. So nothing is beyond doubt. So if I were to go about doubting persistently enough, I would end up doubting everything.

One part of this argument can be summed up in skeleton form as follows:

For any belief we can find a reason for doubting it.
Therefore: We can doubt all our beliefs.

The skeptical arguments that Descartes considered were much more inter-esting than this. They depend on *Descartes' discovery*: there are demon possibilities that undermine many of our beliefs about the world. (For example, the deceiving spirit he imagined, or the possibility that you might be a brain in a vat.) So the skeptical arguments he considered focus on the set of beliefs which are undermined by a given demon possibility. (That is, the beliefs that we would have no reasons for believing if the demon possibility were true.) Then Descartes' claim is that we can doubt all of these beliefs. For we can imag-ine that the demon possibility might be true; and as long as we cannot show that it is not, we have a reason to doubt this whole set of beliefs. So while the basic skeptical argument needs a different reason to doubt each belief, Descartes' skeptical arguments deal with single reasons that cast doubt on whole sets of beliefs. So a *Cartesian skeptical argument* can be stated as follows ("Cartesian" means "about Descartes").

Cartesian skeptical argument

Informal statement   There are demon possibilities, such as the possibility that I might be dreaming, or that a demon might be deceiving me, or that my brain might be hooked up to a computer which is feeding it completely misleading information. For any such possibility there are many beliefs – call them its "victim beliefs" – which are undermined by it. And for most of my beliefs I can think of demon possibilities that cast doubt on them. So I can doubt most of my beliefs.

Part of the content of this argument can be represented in skeleton form as follows:

If demon possibilities are true, then we do not know that the ord-inary beliefs they undermine are true.
Therefore: Until we can show that demon possibilities are not true, we cannot say we know that the victim beliefs that they undermine are true.

Two differences between the Cartesian skeptical argument and the basic skeptical argument are particularly important. The first is that the Cartesian argument is supposed to show a special kind of doubt – until we can show that the demon possibility is not true the victim beliefs remain doubtful. And this leads to the second difference. If we can show that the demon possibility is not true then the doubt disappears. So Descartes' doubt can be a tool for attain-ing certainty: if we can refute demon possibilities then some of the doubts one might have about their victim beliefs will be removed.

Box 5 The Optimistic Skeptic

René Descartes was an early scientist who is now remembered mostly for his philosophical writings, such as the *Meditations* and *Discourse on Method*. But he made important discoveries in physics and mathematics. He was one of the first to understand how telescopes and eyes work on similar principles, and he invented analytic or coordinate geometry, often known as "Cartesian geometry." (Anything to do with Descartes is called "Cartesian," so we speak of Cartesian doubt, Cartesian rationalism, Cartesian coordinates, and there is even a toy called a Cartesian diver.)

Descartes' scientific work was inspired by Galileo. He dreamed that a mathematical physics could explain all of the natural world. (He had a strong preference for mathematical over empirical explanations; in fact, he would spend his mornings in bed thinking about mathematics and philosophy.) He also believed in a sharp distinction between mind and body, so that completely different principles would explain the workings of the mind. This is discussed in Chapter 12, Section 4. (But in his book *The Passions of the Soul* he argued that many emotions can be explained physically, in terms of various liquid- and gas-like "humors" in the body.)

Descartes' optimism about the progress of science is shown by a sad story. He had a daughter of whom he was very fond. She died as a girl, of scarlet fever. Descartes wrote to a friend that it was tragic that God had taken her from him, for in only a few years he would understand the physical world well enough to understand how living bodies work. And then deducing the cures for all diseases would be simple.

Descartes did not live to appreciate quite how difficult the enterprise of explaining all of nature mathematically would be. He traveled to Sweden to discuss philosophy with Queen Christina, who had wide intellectual interests. The Swedish climate and Christina's preference for philosophical discussions in the early morning proved too much for Descartes, and he died in 1650 at the age of 54.

3.6 Doubting Anything versus Doubting Everything

In skeleton form, part of the basic skeptical argument runs:

(a) For any belief, we can find a reason for doubting it.
Therefore we can doubt all our beliefs.

Compare it with the following arguments:

(b) For any number we can find a larger one.
Therefore we can find a number that is larger than all numbers.

(c) **For any food we can find an implement for eating it non-messily. Therefore there is an implement for eating all foods non-messily.**

(d) **For any person there is someone who will love them. Therefore there is someone who will love anyone.**

Do these arguments really show that there is a largest number, an all-purpose eating tool, a universal lover? Of course not: (b), (c), and (d) are completely unconvincing arguments. So perhaps we should reject (a) too.

Here are some ways in which (a) is like and unlike (b), (c), or (d). (More accurately, ways in which (a) may be claimed to be like and unlike (b), (c), (d). You may disagree with some of them.)

Similarities

To (b): there are infinitely many possible beliefs, just as there are infinitely many numbers.

To (c): there are many essentially different reasons for doubt, just as there are many essentially different kinds of food.

To (d): a doubt usually affects just a small number of beliefs, just as a person usually loves only a small number of other people.

Differences

From (b): numbers come in a single linear order, but beliefs have much more complex relations to one another.

From (c): different foods are completely different kinds of things, but beliefs are all the same kind of state of mind.

From (d): a reason for doubting one belief very often can be extended to a reason for doubting others, while someone who loves one other person is rarely led by this to loving others.

Which are more impressive, the similarities or the differences? Should we conclude that (a) is a persuasive or an unpersuasive argument?

3.7 Demon Possibilities, Paranoia, and Fantasy

Here are some common fantasies. Most people have one or another of them at some time in their childhood. They are in many ways like demon possibilities in that if any one of them is true then you do not know a lot of what you thought you did. They differ from demon possibilities in that they focus on grandiose ideas of being very special and on paranoid ideas that other people's attitudes are not what they seem.

(a) You were adopted as a baby, but your parents have decided not to tell you. In fact, they made everyone in your family promise to lie to you whenever the question arises.

(b) As a result of an intrigue in the royal family of your own or another country, the true heir to the throne has been stolen as a baby and raised in a nonroyal household. That child is you.

(c) It is really the twenty-third century. A psychological experiment is being carried out to find out what sort of person would have resulted from the child-raising style of the late twentieth and early twenty-first centuries. A child is being raised by actors who are behaving in ways that people behaved two hundred years before. All the technology and current events are recreated from the past. That child is you.

(d) A spaceship is traveling from earth to a distant galaxy. The journey will take a whole human lifetime, so there is only one human passenger, who is a new-born baby when the voyage begins. Everyone else on the spaceship is a robot, programmed to act toward that one human child as if it were living a normal human family life on earth. That child is you.

(e) A terrible fate awaits one child. (For example, the child is to be sacrificed to hungry aliens.) The child has been selected, but during the ten years before its fate it is being given a normal life. Everyone lies to it about the true facts. That child is you.

Imagine that you are a child being raised by two human parents and living a "normal" life. Consider the effects of the fantasies in the above list. Which of the following beliefs are undermined by which of the fantasies? (All the beliefs are things you think you know, but if some of the fantasies are true then those beliefs could be false. In that case, you would not really know them.) Some of the beliefs may not be undermined by any of the fantasies.

(1) The date on today's newspaper is today's date.
(2) You are living on the planet earth.
(3) $24 + 14 = 38$.
(4) Most of the things your parents tell you are true.
(5) Grass is green.
(6) Those around you have kindly emotions to you.
(7) You are in most respects like others around you.
(8) When those around you speak to you their normal intention is to make you share their beliefs.
(9) Your parents are your parents.
(10) You will eventually die like everyone else.
(11) The earth orbits the sun.
(12) You are the age you think you are.

(13) There were once dinosaurs on the earth.

(14) If you mix blue paint and yellow paint you get green.

This activity could be divided between groups. One group could choose beliefs 1 to 7 and the other beliefs 8 to 14. Each should decide which of the beliefs are undermined by which of the fantasies (a) to (e). Then they should compare their results. Points to compare:

◆ Which fantasy undermines most beliefs? Which undermines least?
◆ Which beliefs are most easily undermined? Which are least easily undermined?
◆ Are the fantasies that the first group finds to undermine 1, 2, 6, and 3 the same as the fantasies the second group finds to undermine 9, 11, 8, and 14 respectively? If not, why?

Divide the beliefs undermined by each fantasy into two classes: (i) those such that if the fantasy is true then they are false; (ii) those such that if the fantasy is true then you have no reason to believe them (though they may be true).

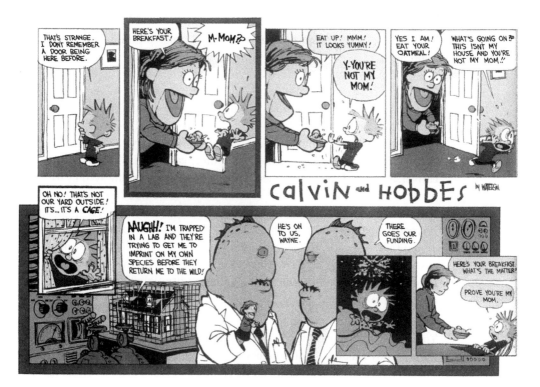

Figure 3.1 Calvin and Hobbes © Watterson. Reprinted with permission of Universal Press Syndicate. All rights reserved.

> ### Box 6 Fossils and Memory
>
> A nineteenth-century English biologist, Philip Gosse (1810–1888), wanted to undermine the evidence from fossils for Darwin's theory of evolution. He argued that when God made the earth only a few thousand years ago He made it complete with fossils in the ground just as if there had been other species of animals millions of years before. The twentieth-century English philosopher Bertrand Russell pointed out that Gosse had discovered a new demon possibility. If God can do this, He can also make a human mind, complete with memories, as if they were memories of five minutes or eighty years before. So perhaps you have only existed for five minutes, long enough to read this paragraph, and during these five minutes you have experienced some of the illusory memories with which you were created, of a lifetime preceding those five minutes, which you never actually had.

3.8 The Matrix

The film *The Matrix* takes place in a world in which all humans are in a situation just like the one Descartes worries about in the first two *Meditations*, or like a brain in a vat. The film centers on a young man, Neo – played by Keanu Reeves – a respectable programmer by day and a subversive hacker by night, who comes into contact with a band of rebels – particularly the leader Morpheus – Laurence Fishburne – and his ace agent Trinity – Carrie-Anne Moss – who show him that humans are being kept in vats by robots and provided with synthetic experience from a computer, called the Matrix. In a crucial conversation with Neo, Morpheus says, "There's something wrong with the world. You don't know what it is but it's there, like a splinter in your mind. . . . The Matrix is all around us. . . . It is the world that has been pulled over your eyes to blind you from the truth . . . that you are a slave . . . born into a prison that you cannot smell or taste or touch." Eventually Neo escapes from his vat and learns to fight the Matrix and its agents. By the end of the film we know that he is the One who will give humanity the chance to escape from the invisible prison.

To make the connection between the film and the demon possibilities described by skeptical philosophers, consider the following:

◆ Neo is in his office when a phone call from Morpheus tells him exactly what to do to escape from Matrix agents who have arrived to arrest him. How does Morpheus know exactly what is going on?

◆ The Matrix agents and rebels in the world of illusion can move in a faster way than ordinary humans. Both have something like magic powers. How can they do this?

◆ When Trinity is being chased by the agents she runs desperately toward a phone booth as agents drive a truck at it. She gets there just as the phone rings, the truck smashes into it, and when the agents examine the wreckage she has escaped. How?

◆ When Neo has agreed to join the rebels and to see the true state of the world, they inject him with a "tracer" so that they can "locate" him. What are they doing?

Although the film sticks consistently to the distinction between the world of illusion and the grim reality, there are hard questions to ask about whether the situation really makes sense.

◆ The heroes move between reality and illusion by using telephones, presumably using modems to transmit files through hacked connections to the Matrix. These are real phones in reality, but in the world of illusion they are illusory phones. The phone in the phone booth that Trinity uses to escape the agents and their truck, for example, is just a package of data in the execution of some program. So how can one manipulate an illusory phone to achieve a real effect?

◆ The campaign against the Matrix largely consists in martial arts encounters with its agents. That is, people in the world of illusion – who just by coincidence look exactly like their real physical bodies – can die. But why should this be fatal for their real physical bodies whose brains are transmitting the files that animate the illusory rebel bodies?

◆ At the end of the film Neo defeats the agents by simply moving faster than they can and then walks into a crowd and suddenly flies above it like a superhero. He now has powers that are greater than any agents of the evil Matrix. But outside the Matrix illusion he is still an ordinary human being subject to disease and the physical assaults of real robots. So what good are his illusory superpowers going to do?

Throughout the film there are hints of a mystical rather than a technological side to things. There is the interview with the woman who can foretell the future. (This scene is wonderful in a way that is hard to describe. I suppose it is mostly the acting.) There is the use of oriental martial arts instead of mechanical warfare, thus making mental preparation more important than equipment. There is the moment when Trinity revives Neo from death at the hands of the agents by telling him that she loves him and that her love is connected with his destiny as the One. The love theme and the theme of seeing the future both link to a theme of fate and of both wanting to choose one's own actions and of wanting to live up to one's destiny. (Are these the same? Or opposites? And why are physical bodies which have escaped from a vat any more free than illusions in a computer program?) And there are the moments at the end of the film when Neo has defeated the agents who were attacking him. His manner for this short time seems to evoke the grace of someone who has achieved a kind of enlightenment, while remaining in the world. He seems like a mythical Zen master. Can we understand this side of the film at the same time as keeping the intended technological interpretation? Or is it meant to suggest that even that is some sort of an illusion?

3.9 How Doubt Can Increase Belief

Sometimes if you doubt one thing you make another more believable. For example, if you doubt that you are awake you make it more believable that you are in bed. If you doubt that diseases are caused by viruses and micro-organisms then you make it more believable that they are caused by magic spells. (So I don't mean that doubting the one thing makes the other *actually* believable, just more *nearly* believable. The *plausibility* is raised.)

For each of these beliefs find another possibility that would become more believable if you were to doubt the belief.

◆ The earth is round.
◆ Life evolved from inorganic matter.
◆ Other people have minds like mine.

Possible answers If I doubt that the earth is round I may find it more believable that the earth is flat. If I doubt that life evolved from inorganic matter I may find it more believable that life was created by a God. If I doubt that other people have minds like mine I may find it more plausible that other people are robots.

The relevance of this exercise is, first, to the simple skeptical argument (see above). Assume that for everything you believe you may be able to find a reason for doubting it. It does not follow that you will ever find reasons for doubting everything simultaneously. For the reasons for doubting one thing may make another thing less doubtful.

There is also a connection with Descartes' skeptical argument. Demon possibilities undermine large numbers of ordinary beliefs. But many demon possibilities increase the believability of some beliefs too. If I suspect that I may be asleep then I am more likely to believe that I am in bed. If I suspect that I am a brain in a vat then I am more likely to believe that all my thought depends on a physical organ, the brain. Descartes' own demon possibility, the evil spirit, was meant not to have this feature. But it is a rather vague possibility; when we describe more concrete or definite demon possibilities they seem to increase as well as decrease the plausibility of some ordinary beliefs.

3.10 Skepticism and Religious Faith

Skepticism is based on doubt, and there are many reasons for doubt and many ways of doubting. Moreover, there are many different ways in which doubt can be used to support or attack a philosophical position. So it is not surprising that in the history of philosophy we find that skeptical positions play many different roles. Sometimes skeptics are attacking religious belief, and sometimes they are defending it. Sometimes skeptics are undermining the authority of science, and sometimes they are upholding it. This section gives a brief history of the different ways different kinds of skepticism have been used to support or undermine belief.

The positions discussed here are:

◆ Socratic skepticism
◆ Protagorean relativism
◆ dogmatism
◆ Pyrrhonism
◆ fideism
◆ Cartesian doubt

When reading this section, first pay attention simply to what these six positions are. Only after that should you think about which ones you agree with or take seriously.

In Greek philosophy, Socrates questioned traditional moral beliefs in order to reveal that people normally do not have good reasons for them. But he thought that there were in fact truths about such things as virtue and justice. So Socrates' method was skeptical but he was not really a doubter. Socrates' views can be contrasted with another Greek of his time, Protagoras, who claimed that when two people disagree neither one is wrong. They are both right for themselves. Or, as Protagoras put it, "humanity is the measure of all things." Just about anything you believe is true for you. This view is called *relativism*. So although Protagoras' method was not skeptical, his theory was meant as a radical challenge to the idea that we can think and investigate and discover which views are true and which ones false.

Another, later, skeptic was Sextus Empiricus. His brand of skepticism is known as *Pyrrhonism* (because many of the ideas come from a philosopher called Pyrrho whose writings have not survived). Pyrrhonism developed at a time when the ancient world was filled with social and religious controversies. Numerous cultures were thrown into contact with one another, and each of a large number of religions, including early Christianity, was trying to persuade people that its particular beliefs were true. Skeptics like Sextus Empiricus wanted to remain above all these controversies. So they opposed *dogmatism*, the philosophical attitude that some of our beliefs can be taken as certain. The attack on dogmatism was meant to show that any view that went beyond the small amount of definite evidence we have on any topic – scientific, religious, or moral – could be doubted. So we should stick with the simple appearances of things, which are certain, and not try to make conjectures about why things are the way they are. As a result, we should not feel disturbed or uncertain about moral or religious matters. Instead we should feel a calm unperturbed indifference to questions which the human mind cannot possibly settle. We should learn not to care.

Once Christianity had become the dominant religion of Europe, and Islam had come to dominate North Africa and the Middle East, the role of skepticism changed again. Now the dominant questions were whether one could show with certainty that the basic beliefs of one's religion were true, so that any-one of sufficient intelligence would have to believe them. Again there were dogmatists and skeptics. The dogmatic position now is that one can prove, say, that God exists and will reward those who obey him. The skeptical position in this context is that religious beliefs cannot be established *by reason alone*. Faith is necessary, where faith is the capacity just to accept what religious leaders, scripture, and perhaps one's natural common sense, tell one. So skepticism shows the necessity of faith. This position is known as *fideism*.

The situation changes again after the Reformation (the rise of Protestantism). Within Christianity there were now more options for belief, and moreover there was much dispute about the reasons on which one should base one's belief. Protestants put more emphasis on the Bible and on one's inner sense of con-viction, and less on the authority and traditions of the Church. Some early Protestants used skeptical arguments to show that one could not know, for example, that religious authority is as infallible as it claims to be. But of course if these arguments are pushed a bit further they suggest that one cannot know that the Bible is true, or know how to interpret unclear passages in the Bible or resolve contradictions in it. So Catholic thinkers of about this period tend to use skeptical arguments to defend a form of fideism: reason is not going to tell us what religious beliefs are true, so we have to accept what the traditions of our society tell us in order to live a decent Christian life. (Both Erasmus (1466–1536) and Montaigne (1533–1592) are in different ways fideists.)

With the rise of science, new claims of certainty emerge. By the time of Galileo (1564–1642), a physical science has appeared that seems to claim an ability to answer questions about the natural world with a precision and definiteness never before achieved, and at the same time to cast doubt on the claims of common sense. (See Section 3 of this chapter, and Chapters 14 and 15.) In the philosophy of Descartes (1596–1650) the skeptical questions raised by the Reformation and by the scientific revolution come together. Descartes wanted to use doubt as a way of eliminating all beliefs that could not achieve the kind of certainty which he thought a rigorous science could achieve, and to do this he wanted the most pervasive doubt possible. So he thought of the evil spirit hypothesis and the cogito (see Sections 5 and 11 of this chapter). His aim was to use a very severe doubt to establish a very great certainty.

To repeat, the six positions discussed here are:

◆ Socratic skepticism (Socrates)
◆ Protagorean relativism (Protagoras)
◆ dogmatism
◆ Pyrrhonism (Sextus Empiricus)
◆ fideism (Erasmus, Montaigne)
◆ Cartesian doubt (Descartes)

There are clear differences between these positions. For one thing, some are more skeptical than others. The more skeptical positions suggest that more of our normal beliefs are false. (For example, the least skeptical position is dogmatism, which suggests that all of our normal beliefs – of the dogmatist, at any rate – are true.) Another difference between them is that some of them are more consistent with conventional religious belief than others. (For example, dogmatism is clearly consistent with religious belief; and Protagorean relativism is not, since it suggests that an atheist's beliefs are true for him or her.)

Arrange the six positions on the graph in Figure 3.2, which classifies them in terms of how skeptical they are, and their consistency with religious belief.

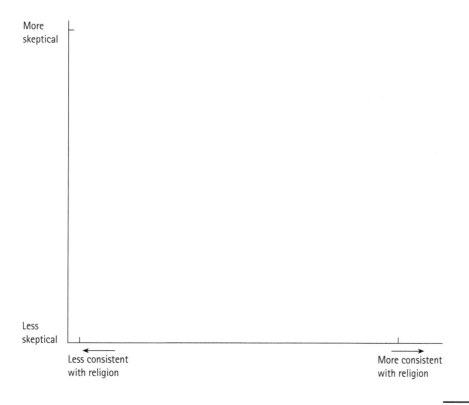

Figure 3.2

3.11 "I Think, Therefore I Am"

Descartes' method of doubt was meant to lead to certainty. It was supposed to allow Descartes to reject all his doubtful beliefs, leaving only the absolutely certain ones, on the basis of which he could establish an absolutely perfect science. But could he really do this?

What Descartes actually did was to find one belief which he was sure could not be doubted. Then he tried to get certainty to spread from this one belief to others.

The one basic certainty was his own existence. He reasoned as follows: I am doubting my beliefs, so whatever else I am doing I am doubting, but I could not doubt unless I existed, so I can be sure at any rate that I exist. Doubting is just one kind of thinking, and any kind of thinking requires a thinker. Descartes sums this up with his famous phrase "I think, therefore I am."

Proving your own existence is not really such a big accomplishment, if what you really want to do is to prove that there is a real world around you, that most of the things you have always believed are true, and moreover that there is a method of discovering the true secrets of nature. Descartes claimed to have done this. In the *Meditations* and in other books he produced a number of arguments to show how, once this one certain belief has been established, many other beliefs fall into place. There is not much agreement among experts on Descartes how this is supposed to work, how he thought he could spread the certainty around.

One possibility, which does seem to fit the sequence of ideas in the *Meditations*, is that he meant to argue from his own existence to that of God, and then to argue that since God is good and trustworthy, he would not allow any demon possibility (such as the existence of a deceiving spirit) to confuse people's sense of what is true and what is not true. This line of argument runs into trouble though, since to prove the existence of God he needs to know just the kind of things that are blocked by demon possibilities. For Descartes presents arguments for the existence of God which have the general character of mathematical proofs. If a malicious demon can make one think that $2 + 3 = 5$ when really $2 + 3 = 83$, then it certainly ought to be able to make one think that a proof of the existence of God is persuasive when in fact it is not.

Another possibility is that Descartes means the proof of his own existence – "I think, therefore I am" – just to show what it is like really to understand why something is true. Once you grasp the idea behind "I think, therefore I am," you see how it could not possibly be false. You see that it is what Descartes called a "clear and distinct idea." You can then compare it with other ideas to see if they are equally persuasive. If they are, you can accept them.

The aim would be first to accept that mathematics is reliable and then eventually to put together a doubt-proof scientific account of the world. And in the sixth and last of the *Meditations* Descartes suggests that, armed with a scientific understanding of the human organism, we can learn when perception is reliable and which of our traditional beliefs are true. Thus after a long detour through science, we finally manage to vindicate at least some of the beliefs that originally succumbed to doubt.

Again there is a problem. Descartes may say that he sees that "2 + 2 = 4" and "God exists" or "There is a physical world" are clear and distinct ideas that are as obviously true, once one appreciates the reasons for them, as "I exist." But this does not give him any reply to a skeptic who refuses to admit that these things do seem clear to him. "Try it yourself and you'll see," says Descartes. "I have and I don't," says the skeptic. Not very satisfactory.

But there is one aspect to this line of thought that is easily missed. Anyone who has done some nontrivial mathematics or some physics, or any other really serious science, sees what it is really to understand something. Once you have seen this, you find it hard to be content with anything less. You no longer accept arm-waving or fuzziness. So there is something to be said for showing someone some really "clear and distinct" ideas and then saying "Don't accept less than this."

Descartes' attempts to escape from his own doubts are thus not very successful. So what? What Descartes' failure suggests is that we will not be able to show that very many of our beliefs are certain. We are not going to get completely doubt-proof reasons for believing that the physical world exists, or that other people have minds, or that it is wrong to kill innocent people. But that does not show that we have no reasons at all to believe these things. Instead of asking for indubitable reasons, we should ask for adequate, persuasive reasons. We have yet to see if even that can be accomplished.

3.12 Doubting Even One's Own Existence

Descartes set a very high standard of certainty – so high that he could not meet it himself. That is, his arguments for the existence of God and for the existence of a physical world around him do not seem to provide the certainty that he wanted. That is not to say that they did not make a good case for the existence of God and the world; but Descartes wanted something much stronger than a very good case. To see quite how high were Descartes' standards for knowledge, remember that he doubted many of his former beliefs because they were undermined by the hypothesis that there might be an evil spirit who fools him into confusions about arithmetic. Descartes claims to have found beliefs that are not undermined by this hypothesis, namely those based on his confidence that he himself exists. But is even his belief in his existence quite as sure as he thinks? If an evil spirit could fool you about whether 2 + 3 is 5 or 7, might it also be able to fool you about whether you existed? Several philosophers have suggested that one's own existence is not really as certain as Descartes claims.

Here is Descartes' presentation, in the second *Meditation*, of his proof of his own existence:

> I suppose, therefore, that all the things I see are illusions; I believe that nothing has ever existed of everything my lying memory tells me. I think I have no senses. I believe that body, shape, extension, motion, location are fictions. What is there then that can be taken as true? Perhaps only this one thing, that nothing at all is certain.

> . . . Is there not a God . . . who puts these thoughts in my mind? That is not necessary, for perhaps I am capable of producing them myself. So am not I, at any rate, something? . . . But I have convinced myself that nothing in the world exists, that there is no sky, no earth, no minds, nor any bodies. So am I not persuaded that I too am not? Not at all, I certainly exist, if I am persuaded of anything, or even think anything. But there might be some deceiver, very powerful and very cunning, who works hard always to deceive me. If he deceives me, then there is no doubt that I exist. And however much he deceives me he will never be able to make me be nothing while I think I am something. So after thinking well and carefully, finally I must conclude . . . that this proposition I am, I exist, is necessarily true whenever I say it or conceive it in my mind.

Here is the reaction to this passage of the English philosopher Bertrand Russell (1872–1970):

> But some care is needed in using Descartes' argument. "I think, therefore I am" says rather more than is strictly certain. It might seem as though we were quite sure of being the same person to-day as we were yesterday, and this is no doubt true in some sense. But the real Self is as hard to arrive at as the real table, and does not seem to have that absolute, convincing certainty that belongs to particular experiences. When I look at my table and see a certain brown colour, what is quite certain at once is not "I am seeing a brown colour", but rather, "a brown colour is being seen." This of course involves something (or somebody) which (or who) sees the brown colour; but it does not of itself involve that more or less permanent person whom we call "I". So far as immediate certainty goes, it might be that the something which sees the brown colour is quite momentary, and not the same as the something which has some different experience the next moment.

And here is the reaction of the French philosopher Jean-Paul Sartre (1905–1980):

> One can ask why the I has to appear with the cogito [Descartes' argument "I think, therefore I am"], since the cogito, if used rightly, is the awareness of pure consciousness, not directed at any fact or action. In fact the I is not necessary here, since it is never united directly to consciousness. One can even imagine a pure and self-aware consciousness which thinks of itself as impersonal spontaneity.

These two passages contain rather similar criticisms of Descartes' "I think, therefore I am." (And this is interesting, because Russell and Sartre are writing in very different philosophical traditions.) They are both suggesting, among other things, that Descartes' argument does not prove his existence. It is not as easy as Descartes supposes to prove to himself that he exists. (Perhaps he can prove that something exists, but he has not proved that that something is him, Descartes.)

In each case Descartes is accused of having overlooked something. Russell says that Descartes has overlooked the possibility that you could know that something was thinking your thoughts but not know that the something was you. (So Descartes not only has to prove that something is thinking, but also has to prove that whatever is thinking "his" thoughts today is the same as whatever thought the thoughts he remembers from yesterday.) Sartre says that Descartes has overlooked the possibility that there could be a conscious experience that does not involve any awareness of self or "I" at all. These are similar points, but they are not the same.

Here are four imaginary situations. Some of them suggest that Russell's possibility can happen, and some of them suggest that Sartre's possibility can happen.

(a) Futuristic scientists take two people, George and Helen, and while they are asleep connect their brains. When they wake up each has a brief flash of memories stored in the other brain. For just a moment George thinks he is a woman of 45 who has had five children, and for just a moment Helen thinks that she is a male fighter pilot.

(b) Elaine falls in love with seductive and domineering Boris. Boris does not want Elaine to have any contact with her parents, and so he tells her false stories about her childhood, as if he were repeating her memories. Over several months these progress from the slightly misleading ("You told me once how your father would forget your birthday") to the completely false ("I'm not surprised you sometimes forget you used to live in Wyoming, since that was the time they beat you every day"). Eventually, Elaine has completely false beliefs about her past. She no longer knows who she is.

(c) After a car crash a young man has brain damage which gives him severe amnesia. He not only has no memories of his past, but also cannot form any new memories. He does not know what he was doing twenty minutes ago. Yet his intelligence and his capacity to reflect on his situation remain unaffected. He thinks: "I have no idea who I am. Perhaps I was created five minutes ago."

(d) Robin has been in a coma for two years. In a desperate attempt to revive Robin the doctors inject a strong dose of a powerful stimulant. Consciousness returns to Robin's brain for ten seconds and forms the thought "What an interesting smell; smelling is really wonderful." Then Robin dies.

Russell's possibility is that you could know that something was thinking your thoughts but not know that the something was you. Sartre's possibility is that there could be a conscious experience that does not involve any awareness of self or "I" at all.

Which of these four stories would show that Russell's possibility can happen? Which ones would show that Sartre's possibility can happen? Which would show that both can happen at once? Which ones could actually happen, now or in the future?

Descartes might accept that situations like those in (a) to (d) can happen, and say that this does not refute what he was trying to prove. He might say any of the following three things:

(1) The "I" in "I exist" is not a physical person in space and time. It is just "whatever is thinking this thought."
(2) After I have proved that I exist I have to go on to prove that my past exists, just as I have to go on to prove that the world around me exists.
(3) "I exist" really just means "thinking happens."

Suppose he did. Each of these replies would make more problems for him. Each makes even harder the job of showing that some of his original beliefs can be known to be true. Which of the replies (1), (2), (3) would produce which of the problems (i), (ii), (iii) below?

(i) Now he can no longer prove with certainty that any thing exists at all.
(ii) Now to prove that he exists he will have to prove that the world has existed for many years past.
(iii) The evil spirit hypothesis will make it impossible now to get from "I exist" to "Descartes exists."

3.13 Degrees of Certainty

The strongest and most ambitious kind of rationalism looks as if it will not work. That is, it does not seem as if just by reasoning and arguing we will be able to find a set of beliefs that we can treat as absolutely certain. In fact, the last section suggests that even your belief in your own existence is not completely certain.

This shows that the strongest and most ambitious kind of rationalism is wrong. It does not show that all rationalism is wrong. It does not show that reason is not a powerful tool, perhaps the most powerful tool, in our attempts to know the world. It does not show that the capacity to think, argue, find new concepts, find new theories and see problems with old ones, is not a very powerful one. But however powerful it is, it is not going to make much of what we believe completely certain. Suppose, though, that we ask for less than total certainty. And suppose that we do not ask reason to give us answers all by itself but allow it to consider evidence, and perhaps even to build on common sense or tradition. What will happen then? Later chapters of this book, particularly Chapters 6 and 11, which are respectively the last chapters of Part I and Part II, try to answer this question.

In this chapter we have seen that many beliefs are not as certain as we might have thought. Surprising doubts can arise. But that does not show that we should expect these beliefs to be wrong. There are still good reasons for believing most of them, even if those reasons are not as absolutely powerful as a strong and ambitious rationalism may want. A more modest rationalism can ask about *comparative* certainty. It can ask which beliefs are more certain and which are less certain. It can filter through all the beliefs we take for granted, not to throw out everything for which we can imagine the slightest doubt but to decide which beliefs look more dubious and which look safer. The really important question is how certain beliefs are after we have thought about them hard and considered many doubts and alternatives. But even on the basis of the thinking we have done in this chapter we can see that there are many beliefs between the obviously doubtful and the extremely certain.

Below are six beliefs that you probably treat as certain. In fact, you would probably think it was insane to doubt any of them.

(1) $312 + 108 = 420$.
(2) You were alive yesterday.
(3) When you wave at a friend your arm moves because you want it to.
(4) Cats are animals.
(5) If Garfield is a cat and all cats are animals then Garfield is an animal.
(6) You see with your eyes.

For each of these, describe an imaginary situation in which you would begin to wonder if it was true. (Remember the evil spirit; remember the brain in a vat possibility; remember Russell's and Sartre's possibilities. But these may all need to be adapted to link with the beliefs above.) Yet even in these situations you would probably only begin to wonder about their truth. For which ones might the wondering get nearer to real doubt? Rank each of them from 1 to 6, with the most certain (hardest to doubt) getting 6 and the least certain (easiest to doubt) getting 1.

Box 7 The Difficulty of Philosophy

Thinking about thinking is central to philosophy, and carefully aimed skepticism is a central tool in thinking about thinking. That immediately makes a problem in understanding philosophy. Often, philosophers seem to be considering completely outrageous claims. Already in this book we have mentioned several such claims: that there is no difference between right and wrong, that science is wrong about the world, that people do not have thoughts and feelings. (None of these has been asserted, just considered.) If someone might be saying something so outrageous, how can you tell if you have misunderstood?

A closely related source of difficulty comes from another similar philosopher's device: finding missing premises. Many arguments we normally find convincing rest on hidden premises which it seems unnecessary to state and mad to doubt. But once they are stated carefully they often seem less secure than one might at first think. And so by looking carefully at the assumptions we make automatically, philosophers can expose many vulnerable beliefs – beliefs about the physical world, beliefs about right and wrong, beliefs about politics. They may be vulnerable because when we think about them we decide they may be false. Or because thinking about them helps us to understand other things about the way we think. Thus it is that philosophy is always a potentially subversive subject. But thus it is that it is always a potentially confusing one.

It helps to distinguish between puzzlement and confusion. If you don't understand what someone says you are confused by it. You may also be puzzled about why the person should say such things. (One reason why you are puzzled is often that you cannot think of sensible missing premises to make valid the arguments the person is implicitly using.) And in philosophy too it is very easy to be confused. But in philosophy, puzzlement is often not a sign of confusion. It is often a reaction to the fact that the things that are being claimed or considered really are very strange. So if you feel lost and uncertain while reading a philosophy book or listening to a philosophy lecture, don't get discouraged. Ask yourself: am I reacting to the fact that I do understand what is being said and it is strange, or to the fact that I don't understand? Very often it is the first rather than the second. That's a good sign.

Conclusions of This Chapter

◆ *If we could discover the truth about the world and about morals just by thinking then we could throw away everything we believe just by habit or authority and start again from scratch.*
◆ *Some theories in physics or philosophy look sensible but when we question them we see they could not possibly be true.*
◆ *Descartes' skepticism was based on doubting a few central beliefs, such that if they were wrong then most of what we believe is doubtful.*
◆ *Descartes wanted to overcome skepticism by proving first that he existed, but it does not seem as easy as he thought to start from your own existence and then deduce complete and certain beliefs about the world.*

Further Reading

Galileo and Descartes

Selections from Descartes' *Meditations* in Part I of John Cottingham, (ed.), *Western Philosophy: An Anthology*. Blackwell, 1996.

René Descartes, *Meditations on First Philosophy*, especially Meditations I, II, and VI in *Descartes: philosophical writings*, translated and edited by Elizabeth Anscombe and Peter Geach. Nelson, 1954.

John Cottingham, *The Rationalists*. Oxford University Press, 1988.

Galileo Galilei, *Dialogues on Two World Systems*. Translated by Stilman Drake. University of California Press, 1953.

Stilman Drake, *Galileo*. Oxford University Press, 1980.

George Macdonald Ross and Richard Francks, "Descartes, Spinoza, and Leibniz", in *The Blackwell Companion to Philosophy*.

Rationalism

Chapters 1 and 2, and Part A of chapter 3, of John Cottingham, *Rationalism*. Oxford University Press, 1988.

Chapter 2 of Martin Hollis, *Invitation to Philosophy*. Blackwell, 1985.

Chapter 10 of Robert M. Martin, *There Are Two Errors in the the Title of this Book*. Broadview, 1992.

Chapter 3 of Adam Morton, *A Guide through the Theory of Knowledge*, third edition. Blackwell, 2002.

*Chapter 1 of Jonathan Dancy, *An Introduction to Contemporary Epistemology*. Blackwell, 1988.

The Matrix

William Irwin (ed.), *The Matrix and Philosophy*. Open Court 2002.

Electronic resources

Routledge Encyclopedia of Philosophy (available online at many universities): articles on Descartes; Galilei, Galileo; Rationalism.

Stanford Encyclopedia of Philosophy (http://plato.stanford.edu/): a priori justification and knowledge; Descartes, René; Skepticism (articles listed here are not yet available as this book goes to press; they should be available soon).

4 Rationalism versus Relativism in Morals

Introduction

Rationalist philosophers are optimistic that we can act certainty about the world or about morals by using logical arguments and similar kinds of reasoning. They consider extreme forms of doubt in order to prove how certain their beliefs are.

Can our beliefs about right and wrong ever be made completely certain? Some philosophers, rationalists about morals, try to determine with logical arguments what we must think right or wrong. But if the moral beliefs of a particular society can be shown to be right then the moral beliefs of other societies must be wrong. Moral relativists think that the moral beliefs of all societies are equally right and so they disagree with moral rationalism.

Can we have certain beliefs about the world around us? Many of our beliefs about the physical world cannot be supported just with logical arguments. . . .

Chapter Objectives

By the end of this chapter you should be able to answer the following questions.

◆ *Why is moral rationalism often based on a principle of impartiality?*
◆ *What factors can increase and decrease the justice of a society?*
◆ *How does Plato think he can prove what an ideal society would be like?*
◆ *What are the arguments for and against moral relativism?*
◆ *How is existentialism similar to moral relativism?*
◆ *What should we expect of a moral philosophy?*

Definitions

The following words used in this chapter are defined in the list of definitions at the end of the book:

existentialism   impartiality principle   moral relativism

4.1 The Appeal of Moral Rationalism

Suppose that someone thought that torturing children was morally good. Or suppose that someone thought that the less liberty the citizens of a country have, the better that country is. Such opinions seem obviously wrong. So obviously wrong that you might think that a little thought would persuade anyone not to hold them. So rationalism is possible in ethics as well as in science. And as in science there are weaker and stronger forms. A very strong moral rationalism claims that we can discover true moral and political opinions just by reasoning. We can prove them, like theorems in mathematics. A weaker moral rationalism will just defend the necessity for clear and logical thinking about morals, and will emphasize the power of rational argument to help us reject unhelpful moral ideas and think our way to better ones.

Moral rationalism is particularly plausible when it is applied to issues about justice and equality. Suppose, for example, that someone is advertising a job but refuses to consider any female candidates. This may seem unfair, unjust, since not all candidates are being treated equally. So we may challenge him to explain why it is not unfair. In so doing we are appealing to a very general principle: unequal treatment is unfair unless there is a good justification for it. That principle looks like a very basic moral truth. In fact it looks rather like "2 + 89 = 91" or "The circumference of a circle is longer than its diameter," something only a very confused person would disagree with.

If we wanted to prove that unequal treatment is unfair unless there is a good reason for it, we might try deducing it from even more basic principles. For example, if one person condemns another for telling lies but then lies herself she will be accused of hypocrisy. She does what she condemns. She may say "it's wrong for others but not for me." But if she does she will be going against a basic feature of morality: it is general and impartial. What is right for one person is right for all people in the same situation. Call this the *impartiality principle*. (It is a feature of Kantian ethics, discussed in Chapter 8.) And the unfairness of unequal treatment can be seen as a special case of this. Most moral systems acknowledge this fact in that they have principles like the golden rule "Do unto others as you would have them do unto you." So one might try to work out an ethical theory that began with such obvious principles and then deduced answers to the moral and political problems we face.

4.2 Four Golden Rules

So many philosophers and religious thinkers have suggested impartiality principles as the basis of ethics that it is very tempting to think that we can deduce all of morality from some such "golden rule." The point of this section is to add a little caution.

Confucius: "What you do not like when done to yourself do not do to others."

Jesus: "Therefore all things whatsoever ye would that men should do to you, do ye even so to them: for this is the law and the prophets" (Matthew 7: 12).

Thomas Hobbes (1588–1679): "that a man be willing, when others are so too, . . . [to] be contented with so much liberty against other men, as he would allow other men against himself. . . . This is that law of the Gospel; whatsoever you require that others should do to you, that do ye to them."

Samuel Clarke (1675–1729): "So deal with every man as in like circumstances we could reasonably expect he should deal with us, and in general we endeavour, by an universal benevolence, to promote the welfare and happiness of all men."

It is remarkable how many people have adopted impartiality principles like these as bases of their ethics. Very often they stress that a principle like this is the fundamental part of morality. (When Jesus says "this is the law and the prophets" he is saying that it will serve to guide one in a way that can sum up what is good in the Jewish moral tradition of his time.) Some of these people are religious thinkers and some, such as Hobbes and Clarke, are trying to found a morality on nonreligious grounds. Clarke, in fact, is trying to make a moral rationalism by deducing moral laws from obvious axioms, in deliberate comparison with mathematics.

But it is also important to see that all these ways of stating "the" golden rule are not exactly the same. Contrast the following claims:

(1) If you want people to do some act to you then you should do it to them.
(2) If you do not want people to do some act to you then you should not do it to them.
(3) If you want people to do acts which benefit you then you should do acts which benefit them.
(4) If you do not want people to do acts which harm you then you should not do acts which harm them.

Which of these are found in which of the four quotations? Some of the quotations may suggest two of them.

Rules (1) to (4) are different. This can be seen by asking what the rules require people to do in various situations. Suppose that we have two people, Rama and Sitta. Rama wants a cup of coffee and does not want to be taken to a rock concert. Sitta wants to be taken to a rock concert but does not want a cup of coffee. Rule (1) requires that Rama give Sitta a cup of coffee, and that Sitta take Rama to a rock concert. What do (2), (3), (4) require of each of them?

In the Rama and Sitta example, which of (1) to (4) are plausible descriptions of how they should treat each other?

Each of Clarke and Hobbes gives two ideas, and each claims that they are the same. But it is not clear that they are the same. Clarke claims that universal benevolence is required if you are to deal with every person as you might expect them to deal with you. We could state universal benevolence as:

(5) If an act benefits someone then you should do it.

Is (5) the same as any of (1) to (4)? Does it follow from any of them? (You can make sure of this by thinking up examples of the Rama and Sitta type.)

Hobbes claims that two rules are the same:

(a) Whatsoever you require that others should do to you, that do ye to them.
(b) Be contented with so much liberty against other men, as [you] would allow other men against [you].

Hobbes is saying that claiming only so much freedom as you will allow others is the same as doing for others what you need them to do for you. Is it? Let us take (a) to be a version of (1), and (b) to be (6) below. So (a) and (b) become:

(1) If you want people to do some act to you then you should do it to them.
(6) If you would not permit someone to do something to you then you should not permit yourself to do it to someone else.

Are these the same? Consider Rama and Sitta again. Suppose that Rama not only does not want to go to a rock concert, he would not permit anyone to take him. But although Sitta does not want a cup of coffee she would allow someone to give one to her. What acts does (1) require Rama and Sitta to perform? What acts does (6) require Rama and Sitta to perform? Are they the same?

4.3 Equality and Justice

This section is meant to help you to see the plausibility of rationalism about one particular ethical topic, the relation between equality and justice.

Imagine a very unequal society. It is divided into three groups: the Tops, the Mids, and the Bots. The groups determine basic aspects of people's lives, and a person's group is an important part of the way they think of themselves. The rules of the society work in terms of these groups. The Tops have most of the wealth and power. They are helped by the Mids, who as a reward have some, but considerably less, wealth and power. The Bots have only enough to survive. In fact they occasionally starve. They have practically no power.

This society seems unjust. It seems unjust because it is unfair, and unfair because it is unequal. It is not easy to define the terms "just" and "fair." Different philosophers work with very different definitions. Let us say that a society is fair when there are good reasons for any differences between how much of the important things in life different people get. And let us say that a society is just when there are good reasons for the ways people are treated. So if a society is fair it is just, but not necessarily the other way around.

Although this society seems unjust, it is not the most unjust society you can imagine. Suppose that you gave the most unjust society possible a score of 0, and the most just society possible a score of 10. What score would you give this society, just based on the description of it above? Write the score in this space.

But this description of the society leaves out a lot of relevant factors. Here are five ways in which the description could be extended or changed.

Sources of power

We do not yet know why the Tops have so much more power, and why the Mids and Bots do not take their power from them. Consider some possibilities:

(a) By chance, the Tops had more military power hundreds of years ago. But the situation that this has allowed them to set up is self-perpetuating: because Mids and Bots have no power they can get no power. For example, they have no weapons so they can get no weapons. In this case, power comes from physical force and physical force preserves power.

(b) The Tops have access to some scarce natural resource, which everyone needs. They guard the secret knowledge of it so that only they can provide it. This gives them wealth and power.

(c) The Tops have social and intellectual powers that are needed by the Mids and Bots. Although the other groups are poorer than the Tops, they are wealthier than they would be without the special skills of the Tops. They know this, so they permit the situation to continue.

Which of these possibilities increase or decrease the injustice of the society? To make your reactions definite, put a number between 0 and 10 in the spaces after each of (a), (b), (c).

The imbalance of power between Tops and the rest of the society is most arbitrary in (a) and least arbitrary in (c). Based on the numbers you put in the boxes, does a more arbitrary imbalance of power make a society more or less unjust?

Numbers

We do not know what proportion of the people are Tops, Mids, or Bots. Again, here are some possibilities:

☐
☐
☐

(a) There are very few Tops, rather more Mids, and very many Bots.
(b) The three groups are about equally divided.
(c) Most people are Mids, with much smaller numbers in each of the other groups.

Which of these possibilities increase or decrease the injustice of the society? Put a number between 0 and 10 in the spaces by each of (a), (b), (c).

The proportion of the population in the bottom group is greatest in (a) and least in (c). Based on the numbers you put in the spaces, does having a greater proportion in the bottom group make a society more or less just?

Unhappiness

Do the people like or dislike their unequal arrangement?

☐
(a) The lives of all of the Bots and some of the Mids are filled with resentment toward those better off than they are.

☐
(b) Many of the Tops feel a lot of guilt about their comparative wealth. They despair of ever producing a more equal society, in part because of the complacency of the Mids and the apathy of the Bots.

☐
(c) The lives of the Mids are dominated by snobbery. They like things the way they are because they can say that they are better than the Bots. The Bots do not resent their situation because they do not spend much time thinking about justice. They accept their lives and doubt that things could be much different.

Which of these possibilities increases or decreases the injustice of the society? Do any of them show that the society is just? Put a number between 0 and 10 in the spaces by each of (a), (b), (c).

The resentment of inequality is greatest in (a) and least in (c). Based on the numbers you put in the spaces, does more resentment of inequality make a society more or less just?

Voluntariness

Did the people ever choose to be in this kind of a society?

☐
(a) Every ten years there is a referendum. At each referendum, a majority votes to keep things the way they are.

☐
(b) Three hundred years ago representatives of all groups met and agreed freely on the basic structure of the society. There has been no meeting since.

☐
(c) The society came about when the Tops invaded the territory of the Bots and enslaved them. There are no elections or referendums.

Which of these possibilities increases or decreases the injustice of the society? Put a number between 0 and 10 in the spaces by each of (a), (b), (c).

Voluntariness is greatest in (a) and least in (c). Based on the numbers you put in the spaces, does more voluntariness make a society more or less just?

Social mobility

Do people remain in their groups for ever?

(a) By doing the right things a person can become accepted as a member of a higher group, and by doing the wrong things a person can sink to a lower group. □

(b) Children are assigned to social groups by a lottery. But once they are in a group they remain there for life. □

(c) Children of Tops, Mids, or Bots are members of those groups, and remain so for all of their lives. □

Which of these possibilities increases or decreases the injustice of the society? Put a number between 0 and 10 in the spaces by each of (a), (b), (c).

Social mobility is greatest in (a) and least in (c). Based on the numbers you put in the spaces, does more social mobility make a society more or less just?

Political arithmetic

By now you should have discovered whether you think that, based just on your reactions to this one case, justice is increased or decreased by each of the factors. Summarize your conclusions in the table.

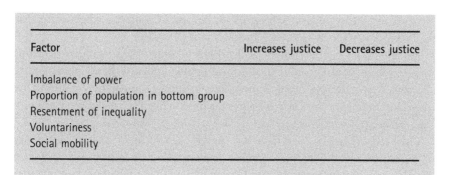

Factor	Increases justice	Decreases justice
Imbalance of power		
Proportion of population in bottom group		
Resentment of inequality		
Voluntariness		
Social mobility		

Compare your table with that of others. (Or compare the table your group has agreed on with the table another group has agreed on.)

If you discuss the possibilities under these five headings you will find that most people agree on many of the factors that make the society more or less

equal. When people disagree they will often find that it is because they disagree on some further question. (For example, they might disagree about
whether parents have a right to hand on wealth and power to their children.)
It is worth trying to state these further questions; some of them are very hard
to put into words.

But it was an imaginary society. Very few of the many possible combinations of the factors above make the relations between the Tops, Mids, and Bots
much like those in any real human society. Yet we can make judgments about
which of them are more and less fair. And some of these judgments are pretty
uncontroversial.

How can we know these things about imaginary societies? One answer
is that by the power of reason – by thinking and discussing and considering
examples – we can discover important truths about justice, or about fairness
or equality. It is not completely unlike the way we can discover truths about
arithmetic by counting imaginary objects. If you find this answer plausible then
you are allowing the possibility of moral rationalism.

4.4 Plato's Moral Rationalism

Plato, in his most famous work *The Republic*, described what he took to be
the ideal form of government. His conclusions are startling to us: the ideal
government, according to Plato, is an undemocratic dictatorship run by a
puritanical elite.

Before considering Plato's reasons for these hard-to-believe conclusions, notice
what is very plausible about it. What is plausible is that it is a moral rationalism which takes the idea of *justice* as its focus.

Imagine that a philosopher is giving a philosophy course and some students
are taking it. She considers giving marks to the students by the following rule:
give As to all the students who smile at her, and fail all the others. This rule
is obviously unfair. It violates a requirement of justice.

Imagine that a government is distributing some good, such as pensions
to the old, or access to education to the young. It distributes it according to
the rule that members of the same ethnic group as the ruling elite are to get
the good, and everyone else is to get nothing. This also obviously violates a
requirement of justice.

Now reflect on what you have just imagined. You have not considered any
complicated social facts or economic theories. You have not used any deep
knowledge of human nature. You have simply used the fact that you can often
tell justice from injustice, in real and imaginary situations.

This suggests that parts of political philosophy may be like mathematics.
We can think out some questions about justice by considering imaginary or
ideal cases, and by using our capacity to reason to make distinctions and draw
conclusions. (There could be a science fiction novel, set on a planet that was

very different from earth and populated by beings very different from humans, such that every reader of the novel was revolted by the injustice of some of these beings.)

Remember that Galileo and Descartes wanted to reject some scientific theories in advance, because when we think about them we see that they cannot be true. In a similar way Plato, and many other political philosophers, want to reject many political systems in advance, because when we think about them we see that they cannot possibly satisfy requirements such as those of justice.

(Warning: Plato lived almost two thousand years before Galileo. If there is an influence here it is that of Plato on Galileo rather than the other way around.)

Now briefly consider Plato's argument for his republic. He comes at the question from two sides. On the one hand he thinks that acting justly must be a good thing for the person who acts justly – it must make his or her life better. So there must be some deep aspect of a person which is satisfied only when the person acts in accordance with justice. So some deep aspect of the mind or soul must reveal the nature of justice. This same quality of justice will be found in a just state: a just city or country. (In Plato's day Greece was a collection of self-governing cities. There was no national government. Greek philosophers think of states the size of a city.) And therefore, according to Plato, a just state must in some way reflect the structure of the mind. Moreover, Plato thinks that the mind consists of desires, will, and intellect. A happy person is one in which all three can operate in harmony, and a just state is one in which there are corresponding social groups that similarly operate in harmony.

Plato's other angle on the question concerns issues about special interests and corruption. He sees clearly the tendency of democratic states to be prey to mass enthusiasms and the agitation of special interest groups. And he sees the tendency of dictators to corruption and selfishness. So, he thinks, a good state must be ruled by people who have no personal stake in the outcomes of their decisions. They will be perfectly impartial decision-makers.

These two approaches come together in Plato's final description of his republic. It is ruled by "guardians," philosopher-kings who own no property and have no private lives. They make all important decisions; their training is in mathematics, philosophy, and ethics, so that they can represent the intellectual part of the mind. Below them there are soldiers and administrators, corresponding to the mind's powers of decision-making, and workers, corresponding to desire. Thus the whole state is a picture of a harmonious mind, sane and contented, free from corruption and special interests.

There is a lot that seems alien, even repugnant, to us about this. Yet Plato has described a society firmly based on equality and impartiality. (He suggests that in many respects women are to have the same rights as men. And access to the governing class is to be by ability, not birth.) If we do not like the society he describes, that may be because there is some other important aspect of a good society that he has left out. But what is it? Suppose we manage to say where Plato has gone wrong, either by showing that his republic does not give a good life to its inhabitants or that there is an even better way of organizing a society. Then we will still have got to our conclusions by reason and imagination. Either way shows the force of moral rationalism.

4.5 Three Arguments from Plato's *Republic*

Below are three well-known passages from Plato's dialogue *The Republic*. In it he is describing his ideal society or state. He imagines it to be a city roughly the size of the cities of ancient Greece, which were independent states not united by any central government.

The first passage is a speech given by Socrates' main opponent in the dialogue, Glaucon. Dots (. . .) indicate where words have been left out, and [square brackets] surround words that are just a summary of what Plato says.

> *Imagine giving both the just and the unjust the freedom to do what they please, and then accompany them in imagination and see where desire will lead them. We will then find the just man acting in the same way as the unjust man because of the self-advantage which every creature by its nature pursues. . . . [Suppose that they have] the power which once came to the ancestor of Gyges [who found a ring which had the power that] when he turned it one way he became invisible, and when he turned it the other way he became visible. When he realized this he immediately arranged to become one of the messengers who went up to the king, and when he was there he seduced the king's wife and with her help set upon the king and killed him and took his kingdom.*

> *Suppose now there were two such rings, and the just man should put on one and the unjust man the other. Then neither one would continue to act justly and to refrain from taking the possessions of others, even though he could safely take what he wished even from the market place, and enter into houses and have sex with anyone, and kill and release anyone, and act in all ways just like a god. . . . And this proves that no one is just by choice but only because they have to be, in that everyone does wrong when he can get away with it. For every man believes, and truly, that there is more to be gained by injustice than by justice. For if anyone who had this kind of power refused to do any wrong or to take other people's possessions, he would be regarded as a pitiable fool by everyone who noticed it, even though they would praise him publicly, deceiving one another because of their fear of suffering injustice.*

The image of the ring of Gyges is striking. But what conclusion is Glaucon arguing for? Here are some things one might take the passage to be suggesting. (Do remember that these are not Plato's conclusions. He makes his character Glaucon suggest them because he thinks they need to be stated clearly and defended forcefully, so that he can refute them.)

(1) Given sufficient temptation, the best people will do the worst things.
(2) No one wants justice for its own sake.

(3) People say that justice is desirable only because it is in their interest to say this, not because they believe it.

(4) There is no difference between acting justly and acting unjustly.

(5) All creatures act from their own interest.

(6) People who act justly are fools.

Divide these six claims into three classes, A, B, and C, as follows:

(A) main conclusions of the passage – that is, claims that Glaucon wants the other claims he makes to support;

(B) incidental conclusions of the passage – that is, claims that Glaucon makes along the way to his main conclusions;

(C) not conclusions of the passage – claims that Glaucon is not making.

Now mark your classification by putting ticks in the table. (Discuss the resulting table with others in your group. Or compare your agreed table with that of another group.)

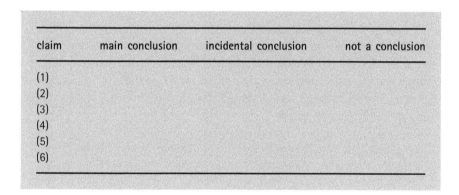

claim	main conclusion	incidental conclusion	not a conclusion
(1)			
(2)			
(3)			
(4)			
(5)			
(6)			

The next passage is from a speech by Socrates, later in the dialogue. Socrates is talking to Glaucon. Glaucon's replies are shown in normal type. They are included in part to show Socrates' style of argument, which involves asking many leading questions. At the end the passage refers to the *guardians*. These are the people who run the republic: they combine the roles of soldiers, judges, lawmakers, and civil servants.

> *We agreed that it is impossible for one man to master many arts. . . . Well, then, don't you think that the business of fighting is an art? . . .*
> True.
> *Does the shoemaker's art require more care than the art of war?*
> Not at all.
> *So we cannot allow a shoemaker to be at the same time a farmer, a weaver, or a builder, if we want shoes to be made well. And similarly we should assign to each person one*

occupation, to which that person is fit and naturally adapted. . . . Are we in any doubt that waging war properly is even more important? But no one can make himself an expert at, for example, checkers or dice who did not practice that and nothing else from childhood? So could someone who is cultivating the soil be at the same time a soldier and a shoemaker, or any other trade? No tool or equipment will make someone an artist or an athlete unless they have knowledge of how to use it and have practiced with it. Are we to believe that someone who just picks up a shield or other weapon will be competent in warfare?

A lot of use tools would be without experience!

The task of our guardians is the most important of all. It would require more leisure than any other business and the greatest knowledge and training.

I think so.

Does it not also require particular kinds of people, suited to the task?

Of course.

At five points Glaucon agrees with what Socrates is saying (*true, not at all,* and so on). Each time he does this Socrates is drawing another conclusion on the way to his final conclusion. State the conclusion that Socrates is drawing at each of these five points. Glaucon does not seem to be giving Socrates much opposition. At which points should Glaucon not have agreed so readily? (What might he have said instead?)

In the third selection Plato is arguing, through the mouth of Socrates, for one of his most philosophically difficult ideas. The idea is that justice is the same thing when it is found in a state or in a single person's character, so there must be some parallel between the structure of a state, at any rate of a just state, and that of the human mind.

We supposed that if we observed justice in something larger than an individual person it would make it easier to understand it in the individual. We agreed that this larger thing is the state, and so we described the best state we could, knowing that justice would be found in the good state. Now we must transfer our considerations back to the individual again. . . .

Now if you apply the same name to a big and a small thing, are they not alike in that respect? . . . So the just man and the just state will be alike in respect to justice. . . . Now the city was thought to be just when the three kinds of people in it . . . performed their functions. And it was moderate, brave, and wise, because of other characteristics of these three kinds of people. . . . And we shall therefore conclude that individual persons must have the same parts in their own minds.

It is clear what the conclusion is here: it is that the structure of the human mind must be similar to that of the ideal state. (In more detail: in both the mind and the state there must be three parts, corresponding to the virtues of wisdom, courage, and obedience. Plato goes on to describe the three parts of the mind as intellect, desire, and will. These correspond to the social classes of leaders, executives, and workers.)

And it is clear what assumptions Plato is using in order to argue for this. He is assuming that justice is the same thing in states and individual people, and that the ideal state has different kinds of people (three kinds, in fact), each doing their assigned task. What is far from clear is how Plato thinks those assumptions lead to that conclusion. Here are some arguments that might be used to get from the assumptions to the conclusion.

(i) A just state has three classes of people doing different tasks.
Therefore a just state has three separate parts.
Justice is the same in states and people.
Therefore the mind of a just person has three separate parts.
Therefore all people's minds have three separate parts.

(ii) A just state has three classes of people doing different tasks.
Therefore there are three tasks that must be performed in a just state.
Justice is the same in states and people.
Therefore the same tasks must be performed in just states and in just people.
Therefore there are three tasks that must be performed in the minds of just people.
Therefore there are three tasks that must be performed in any person's mind.
Therefore there are three parts in any person's mind.

(iii) A just state has three classes of people doing different tasks.
Justice is the same in states and people.
Therefore there are three tasks that must be performed in a just state or a just person.
These tasks will be performed well in a just state or person.
Therefore they will be performed less well in an unjust state or person.
Therefore they will be performed well or less well in any person.
Therefore there are three tasks which are performed in any state or person.
Therefore there are three parts in any person's mind.

Temporarily suspend your disbelief in the assumptions and the conclusions of these arguments. Which of them are the most persuasive? (You may prefer to understand this as: which of these arguments are the least unpersuasive?)

Here are some objections that could be made to the three arguments. Which objections would apply to which of the arguments?

(a) What happens in a just person's mind may be very different from what happens in an unjust person's mind.

(b) One part of a state or a mind can do several tasks.

(c) Compare justice to explosiveness. A stick of dynamite and an atomic bomb are both explosive. But there is very little resemblance between the parts of a stick of dynamite and the parts of an atomic bomb.

(d) Sometimes we use the same word to discuss very different things. For example, "depression" as applied to a weather system is completely different from "depression" as applied to a person. So it would be silly to say, for example, "depression is the same whether it is found in weather systems or in people."

(e) A task that is performed well in a just state or person may not be performed at all in an unjust one.

When these objections are taken into account, which of the arguments ((i), (ii), or (iii)) emerges as the most persuasive? Could it be modified to make it more persuasive yet?

Plato's arguments that the just state and the just person must resemble each other may not persuade you. And his conclusions about what the just state would be like may seem repugnant. It is likely that you will be repelled by the idea that most of the people in the state should have no influence on its policies, but it is also likely that you will be attracted by the idea that these policies should be based on what is wise rather than on simply what is popular. But Plato thinks that the second of these two features requires the first. You should remember that Plato has other arguments too; the *Republic* is a long book. Yet in producing these arguments Plato introduced into philosophy some ideas that will not go away. They include the idea that justice is a basic quality of states, that it concerns the motives of the people in the state and its political structure, and, most importantly, the idea that by using our powers of reasoning and imagination we can describe political systems that are very different from the ones we actually experience.

4.6 Moral Relativism

Moral relativism is the enemy of moral rationalism. Moral rationalism is based on the idea that by reasoning and argument we can discover the true moral and political beliefs. But moral relativism denies that there are any true moral and political beliefs. According to moral relativism, something is not simply right or wrong. It is right *according to a society*, and wrong according to another society. And no society's views on right and wrong are more true than any other's. According to moral relativism, *there are no moral facts*. There are no facts about what is right and wrong; there are only facts about what people *think* is right and wrong.

There is a big difference between facts about what people think and facts about what is true. It is not hard to see how there could be facts about what is truly right and wrong. Suppose, for example, that right and wrong were determined by God's commands. Suppose that there is a God and that what He commands is right and what He forbids is wrong. Then there are simple truths and falsehoods about morality. If God says "Honor your father and mother," then it is true that you should honor your father and mother. (This is discussed in Chapter 13, Section 1.)

Or suppose that right and wrong are determined by what is the only way in which human beings can live the most peaceful and profitable lives together. (This could be a very conservative view, describing a traditional society as the only one in which people can flourish. Or it could be a radical view, describing some social arrangement we have not yet achieved.) Then again there would be simple truths and falsehoods. If in the most workable form of social life people take care of their children then it is true that you should take care of your children. (Something like this is discussed in Chapter 13, Sections 7 to 9.)

If right and wrong were determined either by God's commands or by the best way for people to live together, there would be moral facts. They could be very different from the moral opinions of people in any society. People could be wrong about God's commands, or they could be wrong about the ways in which people can and cannot live together successfully. God could give us very definite and explicit commands, but do so in a whisper, so that even the most inspired or prophetic human was often in doubt about what to do. Or there could be a simple solution to many social problems that people just never thought of. On either of these accounts, what is right or wrong is so quite independently of what people think, just as the facts that $98,765 \times 12,345 = 1,219,253,925$ and that robins eat worms are.

But notice the *ifs*. If morality is God's commands, or if it describes an uniquely desirable way of life, then there are moral facts. But we can make different assumptions about what morality is, and then we can conclude that there are no simple moral facts.

How could moral beliefs not be about moral facts? They could be like beliefs about table manners. In Europe people are supposed to put their forks in their left hand and their knives in their right hand and leave them in those hands. In North America they start off like that but then switch around. In China people use chopsticks. Are there truths of the form "It is good manners to eat in such and such a way"? Of course not. What there are, are truths of the form "In such and such a country it is good manners to eat in such and such a way."

So table manners are a bit like left and right. Although we say "this is to the right of that," what is actually true is that this is to the right of that from a certain point of view. (Paris is to the right of New York looking from the south, but to the left of New York looking from the north.) Similarly, although a parent in Europe or America may say to a child "It is good manners to pick up your knife with

> Moral beliefs might be like beliefs about table manners.

your right hand," what is actually true is that it is good manners in a certain culture to pick up your knife with your right hand.

The point of the analogies should be clear. What places are to table manners, and points of view are to right and left, societies might be to morality. Moral beliefs are not simply true or false but only relative to societies. Some societies have the most peculiar taboos and customs, and relative to those societies very peculiar things are right and wrong. Or so we might argue. To believe this is to believe in moral relativism.

Moral relativism is in some ways a comfortable view. It makes moral knowledge easy. At least, you can easily know what people think is right and wrong. (Knowledge of what really is right and wrong is impossible, since there is no such thing.) You can know what is right according to your society simply by learning the beliefs and standards that are current in it. You learn what it is that parents teach their children and moral authorities such as religious and community leaders urge ordinary people to do, and then you know what is right for people in your society. (And you can learn these things about another society and learn what is right according to it.) Moreover, moral relativism makes it easy to tolerate the different moral views of people in other societies. If you and the people with whom you live think that suicide is always wrong, but people in some other place think that sometimes it is not wrong, then suicide is always wrong according to your culture but not always wrong according to theirs. (Cultural tolerance is discussed at greater length in Chapter 6.)

But these advantages have a price. If moral relativism is true then we can have a kind of moral knowledge. But we can only know what is right and wrong in a culture. Suppose that people in some culture believe that when a man dies it is the moral duty of his widow to kill herself so that she can be with him in the afterlife. Then moral relativism allows us only to say that these beliefs are not our beliefs. According to moral relativism it does not even make sense to say that they are wrong beliefs. So there is no justification for trying to persuade people that they are wrong.

4.7 For and Against Moral Relativism

Here are three arguments for moral relativism, followed by three against it.

For

Cultural variation   The simplest reason for believing in moral relativism is the way moral beliefs vary from one culture to another. If intelligent, kind, and honest people in other cultures have very different beliefs about right and wrong from you, and you do not have any reason to think you have more moral insight than them, then you may think there is something wrong in calling their views false. But it would be equally wrong for them to call your views false. Each view about morality is right, for the people who hold it.

If we put this argument in skeleton form and focus it on a pair of imaginary cultures and a particular moral belief, we get the following:

People in culture A think that suicide is always wrong.
People in culture B think that suicide is sometimes right.
People in both cultures are thoughtful and considerate.
Therefore suicide is wrong for people in culture A but sometimes right for people in culture B.

Think about your reaction to this argument. It helps to pin down your own reactions before you compare them with those of others. Tick one or more of the spaces below. This argument is:

convincing ☐ suggestive but not convincing ☐ doubtful ☐ unconvincing ☐

Knowability   Morality is meant to guide our actions. It cannot do this if we cannot know what is moral. If we can know what is moral then morality has to concern things in and around our everyday lives. The moral beliefs of the communities we belong to are not hard to know and they are intimately connected with our everyday lives. Therefore it is reasonable to take them as defining what is right.

A version of this argument in extremely simplified skeleton form is the following:

Morality can be known.
If morality is about what people in a culture think is right and wrong then it can be known.
Therefore morality is about what people in a culture think is right and wrong.

Think about your reaction to this argument. Tick one or more of the spaces below. This argument is:

convincing ☐ suggestive but not convincing ☐ doubtful ☐ unconvincing ☐

Tolerance   People belonging to different communities and cultures have different ideas about how they should act. If you believe that there is a single objective morality then you must believe that many of these communities and cultures are wrong. But who are you to say that whole cultures, which have developed over thousands of years, are wrong? Moreover, in modern life cultures have to live together, and they cannot do this if they do not respect each other's beliefs about morality. So if we are to live peacefully in a world in which different cultures coexist then we must not believe that some cultures are wrong about what is right. Tolerance requires relativism.

One way of putting this argument into skeleton form is as follows:

We should tolerate other cultures.
If we tolerate other cultures we should believe that their views are not mistaken.
Therefore we should believe that other cultures' views about right and wrong are not mistaken.

Think about your reaction to this argument. Tick one or more of the spaces below. This argument is:

convincing ☐ suggestive but not convincing ☐ doubtful ☐ unconvincing ☐

Against

Awful cultures   At some times and places people have not only done terrible things, but have done terrible things with the permission of their cultures. Terrible things have been considered right: slavery, the abandonment of children, the killing of widows. But these things are simply wrong, whatever the beliefs of people in these cultures. So although people in cultures that believed in slavery, for example, did honestly think that slavery was not wrong, slavery is and was wrong, even for them.

Here is the argument in skeleton form, using the particular example of slavery:

People in some cultures have thought that slavery was right.
Slavery was wrong for those people.
Therefore it is not true that if a culture believes that something is right then it is right for that culture.

Think about your reaction to this argument. Tick one or more of the spaces below. This argument is:

convincing ☐ suggestive but not convincing ☐ doubtful ☐ unconvincing ☐

Moral progress   Cultures develop. All cultures used to have different beliefs about right and wrong than they do now. For example, people in Europe and America accepted slavery 300 years ago, but now realize that it is wrong. More recently, views about the status of women have been changing. Many people no longer believe that it is the duty of a woman to marry and bear children. These have not been arbitrary changes. They came about because we found better ways to lead our lives. So moral progress is possible: sometimes a culture will change its beliefs for the better. But if the later beliefs are better it must be because they are nearer to what is objectively right.

There are many ways of developing and interpreting this argument. In skeleton form one simple one is as follows:

Cultures change their beliefs about right and wrong.
Sometimes the later beliefs are improvements on the earlier ones.
Therefore the later beliefs are more right for the people in the culture than the earlier ones.

Think about your reaction to this argument. Tick one or more of the spaces below. This argument is:

convincing ☐ suggestive but not convincing ☐ doubtful ☐ unconvincing ☐

Argument If someone's moral beliefs are different from yours you can do more than either tolerate or disapprove. You can argue. You can begin a discussion with the person which challenges their views. No doubt in such a discussion the other person will challenge your views too. But often one person will convince the other. Thus racists can be asked why they think that people of different races should be treated differently. If they cannot come up with convincing reasons then they will find themselves under some pressure to change their views. In fact, many of our moral and political views have changed in response to arguments. (Sometimes these arguments go on for decades.) If you can find a convincing argument against a moral belief or practice then you have gone some way to showing that it is objectively wrong. So the mere fact that moral argument is possible shows that moral relativism is not right.

One skeleton argument that can be extracted here is as follows:

We can argue reasonably about morality, and sometimes we can convince one another.
If moral relativism were true there would be nothing to argue about.
Therefore moral relativism is not true.

Think about your reaction to this argument. Tick one or more of the spaces below. This argument is:

convincing ☐ suggestive but not convincing ☐ doubtful ☐ unconvincing ☐

Comparing for and against

Look back at your reactions to these six arguments, as indicated by the spaces you have ticked after each one. Discuss them with others and reconsider any where you find that most others disagree with you. (But don't fold too quickly. The others could all be wrong.) On the basis of these reactions, which arguments do you find stronger: the ones for moral relativism or the ones against it?

Decide what you consider to be the most powerful argument *against* your favored position, guided by your reactions in the spaces and the reactions of others. (If you are *sympathetic* to moral relativism consider the argument *against* it that seems to challenge your view most powerfully, and if you are *unsympathetic* to it consider the most powerful argument *for* it.) Try to refute the argument, either by challenging its premises or by saying why its premises do not support its conclusions. (The skeleton forms may help here, but you can consider anything in the fuller statements of the arguments.)

After you have done this, look at all six arguments again. Do you want to reconsider your decision about whether moral relativism is easier to defend or attack?

Box 8 On Becoming a Martian

All philosophy forces you to consider the beliefs of your own culture as if they were those of a strange and distant people. It makes you an anthropologist at home. For the assumptions that it is usually most profitable to make explicit and question are the implicit ones, the everyday ideas that may seem too obvious even to state. This is especially true of moral beliefs. A moral philosopher has to ask herself why she thinks it wrong to torture and why just societies are better than unjust ones. She has to treat these beliefs as if they were very strange ones, in need of explanation. Some of them are probably beliefs that all human beings take for granted. So in examining them one is acting like a visitor from Mars, for whom all human beliefs are unnatural.

This does not only happen in philosophy. There is a literary technique, too, of describing very familiar things so that they sound strange and exotic. The eighteenth-century Irish writer Jonathan Swift was a master of this. For example, in one episode of his *Gulliver's Travels* he describes the "grand academy of Lagado," where learned but impractical scholars make all sorts of crazy inventions, like turning ice into gunpowder, or building houses by starting with the roof and working down, or trying to breed hairless sheep. It is a Martian picture of a university.

The aim is to give a description of something apparently remote in order to understand some aspect of what is otherwise too near to see. When you see what is going on, things suddenly look different. Assumptions you had always made without thinking now seem strange and dubious. Is this a healthy activity? Only if you also learn how to snap out of it.

4.8 The Ik

One of the arguments against moral relativism appealed to the existence of awful cultures. And one of the defenses of moral relativism appealed to the import-ance of tolerating cultures different from our own. Anthropologists describing the societies they study usually are very careful not to judge the values of the people they are studying, even though these are often very different from the values by which the anthropologists themselves live their lives. One exception to this is the book *The Mountain People*, by Colin Turnbull. Turnbull spent several years living among the Ik, a people who had been forced to move from their former territory and former way of life to a miserable existence on the brink of starvation. Under this pressure they developed a set of attitudes which horrified Turnbull. All affection and cooperation between people, even parents and children, seemed to have disappeared. Here are some incidents recorded by Turnbull as typical.

> *An old man, Lolim, with no occupation that makes him useful to others, is given food and tobacco. The younger people attack him to take his food away. The children ridicule the old man and throw stones at him. His grandson . . . used to creep up behind Lolim and with a pair of hard sticks drum a lively tattoo on the old man's bald head. Once Lolim, trying to cover his poor head with his bony arms, accidentally caught Arawa [his grandson] in the mouth. Instantly Arawa . . . slapped Lolim as hard as he could on the side of the face, knocking the old man to the ground. There were shrieks of delighted laugher, but as the old man lay still, not moving and not even crying, the fun wore thin.*

> *It was rather commonplace, during the second year's drought, to see the very young prying open the mouths of the very old and pulling out food they had been chewing and had not had time to swallow.*

> *When . . . Bula was in great pain and was sitting outside . . . crying, holding her breast under which a little puddle of pus and blood had formed, Atum, her father, took notice of her only to ask if she had to sit there – she was blocking the entrance and her crying gave him a headache.*

> *She . . . had tried to make her way down the mountainside. But she was totally blind and had tripped and rolled to the bottom . . . . , and there she lay on her back, her legs and arms thrashing feebly, while a little crowd standing on the edge above looked down at her and laughed at the spectacle.*

Episodes like these occur in every society, But at this time among the Ik they were normal and typical. Turnbull expresses his dismay. But in fact his feel-ings are very mixed, and he has a complex sympathy for the Ik.

> *[A] This seemed to strike hard at the assumption that there are such things as basic human values, at the very notion of virtue, of goodness even. . . . Yet biologically it*

made good sense. The children were as useless as the aged . . . you can always get more children. So let the old go first, and then the children. Anything else is racial suicide, and the Ik, I almost regret to say, are anything but suicidal.

[B] And I thought of other old people who had joined in the merriment when they had been teased, knocked over or had a precious morsel of food taken from their mouths. They knew that it was silly of them to expect to go on living, and, having watched others, they knew that the spectacle was really quite funny. . . . Perhaps if we had left Lo'ono, she would have died laughing, happy that she was at least providing her children with amusement. But what did we do? We prolonged her misery for no more than a few brief days. . . . At the time I was sure that we were right, doing the only "human" thing. In a way we were – we were making life more comfortable for ourselves, confirming our own sense of superiority. But now I wonder. In the end I had a greater respect for the Ik, and I wonder if their way was not right.

[C] [If the Ik] once possessed in full measure those values that we all hold to be basic to humanity, indispensable for both survival and sanity, then what the Ik are telling us is that these qualities are not inherent in humanity at all, they are not a necessary part of human nature. . . . The Ik have successfully abandoned useless appendages, by which I refer to those "basic" qualities such as family, cooperative sociality, belief, love, hope, and so forth, for the very good reason that in their context these militated against survival.

Here are three simple interpretations of what Turnbull might be saying:

(i)   If conditions are so bad that decency is an obstacle to survival then people should not act decently.
(ii) If conditions are so bad that decency is an obstacle to survival then you cannot expect people to do what they should.
(iii) If you are not yourself subject to awful conditions you have no right to judge the results that those conditions produce in others.

Which of these best fit (A), (B), (C) above? (Perhaps none of them does. In that case, can you provide a better interpretation?) Which, if any, best express your reaction to Turnbull's description of the Ik?

(Think of the advantages as well as the disadvantages of cooperation. Think of the ways people have survived other horrific situations. Think of societies nearer to your own which you do not hesitate to criticize.)

4.9 Law and Morality

Many of the controversial claims that moral relativism makes about morality are much less controversial if one makes them about law. What is legal in one country is often not legal in another. You can drive as fast as you like on the Autobahn in Germany, but you may be arrested if you exceed 55 mph in the

United States. So there are no simple truths like "It is illegal to drive at more than 55 mph." One has to make the claim relative to a legal system and say, for example, "It is illegal in Ohio to drive at more than 55 mph." Moreover, it is pretty plausible that beliefs about the law are really about legal practices, about what legislators have decided and judges ruled. The explanation of someone's belief that it is illegal in Ohio to drive at more than 55 mph is ultimately that the Ohio State Legislature passed a particular bill at a particular time. So a mild "legal relativism," the claim that beliefs about the law are really about legal practices in different legal systems, is true.

The really difficult questions are about the relation between morality and the law. Suppose you think that a law is morally wrong: should you therefore disobey it? Suppose you are traveling in a foreign country, whose legal system you feel no loyalty to: are you obliged to obey the laws of that country?

The important concept here is that of the moral force of law. This is a moral and not a legal concept; it concerns a person's moral obligation to obey a law. Most people do consider themselves to have such an obligation. They consider it morally wrong to break the law. But most people do not think that this is their only or their strongest obligation. So when obeying the law means doing something wrong they will break the law. (A trivial example: you are rushing someone to hospital in your car, someone who may die if you do not break the speed limit. It is your moral duty to preserve their life, and this is stronger than your obligation to obey this particular law.)

Do some laws have more moral force than others? You would probably break the speed limit rather than break a promise to a friend, but you might not break a law against theft rather than break a promise. But this may be because laws against theft forbid acts which are morally as well as legally wrong. However, theft is defined as taking what belongs to another, and this concept of possession ("what belongs to another") is a legal concept, defined by the laws of a particular time and place. (For example, the laws about how property is inherited, about who owns family property, and about children's property rights vary greatly from one legal code to another. See Box 9.) So law and morality are here very closely tangled up with one another.

We can extract from this an argument for moral relativism and an argument against it:

- ◆ *For* What is legally required varies from place to place, and laws often define the concepts (such as property) that morality uses. So what is morally required will vary from place to place.
- ◆ *Against* Some laws have a strong moral force and some do not. This must be because some laws get their authority from more than simply the opinions and practices of the people concerned.

How convincing are these arguments? Record your reactions to them by ticking the appropriate column in the table.

	Convincing	Suggestive	Doubtful	Unconvincing
Argument for				
Argument against				

Now imagine what your reaction would be if the laws where you live were changed in various ways. Some of them might have moral force for you – you might think that you ought to obey them even if the government does not compel you to – and some of them might not. Some, in fact, might seem to you so immoral that you would think that you ought to disobey or obstruct them. Consider the following possible laws:

1. A law making it necessary to pay a large fee to vote in an election.
2. A law making private property in air, so that you have to pay if you breathe air that belongs to someone else.
3. A law requiring everyone to contribute to the relief of famine elsewhere in the world.
4. A law forbidding the telling of racist or sexist jokes.
5. A law forbidding parents from teaching their children the beliefs of unusual cult religions.
6. A law requiring people to display photos of the head of state on their walls.

Which of these would you be morally obliged to obey? Which would it be morally permissible to ignore? Which would you be morally obliged to disobey or obstruct? (In each case you may think the answer is "None.") After discussing these questions with others record your answers with ticks in the table.

Imaginary Law	Obliged to obey	Permissible to ignore	Obliged to disobey
1			
2			
3			
4			
5			
6			

Some of these possible laws might be thought to make problems for the two arguments (*For* and *Against*) above. In fact your reactions to the possible

---

Box 9 **A Puzzle about Property**

I buy a Christmas present for you, and you put it under your tree, intending to open it on Christmas Day. Later, I decide to give you something else instead, so I wrap up the new present in identical wrapping paper and exchange them when you are not looking. Is this theft? Only if the present belongs to you. Do you own it when you have put it under your tree but you have not yet opened it? There is no answer if we are just talking about everyday morality. The rules of a legal system might define ownership more carefully, and then my act might be stealing in one legal system and not in another. Then people living in the jurisdiction of the one system would be more likely to think that my act was wrong. They would think this not just because I was (or was not) breaking the law but because the legal system had shaped the concept of property which their everyday morality used.

---

laws may make you rethink your judgments of how convincing the arguments were.

Did you judge the *For* argument to be "persuasive" or "suggestive," and judge law 2 as one that it might be permissible or obligatory to ignore? If so, find someone who had the same reaction to law 2 and an opposite reaction to the *For* argument, and discuss it with that person.

Did you judge the *Against* argument to be "persuasive" or "suggestive," and judge law 4 as one it might be permissible or obligatory to ignore? If so, find someone who had the same reaction to law 4 and an opposite reaction to the *Against* argument, and discuss it with that person.

(One thing that your reactions may bring out is the fact that "morally wrong" does not mean "ought to be illegal." It is perfectly reasonable to say that something is wrong – people should not do it – but that it should not be against the law.)

4.10 Existentialism

A modern philosophical view which is in some ways like moral relativism is *existentialism*. Existentialism is in fact a name applied to a very varied collection of theories, including ideas about many topics besides morality. But at the heart of most of them is the idea that individual human beings have to choose how they are to live, what they are to value, and what actions they are to perform. We cannot, according to existentialism, get complete guidance from tradition or religious revelation or reason, for in the end it is up to the individual person to choose whether to accept what religion or tradition or reason says.

The original inspiration for existentialism came from the German philosopher Friedrich Nietzsche (1844–1900) and the Danish philosopher Søren Kierkegaard (1813–1855). (Nietzsche argued that Christianity was a religion for weak people who do not want to face the problem of making their own morality, while Kierkegaard argued that Christian faith is something that has to be accepted by an arbitrary choice. Among later existentialists too one finds both Christians and vehement anti-Christians.) In the twentieth century the two most influential existentialists have been the German philosopher Martin Heidegger (1889–1976) and the French philosopher Jean-Paul Sartre (1905–1980). All these thinkers have stressed the fundamental nature of the choices that each person must make. Some of these choices concern things so basic that they can be described as decisions about how one is to exist in one's environment, what kind of a thing one is to be. These are decisions like: "Am I going to live with or apart from others?", "Am I going to make my own decisions or let others make them?", "Am I going to concentrate on the here and now or the abstract and ideal?" Such choices are called *existential* because they concern the way in which one is to exist. Both Heidegger and Sartre stress the difficulties of such decisions, their anguished quality. You make these choices all by yourself, in a terrifying solitude.

The resemblance with moral relativism lies in the emphasis on arbitrary choice. Every person has to choose their morality, and there is no ultimate guidance how to do it. One simple difference from moral relativism lies in the emphasis on individual choice: it is not whole societies or cultures but individual people who have to choose. If morality is relative, according to existentialism, it is relative not to particular societies but to particular people.

There is a deeper difference, though. Existential choices are hard and painful. There is a strong temptation not to face up to them. You can do this by simply accepting the choices of other people about what kind of a person you are or what your role in life is. You can lead the life other people expect you to. Or you can pretend that you do not have the freedom to choose, for example, by letting your responsibilities to other people determine the whole course of your life. To evade existential choices in ways like this is to fail to live fully; it is to be blind to what it really is like to be a free human agent. Existentialist philosophies condemn such evasion.

This aspect of existentialism, the ability of people to choose not to fall into the roles that others assign to them, has influenced feminist philosophers. The writings of the French philosopher Simone de Beauvoir (1908–1986), such as *The Ethics of Ambiguity* and *The Second Sex*, are important here. As de Beauvoir wrote:

> In particular, those who are condemned to stagnation are declared to be happy on the pretext that happiness consists in immobility. This is a notion we will not use. The perspective that we adopt is that of existentialist ethics. Every person is real only by using her projects as a mode of transcendence; she achieves her liberty only by

continually reaching out to other liberties. The only justification for present existence
is its expansion into an indefinitely open future.

Existentialism thus does not offer any definite guidance to an individual human person trying to decide how to live. In fact it denies that there is definite guidance to be had. Hard choices have to be made. But it does provide something like an ethics of choice: to fulfill the potential of a free human being you have to face the depth of your choices with courage, and invent your own way of existing. Then, having made your choices, you must live with them, not pretending that they were forced on you.

4.11 What Is Morality About?

This chapter began by making a case for moral rationalism. The aim was to make you take seriously the idea that we can discover things about politics and morality by the use of reason. Argument, discussion, and analysis can guide us when we want to know how to act. So if this view is right there are definite moral truths and we can know them. In later sections of this chapter very different ideas were discussed. Moral relativism and existentialism allow much less hope that we can get permanent answers about how we ought to act. Although we may be able to know what the morality of some particular culture is, or what our own moral commitments are, there is no definite answer, valid for everyone, when someone asks: "What should I do?"

One very striking difference between these different views is what they think morality is about. At one extreme there are absolutist views like the view that morality consists in God's commands. If that is what morality is about, then although there may be difficulties in finding out what it is that God is commanding, there is a definite objective morality which we can potentially discover. At the other extreme are subjective views like existentialism, which make morality consist in the deep commitments of individual people. If that is what morality is about then there just is no point in looking for ways of discovering definite objective moral truths.

How do we settle questions about what morality is about? Suppose that someone says: "Morality is about the opinions of my guru. That is what I mean by 'morality.' So in order to know what I ought to do I first have to discover what my guru thinks." Is there any way of showing that this person is wrong?

Here is one way in which we can begin to settle these questions. All of us have opinions about right and wrong. Some of these we feel very intensely. For example, think of our reaction to someone who tortures children. Just about everyone will react not only with the abstract thought that this person's action is wrong, but with intense disapproval and loathing. If we think something is sufficiently wrong we hate it and anyone who does it. And then there are real moral problems, situations in which we do not know what we ought to do. For example, think of any case in which human welfare has to be balanced against damage to the environment. (Imagine a group of hunters whose way of life is based on hunting an endangered species of whale.) Should we protect the environment even at the cost of severe human suffering? Most of us are genuinely puzzled by such cases. Although we may have opinions here we usually feel pretty unsure of them. Because of these two kinds of cases there are two rather different requirements for a moral philosophy.

(A) On the one hand a moral philosophy must be in accord with many, at least, of the moral opinions that we feel intensely. Ideally, it should connect them up together in a way that helps us see the deeper values that underlie the things we care about.

(B) A moral philosophy must help us to find our way through the moral problems that really trouble us. It ought to help us to see more clearly what makes a problem difficult, and how we might find a solution to it.

Go back to the person who says "Morality is about the opinions of my guru." Apply the two tests to this view of morality. Is there any reason to believe that the opinions of the guru articulate your most heart-felt convictions, or that they help you think through the moral problems that most puzzle you? Most likely the answer is "No." If the guru's opinions coincide with your own strongly held convictions the reason is most likely to be not that the opinions are his opinions as much as that the guru shares some of the assumptions of your culture. And the guru's opinions on puzzling moral problems are probably more dogmatic than insightful. If that is the case then you can feel pretty secure in rejecting this moral philosophy.

We can apply the same test to more serious theories about what morality is about. We can, for example, ask if moral relativism is going to be a helpful guide when we need to think through deeply troubling moral problems. It is unlikely that it will pass this test. For moral relativism says "pick a culture and see what people in it say." But for a deeply troubling problem the people in the culture will almost certainly either be too troubled or too dogmatic. That is, either they will also be deeply troubled and therefore have no answer to the problem; or they will not see the problem that is tormenting you and thus will have a straightforward dogmatic answer which you will not find satisfactory. What you want is a way in which you and people like you, people in your culture, can discuss the problem, consider relevant facts, and eventually change your moral opinions.

Existentialism is more promising than moral relativism here. It says to people faced with moral problems, "Make a choice, and change your life so as to be consistent with that choice, but make sure that it is a choice you can make freely and live up to." It warns against both cowardice and hypocrisy. That might be more of a guide to thinking through hard moral problems. It could hardly be a complete guide, though.

We should think of morality as concerned with the moral opinions we hold strongly and the moral problems that trouble us. We should take it to be about things which, if we understood them well enough, would explain the strength of our opinions and would help us see our way through our problems. It is important to see that this test could give different answers if different people apply it. Suppose, for example, that you have very straightforward and dogmatic views which say that some holy book gives all the answers to all questions about life. There are no moral problems because all the answers are in the book, which does not need any interpretation or effort to apply. Then you may well say "Morality is going by the book; that is what it's about." And for you that will be an acceptable answer. But it will not be for most of us, just because we do face moral problems about which we are deeply uncertain. We want a moral philosophy that probes rather deeper. (And the person with the straightforward dogmatic views may well also want more from a moral philosophy, if their life changes so that new and bewildering questions arise.)

Thus although this section is generally critical of both moral relativism and moral dogmatism, there is something to be said for them: in different societies it will be natural to rely on different sources of moral advice and solutions to moral problems. And in some societies it will be natural to consider simple dogmatic answers. But in the modern world, in which people have many values which conflict with one another and face many decisions in which it is not at all obvious what the right thing to do is, most people will not find these answers helpful. They will want to understand morality in some different way. (For example, in accordance with utilitarianism, discussed in Chapter 7, or in terms of Kantian ethics, discussed in Chapter 8, or in accordance with social contract theory, discussed in Chapter 13.)

Moral rationalism also seems too simple and optimistic. At any rate, the project of deducing answers to questions about morals as if they were mathematical problems has not had enough success to make it believable. On the other hand, if we start with our moral problems and our moral convictions and try to work toward better and clearer ways of thinking about what we should do, then rational argument and persuasion will have to play a very important part. So there is this much truth in moral rationalism: we can and must think and argue about our values.

One place where both the force of reasoning about morals and its incompleteness can be easily seen is in the impartiality principle, the idea that what is right for one person is right for all people in the same situation. People who treat others in a blatantly unequal way can be asked: "If it is right to treat this person in this way, why do you not treat that person also in the same way?" And then they have to reply by giving a good reason why the differences between this person and that one matter. Perhaps they cannot, and then the force of reason has scored a victory. But perhaps they can, for they may have beliefs about why some differences between people (for example, differences of gender, or of who is related to whom) matter. Suppose, for example, that someone helps their aged mother but refuses to help some unrelated old person. Is this a relevant difference? Is relatedness a morally acceptable reason for unequal treatment? Reason alone is not going to tell you.

Conclusions of This Chapter

> ◆ *The principle that what is right for one person to do is right for any other person in similar circumstances can be used to clarify many moral problems. But it cannot by itself solve many of them.*
> ◆ *If we imagine ways in which human beings could live, and compare them with the way we actually live, we can get conclusions about what a just society would be like.*
> ◆ *Although many people claim to think that right and wrong depend on the rules of a particular culture, when they think hard about this most people become very unsure that it is true. Most people find their opinions about, for example, slavery hard to reconcile with such a moral relativism.*
> ◆ *A philosophy of morals should both respect many of our moral convictions and help us to think through our moral dilemmas.*

Further Reading

Plato's Republic

Selection "Morality and Happiness" from *The Republic* in Part VII of John Cottingham (ed.), *Western Philosophy: An Anthology*. Blackwell, 1996.

Books 4 to 7 of Plato, *The Republic*, in *Collected Dialogues of Plato*, edited by Edith Hamilton and Huntington Cairns. Pantheon Books, 1961.

Julia Annas, *An Introduction to Plato's* Republic. Oxford University Press, 1981.

Chapter 4 of George Sabine and Thomas Thorson, *A History of Political Theory*, fourth edition. Dryden Press, 1973.

Existentialism

Sartre selection "Condemned to be Free" in Part IV of John Cottingham (ed.), *Western Philosophy: An Anthology*. Blackwell, 1996.

Jean-Paul Sartre, *Existentialism and Humanism*. Methuen, 1948.

Robert C. Solomon, *From Rationalism to Existentialism*. Humanities Press, 1978.

Mary Warnock, *Existentialism*. Oxford University Press, 1970.

Rationalism in ethics

Chapter 2 of Peter Singer, *Practical Ethics*, second edition. Cambridge University Press, 1993.

Chapter 5, Part E of John Cottingham, *Rationalism*. Oxford University Press, 1988.

Chapters 1, 2, and 8 of Gilbert Harman, *The Nature of Morality*. Oxford University Press, 1977.

Moral relativism

Colin Turnbull, *The Mountain People*. Jonathan Cape, 1972.
Chapters 1 and 3 of J. L. Mackie, *Ethics: Inventing Right and Wrong*. Penguin, 1977.
Chapter 16 of Robert M. Martin, *There are Two Errors in the the Title of This Book*. Broadview, 1992.

Electronic resources

Routledge Encyclopedia of Philosophy (available online at many universities): articles on Existentialism, Moral Relativism, Plato.
Stanford Encyclopedia of Philosophy (http://plato.stanford.edu/): Callicles and Thrasymachus; *Justice, distributive*; Plato, Ethics and politics in *The Republic*; *Relativism*; Sartre, Jean-Paul; *Utopia* (*italicized* items are available as this book goes to press; the others should be available soon).

5   Induction and Deduction

Introduction

Some philosophers, rationalists about morals, try to determine with logical arguments what we must think right or wrong. But if the moral beliefs of a particular society can be shown to be right then the moral beliefs of other societies must be wrong. Moral relativists think that the moral beliefs of all societies are equally right and so they disagree with moral rationalism.

Can we have certain beliefs about the world around us? Many of our beliefs about the physical world cannot be supported just with logical arguments. Our evidence for them depends not on deduction but on induction. But thinking about induction suggests that very few beliefs about the physical world can be completely certain.

Thus it is unlikely that either our beliefs about morals or our beliefs about the world around us can ever be completely certain. Some philosophers think that this shows that reason is powerless....

Chapter Objectives

At the end of this chapter you should be able to answer these questions.

◆ *What is inductive reasoning?*
◆ *What is simple induction?*
◆ *What is the difference between inductive and deductive reasoning?*
◆ *Why are the conclusions of inductive reasoning always uncertain?*

Definitions

The following words used in this chapter are defined in the list of definitions at the end of the book:

counterexample	*induction-friendliness*	*simple induction*
deduction	*inductive reasoning*	*syllogism*
deductively valid argument		

5.1 Simple Induction

Many philosophers have noticed a pattern of thinking that is now called *inductive reasoning.* It seems to be the basis of many of our beliefs about the world around us. And it seems often to give beliefs in which we can have a lot of confidence. To begin, consider some examples.

First example   You observe that when you put a piece of sodium in a flame it burns with an orange flame. You try burning sodium in different kinds of flames and each sample of sodium burns orange. You try varying other conditions – the time of day, the location of the experiment, the weather – and sodium always burns orange. You conclude that sodium always burns with an orange flame.

Second example   You know about the lives of many people from history books and from what you have been told and from your own experience. In all these lives no one has lived more than 150 years. The pattern seems to be: people are born, they live for a certain number of years, and then they die. So you conclude that no humans are immortal.

Third example   You see objects colliding with other objects. Billiard balls collide with one another, cars with other cars, bats with balls, sometimes trains with other trains or with cars. The pattern seems very varied: sometimes both objects move off in the same direction (bat and ball), sometimes one object comes to a halt and the second object continues in the same direction (car and train), sometimes both objects reverse their directions (two rubber balls). Some patterns never occur: for example, it never happens that two objects meet head on and then both move off at right angles to the line of their collision. Someone explains to you the concept of momentum – the mass of an object multiplied by its velocity – and claims that in all collisions the total momentum after the collision is the same as the total momentum before the collision. This can happen with all the patterns that you have observed, and rules out the patterns that you do not observe. You make careful measurements from controlled collisions (staying away from train crashes), and find that the total momentum afterwards is always the same as the total momentum before. So you conclude that total momentum is preserved in collisions.

These three examples are different in important ways. In the first example you have got all the evidence (the "data," the given facts you are reasoning from) from your own experience. (Though other people's experience will in this case support the same conclusion.) In the second case the data comes from other people's experience; this has the advantage that there is a lot of it, and the disadvantage that you have to trust what other people say and write. In the third case the crucial idea, momentum, is one you probably could not have thought up for yourself. But once it is explained to you, you can check patterns in nature involving it. (The crucial concept in the first example, that of sodium, is also one that you would not have thought up all by yourself. Life and death, in the second example, are rather closer to common sense.)

The examples are similar in one very important respect. In all of them you reason from data which shows a pattern being repeated many times without any exceptions, and you conclude that the pattern will continue to be repeated. This is the simplest kind of inductive reasoning, and aspects of the examples can be summed up in a simple rule. This is the rule of *simple induction*. Simple induction says: if your data consists of evidence that a series of objects of some kind has some property or characteristic, and you know of no object of that kind that does not have that property, then conclude that all objects of that kind have that property.

> Inductive reasoning sees a pattern in the data and projects it to new cases.

◆ *The rule of simple induction:* If your data consists of evidence that a series of objects of some kind has some property or characteristic, and you know of no object of that kind that does not have that property, then conclude that all objects of that kind have that property.

(In the first example the kind is sodium and the property is burning with an orange flame; in the second example the kind is humans and the property is dying; in the third example the kind is systems of physical objects and the property is preserving momentum in collisions.)

5.2 Applying Simple Induction

Everyday life

Below are four conclusions that can be supported by reasoning using simple induction, and five items of data that could be used to support them. They are mixed up together. Which ones are the data and which ones are the conclusions? To see which is which, you have first to think out how reasoning according to the rule of simple induction can lead from one of them to another. (Note that one of the items of data does not support, by simple induction, any of the conclusions, and one of the conclusions is not supported, by simple induction, by any of the items of data.)

(1) All cats hate spinach.
(2) All children in Maine like cola drinks, as do those in New Hampshire, Connecticut, and New York. We haven't yet investigated the other states.
(3) So far everyone who has eaten sand has been constipated, everyone who has eaten tar has vomited, and everyone who has eaten pigeon droppings has had a stomach ache.

(4) All children like peanut butter.

(5) Anyone who eats sand, tar, or pigeon droppings feels bad afterwards.

(6) All American children like cola drinks.

(7) Uncle Albert will always crash his cars.

(8) Uncle Albert had a Rolls Royce and he crashed that; then he had a Chrysler and he crashed that; then a Toyota, a Cadillac, and a Mercedes, all crashed. He hasn't had any other cars.

(9) Cats have always hated spinach.

(10) All English children like peanut butter.

(For example, the data "Uncle Albert had a Rolls Royce and he crashed that; then he had a Chrysler and he crashed that; then a Toyota, a Cadillac, and a Mercedes, all crashed. He hasn't had any other cars" supports the conclusion "Uncle Albert will always crash his cars.")

Remember the rule of simple induction:

◆ If your data consists of evidence that a series of objects of some kind has some property or characteristic, and you know of no object of that kind that does not have that property, then conclude that all objects of that kind have that property.

Mortality

Suppose that you have exact information only about the lives of people living in one town, Urbia. According to this data, in Urbia there was no one in the 1950s above the age of 95, no one in the 1960s above the age of 100, no one in the 1970s above the age of 103, no one in the 1980s above the age of 105, no one in the 1990s above the age of 108.

Here are some conclusions you could draw from this data:

(i) All people eventually die.

(ii) All people in Urbia eventually die.

(iii) All people in Urbia die before the age of 108.

(iv) All people in Urbia die before the age of 150.

(v) As time goes on people will live for longer and longer.

Which of these conclusions can be got from this data by the rule of simple induction?

(The answer is easiest to see if you turn the question around. Can any of these conclusions *not* be got from this data by simple induction? Is there one for which you cannot choose the "kind" and "property" so that simple induction gives the conclusion? For example, with (i) the kind is *all people* and the property is *dying eventually*, and all people of that kind – that is, all people – in your evidence have the property of dying eventually. And you know of no person who does not die eventually. So simple induction allows you to conclude that all people die eventually.)

Some of these conclusions are riskier than others. That is, there is a greater possibility that they are false. Which are the riskiest and which the least risky? Rank them all in order of riskiness. (Think of one conclusion as being *less* risky than another when if the first one turned out to be false then the second one would be false too, but not the other way around. Thus the conclusion that all people in Urbia will die before the age of 150 is riskier than the conclusion that all people in some district of Urbia will die before the age of 150. For if the second conclusion turned out to be false, because there was some person in that district over the age of 150, then the first conclusion would be false too, but not the other way round, since if there was someone over 150 somewhere in Urbia it would not have to be in that district.)

Could someone believe all five conclusions? (Compare (i) and (v), (iii) and (iv), (iii) and (v). Could someone who was thinking carefully believe both of each of these pairs?)

Suppose you had to choose which conclusions to believe, on the basis of this data. Which ones would you choose? (Factors to take into account: how much evidence supports the conclusion, its riskiness, its basic plausibility.)

Microbiology: punk bacteria

You have 400 samples of a hitherto unknown bacterium, *Davidhumecium*. They can be classified into three groups.

◆ In the first group, with 200 bacteria, they all have *green spots, spikes, a purple nucleus*, and *one blue stripe.*
◆ In the second group, with 100 bacteria, they all have *green spots, spikes,* and *a purple nucleus.*
◆ In the third group, with 100 bacteria, they all have *green spots, a purple nucleus,* and *one blue stripe.*

To apply the rule of simple induction you have to decide what you are using as the "kind" in the rule. (The rule says "evidence that a series of objects of some kind . . .") What conclusions can you draw when you take as the kind:

(a) *Davidhumecium?*
(b) *Davidhumecium* with spikes?
(c) *Davidhumecium* with a purple nucleus?

For example, if you take as the kind "*Davidhumecium* with spikes," the rule of simple induction permits you to draw the conclusion that all *Davidhumecium* bacteria with spikes have green spots. For in your data you find that all the

Davidhumecium bacteria with spikes are in the first and second groups, and all of these have green spots.

Here are some possible conclusions. Which conclusions can be drawn, by applying simple induction to which kinds?

(1) All *Davidhumecium* with a purple nucleus have green spots.
(2) All *Davidhumecium* which do not have green spots do not have spikes.
(3) All *Davidhumecium* with a purple nucleus have green spots.
(4) All *Davidhumecium* with green spots have a purple nucleus.
(5) All *Davidhumecium* have green spots.
(6) All *Davidhumecium* have green spots and a purple nucleus.
(7) All *Davidhumecium* have a purple nucleus if they have a green spot.

Suppose you have to decide what conclusion to believe. Which of the conclusions you got with these three ways of applying the rule of simple induction are most believable and which least believable? (Factors to consider: the number of bacteria in each of the three samples, the riskiness of the conclusions as defined in the "Mortality" discussion above.)

5.3 Seeing Patterns in Nature

The aim of reasoning by simple induction is to find patterns in the evidence, in order to get beliefs about the world that we can trust. Imagine, for example, that you want to understand the tides. You want to know how deep the sea will be in the harbor and how high it will rise up the beach, and you want to know why high tides and low tides occur. (You want to know how far up the beach you have to leave your possessions to prevent them being swept away, and you want to know when you have to set sail if you are to get over the sandbank at the harbor entrance.)

The tide does not follow exactly the same pattern every day. But you have a lot of evidence, and you can think of many theories, and you can apply many kinds of abstract reasoning. Still, you are not sure how to combine all these to get a result you can trust. Perhaps you should explain the tides in terms of the rotation of the earth, perhaps in terms of habits the sea has fallen into, perhaps in terms of the influence of the moon and other celestial bodies. But all of these could be wrong. Perhaps the earth does not rotate, or the connections between its rotation and the tides are just coincidences. Perhaps it is quite unreasonable to attribute habits to the sea; perhaps the links between the moon and the tides are coincidences; and perhaps to appeal to the "influence" of the moon is to believe in some kind of magic. It would be nice to be able to think out the problem in advance, to know for certain what kind of a theory, obtained in what way, will be a good one.

Simple induction tells us to look first at the patterns in the data, and not to look for deep or abstract explanations until we are sure what the basic patterns are. So, reasoning by simple induction, we should note how many times a day there is a high and a low tide, and on what days of the year the high and low tides occur. We should carefully note the correlations between the tides and the location and phase of the moon before we make any guesses about how the moon might affect the tides. For we want to find the patterns that really are there before we look for explanations of them.

Is this a good way of reasoning? Will it give us beliefs that we can trust? Is there any way that we can show that induction works? Well, we can show that some alternatives to simple induction do not work. For example, consider this method: first write down all the ideas that occur to you, make sure you think of 365 of them, number them and associate each of them with one day of the year. Suppose the first is the theory that high tides occur after it has rained, so you associate it with January 1; the second is the theory that low tides occur when people are depressed, so you associate it with January 2; and so on. Then accept the theory that corresponds to your birthday.

We know that this method is very unlikely to produce true beliefs. We know this for two reasons. The first is that different people using it will accept different theories, so if one person accepts a true theory another will accept a false one. The second is that there is no connection between the facts that would make the theory true or false and the reasons for accepting the theory. It would be just an accident if the theory were true.

So by thinking in advance we can sometimes know that a way of getting beliefs is not going to work. Can we recognize in advance a good way of getting beliefs, one that will work? By thinking about induction we can see that it has two important features. First, it does not give conclusions that say too much – if a theory is supposed to explain the tides, but it makes lots of claims about angels and seaweed and other possibly irrelevant factors, then there will be many ways in which it might turn out to be false. Second, simple induction gives conclusions that are connected to the evidence in a straightforward way. The reasons for believing a theory of the tides ought to have something to do with the tides (rather than, for example, the birthday of the person making the theory).

So we want very modest theories, which do not say too much, which fit the evidence they are meant to explain. Simple induction is modest and fits the evidence. It aims to prune away all the irrelevant detail and arrive at just the patterns in the evidence. For these reasons induction is an attractive and trustworthy method of reasoning.

But it is a trustworthy method with one rather puzzling feature. For all its modesty, its conclusions will sometimes be false. Consider again the examples in the previous section. For example (from "Everyday Life" example (1)) even though millions of cats have been observed to hate spinach and none has ever been seen to like it, it may still happen that tomorrow a cat is born who will eat nothing but spinach. Or (from "Mortality" example (iv)) although all the people in Urbia for hundreds of years die before the age of 150, in the next century some new medical treatment may allow people in Urbia and elsewhere to live to be 200. Or (from "Microbiology" example (5)) although all *Davidhumecium* observed in that experiment have green spots, there may be in some laboratory somewhere, a single *Davidhumecium* with no green spots.

How much should we trust simple induction then? In order to answer this question we have to understand the difference between induction and *deduction*. The next four sections explain what deduction is and how it is different from induction.

5.4 Deduction 1: Syllogisms

A syllogism is an argument with two premises and a conclusion in which both premises and conclusion are expressed in terms of the concepts "all" and "some." For example:

Some cats eat mice.
All mice are mammals.
Therefore some cats eat mammals.

Some philosophers are ridiculous.
All ridiculous philosophers read Hume.
Therefore someone who reads Hume is ridiculous.

The best-known type of syllogism is of the form:

All As are Bs
All Bs are Cs
Therefore all As are Cs

That means that any argument you get by putting any suitable words in place of A, B, and C will be a syllogism. For example:

All cats are mammals.
All mammals are animals.
Therefore all cats are animals.

and

All Romans are Italians.
All Italians are Europeans.
Therefore all Romans are Europeans.

are syllogisms. And the two more complicated arguments below are also syllogisms.

All animals with feet are animals with toes.
All animals with toes are animals with toenails.
Therefore all animals with feet are animals with toenails.

All people who live in Manhattan are residents of New York City and New York State.
All residents of New York City and New York State live in the United States.
Therefore all people who live in Manhattan live in the United States.

This is called a syllogism in Barbara. (The name comes from an old Latin verse which students used to use to remember the kinds of syllogism. You can think of it as bArbArA, because this syllogism goes All–All–All.) A syllogism in Barbara does not have to use the words "all" and "are" if it uses other words or phrases which mean the same. For example, both the arguments below are syllogisms in Barbara.

Every dog in town has fleas.
All dogs who have fleas scratch.
Therefore every dog in town scratches.

Each computer in the shop has a defect.
A computer with a defect ought to be fixed.
Therefore every computer in the shop ought to be fixed.

On the other hand, all four of the arguments below are *not* syllogisms in Barbara.

(1) Some cats eat mice.
All mice are rodents.
Therefore some cats eat rodents.

(2) Most cats hate spinach.
Most spinach is delicious.
Therefore most cats hate something delicious.

(3) All people living in Alberta are living in Canada.
All people living in Alberta live in Western Canada.
Therefore all people who live in Western Canada live in Canada.

(4) All philosophers are intelligent.
All intelligent people are curious.
Therefore all curious people are philosophers.

In (1) the first premise uses "some" instead of "all." In (2) "most" occurs where a syllogism in Barbara would need "all." In (3) the pattern is:

All As are Bs
All As are Cs
Therefore all Cs are Bs.

And in (4) the pattern is:

All As are Bs
All Bs are Cs
Therefore all Cs are Bs

instead of the Barbara pattern:

All As are Bs
All Bs are Cs
Therefore all As are Cs.

Which of the following are syllogisms in Barbara?

Some philosophers are cruel people.
All cruel people are bad.
Therefore some philosophers are bad.

All grandmothers are grandparents.
All grandparents are relatives.
Therefore all grandmothers are relatives.

God loves everyone.
Therefore God loves me.

All women are people.
All people have rights.
Therefore all women have rights.

Each child in this class has a problem.
Children with problems should get special attention.
Therefore all the children in this class should get special attention.

Nearly all people are kind.
Nearly all kind people can be trusted.
Therefore nearly all people can be trusted.

5.5 Deduction 2: Validity

All syllogisms in Barbara are *deductively valid arguments*. That is, their conclusions are always true when their premises are true. So if you know that an argument is a syllogism in Barbara and you know the premises are true, you can be sure the conclusion is true. If you know that all Lemonmobiles are unreliable and you know that a Machissimo GT is a kind of Lemonmobile (so all Machissimo GTs are Lemonmobiles), then you can be sure that all Machissimo GTs are unreliable. In fact, even if you just believe the premises may be true, you should believe that the conclusion may be true. You should be as sure of the conclusion as you are of the premises.

Other kinds of syllogisms have the same property, for example, syllogisms that have the form:

Some A are B
All B are C
Therefore some A are C.

You should be as sure of the conclusions of these as you are of the premises. If you are sure that some of your enemies are kind and you are sure that all kind people are trustworthy, then you should be sure that some of your enemies are trustworthy. (The reason for using syllogisms in Barbara as the main example in this chapter is that they focus on the word "all," and that makes the relation between deduction and induction clearer.) And there are many other kinds of argument that are like this: if their premises are true their conclusions have to be true. Two other examples are:

If it is Monday I ought to be at work.
It is Monday.
Therefore I ought to be at work.

James is the grandfather of every child in this restaurant.
James is alive.
Therefore every child in this restaurant has a living grandfather.

The first of these (the one about Monday and work) has the pattern or form:

If p then q
p
Therefore q

Any argument which has this form, like any argument that has the form of a syllogism in Barbara, will give conclusions which are as certain as the premises are. The second one (the one about the grandfather and the restaurant) also has a form which gives conclusions that are as certain as the premises. It is harder to state this form in easy language. Just as when talking about syllogisms we used letters A, B, C to represent kinds of things, and just now we used letters p, q to represent whole sentences, we could use the letter R to represent a relation between things, like "being the grandfather of" or "being to the north of." So if R is some relation, and A is some thing, and B is some kind of thing, the second argument has the form:

x has R to every A
x is B
Therefore for every A there is a B which has R to it

This form is also found in other arguments, such as:

The north pole is to the north of every place on earth.
The north pole is on the earth.
Therefore there is one point on earth to the north of every other place on earth.

Do not try too hard to understand this! The point is just that here also there is a general pattern, though it is hard to express in simple language. (Philosophers have invented a new language to describe arguments like this. It is called symbolic logic. Symbolic logic is one of the origins of computer programming languages.)

A deductively valid argument is an argument where the conclusion has to be true if the premises are. Deductively valid arguments come in families, all of which have the same form. Syllogisms in Barbara are one such family; arguments of the form "If p then q. p. Therefore q" (which is known as *modus ponens*) are another. (Logic, which studies the patterns of deductively valid argument, is a large part of philosophy. It is a big subject, with many important and deep discoveries.) So there is another definition of a deductively valid argument. A deductively valid argument is an argument that belongs to a family of arguments of the same form, and when the premises of any argument of this family are true the conclusion is also true. Deductively valid arguments are truth-preserving machines: truth in, truth out.

When the premises of a deductively valid argument are true the conclusion is true. But when the premises are false the conclusion may be true or it may be false. Consider the following syllogisms in Barbara:

(i) **All cats are dogs.**
  All dogs are fish.
  Therefore all cats are fish.

(ii) All cats are dogs.
   All dogs purr.
   Therefore all cats purr.

In (i) the premises are false and the conclusion is false. In (ii) the premises are false but the conclusion is true. Both are deductively valid syllogisms: if you came to believe that all cats are dogs, and you also came to believe that all dogs are fish, then you should also come to believe that all cats are fish. The one pattern that we do not find with a deductively valid argument is: premises true and the conclusion false. (Gold in, gold out. Garbage in, garbage out: but sometimes there's gold in the garbage.)

Below are seven sentences. Use them as premises for three syllogisms in Barbara, such that in the first, both premises are true and the conclusion is true; in the second, one premise is false and the conclusion is false; and in the third, one premise is false and the conclusion is true. (You may have to supply the conclusions yourself.)

(1) All humans can solve mathematical problems.
(2) Anything that can think is a human being.
(3) All people can think.
(4) All humans can change their beliefs.
(5) Anything that can think can solve mathematical problems.
(6) Anything that can think can change its beliefs.
(7) All people are human beings.

5.6 Deduction 3: Venn Diagrams and Counterexamples

A syllogism can be represented as a diagram. The syllogism "All cats are mammals. All mammals are animals. Therefore all cats are animals" can be represented by the diagram in Figure 5.1.

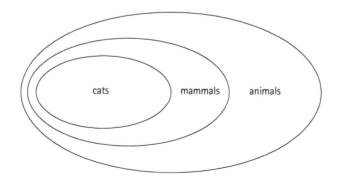

Figure 5.1

You can see that this diagram can just as well represent any other syllogism in Barbara. One shape can represent A and another B and a third C, and as long as the first shape is completely inside the second and the second is inside the third, then the first one will be inside the third. And so it will give a good picture of the reasoning behind "Every A is a B, and every B is a C; therefore every A is a C." Similar diagrams can represent other syllogisms. For example, the syllogism "Some A are B, and every B is a C; therefore some A are C" (as in "Some cats eat rabbits, and every rabbit is an animal with long ears; therefore some cats eat animals with long ears") can be represented by Figure 5.2.

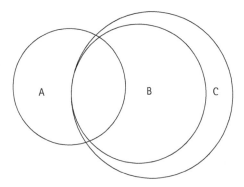

Figure 5.2

Diagrams like this are called *Venn diagrams.* They are useful when we want to show that an argument is not deductively valid. For example, someone might use the following argument:

All cats are mammals.
Some mammals can fly.
Therefore some cats can fly.

We can show that this is not valid by drawing the diagram shown in Figure 5.3. What this diagram shows is that it could be true that all cats are mammals and some mammals can fly, but not true that some cats can fly. It gives a sketch of a world in which cats are mammals and some mammals fly but cats do not. It gives a *counterexample* to the argument.

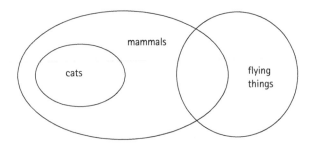

Figure 5.3

A counterexample to an argument is an example which shows that the argument is not deductively valid, by showing how the premises could be true without making the conclusion true. A counterexample is particularly useful when the conclusion of the argument is actually true. For example, consider the argument:

All cats are mammals.
Some mammals eat mice.
Therefore some cats eat mice.

The conclusion of this argument is true. So are the premises. Still, the argument is not deductively valid. The premises do not *show* that the conclusion is true. We can show that the argument is not deductively valid by using the same shaped diagram again (Figure 5.4).

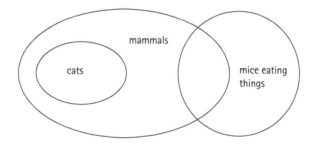

Figure 5.4

What this diagram shows is that arguments of the form:

All As are Bs
Some Bs are Cs
Therefore some As are Cs

are not deductively valid. So if you believe that all cats are mammals and some mammals eat mice, and you want to persuade someone (or yourself) that some cats eat mice, you will have to bring in some other information, besides the information in those two premises. Or suppose that someone claims that some cats eat mice and defends the claim by saying that all cats are mammals and some mammals eat mice. Then in reply you can say "Well, the conclusion seems true, but that is a bad reason for believing it. You might as well argue that some cats fly because all cats are mammals and some mammals fly."

Here are four arguments that are not deductively valid. Give a counterexample to each argument by making a Venn diagram to show how in each case the premises could be true and the conclusion false. Then use the diagram to think up an (invalid) argument of the same form which has true premises and a false conclusion.

(a) **All bats fly.**
 All flying things have wings.
 Therefore all flying things are bats.

(b) **Some philosophers are fools.**
 Some fools are beautiful.
 Therefore some philosophers are beautiful.

(c) **All humans can think.**
 Anything that can talk can think.
 Therefore anything that can talk is human.

(d) **All humans have a right to life.**
 Anything that has a right to life is valuable.
 Therefore anything that is valuable is human.

5.7 Induction versus Deduction

You can be as sure of the conclusion of a deductively valid argument as you can be of the premises. So valid deductive reasoning, reasoning by deductively valid arguments, will always give conclusions that are as certain as the premises. In contrast, inductive reasoning does not have this property. Consider a case of simple induction. Someone sees hundreds of cats, and they are all either black or white, and never sees a cat that is neither black nor white. So she might reasonably conclude that all cats are either black or white. And this would be reasoning by simple induction. But then one day she is sitting in the park and around the corner walks a ginger cat. Any reasoning by simple induction is like this: the premises are that some pattern has happened many times, and the conclusion is that it will always happen. But this conclusion can always turn out to be false.

There are several conclusions we can draw here.

First, *a reasonable conclusion need not be certain.* If you have seen hundreds of black cats and white cats and have no reason to believe there are cats of any other color, it is perfectly reasonable to believe that all cats are black or white. After all, what other reason do most people have for believing that grass is green or yellow (but never black or purple) or that elephants are bigger than ants, except that they have often seen green and yellow grass, and know that elephants have always been bigger than ants?

Second, *induction is not deduction.* Deductive reasoning gives conclusions that are as certain as the premises on which they are based. But inductive reasoning gives conclusions that are less certain than the premises. They may only be a little bit less certain, but still they are less certain. You are *almost* as sure that all elephants are bigger than all ants as you are that all the elephants you have ever heard of are bigger than all the ants you have ever heard of, but still there is that tiny unlikely possibility that tomorrow an elephant-sized ant or an ant-sized elephant will be discovered.

Third, the *conclusion of inductive reasoning can always be false.* Even if the premises on which perfectly reasonable inductive reasoning is based are true the conclusion may be false. The person reasoning by induction may have no reason to know they are false, and their falsity may never be discovered, but still they may be false. Induction is fallible.

The fallibility of induction was first stated clearly by the Scottish philosopher David Hume (1711–1776). Hume realized quite how far-reaching his discovery was. For many scientific theories and many of our ordinary beliefs are based on induction, at least in part. So if our only reasons for believing these things come from induction, or other ways of reasoning no less fallible, then we have to face the possibility that all these beliefs could turn out to be false. Around the corner there might be not only a ginger cat but a stone that rises when dropped, a particle that travels faster than light, a human who lives for ever, . . .

> Further evidence can always show that the conclusion of inductive reasoning is false.

The basic reason why induction is fallible can be made clearer with Venn diagrams, like the ones we used in the previous section. The diagrams we use have to be partial, though; they have to be partially covered up. Suppose that we have a partially covered up diagram like the one in Figure 5.5.

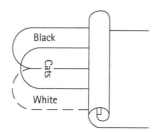

Figure 5.5

Think of what might appear when some of the cover is rolled back, as in Figure 5.6. If diagram (a) shows what is under the cover then all cats are black or white. If either (b) or (c) shows what is under the cover then there are some cats that are neither black nor white. In (b) the conclusion that all cats are black or white is almost true. The ginger cats are a rare exception. But in (c) the conclusion that all cats are black or white turns out to be totally false. All we can be sure from the data in the first, very covered up diagram, is that all cats are black or white if cats are the way the evidence suggests. We can see that a ginger cat would be a surprise. But surprises happen.

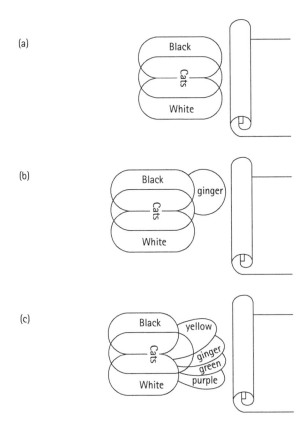

Figure 5.6

5.8 The Induction-friendliness of the World

Deduction gives conclusions that are as certain as the premises. Induction seems a fairly safe and reasonable way of reasoning, even if its conclusions are not as certain as the premises they are based on. But perhaps induction gives conclusions that are *nearly* as certain as the premises they are based on. Perhaps, although induction can sometimes lead from true premises to false conclusions, it will not do this very often. Perhaps the conclusions of inductive reasoning will usually be true.

These are very hard issues. It is easy to see how the conclusions of inductive reasoning could often turn out to be false. When we uncover more data we could discover that many of the conclusions we have based on induction are false. After centuries of observing white swans, Europeans traveled to Australia and saw black swans. After centuries of believing that humans would never fly, we invented first planes and then hang-gliders. And so on.

The questions here go back to the fundamental assumptions of our culture. Imagine yourself back to a preliterate, prescientific culture, living a hand-to-mouth existence in constant danger of extinction. You don't understand the powers that control people's lives. Sometimes the crops fail and sometimes they don't. Sometimes your children die and occasionally they survive. People sometimes recover from disease but often they don't. If you understood the forces behind these things you might be able to anticipate, or even control, them. But you cannot. (How can you react to your plight? More by appeasing than by controlling nature. You might try sacrificing your first-born.)

Now imagine yourself into the world of scientific optimism. Here too your life is affected by forces of nature. But you can predict and to a large extent control them. You know why the crops fail sometimes, and what sorts of things to avoid if you don't want them to. You know what organisms cause which diseases, and what medicines are effective against them. The world seems to be a well-ordered, intelligible place. It has its dangers, but it is generally friendly toward our attempts to know it.

To go from the first attitude to the world to the second is to think that it is governed by laws which are regular and which we human beings can under-stand. The ancient Greeks began to think of the world in this way. They had the concept of *nomos*, of a law which natural events followed. (Not all natural events were equally governed by law, according to Greek conceptions of it. Aristotle, for example, thought that the stars moved in perfectly regular ways, but that down here on earth many things were governed by chance and accident.) And a picture of the world as created by a God who also made human beings in His image reinforces this conception. For our minds are smaller versions of the mind that thought up the laws of nature. Perhaps belief in God is a useful first step toward scientific optimism.

Which world do we actually live in? Well, we don't think of nature as mys-terious, malevolent, and unknowable. But we don't think of her as completely intelligible either. She's not as friendly as we once thought. In the twenty-first century we have behind us the simplicity and elegance of classical physics and the successes of modern medicine. But we have also had to come to terms with quantum physics, which builds unpredictability into the depths of nature, and we appreciate chaos as an intrinsic feature of most natural systems. We no longer expect that predicting the weather, or the course of human history, or the working of the human nervous system, will be a simple application of simple laws.

So we are now somewhere between savage incomprehension and scientific optimism. We think we can understand many features of nature, but we real-ize that some aspects of nature may be less knowledge-friendly than others. And some aspects may be completely beyond our powers of comprehension.

One way in which the world may encourage or frustrate our attempts to understand it is by being receptive or uncooperative to inductive reasoning. Imagine a world which at first seems very orderly. The patterns that people observe over a few instances do not soon afterwards turn out to be wrong. If the first hundred cats that you see are all either black or white then you can safely assume that all cats are black or white. If chocolates have never given you a stomach ache then they won't the next time you eat them. This world can continue like this. If it does, then it is *induction-friendly*. Or it can suddenly change. One day the patterns may begin to fail. Ginger cats, poisonous chocolate, stones that rise in the air. In that case it is *induction-unfriendly*.

A seemingly induction-friendly world could turn out to be induction-unfriendly in another way, too. People could begin to study things they had never studied before (the weather, perhaps), and when they try to find simple patterns in the new domain of study ("red sunset means good weather next day") they find that they often turn out to be wrong. And of course a world that at first seemed induction-unfriendly could seem more induction-friendly when we shift our inquiries to other matters. That is part of what happened when people came to think of nature as being governed by simple knowable laws. They shifted their attention from the chaotic domain of climate, disease, and human fate to the much more predictable domain of astronomy and physics.

How induction-friendly is the world? Will induction give us true beliefs? If the world is very induction-unfriendly then most of the beliefs we form by inductive reasoning will eventually be refuted. Hume pointed out that the conclusions of inductive reasoning can always be wrong. There is never a logical guarantee that patterns that we have observed in the data over thousands of years (the sun rising in the morning, rabbits giving birth to rabbits, pure water quenching thirst) may not prove to have exceptions.

We cannot be certain that the world is induction-friendly.

If we cannot tell by pure logic (by deductively valid reasoning) how induction-friendly the world is, how *can* we tell? By inductive reasoning perhaps. But suppose the world was extremely induction-unfriendly, but took a long time to show it. Suppose that for thousands of years nature seems extremely simple and regular, and then one day all hell breaks loose. The sun doesn't rise every morning, rabbits give birth to puppies, pure water tastes like sand. And, even worse, new patterns that seem to emerge never continue. The induction-friendliness of the world was an illusion: in terms of a larger body of data there are no unrefuted generalizations.

It would be wonderful if we could give good reasons to believe that the world – this world, the universe we actually live in – is induction-friendly. For then we would have shown that reasoning by induction is a good way to get beliefs. But it does not seem that we can.

One thing we do know: the world is at least slightly induction-unfriendly. Often people do form beliefs because they have seen a pattern repeated many times, only to discover that the pattern does not hold for all cases. As a result we know that we will never show that the world is an absolutely ideal place to use inductive reasoning. The best we can get is an idea about where on the friendly–unfriendly scale it lies. So we can at least ask a more sophisticated question now: in what ways can we form a useful estimate of how induction-friendly the world is?

5.9 Diagramming Induction-friendliness

Figure 5.7 is a Venn diagram. Think of it as representing a mini-world. Moreover, suppose that the people in that world observe the data in the world as it is uncovered from left to right. That is, suppose that at first they know only what is revealed in the part of the diagram between line 0 and line 1, and then they learn the information given in the diagram up to line 2, and so on.

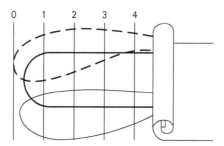

Figure 5.7

You can see that it is a very induction-friendly world. The generalizations that its people form on the basis of a small amount of data are not going to be refuted when more data comes in. By contrast, the diagram in Figure 5.8 represents a very induction-unfriendly world. Generalizations that are formed from incomplete amounts of information are often going to be refuted when more data arrives.

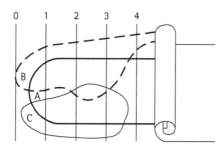

Figure 5.8

Which of the four diagrams in Figure 5.9 – (a), (b), (c), or (d) – represents the most induction-friendly world? Which one is most induction-unfriendly? And what about the two remaining diagrams: which of these is the more induction-friendly of the two?

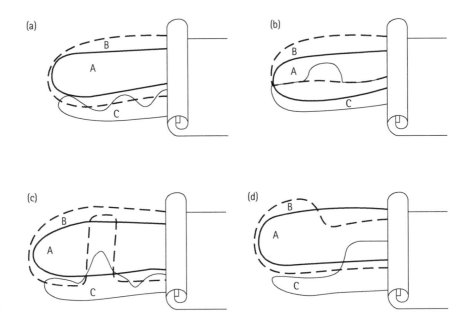

Figure 5.9

5.10 Hume's Discovery: Nightmare or Liberation?

Induction is not deduction. Further evidence could always show that the conclusion of inductive reasoning is false. And we cannot tell by deductive reasoning how induction-friendly the world is. There is no way around these three facts. They set definite limits to the power of inductive reasoning. Hume discovered them; he was the first philosopher to see how important they are. Some philosophers have drawn very grand and exciting conclusions from Hume's discovery.

Often the conclusions have been skeptical. Here is a typical skeptical argument:

> **Many of our beliefs are based on inductive reasoning.**
> **Inductive reasoning can always give a false conclusion.**
> **Therefore: Many of our beliefs could be false.**

Now if we add one more assumption we get a more worrying argument:

> **Many of our beliefs are based on inductive reasoning.**
> **Inductive reasoning can always give a false conclusion.**
> **Therefore: Many of our beliefs could be false.**
> *If a belief could be false then it is not certain.*
> *Therefore: Many of our beliefs are not certain.*

Add yet one more assumption and the argument for skepticism emerges:

Many of our beliefs are based on inductive reasoning.
Inductive reasoning can always give a false conclusion.
Therefore: Many of our beliefs could be false.
If a belief could be false then it is not certain.
Therefore: Many of our beliefs are not certain.
If a belief is not certain then it is not known.
Therefore: Many of our beliefs are not knowledge.

(But are the two extra assumptions true? They are: (a) If a belief could be false then it is not certain; and (b) If a belief is not certain then it is not known. It is not at all obvious that they are true. They will appear again in Chapter 6.)

The possibility that induction might give false beliefs works as a kind of demon possibility, undermining a large category of beliefs. (See Chapter 3, Section 7 on demon possibilities.) Many philosophers have thought that this argument, or others along the same lines, sets up a philosophical nightmare. We know in our bones that induction is a reasonable way to form beliefs, and yet we cannot show, either inductively or deductively, that it will work. And if we cannot then we seem to lose our grip on the difference between beliefs based carefully on patterns found in the evidence, and beliefs based on superstition, or on hearsay or whim.

> The fallibility of induction can be seen as a frightening weakness of reason, or as showing the need for faith.

But there is another way the situation is often seen. Again, it can be expressed as an argument:

Science depends on inductive reasoning.
Inductive reasoning has to be assumed, not proved.
Therefore: Science, like religion, rests ultimately on faith.

Many people fear the pretensions of science, its claim to be the only source of really certain knowledge. They sometimes produce arguments along the lines of this one, to cut it down to a more appropriate size.

Which of these attitudes to induction is right, the skeptical one or the science-limiting one? Or both? In fact, it is hard to make a really good case for either. For if each is spelled out more carefully each makes a number of false assumptions. One of the most important false assumptions is made by both of them. That is the assumption that induction gives true beliefs (but we have problems proving that it does). The skeptical argument assumes that in order to show that we know what we think we do, we would have to show that induction never goes wrong. And the science-limiting one assumes that in science we have an unjustifiable faith that inductive reasoning will always give true conclusions.

But this is false. Much, perhaps most, of the inductive reasoning that people have ever used has resulted in false conclusions. We only remember the successes. But think of all the refuted scientific hypotheses, for which there was originally very good evidence. (Think of Newton's laws of motion, which turned out to be – approximately – true only at low speeds and energies. Think of all the evidence people once had that species do not evolve.) Think of all the practical disasters that have been produced by people assuming that a small sample of the data was representative of the whole.

So we may take it that induction often gives false conclusions. How often? That is a harder question. (It is the question not of *whether* the world is induction-friendly but of *how* induction-friendly or induction-unfriendly it is.) Again there is some inductive evidence, though. It is that induction works much more reliably for some areas than others. There is a list of topics that represent pretty induction-friendly aspects of the world and a list of topics that represent much less induction-friendly aspects. The first list includes the motions of stars and planets and similar objects, the patterns of chemical combination, and some kinds of biological facts (for example, what animals can mate with what other animals, and what will result). The second list includes human interactions, and human social life, and the behavior of subatomic particles.

That is not to say that we should use inductive reasoning for topics on the first list and not for topics on the second list. But it is to say that we should be more cautious about the conclusions that induction leads us to on some topics than we need to be on others. (Especially when the amount of data is small.) And we should remember two important facts.

It is crazy to want to justify induction, if that means wanting to prove that induction won't give you false conclusions, because induction *will* give you false conclusions.

There is an important study that people can and do carry out successfully to investigate which patterns of inductive reasoning will succeed under which circumstances. (It is called statistics!)

5.11 Causation and Induction

How many of our beliefs depend on inductive reasoning? Hume had an argument to show that the reasons for many of our beliefs come from induction. He first pointed out that many of our beliefs are about cause and effect. We believe that if a ball hits a window it will break it – that is, that the impact of the ball will *cause* the glass to shatter. We believe that germs *cause* disease, that being rude to people *makes* them angry. And so on.

And, especially important, Hume pointed out that when we believe in the existence of something that is not immediately present, it is often because we believe that it is the cause of some object or experience that is present. (I believe that my four great-grandmothers existed, though I never met them. I believe so because I think their existence *caused* mine.)

Hume next pointed out that the main source of our beliefs about cause and effect is in our observations of correlations. A correlation is just a regular pattern of one kind of event coming together with or soon before another. We believe that the impact of balls on windows is correlated with windows breaking, and that A's being rude to B is correlated with B's being angry at A. And where do our beliefs about correlations come from? They are just the kind of conclusion that one can get by simple induction. So Hume's argument runs:

Many of our beliefs are about cause and effect.
Beliefs about cause and effect are based on correlations.
Beliefs about correlations are based on inductive reasoning.
Therefore: Many of our beliefs are based on inductive reasoning.

Hume also seems to have argued for a stronger conclusion. His argument can be summarized as follows:

Knowledge of correlations is all that is needed to establish conclusions about cause and effect.
Many of our beliefs are about cause and effect.
Therefore: Many of our beliefs are based only on inductive reasoning.

Is the first premise of this second argument true?

Consider this example: the noon whistle blows in Norman, Oklahoma. At that moment hundreds of workers hundreds of miles north of Norman in Winnipeg, Manitoba, stop work and go to lunch. This happens five days a week for years. Does the whistle in Norman cause the lunches in Winnipeg?

There are also situations in which (a), (b), or (c) occur:

(a) Two kinds of events are correlated – one always happens at the same time or just before the other – and although neither causes the other there is a third kind of event which causes both.
(b) Two kinds of events are correlated, and not only does neither cause the other, but they have no common cause. (There is nothing that causes both of them to happen at the times they do.)
(c) Two kinds of event always occur at the same time though one is the cause of the other, and not the other way round.

Find examples of (a), (b), (c) among the events in the following story.

Paula and her twin sister Johanna live on opposite sides of town, with their husbands. Paula is married to John, and Johanna is married to Paul. John and Paul are also twins. People find this very confusing. Every morning at 7 a.m. an alarm clock rings in each house. The clocks are reset twice a year when summer time begins and ends. Paula has very regular bodily rhythms: because she wakes up at the same time every day, she wakes naturally at the same time as her clock rings. She would wake even if the clock failed. Paula and her alarm clock wake John. Johanna does not have quite as regular a body rhythm as Paula so while she wakes at the moment of the first ring of her clock, if it failed she would not wake. Johanna wakes Paul. At the same time a clock in the center of town, miles from either house, strikes seven.

·(One conclusion philosophers draw from examples like these is that causation and induction are not very tightly linked. We do not usually know that one kind of event causes another just by reasoning by simple induction that they are correlated. Hume's original discussion of inductive reasoning was closely tied to his theory of causation. This can make it confusing to read now.)

5.12 Choosing the Right Concepts

HARDER

There is another reason for thinking that inductive reasoning will give false conclusions. It is a deductive argument; it shows that if simple induction is applied mechanically then it must often lead to false conclusions.

Consider a graph of the population of the earth through time. It might look like Figure 5.10. Compare two ways in which someone before the year 2000 could reason inductively from the data in the graph:

(i) **At all times before 2000 the population of the earth has been less than 4 billion.**
Therefore: After 2000 the population of the earth will be less than 4 billion.

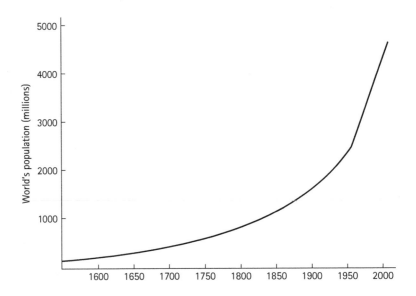

Figure 5.10

(ii) At all times before 2000 the population of the earth has fitted the curve in the graph.
Therefore: After 2000 the population of the earth will fit the curve in the graph.
Therefore: At some time after 2000 the population of the earth will be more than 5 billion.

Both of these are good examples of reasoning by simple induction. But they cannot both have true conclusions. Therefore one of them must have a false conclusion. And in general, inductive reasoning from a single body of data can lead to incompatible conclusions, depending on which patterns in the data you choose to project.

So inductive reasoning will *inevitably* lead to false conclusions.

Why is this problem not more noticeable? One reason is that we choose which properties to use to describe our data, and we choose to use terms that suggest generalizations which we think, given the subject matter, we have a good chance of projecting successfully. So we are always tuning our choice of concepts and our choice of generalizations in order to give inductive reasoning a good chance of giving true conclusions. (And what guides us in this? More inductive reasoning, and our accumulated knowledge of the world.)

There are two important conclusions we should draw from this:

◆ An aspect of the world is only induction-friendly or induction-unfriendly relative to a choice of concepts to describe it.
◆ An important aspect of inductive reasoning is the choice of terms in which to describe the data and formulate the generalizations.

HARDER

Box 10 **Grue**

The American philosopher Nelson Goodman found a particularly dramatic illustration of this point. Define an object to be *grue* if it is either green and we see it before 1 January 2050 or blue and seen after that time. Now we have seen many samples of green emeralds, and none that was not green. But they were all grue, since they were seen before 1 January 2050. So all the emeralds we have ever seen have been grue. So, reasoning by simple induction, we may conclude that all emeralds are grue. But this means that emeralds seen after 1 January 2050 will be blue. But that is crazy.

Conclusion: inductive reasoning gives crazy results if you pick out the wrong properties of objects to use it with. (But what then are the right properties?)

Conclusions of This Chapter

♦ *Inductive reasoning, unlike deductive reasoning, leads to conclusions that are less certain than the premises on which they are based. Inductive reasoning does not exclude the possibility that a counterexample may appear.*

♦ *We have to learn how many of the conclusions we get by inductive reasoning will be false in the same ways that we learn any other fact about the world: by induction, by trial and error, and by conjecture.*

♦ *The fact that we cannot be certain how induction-friendly the world is does not show that we do not know anything or that science is just guesswork. What it does show is that we have to think very carefully about how to reason from small samples to large populations.*

♦ *Inductive reasoning is one of the main sources of our beliefs about causes and their effects. But inductive evidence that one kind of event is followed by another does not by itself show that the first kind of event causes the second kind.*

Further Reading

On induction

Chapters 2 and 3 of Merilee H. Salmon, *Introduction to Logic and Critical Thinking.* Harcourt Brace Jovanovich, 1984.

Chapter 6 of Willard Quine and Joseph Ullian, *The Web of Belief.* Random House, 1978.

Chapter 4 of Adam Morton, *A Guide through the Theory of Knowledge,* third edition. Blackwell, 2002.

Chapter 9 of Robert M. Martin, *There Are Two Errors in the the Title of this Book.* Broadview, 1992.

Chapters 1 and 2 of Brian Skyrms, *Choice and Chance.* Dickenson, 1966.

*Chapter 13 of Jonathan Dancy, *An Introduction to Contemporary Epistemology.* Blackwell, 1988.

*Nelson Goodman, *Fact, Fiction, and Forecast,* fourth edition. Harvard University Press, 1983.

On deduction

Chapter 9 of Merrilee H. Salmon, *Introduction to Logic and Critical Thinking.* Harcourt Brace Jovanovich, 1984.

Samuel Guttenplan, *The Language of Logic.* Blackwell, 1986.

Chapters 5 and 6 of Robert M. Martin, *There Are Two Errors in the the Title of this Book.* Broadview, 1992.

Electronic resources

Routledge Encyclopedia of Philosophy (available online at many universities): articles on Induction, epistemic issues in; Inductive inference.

6 The Retreat from Certainty

Introduction

Can we have certain beliefs about the world around us? Many of our beliefs about the physical world cannot be supported just with logical arguments. Our evidence for them depends not on deduction but on induction. But thinking about induction suggests that very few beliefs about the physical world can be completely certain.

Thus it is unlikely that either our beliefs about morals or our beliefs about the world around us can ever be completely certain. Some philosophers think that this shows that reason is powerless. But reason is not powerless, since some uncertain beliefs are more reasonable than others. Once we see this we can begin to understand how we can live without certainty.

Chapter Objectives

By the end of this chapter you should be able to answer the following questions.

- ◆ *Why did Hume think that many beliefs are based on habit rather than reasoning?*
- ◆ *Why did Hume think that any desire is as reasonable as any other?*
- ◆ *In what ways is Hume's understanding of reason too narrow?*
- ◆ *What problems does Mill's harm principle run into?*
- ◆ *How can you think that something is wrong and still tolerate it?*

Definitions

The following words used in this chapter are defined in the list of definitions at the end of the book:

harm principle   *incoherence*   *incoherent desire*

6.1 Feeble Reason?

How powerful is reason? The past five chapters were about the idea that we can think out the best ways of investigating the world and living our lives. One thing they have shown is the difficulty of defending extreme rationalism. That is, it seems pretty doubtful that by pure reason – by using simply our powers to think, argue, and imagine – we can get the answers to important questions. Reason alone will not tell us what the laws of nature are, whether there is a God, or how induction-friendly the world is. Neither will reason alone tell us the best way for an individual person to live her life or the best way for a society to be organized. (Note that these things are "pretty doubtful," not impossible. Pure thought may still have some surprises for us.)

Some philosophers react to the limitations of pure reason as if these show that reason is powerless, as if these limitations show that reasoning will not even be an important part of the search. (One philosopher who thought something like this is David Hume, whose views are discussed later in this chapter.) When this reaction is applied to science it can produce a form of skepticism. This says: "Since we cannot discover by reason alone what the world is like or how we should investigate it, nothing is certain, so we do not really know anything." When it is applied to ethics it can produce a form of moral relativism. This says: "Since we cannot by reason alone discover how we should act, any values are as good as any others."

The main aim of this chapter is to resist these reactions. Reason *is* very limited in its powers. It cannot accomplish much alone. But it is an essential ingredient of any attempt to understand the world or to think out how we should act. So the limited power of reason does not mean that there is no difference between knowledge and ignorance or speculation. And it does not mean that any values are as good as any others.

6.2 Hume on the Power(lessness) of Reason

The central aim of David Hume's philosophy is to undermine the claims of reason, both in science and in morals. When we try to get true beliefs about the physical world, and when we try to decide what actions we should perform, according to Hume, we depend on our intellects less than we think. In each case he thinks that one of the major factors shaping our beliefs looks at first sight as if it is provided by reasoning, but is in fact provided by something else. His conclusion about our beliefs is that they depend more on *habit* than on reasoning. And his conclusion about our actions is that they depend more on *emotion* than on reasoning.

Hume argued that our beliefs depend more on habit than on reasoning and that our actions depend more on emotion than on reasoning.

Habit and belief

Most of our beliefs about the world around us, Hume thinks, are based on simple induction. One reason for his thinking this was that he thought there was a close connection between simple induction and beliefs about causes (see Chapter 5, Section 11.) Another reason arises from his empiricist theory of thinking (see Chapter 9). Hume realized that inductive reasoning is very different from deductive reasoning, and that there is no simple guarantee that inductive reasoning will give true conclusions. So, he thought, there is no convincing reason to believe that the conclusions of inductive reasoning are true. We have no reason to be certain that the sun will rise tomorrow, or that bread will continue to be nourishing, or that other people will act in foreseeable ways.

If we have no reason to be certain of these things, why do we act as if we were convinced of them? According to Hume, the answer lies in the nature of inductive reasoning. It consists of seeing patterns in the data and projecting them. Why do we project them? Because, Hume says, we have got used to them. We have fallen into the habit of expecting the sun to rise, bread to be nourishing, people to act as they always have; and out of mental inertia we go on expecting these things. It is because of this mental inertia, habit, rather than because of reason, that we hold most of our beliefs.

Action and emotion

Suppose you are deciding what to do, given your situation. You have two things to make up your mind about. One of them is what you want, and the other is how to get it. And, Hume thinks, these are very different. The second, how to get what you want or what is the best means to the end you have chosen, is mostly a matter of having an opinion about the relevant facts. If what you want is to climb Mount Everest then you need lots of opinions about weather, equipment, and geography. And since these are opinions about the world they are mostly the results of habit, Hume thinks. But you also have to make up your mind about what you want. *Do* you want to climb Mount Everest? Wouldn't you prefer a holiday in Hawaii or a year earning money? Hume's important claim here is that reason does nothing to tell you what to want.

He thinks this because he believes that desire is arbitrary. You can want anything at all, and then think how to achieve it. You can want to be eaten by dinosaurs, and then think how to design a time machine or reconstruct dinosaurs in the present day. You can want to appear completely ridiculous. It is only after deciding or realizing what you want that thinking begins, when you are considering the best way of achieving what you want.

We tend not to realize how arbitrary desire is, Hume thinks, for two reasons. The first is that human beings tend to want much the same things.

They usually want happiness, success, the respect of others, and they usually do not want pain, death, or humiliation. But that is not because it is against reason to desire death or humiliation. It is just that human emotions do not usually work that way.

Among the typical human emotions is benevolence. Most people have some sympathy for other people, even though it has definite limits and is felt more strongly for some people than for others. As a result, people rarely have really evil desires. But this is again because of our emotions rather than because of reason. As Hume puts it, "It is not contrary to reason to prefer the destruction of the whole world to the scratching of my finger." (The next section, 6.3, says more about this mysterious quote.)

The other reason we tend not to realize how arbitrary desire is, says Hume, is sloppy reasoning. We think we can show that our moral values are right, that people ought not to desire various bad things. We naively assume a sort of moral rationalism. But really there is no way of proving what people should want. In fact there is no way of proving that any values are right except by assuming the very values we want to prove. You can't deduce an "ought" from an "is." (Another famous quote – again see Section 6.3.)

For Hume, therefore, science and morals are alike, in that in each case we mistakenly give reason a role that in fact is played by something else. In science, in fact in all our beliefs about the world around us, it is habit that is the main factor. And in morals it is emotion. (And habit and emotion work, he says; they are generally reliable guides. Hume was writing a century before Darwin, but he almost seems to say that we have evolved to have the habits that we need to survive in the physical world and the emotions that we need to survive in the social world.)

Box 11 David Hume

David Hume (1711–1776) is the most famous Scottish philosopher. As a very young man he was moved by religious enthusiasm, but not long after, in his twenties, he wrote his philosophical masterpiece *A Treatise of Human Nature*, which argues for a generally skeptical position. The book was a failure, in part because it is hard to read. He then had a career as an author of nonphilosophical books and held public offices, writing his *Inquiry into Human Understanding*, *Inquiry into Morals*, and *Dialogues on Natural Religion* as popular expositions of his earlier views. There is a way in which Hume's life mirrors his philosophy, for he argued both for skeptical conclusions and for the practical necessity of ignoring them. So in his life he first argued that we cannot know what the world is like or what we should do, and then set about a life of practical action.

6.3 Four Famous Passages from Hume

Below are four famous quotations from Hume. Each one is quoted first in Hume's own words and then translated into modern English.

(A) Where a passion is neither founded on false suppositions, nor chooses means insufficient for the end, the understanding can neither justify nor condemn it. It is not contrary to reason to prefer the destruction of the whole world to the scratching of my finger. (Treatise, Book II, part III, section 3)

[Thought can neither justify nor condemn an emotion, unless it is based on a false assumption or makes a mistake about which means will lead to which ends. It is not against reason to prefer the destruction of the whole world to my finger getting scratched.]

(B) In every system of morality which I have hitherto met with, . . . the author proceeds for some time in the ordinary way of reasoning, and establishes the being of a God, or makes observations concerning human affairs; when of a sudden I am surprised to find, that instead of . . . is, and is not, I meet with . . . ought, or an ought not. . . . [It] seems altogether inconceivable, how this new relation can be a deduction from others, which are entirely different from it. (Treatise, Book III, part I, section 1)

[Systems of morality usually begin with reasoning about matters of fact, for example about God or about human psychology. Then suddenly they switch, and instead of saying "is" and "is not" they begin to say "ought" and "ought not." But premises about "is" do not lead to conclusions about "ought."]

(C) We assert that, after the constant conjunction of two objects – heat and flame, for instance, weight and solidity – we are determined by custom alone to expect the one from the appearance of the other. . . . No man, having seen only one body move after being impelled by another, could infer that every other body will move after a like impulse. All inferences from experience, therefore, are effects of custom, not of reasoning.

Custom, then, is the great guide of human life. (Enquiry concerning Human Understanding, section V, part 1)

[My claim is that when two things repeatedly occur together, for example, flame leading to heat, or an object's being solid and its having weight, then we become accustomed to expect one when the other appears. No one who had seen only one object move after another collides with it could deduce that all objects will move when other objects collide with them. All the conclusions we draw from experience, therefore, are really the results of habit, not of reasoning.]

(D) When we run over libraries, persuaded of these principles, what havoc must we make? If we take in our hand any volume; of divinity or school metaphysics, for instance; let us ask, Does it contain any abstract reasoning concerning quantity or number? No. Does it contain any experimental reasoning concerning matter of fact

and existence? *No. Commit it then to the flames: for it can contain nothing but sophistry and illusion.* (Enquiry concerning Human Understanding, *section XII, part 3*)

[Imagine what it would be like if we went through a library keeping my philosophy in mind. Take any book, for example a theology book or an old-fashioned philosophy book. Ask: "Does it contain any mathematical reasoning?" No. "Does it contain any reasoning about the physical world, based on evidence?" No. Burn it, then, for it can contain nothing but fraud and illusion.]

Which of the passages from Hume is arguing for which of the positions below?

(a) You cannot deduce an ought from an is.
(b) Desire is arbitrary.
(c) We should not take seriously any theory that is neither mathematical nor scientific.
(d) Inductive reasoning is founded on habit.

Which of the following arguments *against* the position expressed in passage (A) has the most force?

(1) Hume's little finger is part of the world, so destroying the whole world would destroy his little finger too; so he should see the destruction of the world as worse.
(2) It would be against reason to want not to be able to reason, so wanting some things, for example, intellectual enslavement, would be against reason.
(3) It is unreasonable to want pain, so when choosing two options it is reasonable to want the least painful one.
(4) A creature that preferred the destruction of the world to the destruction of its little finger would be so different from any actual human being that there is no point debating what it would be reasonable for it to want.
(5) It is reasonable to want to satisfy your desires, so it is against reason to prefer the option that would mean getting less of what you want.

What is the relation between passage (D) and passages (A), (B), (C)? Which of the descriptions below seems most accurate?

(i)   (D) is the inevitable consequence of the opinions described in (A), (B), (C).
(ii) (D) is completely contrary to what is expressed in (A), (B), (C).
(iii) (D) expresses a point of view for which (A), (B), (C) could be a partial justification.
(iv) All four, (A), (B), (C), (D), are simply expressions of a blind antireligious bias.

6.4 Four Kinds of Irrationality

Below are four examples of people thinking and behaving in self-defeating ways.

Logical incoherence   Albert believes that the constellations in the sky at the moment of your birth determine every detail of your subsequent life. He also believes that twins often have very different lives (even twins born by caesarean section at the very same instant). When it is pointed out to him that his beliefs about the influence of constellations contradict his beliefs about the lives of twins, he refuses to modify either belief.

Inductive incoherence   Bertha wants to know whether all gerbils are grey. She examines fifty gerbils in her friends' houses and in pet stores and they are all grey. So she feels fairly certain that all gerbils are grey. She says things like "I'm eighty per cent certain that all gerbils are grey." Then she is in an enormous pet shop and passes a cage containing three hundred gerbils. They are all grey, and in fact are no different in color from any of the gerbils she saw earlier. But now she feels less certain that all gerbils are grey. She says things like "I'm sixty per cent certain that all gerbils are grey."

Inappropriate choice of means   Carlos' main aim in life is to surf on the Pacific Ocean. He believes that he will be able to do this only if he takes a job near the Pacific coast. He is offered a job in Los Angeles and one in Rome. He likes both cities the same and both jobs the same. He takes the job in Rome.

Incoherent desire   Dolores is deciding what to study. She wants most of all to become a doctor. She has been accepted for medical school. She also would like to become an accountant, though much less than she wants to become a doctor. She has been accepted for an accountancy course. She decides to go on the accountancy course.

In each of these cases the person is acting in a self-defeating way. Albert's beliefs cannot all be true, Bertha's beliefs get less rather than more likely to be true as she considers more evidence, Carlos acts in a way that blocks what he wants, and Dolores chooses the option that she wants less rather than the one she wants more. (In each case more details could be added so that the person's behavior was not so self-defeating. Dolores might have reasons for thinking she would not succeed in medical school. Bertha might have seen something else in the pet store that changed her ideas about the colors of animals. It is also easy to fill in details so that the behavior is thoroughly irrational.) But the four cases are very different.

According to Hume, reason is concerned with thinking that leads to certainty and with the choice of means to ends. Thus Hume would probably be able to account for what is irrational

> Hume's skepticism comes partly from his very narrow understanding of reason. We can think well or badly in more ways than he considers.

about Albert and Carlos. Bertha and Dolores are a problem for his view, though. In both cases something is going wrong in a domain that Hume excludes from reason. In the Bertha case it is inductive reasoning, which Hume says is the result of habit rather than reason. And in the Dolores case it is the choice of desire, which Hume says is a matter of emotion rather than reason.

The important point here is not how we use the word "reason". Whether or not we say that the irrationality or self-defeating quality found in Bertha's and Dolores' behavior is a failure of reason, it is clear that some kind of thought process has gone wrong. And each of these thought processes has definite patterns which it follows when it is going wrong and when it is going right. In Bertha's case these are the patterns of good inductive reasoning. And in Dolores' case (and also in Carlos') these are what philosophers call "practical reasoning," the way in which a person's beliefs and desires interact to produce the person's actions.

Two very important conclusions can be drawn here.

◆ *We can study many forms of good and bad reasoning.* Inductive reasoning and practical reasoning can go wrong just as deductive reasoning can. They can make it less likely that our beliefs will be true or that we will accomplish our aims. Philosophers (and statisticians and psychologists) study the patterns of good and bad reasoning and try to describe them in useful ways.

◆ *Habit and emotion come in more and less rational forms.* Suppose that we classify the thought processes in inductive reasoning and practical reasoning as habit and emotion. This should not hide the fact that some of these habits and emotions are effective ways of achieving our aims and others are less effective.

(A) to (H) below are cases of behavior that might be thought to be irrational. Which of them fall into which of the following categories?

(1) logical incoherence
(2) inductive incoherence
(3) inappropriate choice of means
(4) incoherent desire
(5) some other kind of irrationality
(6) no irrationality at all

Some cases may fall into more than one category. You may want to classify them so that some category does not apply to any of these eight cases.

(A) Alice is buying a new car and is choosing between a Cord and a Huppmobile. The most important factor for her is reliability. She reads in consumer magazines that Cords are more reliable than Huppmobiles, and several of her friends who have Huppmobiles complain that they break down all the time. But she is very attached to her uncle Fred, who has a Cord that is a real lemon, rarely out of the garage for more than a few weeks. She decides to buy a Huppmobile.

(B) Bruno thinks about his life and decides that he does not enjoy anything he is doing. He realizes that some other people could be happy if they had a chance, and so he abandons all attempts at achieving happiness for himself and devotes his life to the care of others.

(C) Carlotta is choosing a new car. She prefers a Chrysler to a Ford. She also prefers a Ford to a Volkswagen. And she prefers a Volkswagen to a Chrysler.

(D) David falls in love with a woman who despises him. They get married and are divorced within six months. He is extremely unhappy. He then falls in love with another woman who despises him and again marries and soon separates. Again he is extremely unhappy. Then it happens a third time.

(E) Elizabetta believes that all men are stupid callous brutes. She is in love with Zeno and she thinks that he is the most intelligent, sensitive, and refined person on earth.

(F) Frank wants to prove a very difficult and famous unproved conjecture in mathematics. He quits his job and lives on charity, spending all his time trying unsuccessfully to find a proof. He often despairs of ever succeeding, but continues in the quest.

(G) Germaine falls very ill with arthritis and finds walking painful. She is offered a drug that will alleviate the pain. But she says that it is her fate to be crippled and she must accept it.

(H) Henrik knows that years divisible by four are leap years and have 29 days in February. On Thursday February 8, 1996, he says to a friend "I'm not free for lunch today, so let's meet in four weeks' time, on Thursday March 8."

Box 12 The Gambler's Fallacy

You see a coin tossed ten times. It comes down heads every time. It is about to be tossed again. Which way do you expect it to come down? Inductive reasoning and probability theory suggest that you should either think that the coin is biased and so expect another head, or put the run of heads down to chance and expect that heads and tails are equally likely. Yet some people will expect the coin to come down tails next time. They think: a run of eleven heads in a row is even more unlikely than a run of ten heads, so the coin will probably come down tails on the eleventh throw. This is called the gambler's fallacy. It is a mistake. (It is worth trying to say very explicitly why it is a mistake.) Reasoning like this, people sometimes shelter under lightning-struck trees, thinking that lightning rarely strikes the same place twice. And in bombardments people sometimes sit in bomb craters, thinking that the probability of a bomb hitting the same place twice is very low. Psychologists studying how people reason with probabilities say that almost everyone is susceptible to some form of the gambler's fallacy. Though it is not good reasoning, it corresponds to some habit of the human mind.

6.5 Degrees of Certainty

Even when our beliefs are not certain our evidence gives better support for some than for others. If you have seen thousands of swans and they have all been white, and you have no information about black swans, then you have fairly strong reasons for believing that all swans are white. You have better reasons for believing that all swans are white than that, say, some swans are white, some black, and the rest green. And you have better reasons for believing that all swans are white than someone does who has only seen three white swans. Most beliefs are uncertain, but some are more certain than others.

This is why we should not take the fact that reason cannot often give us certainty as a ground for thinking of reason as powerless. Reason – thinking, arguing, considering evidence – can tell us a lot about which things it is more reasonable to believe. Which is not to deny that sometimes the most reasonable thing to believe will be false. There are black swans.

The same is true in ethics. The limits of the power of reason in ethics are less clear. It is still possible that some very deep and logical analysis will show that some particular values have to be part of any moral code whatsoever. Perhaps we can show that some prohibitions on slavery and on murder are like this, without having to take into account facts about human psychology and human society. Perhaps. But suppose that the power of reason in ethics is as limited as it is in science. Does it follow that any values are as good as any others?

No, it does not. Even if we can never be certain about which things to value – what acts to recommend and what to condemn, how to organize society and what ways to live our lives – some values can be preferable to others, and we can even have justified opinions about which ones they are. Some beliefs about right and wrong can be more certain than others, even if none is totally certain.

This is a subtle point. The claim is not that we *must* take some beliefs about right and wrong to be more certain than others. It is that we *can* feel more certain about some moral beliefs than about others, without either contradicting ourselves or having to retreat to moral rationalism. One way to see that this is a possible and defensible attitude is to look at views that many people hold concerning when one should tolerate other people's different values.

6.6 Valuing Values

Our tolerance for the values of other cultures, when they differ from ours, depends a lot on what those values are like. Suppose there is a faraway imaginary culture which believes that all women past childbearing age should be burned to death to appease the forces of nature. People in this culture find the sight of middle-aged women abhorrent, an affront to what is natural. These are their values; they think that it is *wrong* to allow middle-aged women to live. The forces of nature will be offended, and they have a deep reverence for what they consider natural.

Imagine that you are living in interaction with these people. You realize that some middle-aged women accept their fate as correct and just, but some do not, and do not look forward with resignation to being burned. You could try to rescue some of them. Moreover, you can try to influence people in their culture. You can argue with them, show them how people in your culture live perfectly happily without burning anyone, or try to get them to feel some sympathy for their victims. Or, on the other hand, you could respect their values by keeping your opinions to yourself and not interfering in their customs.

Contrast this imaginary culture with another one. When you visit this second society you see no one burned; in fact no one is even punished. Children act in ways that seem to you to be intolerably disrespectful to their parents and are not even told off. People also live their sexual and emotional lives in ways that seem to you irresponsible and potentially disastrous. But the catastrophes that you expect somehow do not occur. They do forbid some acts; and there seems to be an intricate network of rules determining, for example, when one person must have a long and serious discussion with another person. You find their rules and values very puzzling; they are hard to get the hang of, but people in this culture do fail to condemn many things that you consider wrong. Again, you have the options of interfering or leaving them alone.

Some people would react in the same way to both cultures, either condemning and interfering with both or respecting and tolerating both. But many people would react differently to them, condemning and interfering in the first case and respecting and tolerating in the second. One basic reason would lie in the difference in our attitudes, on the one hand, to burning people alive and, on the other, to different patterns of family and sexual life. We have no doubt that burning people alive is a simply horrible thing to do, which can hardly ever be justified. But we have less confidence that the rules we apply to run our family lives and to regulate the emotions we feel to others are the only or the best ones. So we are less prepared to condemn until we see definitely evil consequences flowing from other people's different habits.

Even people who will not react differently to these two cases may react differently to some such cases. For almost everyone holds some of their values with greater confidence than others. It is more certain that some things are wrong than that others are. We value values, and we value some of our values more highly than others. Thus we think that attaching a value to family life and emotional bonds between people is a good thing, but the precise values by which people of one's own or another culture accomplish this are not particularly important. And we attach a very strong negative value to inflicting suffering on people. So we are ready to condemn any system of values that involves it.

We not only value some values more than others, we also value the having of values. And we value their being chosen freely and deliberately.

Contrast two people. Arthur has been raised very strictly in a community of kind, considerate, honest people, who have instilled in him an unflinching obedience to a very strict moral code. As a result he too is kind, considerate, and honest. But his kindness, consideration, and honesty are the result of a mechanical obedience to his upbringing.

Bertha, on the other hand, has been raised in an atmosphere of moral uncertainty, and has had to think out her rules for herself. She too has opted for kindness, consideration, and honesty. But her choice of acts is not mechanical. She has no rigid code to guide her and must think out each situation in its own terms.

Suppose now that Arthur's code is actually a very effective one, in that the actions it leads him to are generally kinder, more considerate, and more honest than the actions that Bertha chooses after long deliberation. Would you prefer to be like Arthur or like Bertha? Which would you prefer your children to be like?

Many people would prefer to be like Bertha, and they would try to raise children who are more like her. That is, they value freely chosen and thoughtfully followed values more than unthinkingly accepted ones. And they do so even if there is a cost to this, in terms of other things they value. (You want your children to think for themselves, even if it means that they will do some things you disapprove of. Up to a point, only!)

And in fact the contrast between Arthur and Bertha gives another reason for reacting differently to the two societies contrasted above. The first was a dogmatic society: people in it had a faith that was not to be questioned, that the forces of nature must be appeased in the way their customs demanded. The second was a debate-centered society: its customs gave an important place to talk and argument – indeed, made them compulsory. So, whether or not it was in fact a good place to live, where people related as they should, it was a place where people lived by values that they had had some chance to challenge.

What does this all show? It does not show that the second society is definitely better than the first, or that it is better to be like Bertha than like Arthur. It does not show that anyone who has the opposite preferences is wrong. What it does suggest is that it is *possible* to think that some values are more certain than others. There is nothing illogical or ridiculous about it. And, as we will see in the last section of this chapter, there are even advantages to it.

6.7 How Tolerant Are you?

Most people are torn between tolerance of the values of other people, which may be based on ideas or preferences that we do not understand, and dislike of values that seem wrong, especially those that seem to involve cruelty or hatred. Different people resolve the conflict differently. Some people are extremely tolerant of other people's values, allowing others the right to hold and follow even those values that seem to them repulsive. Others are extremely intolerant, thinking that others should not hold and follow values that are from their point of view wrong.

This section is based on a questionnaire, which should help you to determine where between these two extremes your attitude lies. Write an a, b, or c in the space provided.

(1) You are a landlord and you discover that your tenants participate in religious customs which offend you. (They make sacrifices to devils, perhaps.) Do you: (a) ignore their customs; (b) argue with them; (c) ask them to leave? ☐

(2) You have a friend who sincerely believes that he should kill himself. You argue with him for a long time and are convinced that he has thought out the issue for himself and is not just in the grip of a depression. Yet you think he is mistaken; you think that it would be wrong for him to kill himself. Do you (a) refrain from interfering; (b) insist on continuing the argument; (c) have him taken into protective custody? ☐

(3) You are the parent of a 16-year-old child who wants to join a religious group that believes its members should devote their entire lives to serving their guru, hand over all their possessions to a foundation controlled by him, and wander the streets converting others. You think this is a waste of her life. Do you (a) let her do what she wants; (b) insist that she see a counsellor; (c) use your parental authority to prevent her? ☐

(4) You edit a local newspaper that has a column in which local religious groups explain their beliefs. One group's submission is a vehement argument for the forcible suppression of all other religious and secular doctrines. Do you (a) print it without comment; (b) print it beside an editorial describing the dangers of their beliefs; (c) refuse to print it? ☐

(5) You are the editor of a magazine, and proponents of an alternative medical technique for treating cancer want to buy advertising space. There is statistical evidence that the treatment has no effect, but desperate people will pay a lot of money in a search for a cure. Do you (a) take the advertisement; (b) take it and also print a commentary by a medical researcher; (c) refuse it? ☐

(6) You are a legislator considering how you should vote on a measure that would make some acts illegal which are harmless to anyone besides those who perform them, but which you consider to be morally wrong. (Try to think of a particular example.) Do you (a) vote against prohibition; (b) abstain; (c) vote for prohibition? ☐

(7) You are a legislator in a country in which the public behavior of one small group, involving nudity and obscene language, deeply offends a majority of very traditional people. You do not yourself think this behavior wrong. Restrictions on the behavior of this group are proposed. Do you (a) vote against; (b) abstain; (c) vote for?

(8) In your community there is a group of people whose religion entails strange views about arithmetic. They think that it is false that $666 + 111 = 777$. And in fact they find it deeply offensive that anyone should make this claim, and want their children to be excused from arithmetic classes in school. Do you (a) permit the children to be excused; (b) leave the choice to individual teachers; (c) insist that the children study arithmetic?

Force yourself to choose one of the three options for each situation. Mark your choices in the boxes. Give yourself 0 points for every (a), 1 point for every (b), and 2 points for every (c). Then assess your scores as follows:

0–3: you are very tolerant of moral positions different from your own;
4–7: you are fairly tolerant of moral positions different from your own;
8–11: you are fairly intolerant of moral positions different from your own;
12–16: you are very intolerant of moral positions different from your own.

If you are, according to this test, very or fairly tolerant, it may be because your own confidence in your moral beliefs is low, or because you think others have a right to their own beliefs, however wrong they are. An indication of which of these is the source of your tolerance may be got from looking more closely at your answers. If you picked more (a) answers for questions 1, 2, and 3 than you did (on average) in the questionnaire as a whole, this suggests that the reason is your low confidence in the correctness of your own values. Call this type 1 tolerance. If you picked more (a) answers for questions 4, 5, and 8 than you did (on average) in the questionnaire, this suggests that the reason is that you think others have a right even to very mistaken beliefs. Call this type 2 tolerance.

If you are, according to this test, very or fairly intolerant, it may be because your own confidence in your moral beliefs is high, or because you believe in a unified society with a single set of shared values. If you gave more (c) answers for questions 1, 2, and 3 than you did (on average) in the question-naire as a whole, this suggests that the reason is that your confidence in your own moral values is high. Call this type 1 intolerance. If you gave more (c) answers for questions 4, 6, 7 than you did (on average) in the questionnaire, this suggests that the reason is that you believe in a unified society. Call this type 2 intolerance.

You may have found questions 6 or 7 hard to answer. With 6, some people may find it hard to imagine what acts would be wrong but do no one any harm. With question 7, some people may find it hard to imagine how they could not disapprove of such offensive behavior. Questions 6 and 7 are worth discussing in groups of four or more people – containing, if possible, one type 1 tolerant person, one type 2 tolerant person, one type 1 intolerant person, and one type 2 intolerant person.

6.8 Mill on Freedom of Expression

John Stuart Mill, an English philosopher who lived from 1806 to 1873, wrote his classic defense of individuality, *On Liberty*, in 1859 (with help from Harriet Taylor). The book as a whole is intended as a defense of a single claim, which is often called *Mill's harm principle*. In his words:

> the sole end for which mankind are warranted, individually or collectively, in inter-fering with the liberty of action of any of their number is self-protection. That the only purpose for which power can be rightfully exercised over any member of a civilized com-munity, against his will, is to prevent harm to others. His own good, either physical or moral, is not a sufficient warrant. He cannot be rightfully compelled to do or forbear because it will be better for him to do so, because it will make him happier, because, in the opinions of others, to do so would be wise or even right. These are good reasons for remonstrating with him, or reasoning with him, . . . but not for compelling him . . .

The basic principle here is that the only reason a society can prevent some-one doing something is that it harms someone else. This may sound like a sentiment we would all accept. But there are two important problems with it.

(A) Sometimes people do things which harm only themselves (or harm them-selves much more than they harm anyone else), but to allow them to do these things would seem to neglect a duty we have to them.
(B) Sometimes an act which might at first appear only to harm the person who does it produces harm to others because of their attitudes or values.

Here are some situations in which one or both of these two problems arise. Which of the two problems arises in each situation?

(i)   Religious people who are offended that atheists do not believe in God, or atheists who are offended that religious people do believe in God;
(ii)   People who want to commit suicide, because of the influence of drugs or depression;
(iii) Parents who are distressed to know what their children do;
(iv)   Children who want to drop out of school;
(v)   People who do not save for their old age, or people who do not wear motor-cycle helmets;
(vi)   People who are distressed at what others know about them.

One reaction to these examples and these problems is to revise the principle. Here are three possible revisions.

(1) The only reason a society can prevent a sane, rational, adult doing something is that it harms someone else.
(2) The only reason a society can prevent someone doing something is that it causes someone else physical or financial damage.
(3) The only reason a society can prevent a sane, rational adult doing something is that it causes someone else physical or financial damage.

These may also seem wrong. While Mill's original harm principle might seem too strong, in that it could be used to allow society to forbid acts that should not be forbidden, these may seem too weak, in that they fail to allow society to forbid acts that should be forbidden. There may be interesting differences, on which of (1)–(3) is preferable and whether any of them are too weak, between people with different scores on the tolerance questionnaire in the previous section.

In chapter 2 of his book Mill defends the right of individuals to express their beliefs freely, even when those beliefs contradict widely held political, religious, or moral beliefs. He is defending the right to be skeptical.

He takes for granted that it is good to have true beliefs and that the operation of free discussion and reasoning will lead to the truth. His method of argument is to consider reasons why one might think that in spite of this, free discussion should not be allowed on some topics. He then tries to show that these arguments have no force. (This is a common method in philosophy. To defend a position, you think of arguments against it. Then you refute these arguments.)

One type of consideration he discusses runs as follows. Suppose we already know the truth about some matter. Then more free discussion of it can only lead to confusion and error. Two of his refutations of this argument are particularly important. The first stresses the greater benefits of free discussion even if it does result in some falsehoods. To quote Mill again:

> *Truth gains more even by the errors of one who . . . thinks for himself than by the true opinions of those who only hold them because they do not suffer themselves to think. [This is] indispensable to enable average human beings to attain the mental stature of which they are capable. There have been . . . great individual thinkers in a general atmosphere of mental slavery. But there never has been, nor ever will be, in that atmosphere an intellectually active people.*

There are two distinct claims being made here. One is that there is a benefit to the life of a community and its individual members from living in an atmosphere of free discussion. (One in which there is a value attached to the free choice of values.) The other is that by questioning even well-established beliefs we learn valuable things.

The two claims here are:

(I) Free discussion is a social good.
(II) Free and questioning discussion often leads to discovery of the truth.

For each of the following topics, which of (I) or (II) (or both, or neither) is plausible?

(a) Religious questions about immortality and the afterlife;
(b) Scientific questions about the nature of matter;
(c) Questions about good and bad art;
(d) Questions about arithmetic, such as whether $7 \times 23 = 161$.

Does (II) show that (I) is true? That is, is the reason that free discussion is good for a society (supposing that it is) that free discussion leads to the truth? Do (a) and (c) support this idea?

Some of the valuable discoveries that come from free discussion concern our reasons for our beliefs. As Mill elaborates the point:

> *Strange that [people] should imagine that they are not assuming infallibility when they acknowledge that there should be free discussion on all subjects which can possibly be doubtful, but think that some particular principle or doctrine should be forbidden to be questioned because it is so certain, that is, because they are certain that it is certain. To call any proposition certain, while there is anyone who would deny its certainty if permitted . . . is to assume that we ourselves . . . are the judges of certainty, and judges without hearing the other side.*

One way of putting Mill's point here is this: we have beliefs, and we regard some of them as more certain than others. These beliefs about which of our beliefs are more certain are important. For example, they affect such things as our choices of what to reconsider when faced with surprising evidence or paradoxical arguments. So we should try to achieve some degree of certainty about which of our beliefs are certain (or which beliefs are more certain than which others). We need to think hard about what one might call the map of certainty among our beliefs. But the best way to do that is by being intelligently skeptical.

But could we become absolutely certain about which things were more and less certain? Then perhaps we could be dogmatic and repressive about the things we were certain were certain. To some extent we are. If a sect comes to believe that $77 + 7 = 100$, we do not think that their beliefs should be respected in the school curriculum. On the other hand we assume, as Mill implicitly does, that on many moral, political, and religious matters, although we may have firm convictions, we are less certain that our conviction is justified. We are certain, but not certain about our certainty. Then, according to Mill, we should tolerate views that we feel certain are false.

6.9 Toleration in Science

If you have faith in science then you may believe that many scientific theories are now established beyond doubt. There may be a tension between this and your commitment to freedom of expression. This section explores that tension.

(A) You are the editor of a scientific journal and you are sent a paper which gives evidence that measles inoculation damages children more often than had been supposed. You expect that further studies will suggest that the conclusions of the paper are too strong. But you also expect that if you publish the paper it will be reported in the popular press and parents will resist having their children inoculated. Then measles will spread and more children will die from it than could possibly have been damaged by inoculation. What would you do?

(i)   Publish the paper anyway, just the same as any of the other articles in the journal;
(ii) Refuse to publish it;
(iii) Send it out to referees, and publish it only if in their opinion it meets a higher scientific standard than most of the articles you publish;
(iv) Publish it together with an editorial warning against taking it too seriously;
(v)   Hold it, in the hope that another study with opposite conclusions will come along soon, so you can publish both in the same issue.

(B) You are the administrator in charge of a large telescope. You are approached by representatives of a small religious group. They believe that God intended that man should take the snail as a model to follow in life. (Snails show no aggression to one another. Moreover they are hermaphroditic, so each snail has the experience of both sexes.) Snail worship is deeply important to them and gives meaning to their lives. They would like to search the heavens for spiral galaxies whose shape could be taken as signs from God of the significance of snails. So they want the use of your telescope. To let them use it you would have to delay or cancel work on several scientific projects. These projects are not extremely important but they are investigating standard astronomical topics. Do you let the snail-worshipers use the telescope?

If *Yes*, is the reason the importance that snails have in their lives? Would a "No" answer be intolerant of their religious beliefs? If *No*, do the reasons include the fact that their beliefs about snails seem to you absurd. Or that they are scientifically unfounded? Are you showing a prejudice against their religion in denying them the use of the telescope?

(C) You live in a village, populated by respectable middle-class Christians. Into the village move a family of slovenly dressed, moon-worshiping, new-age mystics. They claim to be druids. They buy the grocery store. You and all the other previous inhabitants of the town decide not to patronize the store. You organize a car pool so that everyone can buy groceries at the next town. When the newcomers' van breaks down no one will give them a lift to go into the city to get spare parts. Your children are not allowed to play with their children. But you do them no direct harm. You do not throw things at them or speak abusively or damage their possessions. Still, their business fails and they leave, to live in cardboard boxes in the city.

Were you acting intolerantly? Were you violating any right of the newcomers to have their beliefs respected?

Discuss your reactions to each case with others in your group. Then see whether other groups have the same reactions. If not, what are the reasons for your different reactions? Do you disagree more about (C) than about (A) and (B)? (Or do you disagree about (A) and (B) more than about (C)?) This may suggest that your tolerance of disagreements about science is different from your tolerance of disagreements about cultural and moral matters.

| 6.10 Making Uncertainty Pay

There is no way of acquiring beliefs that will guarantee truth. And only the most trivial knowledge-giving strategy comes with a guarantee even that it will fairly often give true results. The fallibility of induction shows that. Complete certainty is unattainable. If that's what you expected from reason you are going to be disappointed.

And if you expected reason – or reflection or wisdom or even philosophy – to give you certainty about how you should act, you are also likely to be disappointed. Moral rationalism still has a lot of force, but moral dilemmas and conflicts of values are a fact of life.

Does this show that thinking is too feeble to be central to our conclusions about life and the world? Can we only follow our moral and practical instincts, trusting that they will work out for the best? Hume draws these conclusions. But they are *not* inevitable. For as the previous section has argued, the fact that we cannot achieve certainty does not show that some ways of acquiring uncertain beliefs are not better than others. No house will stand for ever, but there is still a difference between a mansion and a shack. And the fact that reason alone will not tell us what to want does not show that, given our wants, some ways of satisfying them are not better than others. *To abandon certainty is not to abandon reason.*

In fact there is something more positive to say. Suppose you think that there are truths we have yet to discover, both about the nature of the world and about how human beings can live well together. How are we to learn them, if certainty is generally beyond us? The last section of Chapter 4 ("What is

Morality About?") suggested a way. It suggested that if we know which of our moral beliefs are more and less certain, and which moral problems we find really puzzling and hard to think through, then we know what to look for in a theory of morality. It should help us think through the puzzling cases while leaving many of our present certainties intact. If this is right then it gives a reason why we should be more tolerant of some differences of moral culture than of others. The imaginary culture of "Valuing Values," Section 6 above, which burns people alive, conflicts with values about which we have almost no doubts; while the imaginary culture which seems peculiarly permissive challenges our values on points that are for many of us deeply troubling: what is the point of punishment, and why do some aspects of our emotional lives mean so much to us?

The central idea here is thus: *know which of your beliefs are more and which are less certain; know what your deep and unsettled problems are.* If you do you will have a chance of recognizing an improvement on your own values when you encounter it. But the point does not just hold for ethics. It holds for all our beliefs. We cannot have many completely certain beliefs, but if we are to improve our inevitably uncertain ones we need to know which of our beliefs are less adequate and which we think we can safely build on. We need to know where the puzzles lie. That means that we should shift our aim, from the search for certainty to a search for clarity about which of our beliefs are more and which less certain.

So instead of having to accept a paradox we have to solve a problem. Can we think about thinking without making the certainty assumption? Can we accept the fact that certainty is unattainable while maintaining that there is a distinction between the reasonable and the unreasonable in belief, and between better and worse ways of acting? How can we live in an uncertain world? That is the theme of Part II of this book.

Conclusions of This Chapter

◆ *All kinds of reasoning – inductive reasoning, moral reasoning, reasoning about practical matters – can be performed in better and in worse ways, and we can study what makes any kind of reasoning give more or less satisfactory results.*

◆ *When we find that a belief or a way of reasoning is wrong we have to weigh our disagreement with it against the value we place on people having and living by their own beliefs and values.*

◆ *Mill's harm principle, which says that an action or opinion should be tolerated as long as it does not harm anyone except the person concerned, can give some guidance when we disapprove of the values or beliefs of others. To apply it we have to decide what is to count as harm.*

◆ *We can keep open the possibility of progress in morals and science if we are aware of which of our beliefs are more and which less certain and if we can see the problems even of beliefs which we consider certain.*

Further Reading

On Hume

Selection from Hume's *Enquiry* in Part I of John Cottingham (ed.), *Western Philosophy: An Anthology*. Blackwell, 1996.

David Hume, *An Enquiry into Human Understanding*, chapters 4 and 13; and *An Enquiry concerning the Principles of Morals*, appendix 1, in *Hume's Enquiries*, edited by A. Selby-Bigge. Oxford University Press, 1966.

Barry Stroud, *Hume*. Routledge, 1988.

Terence Penelhum, *David Hume: An Introduction to his Philosophical System*. Purdue University Press, 1992.

Peter Jones, "Hume," in *The Blackwell Companion to Philosophy*.

On decision-making

Chapter 4 of Robert M. Martin, *There Are Two Errors in the the Title of this Book*. Broadview, 1992.

David A. Welch, *Decisions, Decisions: The Art of Effective Decision-making*. Prometheus Books, 2002.

On Mill

John Stuart Mill, *On Liberty*, in *Essential Works of John Stuart Mill*, edited by Max Lerner. Bantam Books, 1961.

William Thomas, *Mill*. Oxford University Press, 1985.

On freedom of expression

Anthony Skillen, "Freedom of Speech," in Keith Graham (ed.), *Contemporary Political Philosophy*. Cambridge University Press, 1982.

*Thomas Scanlon, "A Theory of Freedom of Expression," in Ronald Dworkin (ed.), *The Philosophy of Law*. Oxford University Press, 1977.

*C. E. Baker, *Human Liberty and Freedom of Speech*. Oxford University Press, 1989.

Electronic resources

Routledge Encyclopedia of Philosophy (available online at many universities): articles on Freedom of speech; Hume, David; Mill, John Stuart.

Stanford Encyclopedia of Philosophy (http://plato.stanford.edu/): *Freedom of speech; Hume, David; Mill, John Stuart*; Practical reason (*italicized* items are available as this book goes to press; the others should be available soon).

Postcard History of Philosophy I

This is a very brief history of philosophy from the point of view of the themes discussed in Part I of this book. But not every idea or philosopher mentioned in the history is discussed in Part I. *Italicized* names are discussed in the book, in Part I or elsewhere. (For page references see the index.)

The largest single source of contemporary philosophical ideas is classical Greek philosophy. A combination of influences from Africa and the Middle East led philosophers living throughout the Mediterranean region, and usually writing in Greek, to doubt the beliefs of their culture. *Socrates* (fifth century BC) argued that we know much less than we think we do. "I only know that I know nothing". His pupil *Plato* (fifth–fourth century BC) saw in mathematics a source of certainty, and wanted to get beliefs about morals and politics by similar ways of reasoning. But Plato's pupil *Aristotle* (fourth century BC) put a greater weight on experience and on traditional authority.

Greek ideas were developed by Islamic and by European Christian philosophers, against a background of religious belief. After about AD 1500 the rise of Protestantism and the emergence of modern science gave questions about certainty a different emphasis. Early scientist-philosophers, such as *Descartes* (seventeenth century) were rationalists, hoping for a way to get absolutely certain knowledge about the world. Rationalist philosophy was succeeded by *empiricism*. Empiricists argued that knowledge must be based on experience as much as on reason. *Hume* (eighteenth century) argued for a skepticism about knowledge, partly because of his realization that inductive reasoning will never lead to certainty. Hume was not a skeptic about morals, but he did argue that our ideas of right and wrong must be based on our experience of human nature.

Twentieth-century philosophy tends to emphasize the impossibility of certainty, especially in science. Two extreme expressions of this are existentialism and relativist philosophy of science. Existentialism, in the writings of *Heidegger, Sartre,* and *de Beauvoir*, argues that human beings must invent the values by which they live, and in fact that each person must make his or her own values. Relativist philosophy of science, as found in the work of Thomas Kuhn and Paul Feyerabend, argues that changes of scientific belief produce different rather than better or truer theories. Most contemporary philosophers are neither existentialists nor relativists. But they tend to agree that we have to learn to guide our lives with probabilities rather than certainties.

Part II Life in An Uncertain World

Here is an outline of the sequence of topics in Part II. At the beginning of each chapter the thread of prose will reappear in a way that shows the connection of the chapter with the whole of Part II.

Reason is not powerless, since some uncertain beliefs are more reasonable than others. We need ways of thinking about morals and science that give us reasonable beliefs in terms of changing and uncertain evidence.

Utilitarianism determines the right action in a situation in terms of its consequences. We can use our uncertain information about what might happen if an action were to be performed, to decide what we should do. In some cases this means performing actions that run contrary to traditional morality.

Moral beliefs that are nearer to traditional morality can be got from Kantian ethics, which gives a way of finding moral rules that we can follow whatever the consequences of following them. Kantian ethics emphasizes the motive behind an action, which is ignored by utilitarianism.

Outside ethics an influential way of responding to changing evidence is described by empiricism. Empiricism tries to provide beliefs that are based in a reasonable way on evidence, while keeping the risk of error to a minimum. It does this by considering only evidence which concerns what we perceive and allowing only beliefs that use concepts based on perception.

Empiricism has difficulty explaining why many commonsense and scientific beliefs are reasonable. For example, it makes it hard to understand why it is reasonable to believe that other people have minds and experiences like yours. More powerful ways of basing beliefs on evidence are provided by the inference to the best explanation, the falsificational method, and the hypothetico-deductive method. These are all attempts to describe the kinds of reasoning used in science.

From the debate between utilitarianism and Kantian ethics, and from the problems of empiricism, we can see ways of responding to the false-belief trap of Part I. For we can see how we can sift through our moral and scientific beliefs, finding new ways of testing and connecting them, so that we have a hope of eventually rejecting the ones that are false.

Aims of Part II

By the end of Part II you should be able to

◆ *understand two classic philosophical theories, empiricism and utilitarianism;*
◆ *understand how both of these theories deal with risk and subjectivity;*
◆ *understand why many philosophers reject utilitarianism in favor of Kantian ethics;*
◆ *understand why many philosophers reject empiricism in favor of more informative methods.*

7 Utilitarianism

Introduction

Reason is not powerless, since some uncertain beliefs are more reasonable than others. We need ways of thinking about morals and science that give us reasonable beliefs in terms of changing and uncertain evidence.

Utilitarianism determines the right action in a situation in terms of its consequences. We can use our uncertain information about what might happen if an action were to be performed to decide what we should do. In some cases this means performing actions that run contrary to traditional morality.

Moral beliefs that are nearer to traditional morality can be got from Kantian ethics, which gives a way of finding moral rules that we can follow whatever the consequences of following them. Kantian ethics emphasizes the motive behind an action, which is ignored by utilitarianism.

Outside ethics an influential way of responding to changing evidence is described by empiricism....

Chapter Objectives

By the end of this chapter you should be able to answer the following questions.

◆ *What according to utilitarianism makes an action morally right?*
◆ *What is the difference between utilitarianism and hedonism?*
◆ *What arguments can be used to defend utilitarianism?*
◆ *Why does utilitarianism sometimes recommend actions that go against conventional morality?*

Definitions

The following words used in this chapter are defined in the list of definitions at the end of the book:

altruism	*moral hedonism*	*utilitarianism*
epicureanism	*psychological hedonism*	*utility*

7.1 Naive Utilitarianism

Utilitarianism is a moral theory. It describes a class of actions and recommends them as the ones that we should perform. The basic idea of utilitarianism is very simple, though when philosophers get to work on it they invent some very subtle and complicated variations on the basic idea. Here is a statement of a very simple utilitarianism:

◆ *Naive utilitarianism* The right action is the one which brings about the greatest amount of pleasure or the least amount of pain.

("Brings about," "greatest amount," "pleasure" and "pain" are all pretty slippery ideas. They may look clear but really they hide problems and difficulties. More sophisticated versions of utilitarianism are usually made by taking this very simple version and clarifying or replacing one of these four terms. Some more sophisticated versions are discussed in this chapter and the next.)

> Utilitarianism says to act so as to maximize pleasure and minimize pain.

Consider some straightforward examples. Suppose that two people are stranded in the desert. They know they will be rescued in six hours. One of them has a bottle of water and since she is thirsty she drinks half of it. She can save the other half for the thirst she knows will return in a couple of hours. Or she can give it to the other person, who will suffer extreme dehydration if he does not get a drink soon. According to naive utilitarianism she ought to give the other person the remaining water. For if she saves it for herself she will avoid some painful thirst, but if she gives it to the other person she will avoid his having a much more painful experience.

Or imagine that you are an administrator deciding where to build a hospital. It could be built in either of two districts. In district A 2000 people will be served by it, who at present have no accessible hospital. In district B 4000 people will be served, who also have no hospital at present. According to utilitarianism you ought to build the hospital in district B (other factors being equal), since that way more people will gain, and presumably the balance of overall pleasure over pain will be greater.

Finally, imagine that you are an 18-year-old woman choosing between going away to college and staying at home to take care of your aging mother. If you stay at home you will be committed to a gap of several years in your education. You may in fact lose so much time that by the time you can resume your education it will be much more difficult to enter your chosen profession. And there will also be a big delay before you can consider starting a family. If you go off to college your mother can be taken care of by a nurse, and her mental and physical state is so low that she will not appreciate the difference. Utilitarianism says not just that you may go to college and leave your mother to be taken care of by a nurse, but that you *should* go. For if you do not go you will suffer, and if you do go your mother will not suffer more than she would have if you had not.

Although these are very simple examples they bring out some basic features of utilitarianism. It is a moral theory that focuses on actions: it discusses what you should do, rather than what your motives should be or whether you are a good or bad person. It is a fairly simple theory that takes into account fairly straightforward qualities of actions. In particular, it takes into account the consequences of an action – what will or may happen if you do the action. Lastly, it is a theory that can sometimes give different answers to those given by traditional morality. This is brought out by the last of the above examples.

7.2 Choosing the Utilitarian Action

Five situations are described below. In each of them a person has to decide what to do. Which of the actions listed for each situation would be recommended by naive utilitarianism? (You may be able to think of other actions that would be even more recommended by naive utilitarianism. But to keep it simple stick to the choices listed.)

(a) Zenobia has been left a fortune by her aunt. She has a well-paying job, which she finds satisfying and which gives her a comfortable life. Her aunt had another niece, Yolanthe, who is very poor. Yolanthe is a single parent, struggling to raise four children while working at a very badly paying job. The aunt did not leave her fortune to Yolanthe because they had a disagreement about politics twenty years earlier. Should Zenobia:

    (i)   spend the money on luxuries for herself?
    (ii) give the money to Yolanthe?
    (iii) split the money between herself and Yolanthe?

(b) Xerxes is Wolfram's best friend. Wolfram is devoted to Vita, who is married to someone else but who is distantly polite to Wolfram when they meet. In fact Vita thinks that Wolfram is a creep, and is polite only out of good manners. But Wolfram thinks that she must secretly adore him as much as he adores her. If he learned her true attitude he would be heartbroken. The main prop of his existence would be removed. Wolfram often asks Xerxes: "She does love me, doesn't she?" Xerxes knows the truth. Should he:

    (i)   tell Wolfram that Vita loves him?
    (ii) tell Wolfram that Vita thinks he's a creep?
    (iii) evade the question?

(c) Umberto is a plastic surgeon specializing in the repair of birth defects. He lives in a part of the country where there is no one else with his skills and qualifications. Umberto has two children, who he sees very little of because he spends long hours at the hospital. He is a nice father and his children want to see more of him. He would not earn significantly less money if he decided not to work on weekends and to take holidays with his children. And his children would be happier. But hundreds of other children would then not get the operations that they need in order to live normal lives. Should he:

   (i)   spend the same or even less time with his children?
   (ii) spend much more time with his children?
   (iii) spend somewhat more time with his children?

(d) Tamara is a kind person who always finds time to discuss other people's problems with them. She is studying for her exams in her final year at college. The results are very important to her as they will determine whether she gets into law school or not. The evening before an important exam in a subject she finds difficult (advanced moral philosophy), a friend telephones her. He is upset because his girlfriend has told him he is a selfish pig. He wants to talk to Tamara to be reassured that he is not as selfish as his girlfriend said. She knows that if she lets the conversation start it will take up most of the evening and she will become too involved in his problems to be able to do some last-minute studying and then get to bed early. But if she tells him to phone again in a few days' time he will have an unhappy evening wondering why everyone thinks he is selfish. Should she:

   (i)   tell him to phone again next week?
   (ii) talk to him until he calms down?
   (iii) set a limit of half an hour and end the conversation after that long?

(e) Sumiko has always wanted to be a doctor. She has been provisionally accepted by three medical schools, A, B, and C, provided she does well at interviews with each of them. A classmate, Randolph, is also applying to medical schools. He would make a very good doctor but does not have a very strong academic background. He has been provisionally accepted by C only, and is hoping he does well enough at the interview. Randolph asks Sumiko to withdraw from the interview with C, so that there will be a greater chance that they might take him. If she does then there will be a greater chance that C will accept him, but there is also the slight danger that A and B will not accept her after her interviews, so that in withdrawing from C she would then have lost her chance of becoming a doctor. Should she:

(i)   refuse, and apply to all three schools?

(ii) agree, on condition that when he becomes a doctor he pay her a large sum?

(iii) agree, and refrain from applying to C?

In each of the cases (a) to (e), is the action recommended by utilitarianism the action you would choose? If not, is the reason because:

(1) You are not a moral enough person to do what utilitarianism asks.

(2) Utilitarianism ignores some moral duties we have to others.

(3) Utilitarianism ignores moral duties we owe to ourselves.

(Different reasons may apply to each of the five cases, of course.)

7.3 Pleasure, Pain, and Consequences

Naive utilitarianism was defined as saying that *the right action is the one which brings about the greatest amount of pleasure or the least amount of pain.* The concepts of "bring about," "greatest amount," "pleasure," and "pain" are all potential troublemakers. Each of the cases below is one in which it is not obvious how to interpret naive utilitarianism. That is, in each one it is hard to be sure what action naive utilitarianism really suggests.

In each of the following cases discuss the difficulty in applying the rule that *the right action is the one which brings about the greatest amount of pleasure or the least amount of pain,* and decide whether the difficulty is related to a problem about *pleasure, pain, greatest amount,* or *brings about.*

(A) You are on the finance committee of a large city. You have a sum of money to allocate, which can be used either to fund a soup kitchen for homeless people or to start a city art gallery. No one else will start the soup kitchen if you do not, and homeless people will suffer. But the number of homeless is fairly small, and in your city there are many art students and other citizens interested in art who would get a lot of satisfaction from a well-chosen display of old and new paintings. Does naive utilitarianism tell you what to choose?

(B) A friend phones you and asks you to come around to do him a favor. You arrive and find him strapped into a machine which will apply low-voltage electric shocks to various parts of his body. The voltage is not enough to do him serious harm but is enough to cause a lot of pain. He says "Please do it. I like pain." Does naive utilitarianism tell you what to do?

(C) You are on a committee of inquiry into an application to build a nuclear reactor near to a large city. The reactor is of a very advanced and efficient design and will produce electricity at a very low price if located there. Moreover, it is safe in that the probability that it will do any harm at all to the health of the people in the city is very very small. On the other hand the probability is not zero – there is an extremely tiny chance of a catastrophe – and if the worst catastrophe occurs thousands of people will lose their lives. Does naive utilitarianism tell you what to choose?

(D) You are the warden of a national park. In the park there is a beautiful canyon, which is breathtaking to look into and whose rim presents an awe-inspiring silhouette against the sky. A safety committee argues that although it would spoil the vista you should put a fence along the rim. For somebody might jump over and then they and their dependants would be hurt. You reply "No one could fall over that rim – it isn't steep enough – so they would have to deliberately decide to jump over. And that would make any harm a consequence of their choice, not of mine." Does naive utilitarianism tell you what to do?

7.4 Hedonism

Utilitarianism can demand that people sacrifice their own pleasure for the greater pleasure of others. For utilitarianism bases action on pleasure and pain. And since it recommends creating as much pleasure as possible and as little pain as possible, it clearly takes pleasure to be desirable. But it does not say to create as much pleasure *for oneself* as possible. So it does not say that you should take your own pleasure as more desirable than anyone else's.

There is another attitude to pleasure and pain, called *hedonism*, which also takes pleasure to be desirable. But hedonism says that the most important thing for you is *your own* pleasure. So while utilitarianism can be a philosophy that calls for a lot of self-sacrifice, hedonism is a philosophy that focuses on the choices that involve the most overall pleasure for yourself.

In fact hedonism comes in two forms. According to hedonistic psychology, or *psychological hedonism*, people always act so as to obtain pleasure and avoid pain. Psychological hedonism supposes that there is a fundamental law of human psychology: that people always choose what they think will bring them the most pleasure and the least pain. People's actions are always directed to their own pleasure, according to psychological hedonism, even when they do not know or admit it. Consider, for example, someone carrying out a long, boring, painful project (reading a philosophy book, perhaps). According to psychological hedonism, this person would have to be either obtaining pleasure from the project or anticipating some pleasure that would come from having read it. (And if the person says "No, it is a painful bore, but I want to do it," the hedonist replies "See, you want to: it gives you pleasure.")

Psychological hedonists have to account for the behavior of *altruists*, people who act so as to increase other people's pleasure. (Or decrease their pain, or generally improve their lives.) Altruists will act for the sake of someone else even if it decreases their own pleasure or causes themselves pain. Hedonists tend to say that such people must obtain more pleasure from serving the interests of others than they would from serving their own interests. (So in a way they are not being altruistic: they act only for their own sake.)

Most modern philosophers and psychologists think that psychological hedonism is confused. Its plausibility comes from two of its assumptions. The first is that when people act they usually do so because of their *desires*. (People act to get what they want.) And the second is that when people satisfy their desires they very often feel pleasure. But even if these were both true, that would not prove psychological hedonism. For what is plausible is that people *usually* act because of their desires and *often* get pleasure when their desires are satisfied. This does not mean that people *always* act in order to get pleasure. For it allows that people can also often act in ways that do not bring pleasure, and it allows the possibility that any pleasure someone gets from satisfying a desire might be incidental, not the basic reason why they acted. The example of altruism shows how hard it is to believe that whenever someone acts the aim is to produce their own pleasure. For while there may be very few people who always act altruistically, it seems hard to deny either that there are a few saintly individuals who strive always to help others whatever the cost to themselves, or that almost everyone from time to time does something just because it does someone else good.

The other form of hedonism is *moral hedonism*. It is the view that people *ought* to act to get pleasure and avoid pain. That is the way they can have the best lives. Suppose someone faces a choice between two options. What they ought to do, according to moral hedonism, is to see how much pleasure and how much pain each option would lead to for them personally, then to try to balance the pleasure off against the pain, and finally to choose the option that gives the greatest balance of pleasure over pain. This is just like naive utilitarianism except that it considers only the pleasure and pain of the person making the decision. But this one little difference is really important. Suppose that a utilitarian and a hedonist are given an opportunity to give other people a lot of pleasure at very small cost to themselves. The utilitarian takes the opportunity, considering the personal loss to be outweighed by the greater total pleasure that results. But the hedonist says "What's in it for me?"

So you can be a moral hedonist without being a utilitarian. And you can be a utilitarian without being a moral hedonist. (Though both positions count pleasure as the central good thing in life.) You can also be a moral hedonist without being a psychological hedonist. For you could believe that although people ought to go for their own pleasure, they in fact do not, being held back, for example, by altruism. And you can be a psychological hedonist without being a moral hedonist if you believe that people's moral duty is to be altruistic, but that altruism is impossible for people, since they can aim only at their own pleasure. (You could also think that in fact people always act so as to give pleasure to everyone around them as well as themselves. No philosopher has ever defended this position, but we might call it psychological altruism.) All these views are different. Their relations are explained by the definitions and the table below.

◆ utilitarianism: *duty* to maximize *everyone's* pleasure
◆ psychological hedonism: everyone *in fact* maximizes *their own* pleasure
◆ moral hedonism: *duty* to maximize your *own* pleasure
◆ (psychological altruism: everyone *in fact* maximizes *everyone's* pleasure)

	Moral duty	Psychological fact
Everyone's pleasure	Utilitarianism	(Psychological altruism)
Own pleasure	Moral hedonism	Psychological hedonism

Below are four arguments. Each defends one of the four positions just described. Which one defends utilitarianism, which one defends moral hedonism, which one defends psychological hedonism, and which one defends psychological altruism?

(1) The human race has survived because people have taken care of one another.
Therefore people naturally want one another's welfare.
Therefore people naturally want one another's pleasure.
(2) If you are moral you care about other people's welfare as much as your own.
Pleasure is an important part of welfare.
Therefore if you are moral you should try to increase everyone's pleasure.
(3) People act in order to get consequences they want.
People want consequences when they are pleasant for them.
Therefore people act in order to get pleasure for themselves.
(4) People are unhappy when they deny themselves pleasure.
Therefore people would be happier if they acted to get pleasure.
Therefore the greatest pleasure would be produced if people acted to get their own pleasure.

7.5 Four Styles of Advice

Below, four people ask advice from four philosophers – Uno, Dua, Tria, and Quartius. One of the philosophers is a utilitarian, one is a moral hedonist, and one is a psychological hedonist. Which one is which? (Pay attention to the reasons the philosophers give for their advice, and not just their conclusions.) One of the philosophers belongs to none of these schools.

(a) **Troubled person 1:** Since childhood I have wanted to be a scientist. I studied mathematics and physics in college and now I am preparing to do a Ph.D. What I want most to work on is very abstract problems about the theory of relativity, which have no practical application at all. They really interest me. But sometimes I think I ought to do something which will repay society for the costs of my education, and relieve some of the suffering in the world. Perhaps I should do research on medical applications of particle accelerators.

Uno: Your first task is to overcome your guilt. Only then can you be at peace with yourself and really enjoy whatever it is you choose to do.

(b) **Troubled person 2:** I am living with my husband and my three children. I do not love my husband but he is a kind man who treats me well. I have recently met another man who I do love. He wants me to run away with him and live in another country. I really want to go, but I feel unsure what I should do.

Dua: If you stay with your family you may be less happy than if you leave, but your husband will probably be happier, and your children will certainly be happier. So we are weighing a small increase in the happiness of one person – you – against a much larger decrease in the happiness of four people. It seems obvious you should stay at home, learn to love your husband, and hope that your friend moves far away without you.

(c) **Troubled person 3:** I am puzzled by my own behavior. I wanted to be a veterinarian but after six months at vet school I got bored and quit. Then I decided to go for a career in the film industry so I got a job as an assistant to a director. But much of the preparation for filming was really boring and when we were actually making a film we would have to get up incredibly early in the morning. So I left that job and now I am working for a firm of environmental consultants. I am really committed to preserving the environment, but the work seems so trivial and so cynically media-oriented that I am thinking of finding something else to do.

Tria: The first step toward wisdom is self-knowledge. You expected to enjoy all these activities but in fact doing them gave you no pleasure. So you should stop thinking in terms of grand ambitions and idealism and instead think what simple activities give you pleasure. Only when you actually enjoy some occupation will you be able to continue doing it.

(d) **Troubled person 4:** My parents were very unhappy people and I have always been determined not to live a life as miserable as theirs. So my life is a search for pleasure. The trouble is, it does not seem to be working. The drugs I take often make me feel great, but they always leave me feeling awful afterwards. The adventures I get into are a lot of fun but usually result in my being in trouble and short of money. My lovers are exciting people but in the end they always treat me badly. But I cannot think of anything that would give me greater happiness.

Quartius: You are confusing happiness and pleasure. In fact they are very different. Pleasure is momentary, and you often pay for it later with pain or boredom. Happiness is a continuous sustainable state, which has no bad consequences. So if it is happiness you are after you should not look for short-lived pleasures but look instead at the whole stretch of your life and see what satisfying or pleasant activities will be good for you in the long run.

The philosopher who was not a utilitarian, a moral hedonist, or a psychological hedonist was an *Epicurean*. Epicureanism (named after the Greek philosopher Epicurus, who lived in the third century BC) is a careful and moderate version of moral hedonism. It suggests that we make our lives pursuits of pleasure, but in such a way that pleasures don't produce pains. It suggests a life focused on the careful pursuit of moderate, sustainable pleasures. In fact it claims that happiness, or the good life, is best achieved by living a modest life in which pleasure can be obtained from one's own resources to appreciate thought and beauty.

7.6 Bentham and Mill

Bentham formulated naive utilitarianism as a guide for legislators. Mill tried to be more subtle about pleasure and pain, and to apply the theory to individual moral decisions.

Utilitarianism is associated with two English philosophers, Jeremy Bentham (1748–1832) and John Stuart Mill (1806–1873). Bentham invented utilitarianism, intending it mostly as a guide for lawmakers. Mill then grappled with the problems of trying to make the theory apply to moral problems faced by individuals.

Bentham assumes that the aim of a lawmaker (or public administrator) is to further the common good or public interest. If the effects of one piece of legislation would be more in the interest of the community than the effects of another, then it would make a better law. But communities are nothing more than the sum of their members, according to Bentham. So the interest of the community can be nothing more than the sum of the interests of its members. At this point Bentham brings in pleasure, assuming that one law would be more in a person's interest than another if it would bring that person more pleasure or less pain than the other would. Let us think of pleasure and pain as opposite sides of the same quantity, and say that if an action or a law brings a greater balance of pleasure over pain then it brings more happiness. The conclusion is that the best law is the one that creates the greatest sum of happiness among the members of the community. This can be summed up in Bentham's famous phrase, that the best legislation is that which creates the *greatest good for the greatest number*. That is, the greatest amount of happiness, the most pleasure or the least pain, for the greatest number of people.

Bentham thought that pleasure and pain could be measured fairly precisely, and that one could often know how much pain or pleasure a possible law would cause for how many people. He thus thought that we can in principle calculate the value of proposed laws. Legislation can become an exact science. In this respect he was one of the first people to propose a kind of social engineering, in which experts would be able to oversee a society's development in a way that minimizes misery and promotes public welfare.

Mill inherited these ideas from Bentham. He went further, though, and argued explicitly that the value of any action, not just legislation, consists in the balance of happiness over unhappiness in its consequences. (Bentham had only hinted at this.) Mill was also more sophisticated than Bentham, and saw many problems that Bentham had ignored. One was that the idea of pleasure as a simple aim motivating all action is suspect. Another was that a utilitarian philosopher has to be able to give a reason why we should solve moral problems by calculating the happiness resulting from actions. There are so many other ways of getting answers to the problems facing us – for example, by consulting traditional moral codes – that it is natural to ask: why do it this way?

(Bentham had not seen the force of this question because his emphasis was on legislation, and he thought that it was obvious that legislation should work toward the good of the community and obvious that the good of the community is the sum of the good of the individual members.)

Although Mill also presented an abstract argument to defend utilitarianism, his main defense of it was the claim that it represents a sensible continuation of commonsense moral ideas. He claimed that ordinary ideas about blame, justice, and virtue can be translated into utilitarian terms, and that the result is a set of ethical ideas which could be used by people in a modern liberal society acting freely and respecting one another.

Mill's response to worries about pleasure was to distinguish between higher and lower pleasures. Lower pleasures are essentially simple physical ones: eating, drinking, sex (not that he mentions it), and the like. Higher pleasures are those associated with intellectual or artistic activity. The most important higher pleasure is that of self-development, of making your own life.

Box 13 John Stuart Mill and Harriet Taylor

John Stuart Mill lived through a time of great intellectual change, which affected him in deep and personal ways. A child prodigy, at primary school age he could read several languages and help the work of his philosopher father, who was a follower of Bentham. In his twenties he suffered a severe depression from which he recovered partly by reading romantic poetry, particularly Wordsworth. Ever afterwards, he searched for a philosophy with more room in it for human emotions than the one in which he had been raised. Soon after, he met Harriet Taylor, whom he admired intellectually and loved intensely. Together they wrote *The Subjugation of Women*, one of the inspirations of modern feminism. Mill worked for much of his life as an administrator in the East India Company, which in effect ran India as part of the British empire. While performing this demanding job he wrote many books on philosophy, politics, and economics. He was a member of the British parliament for thirteen years.

Mill argues that we can give higher pleasures a priority in evaluating the consequences of an action. (And the importance of the pleasure of self-development is crucial to his defense of the ideal of the free independent individual.) This move can be seen in three ways. It can be seen as a betrayal of his basic utilitarian convictions, by accepting an idea – that some pleasures are more important than others – that is inconsistent with them. It can be seen as merely a matter of terminology: intellectual and artistic activities may give us more pleasure than sensual ones. Or it can be seen as an anticipation of something many contemporary philosophers would say: distinguish between how much pleasure something gives, and how much you want it.

7.7 Quotations from Bentham and Mill

Bentham on utility and community

> By utility is meant that property in any object, whereby it tends to produce benefit, advantage, pleasure, good, or happiness (all this in the present case comes to the same thing) or . . . to prevent the happening of mischief, pain, evil, or unhappiness.

> . . . The interest of the community is one of the most general expressions . . . : no wonder that the meaning of it is often lost. When it has a meaning, it is this. The community is a fictitious body, composed of the individual persons who are considered as constituting . . . its members. The interest of the community then is, what? – the sum of the interests of the several members who compose it. (Principles of Morals and Legislation, *chapter 1)*

Here is a little fable that relates to this quote from Bentham:

> *Once upon a time three friends, Silas, Henry, and Elizabeth, decided to get away from the big bad city and live a healthy life by themselves. In fact they decided to form a little community which would discover the route to true happiness. They bought a farm in the foothills of the mountains and began to experiment with ways of living.*
>
> *For a year things went well. They were happy to be away from the rat race, and they got on well with one another. Several other people were considering joining the community. Then things began to fall apart. First Silas discovered an interesting plant in one of the fields. If you chewed it you got wonderfully pleasant sensations. Soon Silas did not want to do anything except find and chew the plant. He stopped working on the farm or discussing philosophy with his friends, and they became very angry with him. They would suggest that he stop chewing the plant but he would reply that it gave him the greatest pleasure he had ever known. Silas reacted very emotionally to criticism from Henry and Elizabeth, in part because of the influence of the plant, and would spend the evenings crying. His former happy personality had disappeared. Finally Henry and Elizabeth had a showdown with Silas. They told him that if he did not change they would leave the farm and go back to the city. Silas pointed out that this would be the end of the community they were all so committed to. They replied that they would be better off without the community.*

This fable suggests reasons for doubting two of Bentham's assertions:

(1) that "benefit, advantage, pleasure, good, or happiness" all come to the same thing;

(2) that the "interest of the community then is . . . the sum of the interests of the . . . members who compose it."

Which aspects of the fable suggest reasons for doubting (1), and which suggest reasons for doubting (2)?

Mill on kinds of pleasure

> *It is quite compatible with the principle of utility to recognize the fact that some* kinds *of pleasure are more desirable and more valuable than others. It would be absurd that while, in estimating all other things, quality is considered as well as quantity, the estimation of pleasures should be supposed to depend on quantity alone.*
>
> *If I am asked what I mean by difference of quality in pleasures, or what makes one pleasure more valuable than another, merely as a pleasure, except its being greater in amount, there is but one possible answer. Of two pleasures, if there be one to which all or almost all who have experience of both give a decided preference, irrespective of any moral obligation to prefer it, that is the more desirable pleasure.*
>
> *Few human creatures would consent to be changed into any of the lower animals, for a promise of the fullest allowance of a beast's pleasures; no intelligent human being would consent to be a fool. . . . A being of higher faculties requires more to make him happy, is capable probably of more acute suffering, . . . than one of an inferior type; but in spite of these liabilities he can never really wish to sink into what he feels to be*

a lower grade of existence. . . . It is better to be a human being dissatisfied than a pig satisfied; better to be Socrates dissatisfied than a fool satisfied. And if the fool, or the pig, are of a different opinion, it is because they only know their own side of the question. The other party to the comparison knows both sides. (Utilitarianism, chapter 11)

Bentham (in the quotation at the beginning of this section) talks of "benefit, advantage, pleasure, good, or happiness (all this in the present case comes to the same thing)." Would Mill agree with the "comes to the same thing"?

Mill ends "the other party . . . knows both sides." The other party is a human being in comparison with a pig, or Socrates in comparison with a fool. Why does Mill have to claim that a human, or a wise person, knows what the pleasures of a pig, or a fool, are like?

Is this claim plausible?

7.8 Arguments for Utilitarianism

As John Stuart Mill understood, utilitarianism is not obviously true. Someone could reasonably ask: why should I always act so as to increase the total of happiness in the world? And there are other moral philosophies, for example moral hedonism, or the Kantian ethics discussed in the next chapter, which give very different answers to the question "What should I do?" So it would be much more satisfactory if there were convincing arguments one could give to defend utilitarianism.

First consider two very unsophisticated reasons why someone might favor utilitarianism as a moral theory.

The first of the two is the *argument from moral minimalism*. Moral skeptics and relativists often point to the variety of moral codes found among people. But one explanation of the variation in morals is that people in different times and places have different beliefs. In particular, they have different beliefs about what actions will have what effects and about what the consequences of different social arrangements will be. For example, people disagree about whether children who are allowed to make their own decisions from an early age will grow up to have happy and successful lives. And they disagree about whether arranged marriages are likely to be happy ones. But they all use these different beliefs to deduce the same thing: what patterns of action will lead to more pleasure and less pain in people's lives.

So underneath the variation in moral beliefs there is a constancy: people agree that pain is bad and pleasure is good. Therefore – according to the argument from moral minimalism – utilitarianism provides a minimal core to many different moral views.

The second of these arguments to support utilitarianism is the *argument from altruism*. It runs like this. Morality consists in treating other people with the same consideration as you treat yourself. (To "love thy neighbor as thyself.")

Some things are in your interest and some are in the interests of other people, but what morality demands is that we ignore that distinction between one person and another and let each person's interest be a reason for each other person's actions.

As a result, if one is to act morally one must take another person's pleasures and pains as seriously as one's own. So – according to this argument – one must aim at maximizing the general happiness, not just one's own. But to have this aim is to adopt utilitarianism.

A more sophisticated defense of utilitarianism was given by John Stuart Mill. In chapter 3 of *Utilitarianism*, Mill begins with an assumption which many, including moral relativists, could accept:

> the . . . sanction of duty, whatever our standard of duty may be, is one and the same
> – a feeling in our own mind; a pain, more or less intense, attendant on violation of duty.
> . . . This feeling . . . is the essence of Conscience.

He then observes that utilitarians can attach their consciences to the duty of increasing pleasure and decreasing pain, just as people who have other ethical beliefs can attach their consciences to other duties. So utilitarianism is a *possible* morality, even if it is not the only possible one. He goes on to argue that as society develops, people come more and more to identify with the good of the whole society, so that they will not count their own interests as specially important in comparison with those of others. So, he thinks, as society develops, the utilitarian conscience will come more and more to represent not just a possible morality but the morality which social harmony requires.

In the next chapter of *Utilitarianism*, the fourth, Mill seems to argue for something stronger, that we can "prove" that our duty is to create the maximum amount of pleasure. He writes that:

> The only proof capable of being given that an object is visible, is that people actually
> see it. The only proof that a sound is audible, is that people hear it. . . . The sole evid-
> ence that it is possible to produce that anything is desirable, is that people do actually
> desire it. . . . No reason can be given why the general happiness is desirable, except that
> each person, so far as he believes it to be attainable, desires his own happiness. This,
> however, being a fact, we have not only all the proof which the case admits of, but all
> which it is possible to require, that happiness is a good: that each person's happiness
> is a good to that person, and the general happiness, therefore, a good to the aggregate
> of all persons. (Utilitarianism, chapter 4)

This looks at first like an argument why everyone must value the general happiness, running along the following lines:

People desire happiness.
Therefore happiness is desirable.
Therefore happiness is good.
Therefore the general happiness is a social good.

But if this is the argument it is a very bad one. "Happiness is desirable" must mean simply "happiness can be desired," if it follows from "people desire happiness." But then it does not show that happiness is good, since people can desire many bad things. And even if we allow that happiness is good, it does not follow that the general happiness is a social good, since something could be good for individual people but bad for the society they were members of. (See the discussion of Bentham at the beginning of the previous section.)

In fact, Mill goes on to explain that he means something different, and less crude. What he really means is that people are psychologically constituted so as to think of happiness as something to aim for. When we analyze the ideals and values that different people subscribe to we find that the reason people hold them always comes down to the appeal to humans of human happiness. So the utilitarian ideal of maximizing the general happiness is the right sort of thing to function as a moral aim in human life. In skeleton form this argument runs:

> **People's moral ideals always involve the happiness of individuals. Therefore moral ideals always make the happiness of individuals a central aim of society.**
> **Utilitarianism makes individual happiness a social aim. Therefore utilitarianism is a possible moral ideal.**

This is a better argument. But its conclusion is a lot weaker. And its premises could be challenged. Someone could doubt that moral ideals are always based on the happiness of individuals (rather than, say, the stability of families and societies). And someone could doubt that utilitarianism does take individual happiness as its aim. After all, according to utilitarianism we should sometimes sacrifice the happiness of the individual for the happiness of a greater number of others.

7.9 Objecting to the Arguments

We have seen four arguments for utilitarianism.

(1) The *argument from moral minimalism* One explanation of the variation in morals is that people in different times and places have different beliefs. In particular, they have different beliefs about what actions will have what effects and about what the consequences of different social arrangements will be. But they all use these different beliefs to deduce the same thing: what patterns of action will lead to more pleasure and less pain in people's lives. So underneath the variation in moral beliefs there is a constancy: people agree that pain is bad and pleasure is good. Therefore utilitarianism provides a minimal core to many different moral views.

(2) *The argument from altruism* Some things are in your interest and some are in the interests of other people, but what morality demands is that we ignore that distinction between one person and another and let each person's interest be a reason for each other person's actions. As a result, if one is to act morally one must take another person's pleasures and pains as seriously as one's own. So one must aim at maximizing the general happiness, not just one's own. But to have this aim is to adopt utilitarianism.

(3) *Mill's apparent argument*

People desire happiness.
Therefore happiness is desirable.
Therefore happiness is good.
Therefore the general happiness is a social good.

(4) *Mill's actual argument*

People's moral ideals always involve the happiness of individuals.
Therefore moral ideals always make the happiness of individuals
a central aim of society.
Utilitarianism makes individual happiness a social aim.
Therefore utilitarianism is a possible moral ideal.

Below are six points someone might make in objection to one or another of these four arguments.

(i) Some value systems are based on an ideal of doing one's duty even when no one is benefited by doing it.
(ii) People desire addictive drugs, but addictive drugs are not desirable.
(iii) Not all ideals involving happiness are moral ideals.
(iv) Some cultures believe that suffering is noble.
(v) There are other ways of respecting another person's situation, besides including their pleasure or pain in a common total.
(vi) Even if each person's happiness is a good thing, the good of society may not be the same as the total happiness of everyone in the society.

Which points are objections to which arguments? (Do not worry whether the claim made in each point is true. For each one, the aim is to see which argument or arguments it would block, if it were true.)

 Which points are objections to a *premise* of an argument, and which to the *reasoning* that leads to a conclusion?

7.10 Two Controversial Recommendations

The deathbed promise Your wealthy aunt Croesa is dying. You visit her and she whispers in your ear that she will give you the contents of her jewel box. You know it contains diamonds and rubies worth tens of thousands. She will give you this if you promise that you will sell the gems and give the money to her nephew George. George is a notorious drunkard and wastrel who will lose the money within days, on alcohol, horses, and general loose living. (George is so notorious that Croesa does not want to mention him in her will. It might be used as evidence that she was not of sound mind.) Two possible actions occur to you:

(i) You could make the promise, and then keep it.
(ii) You could make the promise and then sell the gems and give the money to famine relief, or cancer research, or a home for abused children.

The dangerous baby You are a medical professional working in an intensive care ward for children. Two babies come simultaneously to the ward. Baby A is in acute need: it is very likely that if he is not admitted into intensive care he will die. You know, however, that baby A has a rare genetic trait that makes it very likely that if he survives he will grow up to be an aggressive psychopath. Most people with his condition become violent rapists or serial killers. Baby B, on the other hand, while in serious need of medical attention, is in somewhat less desperate a condition. And you know nothing about baby B to make you apprehensive about the adult he may grow into. There is only one place in the intensive care ward: to introduce more than one baby would be to take some other baby off life-sustaining equipment. Do you:

(i) Allow baby A into intensive care.
(ii) Allow baby B into intensive care.

Both of these are very unrealistic situations with implausibly limited choices of action. But take them seriously enough to ask yourself which of the two actions you would choose in each case.

Which action will utilitarianism recommend in each case? (Suppose that it is applied in a very straightforward way. Do not consider very long-term consequences of the decisions.) In each case utilitarianism, applied mechanically, recommends an action that many people think wrong. Do you see why? What moral factors does it ignore? Might it be right to ignore them?

7.11 The Appeal of Utilitarianism

Utilitarianism has three basic features that make it an attractive position to many people: simplicity, naturalness, and balance. They are also the features that make many others reject it. To state these features is not to defend or attack the theory. But it does help to explain why philosophers would try to find arguments to defend or attack it, and why they might try to include some of these features in other moral theories.

> Utilitarianism has the qualities of simplicity, naturalism, and balance. Utilitarianism endorses no general rules, but is troubled by no conflicts of value.

Simplicity

Utilitarianism is a simple moral theory. It is easy to state in quite untechnical language. But it is simple in a more important way, too. The variety of moral ideas it appeals to is very limited. It really appeals to only one moral idea: the value of a consequence of an action (which naive utilitarianism measures in terms of pleasure and pain). In contrast to this, in unphilosophical moral discussions we talk about "rights" and "obligations" and "duties" and "fault." We make complicated judgments about people's moral characters (they are brave or cowardly, trustworthy or untrustworthy, sensitive or callous, and so on). And we relate these judgments to conclusions about what we should do next.

This may seem like evidence that utilitarianism is too simple-minded to be right. Perhaps it is. But it also gives it a capacity to cut through the jungle of competing moral claims on a tangled issue. Consider, for example, some dispute that has a long and complicated history (Palestine or Northern Ireland, say). Partisans of one side will allude to long lists of past misdeeds, past promises, inherent rights of groups of people, and the like. Partisans of the other side will produce an equally long and complicated list. The utilitarian technique to cut through all this is to look just at the future and ask: what are the attainable options, and for each of them how many people will gain, and how many suffer, and how much? These may not be easy questions to answer, but they are clean and simple and clear.

Naturalism

Pleasure and pain are very real. No one could doubt their existence, or be puzzled about where in the world to find them. For they are central elements of human experience. Contrast this with human rights, divine commands, or ultimate ends of human life. These may all be real too. But they are all moral concepts, and they do not have an obvious place in nature. We would have to think very carefully about what they are and how they relate to our lives.

Again, one may take this as evidence for shallowness rather than truth. But it does provide a utilitarian with an answer to worries of the form "What in the real world is morality about?" The answer is that it is about human suffering and how to avoid it.

Balance

According to utilitarianism, the value of an action depends on its consequences. So one should choose an action depending on what you expect its consequences to be. The consequences of an action can depend on very fine details of the circumstances in which it is performed. Suppose you tell an innocent lie to a friend to avoid having lunch with her. That may have good consequences if it allows you to finish an essay on time. But it will have bad consequences if it adds to her feeling of social rejection just enough to push her into a serious depression. So we cannot say that telling lies for social convenience is always right or always wrong: in any particular case the good and bad consequences have to be balanced off against one another.

There are thus very few general rules that a utilitarian will endorse. All rules like "do not kill" or "do not tell lies" or "keep promises" are "rules of thumb," generalizations that may hold most of the time but are only a time-saving substitute for thinking an issue out thoroughly. Inasmuch as this seems to sanction promise-breaking or the occasional killing, this may seem a repulsive feature. But it can also seem to be facing up to reality, given that very few of us would think that it is right to keep promises or tell the truth always.

One important aspect of balancing is *conflict of values*. Suppose that you subscribe to an ethics of moral absolutes. To be specific, take them to be given by the Jewish and Christian Ten Commandments. Then you should always honor your mother and father, and you should never kill. But suppose your mother and father plead with you to kill someone. What do you do then? You have to decide which commandment has priority. (The prohibition on killing obviously has priority, you might say. But many cultures have considered family honor more important than avoiding murder.) Any really comprehensive system of morality will have to have some way of resolving conflicts between values. (A traditional morality usually has implicit ways, which people learn without really being aware of them.) Utilitarianism has only one value – moving the overall pleasure/pain balance in the pleasure direction – so basic conflicts will not arise within it.

HARDER | ## 7.12 Utilitarianism and Risk

Risk and decision-making   Given that the world is such an uncertain place, most of our decisions involve choices between unknowns. We usually have far from perfect knowledge of the consequences that the actions we are considering could have. This makes all decisions harder, not just those involving some moral considerations. This section describes one technique for making decisions when you know only how probable various consequences of your actions are. The interesting thing that emerges is that something a bit like utilitarianism emerges. For the technique can be described as: go for the greatest good in the greatest number of equal possibilities.

To begin, consider a feature you surely would like your decisions to have. You would surely like them to *avoid foolish risks*. Consider, for example, how you might think out this problem. An ordinary, fair, six-sided die is about to be thrown. You have to write either the letter A or the letter B on a card. You will then get a pay-off depending on what letter you have chosen and what number is uppermost when the die has been rolled. The pay-offs are as follows:

	A	B
1	$24	$6
2, 3, 4, 5, 6	$0	$6

(You can see that this could represent many real situations. Perhaps there is a 1/6 (one in six) chance of fair weather, and a 5/6 chance of rain; A represents the consequences if you go to the beach, and B if you stay at home.)

Choosing A is the risky strategy here. It represents a gamble between a small possibility of a good result and a larger possibility of a bad result. B on the other hand represents a certainty of a middling result.

Is the gamble worth it? You could reason as follows. There are six equal possibilities, depending on which number comes up on the die. If you choose A then in one out of the six possibilities you get $24 and in the remaining five you get nothing. So on average you can expect to get $24 divided by 6 – $4. On the other hand, if you choose B you will get $6 whatever happens. So the gamble is not worth it.

A decision-making method should also *identify worthwhile gambles*. Modify the same situation slightly. Raise the jackpot for the gamble and increase the probability of getting it, but leave everything else unchanged. So the pay-offs might be:

	A	B
1,2	$42	$6
3, 4, 5, 6	$0	$6

(The sun is a little more likely to shine, and you like a good time on the beach a bit more.)

Thinking through this changed situation in the same way we see that if you choose A then in two out of the six possibilities you get $42 and in the remaining four you get $0. So you can expect to gain on average $14 if you choose A. But if you choose B you can expect to gain $6. So (thinking just in money terms, and if taking the risk isn't in itself a factor) you should see this as a worthwhile gamble.

The reasoning in these two examples followed a very simple rule. To make it perfectly explicit, it can be broken down into five stages:

(1) List your options (the acts you are choosing between).
(2) List the factors which might affect how desirable the consequences of choosing any of your options are.
(3) Think out the probability of each of these factors occurring, if you have chosen an option. That is, think of the future as divided into a number of equally probable outcomes, and think in how many of these futures each of these factors is found.
(4) Think out how desirable the consequences of each option would be, if each of these factors was present.
(5) Choose the option which gives the best average result, in all the possible futures.

It is here that the resemblance to utilitarianism emerges. Choosing the option which is best on average can be described as going for the greatest good in the greatest number of equal possible futures. (It takes the average over your possible futures in much the same way utilitarianism treats the average over actual people.)

These things combine when the decision involves a number of people and a number of possible futures. Then the utilitarian rule for solving a moral problem breaks down into essentially the same five steps, with a few extra complications:

(1) List your options (the acts you are choosing between).
(2) List the factors which might affect how desirable the consequences of choosing any of your options are *for each of the people involved.*
(3) Think out the probability of each of these factors occurring, if you have chosen an option. That is, think of the future as divided into a number of equally probable outcomes, and think in how many of these futures each of these factors is found.
(4) Think out how desirable the consequences of each option would be, *for each person,* if each of these factors was present.
(5) Choose the option which gives the best average result, *for all the people* in all the possible futures.

To see how a utilitarian decision could be made following these five steps, go back to an example in Section 1 of this chapter. Imagine that you are an administrator deciding where to build a hospital. It could be built in either of two districts. In district A 6000 people will be served by it, who at present have no accessible hospital. In district B 12,000 people will be served, who also have no hospital at present. In either district, if the hospital is built then in a ten-year period out of each 1000 people 10 people will live who would otherwise have died. Suppose that district A is near a busy airport and there is a 1 in 1,000,000 chance of a major disaster at the airport in the next ten years, in which a hospital would save the lives of 100 people. Which district should get the hospital?

(1) The options are: build the hospital in district A or build it in district B.
(2) There are 18,000 people involved. The factors which affect them, besides whether the hospital is built, are whether there is an airport disaster. But this affects only the people in district A.
(3) The probability of an airport disaster is 0.000001. Thus in 999,999 possible futures the disaster does not happen, and in 1 it does.
(4) (a) Consider first the 6000 people in district A. If the hospital is built in A and there is no airport disaster then 60 will live who would otherwise die. If the hospital is built in A and there is an airport disaster then 160 will live who would otherwise die. If the hospital is built in B then 0 in district A will live who would otherwise die.
    (b) Consider next the 12,000 people who live in district B. Whether or not there is an airport disaster (in A), if the hospital is built in A then 0 in district B will live who would otherwise die, and if the hospital is built in B then 120 will live who would otherwise die.
(5) If the hospital is built in district A then there is a 0.999999 chance that 60 lives will be saved, and there is a 0.000001 chance that 160 lives will be saved. So the average number of lives saved is $(0.999999 \times 60) + (0.000001 \times 160) = 60.0001$. If the hospital is built in district B then 120 will live who would otherwise die.

Therefore more lives are saved, on average, if the hospital is built in B.

This example is much simpler than most real-life public policy problems. For one thing, everything was thought out in terms of a ten-year timescale. And for another thing, the only factor taken into account was the number of lives saved, which we can assume will very roughly correlate with suffering avoided. But it is enough to show how utilitarian thinking applies to problems of public policy. And it illustrates one frequent consequence of this thinking: it takes the emphasis away from dramatic but unlikely possibilities and shifts it to the accumulation of undramatic everyday facts.

HARDER

Box 14 Marginal Utility

After philosophers such as Mill had developed the idea of utility it was taken over by economists, who still use it. One important development, due in part to the "Austrian school" of economists in the late nineteenth and early twentieth centuries, was the idea of marginal utility.

Suppose you are giving money to people. Different people will get different benefits from being given, say, $100. A homeless person on the street may benefit by having decent meals for a week. A student may be able to buy a textbook that would otherwise have been too expensive. A multimillionaire may be quite indifferent to so small a sum. This suggests that the amount of benefit to someone from being given an amount of money may depend on what they already have. (This will hold whether we think of benefit as pleasure, or in other terms.) The more money you have the less benefit you will get from a small increase in your wealth.

So if we graph utility (that is, pleasure or other benefit) against wealth, we will typically get a curve of the general shape shown in Figure 7.1.

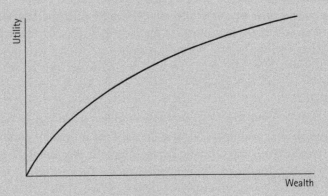

Figure 7.1

The idea that as wealth increases the utility of each additional small increase diminishes is known as the *diminishing marginal utility of money.*

Many goods besides money can be argued to have a diminishing marginal utility. One consequence of these ideas is rather striking. Suppose we are distributing money to people who have different levels of wealth. We clearly will not produce the most overall utility if we give the money to the richest, as their utility increases very little with each additional dollar. So we might give it to the poor. But if we give so much to any poor person that they become rich, then obviously we begin to run into the same problem. The greatest amount of utility is produced if we distribute the money so that, after the distribution, people's wealth is as near to equal as possible.

This is obviously too simple and general an argument to be applied mechanically to real social situations. But it does provide an interesting utilitarian argument for equality.

Conclusions of This Chapter

◆ *Utilitarianism is based on the idea that what is valuable is the happiness of individual people. But it is not the same as hedonism because it insists that each person must take into account the happiness of all other people.*

◆ *Three advantages of utilitarianism as a way of making moral decisions are (a) that it uses only simple concepts like the effects of an action and the happiness or unhappiness of people affected, (b) that it considers things such as pleasure and pain which are undeniably real, and (c) that it has a way of balancing the good and the bad effects of any action.*

◆ *Two disadvantages of utilitarianism are (a) that it can justify any action, even murder or rape, under suitable circumstances, and (b) that it requires that we know all the consequences of every action.*

◆ *If we apply utilitarianism to many real life moral problems we need to take account of the fact that the consequences of actions are often uncertain. The natural way to solve this problem is to consider all possible consequences of an action, giving more weight to the more probable ones.*

Further Reading

Mill and Bentham

Selection from Mill's *Utilitarianism* in Part VII of John Cottingham (ed.), *Western Philosophy: An Anthology*. Blackwell, 1996.

John Stuart Mill, *Utilitarianism*, in *Essential Works of John Stuart Mill*, edited by Max Lerner. Bantam Books, 1961.

Chapters 1 and 2 (chapters 3 and 4 are also relevant) of Jeremy Bentham, *The Principles of Morals and Legislation*. Hafner, 1948.

Alan Ryan, *The Philosophy of John Stuart Mill*, second edition. Macmillan, 1987.

Utilitarianism

Chapters 1 and 8 of Peter Singer, *Practical Ethics*, second edition. Cambridge University Press, 1993.

J. J. C. Smart and Bernard Williams, *Utilitarianism For and Against*. Cambridge University Press, 1973.

Chapter 13 of Gilbert Harman, *The Nature of Morality*. Oxford University Press, 1977.

Chapter 6 of J. L. Mackie, *Ethics: Inventing Right and Wrong*. Penguin, 1977.

Electronic resources

Routledge Encyclopedia of Philosophy (available online at many universities): articles on Bentham, Jeremy; Mill, John Stuart; Utilitarianism.

Stanford Encyclopedia of Philosophy (http://plato.stanford.edu/): Bentham, Jeremy; Consequentialism; *Egoism*; *Mill, John Stuart* (italicized items are available as this book goes to press; the others should be available soon).

8 Kantian Ethics

Introduction

Utilitarianism determines the right action in a situation in terms of its consequences. We can use our uncertain information about what might happen if an action were to be performed to decide what we should do. In some cases this means performing actions that run contrary to traditional morality.

Moral beliefs that are nearer to traditional morality can be got from Kantian ethics, which gives a way of finding moral rules that we can follow whatever the consequences of following them. Kantian ethics emphasizes the motive behind an action, which is ignored by utilitarianism.

Outside ethics an influential way of responding to changing evidence is described by empiricism. Empiricism tries to provide beliefs that are based in a reasonable way on evidence, while keeping the risk of error at a minimum....

Chapter Objectives

By the end of this chapter you should be able to answer the following questions.

◆ *How is a morality that looks at motives different from one that looks at consequences?*
◆ *What is Kant's "categorical imperative"?*
◆ *How can you defend the idea that there are things no one should ever do?*
◆ *How do both consequentialist and deontological moralities sometimes ask more from us than conventional morality does?*

Definitions

The following words used in this chapter are defined in the list of definitions at the end of the book:

categorical imperative   *consequentialism*   *deontology*

8.1 Means and Ends

Is it sometimes right to lie? It might be if telling the truth might lead to someone getting killed. Is it sometimes right to kill someone? It might be if the alternative was that even more people got killed. To think this way is to judge actions in terms of their *consequences*. Utilitarianism focuses on the consequences of actions, and this leads to both its attractive and its worrying features. It provides a clear and simple attitude to morality at the price of ignoring many aspects of it which are central to most people. It ignores such things as motives and principles. These are not ignored by a rival tradition in moral philosophy, which comes from philosophers who are influenced by the German philosopher Immanuel Kant (1724–1804). Kant's ethics emphasizes the importance of motives, of acting on principle and of adhering to general rules of conduct. To bring out your sympathies for Kantian ethics consider two examples.

> Kant's ethics emphasizes motives, general rules, and not treating people as means. The effect of these is very different from thinking in terms of consequences.

(a) Fire in a movie theater. You are a teacher taking a group of schoolchildren to a film. You and the children are sitting in an upstairs balcony in the theater, an old one converted decades ago from a stage theater. In the middle of the show someone cries "fire" and there is a strong smell of smoke. The audience begins to panic and rush for the exits. You fear that the children will be trampled by the crowd so you herd them in an orderly way toward the nearest door, as flames begin to lick up the walls toward the ceiling. When you get to the door you discover that it is a large plate glass door which cannot be unlocked from the inside. In front of it there is a man who has stopped, frozen in panic. Every second counts and so you seize him by the shoulders and smash him against the glass. The glass cracks and you push him through it, leaving a hole big enough for the children to step over his bleeding and unconscious body. You get them all out just before the ceiling of the theater falls down, killing the man and everyone else left inside.

Suppose that you know that what you do to the man will probably cause his death. Are you justified in doing it, in killing him, to save the lives of the children?

(b) The Mission. In the film *The Mission* a priest is protecting a group of Amazonian Indians against the attempts of Spanish settlers to enslave them. He sets up a safe haven for them in the jungle. However, a messenger arrives who reports a complex deal that has been struck between the church and the Spanish and Portuguese governments. The deal requires that the church relinquish its rights in this area. If the deal is not adhered to, wars will break out elsewhere in the world and many people will suffer and die. Many more will suffer than if the mission is abandoned. The priest refuses to abandon the

mission. But he no longer has the protection of the church, and military force is used to subdue the Indians. Cannons fire at children.

Can the decision to abandon innocent people to military aggression be justified by a calculation that on balance, all over the world, fewer people will suffer if you do?

Most people will have many conflicting reactions to both these cases. But one of them is likely to be something like: *there are things that you just cannot do to people.* This reaction conflicts sharply with the whole spirit of utilitarianism. Utilitarianism says that you must evaluate each action by its consequences, but the reaction says that there are some actions that no possible consequences could justify. Some means cannot be justified by any ends.

It is natural enough to have these reactions to such cases. But can we make a systematic theory around them? One that captures a range of our standard moral beliefs and helps us think through moral dilemmas. The most famous attempt to make such a theory is Kant's.

Kant's ethics focuses on motives, rules, and the way we treat people. To see how these are related, consider the two examples again. In the example of a fire in a movie theater your motive is first to get the children out safely. You are acting in your role as teacher, which means following the rule "put the safety of the children first." When the man blocks the door, you consider the action of smashing him through the glass and probably causing his death. But then you may be shifting to another motive. Suppose you choose the action. You are then doing something that means trying to harm the man, violating the rule that you should never deliberately kill someone.

Suppose that you do smash the man through the glass, and that he dies. You might defend yourself by saying "but my aim was not to kill him; I was trying to save the children." If you say this you are thinking of the man as a means to the aim or end of saving the children. But this, according to Kant,

Box 15 Immanuel Kant: The Quiet Revolutionary

Kant never left his home town of Königsberg in Prussia (then German, now part of Russia). He lived quietly there, teaching at the university for most of his life, while around him the French and American revolutions occurred and people throughout Europe began to think and act in a more modern way. In fact, his writings mark an important change to modern ways of thinking. His most famous book, the *Critique of Pure Reason*, argues that our knowledge always has to assume a background of beliefs which are imposed by us and cannot be justified. In ethics, in *The Critique of Practical Reason* and *Foundations of the Metaphysics of Morals*, he argued for a system of moral absolutes that can be known in terms of reason. Faith or authority are not needed. His political writings anticipated problems of world peace, and recommended a global institution like the United Nations.

is a moral mistake: in fact, one of the really basic mistakes in moral thinking. To act morally, according to Kantian ethics, is to act according to motives that never think of people as means, but always as ends. You should never think of people as if they were just tools to be manipulated to achieve some end, even when that end is a very desirable, or even a morally good, one.

8.2 Motive, Rule, and Means

(A) Below are three examples of an action performed in a given context. In each case say: (a) what the person's motives were, (b) what general rules he or she was following, and (c) what consequences were means to what ends for that person.

For example, in the case of *The Mission* above, if the priest abandons the mission in order to help prevent wars elsewhere in the world then one possible set of answers would be:

(a) *motives*: to reduce the suffering of people throughout the world;
(b) *general rules*: act so as to lessen the number of people who die;
(c) *means/ends*: the fate of the Indians – allowing them to be enslaved by the colonists – is treated as a means to preventing war.

And if the priest refuses to abandon the mission then a possible set of answers would be:

(a) *motives*: to preserve the well-being of these particular people;
(b) *general rules*: act so as to fulfill your responsibilities to those who rely on you;
(c) *means/ends*: resisting the Spanish troops is a means to freeing the Indians.

Now here are the three examples:

(1) A woman is about to get married. She plans a big wedding, in June. She has an aunt who is a menace at such occasions. The aunt drinks too much and then sings bawdy songs and tells scandalous stories about members of the family. (Worse yet, the stories tend to be true.) The woman devises a plan. She phones her aunt and tells her that the wedding must be postponed for a month because the best man cannot manage the original date. So the aunt takes her usual June holiday. When the aunt gets back from her holiday she finds a letter telling her very apologetically that the best man changed his plans yet again so they went back to the original date.
(2) You are negotiating with terrorists for the return of hostages. You believe that if you pay (in money or weapons or whatever) for their return the

result will be more hostage-taking in the future. Fewer lives may be lost in the long run if you refuse to play along, whatever they threaten to do to the people they have captured. On the other hand, if you refuse to do anything these actual people may die, and will certainly suffer terribly. You decide not to pay anything to the terrorists.

(3) A doctor is directing a research project into the effect of a new drug on cancer of the spleen. One experiment involves a group of patients in whom the cancer is very advanced and is not responding to other treatments. Half of these patients are treated with the drug and half of them with a harmless placebo which will have no physical effect. Neither the patients nor those dealing with them know who is being treated with the drug and who is receiving only the placebo. The trial is supposed to last for a year, but after six months the computer analysis shows that far fewer patients are dying among those being given the drug than among those being given the placebo. If the patients receiving the placebo are given the drug then the experiment will not have the same scientific weight: it will not show so convincingly the effect of the drug. And, after all, the difference between the two groups may be a random fluke. On the other hand, the data after six months makes a good case for believing that the drug is very effective and that if the patients on the placebo are switched to the drug fewer of them will die. The doctor continues with the experiment without changing the patients' medications.

(B) Compare your lists of motives, rules, and means/ends with those of others. If they are different, is it because one of you has missed something important about the situation? Or is it because there are two equally good ways of describing the rules that apply? It is an important problem with Kantian ethics that most actions fit with several rules.

(C) In each of the three cases above the person's action can be criticized morally. (It can also be defended, but it is the criticism that is important now.) In each case it can be argued that something is wrong with the person's motive, the general rule that describes their action, or their choice of means to an end. For each of (1), (2), (3) say what is questionable about the motive, the rule, or the choice of means.

8.3 Kant's Argument

Applying the ideas of motive, rule, and means/end to examples like those we have been considering, we can see how much is left out if we only consider the consequences of actions. There are all the factors that lead up to an action as well as all the effects that follow on from it. But this does not give us an alternative moral theory. It does not tell us what motives, what rules, and what relation between means and ends are morally good. Kant's moral theory is designed to tell us these things.

Kant begins from the conviction that we should focus on motives rather than consequences. Or, as he puts it, it is the will that is good or bad, and nothing can have moral value in the absence of a good will. Good intentions are necessary for right action. And the fundamental good intention is to do what is right. This may seem to take us round in a circle. But, says Kant, we can already see from this the irrelevance of the consequences of an action. For to evaluate an action by what follows from it is to ignore the reason why it was performed.

The first step was to say that a right action is one that comes just from the desire to do good. But the desire to do good is not just the desire to be nice, or to have others approve of you. For Kant it is the desire *to be moral*. Right action is action that is shaped by the idea of morality. So Kant shifts his emphasis. Right action is important, but it is in a way misleading to think in terms of it. We understand morality better if we understand what it is to want to be moral. Kant assumes that to want to be moral is to want your actions to fit into general moral rules. For what is right for one person must be right for anyone else in the same circumstances. (Remember the discussion in Sections 1 and 2 of Chapter 4, of how morality is general and impartial.) So, he argues, to want to do right is to want to conform to a moral law. And laws are general rules about how people should act. So to act rightly is to act in a way that could be a general law for human action.

Suppose, for example, that you are in a difficult social situation and the easiest way out is to tell a lie. (It may have good consequences for other people besides yourself.) Kant would have us look beyond the immediate action and ask, what is the motive? Could the motive be taken as a general moral rule? Your motive for lying would be to get out of embarrassment. This would not be a morally acceptable motive unless it could be reconciled with some general and impartial rule. One rule might be: "Always tell lies when it gets you out of trouble." That would obviously not be a rule that could regulate the way everyone treats everyone else.

At this point we have got to one of Kant's most basic ideas, which he called the *categorical imperative*. It says: *Act only from motives which you could want to be general principles regulating everyone's actions.* Many motives, such as lying or killing, could not be turned into general principles of action, Kant argues, because the "laws" in question ("always lie," "always kill") would be ones that just could not function as rules governing everyone's behavior. (Sometimes, as in the case of lying, they would undercut their own existence: if everyone lied there would be no point in speaking, and thus no lying.)

Kant then shifts emphasis again. He has been arguing that all that is morally valuable in an action is the motive that lies behind it. So what is valuable about people is that they

> The categorical imperative says: Act from motives that could govern everyone's actions, or treat people as ends and not as means.

can act for motives, and are capable of doing good. People are free agents who make their own decisions of their own free will, and it is for this potentially good will rather than anything else that a person should be valued. So to treat a person as anything but a bearer of a unique individual value – his or her own potentially good will – is wrong. Thus the second formulation of the categorical imperative: *Treat others always as ends, never as means.*

Consider again the case of social lying. Think of the person you are planning to lie to. Their reaction to the truth is a possible source of embarrassment to you, so you are thinking of keeping the truth from them. But to do this would be to treat the person just as a source of embarrassment, and not as a free agent whose desire to know the truth is as valuable as your own. Or, to put it a bit differently, you are not operating by rules that that other person might also approve of.

Kant's ethics has, as we can see, two basic moral principles. The first is to act in accordance with general rules that you could want everyone to abide by. The second is to treat people as ends rather than as means. Kant thinks that these two principles are really different ways of saying the same thing. But many later philosophers, including some who have generally agreed with Kant, have disagreed on this point. In fact, it is not easy to see quite how to relate the two principles, partly because Kant is never as clear as he could be about what it is to treat someone as an end. But here is one fairly simple connection between them. One way of thinking about what it is to treat someone as an end is to say: *they* have a say in what rules should apply to

Box 16 Kant and Christianity

Many features of Kant's ethics have obvious relations to Christianity. For example, the idea that to want to act morally is to want to act as if in obedience to a set of general laws would naturally arise if one thought of morals as being commanded by God. And the first formulation of the categorical imperative resembles the Christian golden rule: do unto others as you would have them do unto you. (But it isn't the same.)

Moreover, the emphasis on treating people as ends and not as means fits well with the Christian conception of each individual as having an individual soul which is of inestimable worth.

One central feature of Kant's ethics may worry some Christians, however. Since he avoids paying any attention to the consequences of actions, he sees the desire for salvation, or the fear of hellfire, as morally unworthy emotions. If I help my neighbor not because I want to act morally but because I want to please God, and want God's reward, then according to Kant I am not acting rightly.

your interactions, they are not just tools with no input into how they are treated. So if you treat someone as an end you will abide by general rules that they would accept as regulating both your and their conduct. So if this is what we mean by treating people as ends rather than as means, then treating people as ends commits us to following general rules.

8.4 Evaluating Kant's Argument

Kant's main ethical argument, as found in his book *Foundations of the Metaphysics of Morals*, can be put very briefly as follows. (This summary cannot do justice to his rich and complicated – and confusing – way of arguing. It surely leaves out some important features.)

(1) Only motive matters in the rightness of an action.
(2) Therefore: The only good desire is the desire to act morally.
(3) Moreover, the desire to act morally is the desire to act in accordance with a moral law.
(4) Therefore: To act morally is to act in accordance with a general law-like principle that one could want to govern everyone's actions.

Below are four points that could be made in criticism of this argument.

(i) Someone can do a morally admirable action for self-centered ends. For example, someone could have a passionate obsession with another person. That other person is trapped in a burning building and the obsessive lover rushes in and saves the other. That was not an act done out of the desire to do good, but it was heroic, and thus morally admirable.

(ii) Moral actions could be thought of as acts coming from kindness or compassion, and there might not be any general law or principle governing them. In fact, in some cases compassion might require a violation of what in general would be a moral principle. So, for example, if someone had a fatal disease but could not bear to know it, compassion might require lying to them.

(iii) Two people might make a contract to govern their relationship. For example, spouses might say to each other: "You may cause me any amount of harm, even death, if it is necessary to prevent harm coming to our children." Then their actions would be governed by a moral principle that they might not want to govern all human relations.

(iv) Someone can act from the best of motives but make such a mess of things that the result is disaster for all concerned. Well-meaning bunglers are not evil,' but often what they do is morally wrong. Stupidity is a vice just as cruelty is.

One of these points can be taken as an objection to premise (1), one as an objection to premise (3), one as an objection to the inference from (1) to (2), and one as an objection to the inference from (3) and (2) to (4). Which is which?

8.5 Consequentialism versus Deontology

In many moral disputes people disagree along utilitarian versus Kantian lines. In fact, on many difficult moral questions a single person can be pulled in two directions, one of which is utilitarian in spirit and the other Kantian. So most people find it very hard to believe that either utilitarianism or Kantian ethics gives what they would intuitively think of as the right answers to all moral problems. (Of course, our intuitive reactions are sometimes wrong. So it is possible that if we think hard enough and revise our values enough we can turn ourselves into fully consistent utilitarians or Kantians.)

The ways in which difficult moral questions pull us in different directions can be described in terms that are more general than the contrast between utilitarianism and Kantian ethics. For each of these positions is just one of a wide range of possible moral positions, and the contrast between the two *kinds* of moral positions is deep and important. The contrast is between *consequentialist* moral views and *deontological* ones.

◆ A consequentialist morality defines the rightness of an act in terms of its consequences: what will follow if the act is performed.
◆ A deontological morality defines the rightness of an act in terms of its relation to acts which are forbidden or obligatory: acts which people either must never do or must always do.

Utilitarianism is a consequentialist morality because it considers how much pleasure or pain there is in the consequences of an action. Kantian ethics is deontological because it defines a right act as one which fits a rule that everyone could always follow (or, closely related to this, because it says "*always* treat people as ends and not as means").

Utilitarianism may not be right. Nor may Kantian ethics. But neither of them is a ridiculous view. It is easy to think up ridiculous consequentialist or deontological moralities. For example, a ridiculous consequentialist morality might say that the right action is the one that causes the greatest number of marriages to happen. And a ridiculous deontological morality might say that the right action is the one that involves never disobeying a police officer

Yet there are many consequentialist and deontological moralities that are not at all ridiculous. For example, one might consider a morality that had as its basic rule: "Never break a promise." People living by this morality would be very careful and explicit about the promises they made to each other, which would probably govern a lot more of their lives than most of us make promises about, and then they would try never to break them. This would be a deontological morality. Or one might consider a morality that had as its basic rule: "Do whatever will give people the most freedom." People living by this morality would be very careful not to restrict one another's liberty; very often they would have to balance the opportunities and restrictions that one action would impose on people with those that another would impose. (If parents give teenagers a lot of money and freedom, the teenagers will have more freedom now but may not choose an education that would open up more freedom to them later.) This would be a consequentialist morality.

8.6 Diagnosing Disagreements

Below are three disagreements between people. In each case one person is taking a generally consequentialist line and the other a generally deontological line. Which is which, in each disagreement? (Watch out: in (c) there are three people.)

(a) **Martha:** I read a disturbing thing in the paper today. A drunk man was cursing at a police officer, and the officer shot him dead because he suddenly reached in his pocket. He didn't in fact have a gun, and even if he had there must have been other ways of disarming him. Surely that is murder.
Norbert: Well, you don't realize how dangerous some people can be. Suppose there had been children around. You wouldn't want a drunk shooting at a policeman and stray bullets hitting bystanders. You just don't want to take the chance.
Martha: You often have to take chances, if the alternative is killing an innocent person.
Norbert: I wonder how far you would push that. Suppose a crazed gunman was walking down the street, preparing to kill dozens of people. Wouldn't the police be justified in shooting him first?
Martha: Even then that's a last resort. Violence is not a good preventative for violence.
Norbert: Suppose someone had an atomic bomb, and was going to blow up New York, and shooting him was the only way to prevent this.

(b) **Ottavia:** I don't understand these grandchildren of ours. They talk back to their parents; they don't care for the family; they don't want to continue the family business. They want to be artists, scriptwriters, actors even. I never thought my daughter could have children like that.
Paolo: But that's what they want to do. It's different for them. They grew up in a different world. If they went into your business they'd feel frustrated.
Ottavia: And they're not going to feel frustrated, spending years trying to be creative and then often failing? Do you know how many unemployed artists there are? No one ought to live like that.

Paolo: Yes, they may be unhappy at times. And they may make their mother unhappy sometimes. But it's what they want. And it's what she wants for them. More people get what they really want that way.

Ottavia: Now you're sounding like one of them. What's going to happen to the business?

(c) **Quinn:** You realize that your uncle Lloyd has lung cancer, and hasn't long to live. Who do you think he'll leave his money to? There's certainly lots of it.

Roberta: A year ago he said he'd make me his heir, if only I promised to join that funny little church of his.

Quinn: Promise then! Go to a few meetings, and then when he's dead you can do what you want.

Sandra: That's awful. Roberta's known this man since she was a baby. He's her godfather, in fact, and you're proposing that she treat him like a sucker, just someone to exploit.

Roberta: Well, if you knew him as well as I do you might have fewer compunctions. But I agree I shouldn't do it. I'd have to tell my children, and then they'd start treating me the same way, telling lies and breaking promises.

Quinn: Be more imaginative. Tell your children you've seen the light and Lloyd's church is the only way. Then six months later lose your faith.

Roberta: That's not realistic. It wouldn't work. Once you start telling lies it spreads. So I'll stick to being honest: the results are better for everyone.

Sandra: I think you're both disgusting.

In (c), the third of the above dialogues, it is hard to classify Roberta's position. In some ways it is consequentialist and in some ways deontological. How does it tend toward each position?

8.7 When it Might Be Right to Lie and Break Promises

Taking your mother's advice

A child, Fernando, has a tendency to tell lies. His mother reprimands him for this. The occasion for the reprimand was an episode when a visitor came to the door to ask for Fernando's father. Wanting his father to play with him rather than talk to the visitor, Fernando told her that his father was not at home. Fernando's mother makes him promise always to tell the truth to people who come to their house.

The next day the doorbell rings and Fernando answers it. At the door is a wild-eyed man with a shotgun in his hand. He utters a string of wild violent-sounding threats, ending with "And is your [expletive deleted] father at home?"

Should Fernando tell the truth? Should he keep his promise not to mislead people who come to the house? You don't have to be a moral subversive to say: of course not.

(a) Is there anything else Fernando's mother could have made him promise *never* to do, which would have prevented most of his lies without running into the problems this story reveals?

(b) Is there some clever way in which Fernando could actually never tell a lie or break a promise, without having effects he would not want to have? Could he, for example, exploit the difference between what is false and what is misleading? Would this be of any relevance morally?

(c) Suppose that someone resolved never to tell any lies or break any promises, whatever the circumstances. Could they live a very restricted life so that they did not bring disaster on all around them? What would this life be like?

Casablanca

The film *Casablanca* is set in Morocco at the beginning of the Second World War. An anti-Nazi writer, Victor (played by Paul Henreid), and his wife Ilsa (Ingrid Bergman) arrive in Morocco as refugees. Victor needs to escape to America to continue the struggle, but he does not have the necessary documents. Ilsa meets a club owner, Rick (Humphrey Bogart), with whom she had been in love in the past. Toward the end of the film Rick persuades Ilsa to run away with him, leaving Victor behind. In fact, he is making it possible for Victor and Ilsa to leave together to continue their anti-Nazi work. She only realizes this at the last moment, and then he tells her that his feelings for her are an attachment to past and not present passion, which is also false. (And "I'm not much good at being noble, but it isn't hard to see that the troubles of three little people don't amount to a hill of beans in this crazy world.")

Rick has lied to Ilsa in order to be part of the struggle against something evil. And the motives are self-sacrificing ones. What stronger justification could be given?

A strong deontologist should not be completely silenced by this. There are replies that can be made. Here are three.

(a) If people are strong enough and reasonable enough they should be able to decide on the right action without having to lie. Rick should be able to persuade Ilsa that her duty lies with her husband and the struggle against the Nazis.

(b) In lying to Ilsa, Rick is treating her as someone who cannot see the right course of action without being manipulated. This is demeaning to her, and sexist. He should have found a more honest method.

(c) Rick is not really lying to Ilsa. She knows he still loves her, and she knows that she should really leave with Victor. So Rick is just allowing her to act on her own realization of the truth.

There is some force to each of these. Which one gives the strongest and which gives the weakest defence of "never lie," in the face of the *Casablanca* example?

8.8 Strong Deontology

HARDER

There are many deontological and consequentialist moralities. For example, there are consequentialists who evaluate the consequences of actions not in terms of pleasure and pain but in terms of whether people get what they want. The best outcome, then, is the one in which the larger number of people satisfy the greater number of their desires. (In dialogue (b) of Section 6 above, Paolo was expressing a view of this sort.) And there are positions on the borderline between consequentialism and deontological ethics. One such position is *rule utilitarianism*, which says that the right acts are the ones that are in accord with the right rules, and the right rules are the ones which if everyone followed them would have the best consequences. (You can then define "best consequences" in terms of pleasure, or the satisfaction of desires, or in some other way.) (In dialogue (c) of Section 6 Roberta was expressing a rule-utilitarian view.)

But while these positions can narrow the gap somewhat, a basic fact remains. Thinking in terms of the consequences of an act is very different from thinking in terms of the reasons for an act. A really strong deontological morality will insist that some kinds of action are forbidden whatever their consequences. For example, on such a view there might be no reason that could ever justify killing someone. (Or torturing them or raping them – different deontological moralities will have different lists of absolutely forbidden acts.)

> A moral theory can focus on many consequences besides pleasure and pain.

An absolute prohibition will not fit into a consequentialist way of thinking. For according to any consequentialist theory you should look at all the consequences of an act (or a rule) and weigh them up, and in some cases even the most awful action may be justified. To see the gap between this and an absolute prohibition consider two cases.

(a) *A lie to prevent lies.* You have applied for a job, and have been invited to an interview. The résumé you submitted with your application made a false claim about your qualifications. Now you learn that one of the people on the interviewing panel has the experience necessary to catch you out. You know that if you are confronted with your lie you will not simply admit to it, but will produce a complex and ingenious story to cover up what you have actually done. You don't want to see yourself telling such fantastic lies, so you consider telephoning to say – falsely – that you have accepted another job and will therefore not be coming to the interview.

(b) *Killing to prevent yourself killing.* A young German officer in the Second World War does not share Nazi ideology. He thinks that the persecution of the Jews is wrong. His superior officer is proposing to put him in charge of a concentration camp, and he knows that he does not have the moral courage to refuse. If he is given this job he will carry it out obediently and as a result will be implicated in the deaths of many innocent people. There is an alternative posting, to the western front. But to earn that he will have to prove his fanatical devotion to party ideas. To show this he arranges for his superior officer to be present when he shoots a prisoner-of-war who has refused to salute the Nazi banner. The commander is impressed and posts him to the front.

In each of these cases someone does or considers an action which would prevent that same person from doing more actions of the same kind. A lie that prevents lies, and a murder that prevents murders. (Your own lies and your own murders.) According to consequentialist theories such actions should be chosen, for the consequences of choosing them are better than the consequences of not choosing them. (Or, at any rate, according to consequentialist theories this is so if there are situations that are really like this. In stories like the two above it is possible to doubt whether doing the forbidden act really has the better consequences.) But would it be right to choose to do something really awful – murder, genocide, rape, torture – even to prevent oneself from doing more awful things later? Many people would think that the action in (a) is acceptable (though there must be many other ways out of the person's dilemma). To that extent they do not think that there is an absolute prohibition on telling lies. But murder, as in (b), is far more serious than lying. Can cold-blooded murder really be justified by its consequences?

If you say no, if you think that there are some acts which cannot be made right whatever they cause or prevent, then your morals are deontological. (You will not kill a baby to prevent the deaths of millions of people.) If you think that sometimes the best action may involve lying, breaking promises, even killing in sufficiently desperate circumstances, then your morals are probably consequentialist. It may seem easier to be a consequentialist. For then you can sometimes do things that a deontological morality would not allow. But it is not always this way.

Sometimes a consequentialist morality can ask you to do things that a deontological morality might not. Consider the following example.

Suppose you live and work in a rich country. You give your family a standard of living that is considered adequate but not luxurious in your country. But it would be beyond the dreams of many people living in poor countries. You are struck by media coverage of a famine far away. You want to give some of your savings and income to feed starving children. How much of your resources should you divert from your own family to starving non-relatives? You apply utilitarian theory to the problem and it says: give until you have reduced your family's income to the point where if you reduce it any more you will be worse off than the people you are helping. That way the total amount of pleasure will be increased and the total amount of pain will be minimized, even though your family will be a lot worse off than they would have been if you had been more complacent about your duties.

But to reduce your family's income this much would be to impose real hardship on them, by the standards of people in your country. You will probably be condemned for it. Contrast this with "conventional" morality, which simply says "Be charitable." You can be charitable without sacrificing yourself and your family anything like as much as utilitarianism demands. So in this case utilitarianism – a consequentialist theory – is very demanding. It requires a lot of moral commitment to follow it. The basic reason is that utilitarianism requires us to consider the consequences of our actions *for all people*.

HARDER

8.9 The Demands of Morality: the Case of Famine

Below are four arguments why an action should or should not be performed. Two of them assume a consequentialist point of view and two of them assume a deontological point of view. Which is which?

(1) Famine relief is often targeted at children, and news coverage of starving children often gets to people's consciences when nothing else will. But in fact in a situation of extreme famine, saving the children is often not the best thing to do. One reason is that badly malnourished children are likely to have suffered irreversible damage to their brains and other organs, so that they will never be healthy productive people. Another is that if the children survive but their parents die they will require long-term support, while if the parents are helped to survive until the next harvest, even if the children die, new children can be produced and the society can continue. For both reasons there is less long-term misery if in these extreme situations aid is directed at adults rather than children.

(2) Letting someone die is really the same as killing them. If you are walking by the bank of a river and you see someone drowning and you do nothing to save them then you are as guilty as if you had shot at them. Similarly, if you know that people are starving and you do nothing to relieve their plight then you are as responsible for their deaths as if you had sent them poisoned food. Therefore when you become aware of famine you have a duty to direct some of your resources to alleviating it.

(3) By having and caring for children you are implicitly promising them that you will make their lives as good as you can. And implicit promises are just as binding as explicit ones. Breaking them is just as bad. But to most of the people in the world you have made no promises, explicit or implicit. In particular, you have not promised to feed them. So although you have an obligation not to violate basic rights of people you do not know, you are not under any obligation to make their lives good. So in any conflict of interest between your obligations to your family and your obligations to people you do not know, it is your family that should win. It is your family that you are morally obliged, by your own implicit promises, to support, rather than people far away, no matter how hungry they are.

(4) Famine relief often helps people who go on to live miserable lives. Sometimes people who survive because of famine relief die in the next famine; sometimes they live longer than that and contribute to the overpopulation of their countries, so that there is more famine in the future. In this way misery is perpetuated and increases. A better course of action is to offer development aid but not famine relief. Development aid buys economic progress; it does not buy food. Thus although more people may die, less misery is produced.

Which of the four arguments makes the strongest case for a moral duty to relieve starvation? Which argument makes the strongest case for there not being any such duty? Suppose that someone using the strongest argument for there being such a duty is debating with someone using the strongest argument for there not being any such duty. What is the most effective point each could make against the other?

Suppose that you were convinced by one of these arguments. Which ones would impose the strongest obligations on you – oblige you to do things you might otherwise be reluctant to do – and which ones would impose the weakest obligations? Rank the four arguments in terms of the strength of the obligations they impose.

8.10 Morality in an Uncertain World

Below, there is a scrambled dialogue between two students who have been working through this chapter as part of a philosophy course. The contributions of the two speakers have been put in the wrong order. They need to be rearranged to see what the dialogue actually is. In order to do this you have to think which statements make sense logically as replies to which other statements. And to do that you will have to think about some of the themes of this chapter. So, put the statements below into order so they make sense as a dialogue about this chapter. (One way to do this is to photocopy the dialogue, cut the statements into separate strips, and then rearrange them until you find the arrangement that makes the most sense.)

Jerry: I'll buy that.

Manuella: The danger is of not having any firm rules to follow. Utilitarianism says to work out the consequences of each action you consider. You can't cling to anything safe like "don't kill." And as a result you can end up miscalculating and doing something really awful.

Jerry: Dangerous? I don't understand. There is no danger in doing the right thing.

Jerry: But the alternative is blindly following rules. Can't that cause disasters too?

Manuella: This chapter was a bit of a revelation to me. I had not realized my moral feelings were so traditional. I had been sympathetic to utilitarianism but now I see that often what it recommends is too dangerous.

Manuella: Nothing can go too badly wrong if you just never do anything forbidden. No one can ever blame you for refusing to kill.

Jerry: Actually I don't. I've come to share your feeling that utilitarianism makes it too easy to play God and pretend that you can see all the consequences of everything you do.

Manuella: So what we need is some way of accepting that any general rule will sometimes lead to trouble, while still giving us some rules to guide us.

Jerry: You can be blamed for not telling a lie, when telling the truth would cause someone's death. There are disasters in wait whatever your philosophy. But I see what you meant about "dangerous" now. Kantian ethics is looking for certainty about morals, even if you can never get it.

Manuella: So you really think if we accept that things can always go wrong we should be utilitarians?

Conclusions of This Chapter

◆ *Kantian ethics is based on the moral idea that what leads to an action – its motives – is as important as what follows it – its consequences.*

◆ *Kant's categorical imperative says (i) act according to rules everyone could follow all the time, (ii) never treat people as means to an end, and (iii) the ultimately good motive is the desire to act morally. Each of these is an important idea and can be defended, but they are different.*

◆ *Kantian ethics is a special case of deontological ethics, and utilitarianism is a special case of consequentialism. Some deontological ethics can resemble utilitarianism and some consequentialist ethics can resemble Kantian ethics, but the resemblance can never be perfect.*

◆ *Someone who follows a Kantian morality very literally will never tell lies and always keep promises. This may result in a difficult and restricted life. On the other hand someone who follows a utilitarian morality very literally will judge each of their actions by the effect it has on every other person on earth. That too will lead to a life that is difficult and restricted, but in different ways.*

Further Reading

Kant

Selection from Kant's *Groundwork of the Metaphysic of Morals* in Part VII of John
 Cottingham (ed.), *Western Philosophy: An Anthology*. Blackwell, 1996.
Immanuel Kant, *Foundations of the Metaphysics of Morals*, especially section 2, trans-
 lated by Lewis White Beck, with critical essays edited by Robert Paul Wolff.
 Macmillan, 1985.

Kantian ethics

Chapter 9 of Peter Singer, *Practical Ethics*, second edition. Cambridge University Press,
 1993.
Chapter 6 of Gilbert Harman, *The Nature of Morality*. Oxford University Press, 1977.
Onora O'Neill, *Acting on Principle*. Columbia University Press, 1975.
J. J. C. Smart and Bernard Williams, *Utilitarianism For and Against*. Cambridge Univer-
 sity Press, 1973.
Chapter 7 of J. L. Mackie, *Ethics: Inventing Right and Wrong*. Penguin, 1977.

Electronic resources

Routledge Encyclopedia of Philosophy (available online at many universities): articles
 on Deontological ethics; Kant, Immanuel; Kantian ethics.
Stanford Encyclopedia of Philosophy (http://plato.stanford.edu/): Consequentialism;
 Ethics, deontological; Kant, Immanuel (articles listed here are not yet available as
 this book goes to press; they should be available soon).

9 Empiricism

Introduction

Moral beliefs that are nearer to traditional morality can be got from Kantian ethics, which gives a way of finding moral rules that we can follow whatever the consequences of following them. Kantian ethics emphasizes the motive behind an action, which is ignored by utilitarianism.

Outside ethics an influential way of responding to changing evidence is described by empiricism. Empiricism tries to provide beliefs that are based in a reasonable way on evidence, while keeping the risk of error at a minimum. It does this by considering only evidence which concerns what we perceive and allowing only beliefs that use concepts based on perception.

Empiricism has difficulty explaining why many commonsense and scientific beliefs are reasonable. For example, it makes it hard to understand why it is reasonable to believe that other people have minds and experiences like yours....

Chapter Objectives

By the end of this chapter you should be able to answer the following questions.

◆ *What are the basic principles of empiricism?*
◆ *Why is empiricism friendly to science and unfriendly to speculation?*
◆ *What is the idea idea?*
◆ *How have empiricists suggested defining concepts in terms of perception?*
◆ *Why may the search for certainty lead to doubt?*
◆ *Why does empirical evidence not have to be completely safe?*

Definitions

The following words used in this chapter are defined in the list of definitions at the end of the book:

belief   *empirical evidence*   *idea*
concept

Empiricism is one of the most influential strands in Western thought. It is defined in Section 2, "The Appeal of Empiricism." But before reading that you may want to see if your views are already friendly or hostile to empiricism. So take the test in Section 1: "Are You an Empiricist?"

Empiricism is actually a family of theories, all of which encourage us to collect evidence for our beliefs and discourage us from speculating beyond the evidence we have. A variety of empiricist opinions is found in Section 3, "Some Empiricist Views." The first influential empiricism was the school of British Empiricists. Its fundamental concept was that of an "idea," discussed in Section 4, "The Idea Idea," after which Section 5, "Translation Exercises," is meant to help you understand what the British Empiricists were trying to get at with their concept of an idea. Some arguments of the founder of British Empiricism, John Locke, are discussed in Sections 6, "Locke's 'Way of Ideas',", and 7, "Locke against Innate Ideas."

Empiricism as it has developed more recently focuses on two questions: how we can find evidence for our beliefs, and how we can acquire concepts. Some basic distinctions are discussed in Section 8, "Concepts, Beliefs, and Sensations." How we can acquire concepts is discussed in Sections 9, "Ways of Defining Concepts," and 10, "Barriers to Concept Acquisition." How we can find evidence for our beliefs is discussed in Sections 11, "Empirical Evidence," and 12, "Adequate Evidence?"

9.1 Are You an Empiricist?

Below are short descriptions of four topics about which people have beliefs. In fact they are topics where people's beliefs very often differ drastically. After the description of each topic there are three possible attitudes to the topic. Choose the attitude that fits your own view of the topic best. You must pick one of the three. ("Don't know," or "somewhere in between," or "none of the above" are not allowed.)

Society   It is very hard to understand how complex human societies work. What makes crime more common in some places than others? What makes families stable? What factors encourage or prevent suicide? What institutions are needed for a democratic government to be possible? We do not have very good answers to any of these questions. One reason is that human societies are so complex, consisting of millions of people each with their own thoughts and motives. Another is that societies are composed of human beings, who have the capacity to make decisions in ways that are very hard to predict. Here are three reactions to this situation.

(a) We must collect more statistics about human behavior and about patterns of human life, and we must study them with the most advanced statistical methods we have.

(b) We must think about what human society essentially is, and in particular about the purposes for which people live together. We must think about justice and happiness. Then we will understand the ideal to which all our societies are approximations.

(c) We must develop the capacity to feel what it is like to have another position in society. Rich people must understand what it is like to be poor, and poor people what it is like to be rich. So people who study society must develop their capacities for imagination and understanding to the utmost.

Parapsychology   People often tell stories about ghosts, telepathy, telekinesis, precognition, and other phenomena which seem to contradict what is physically possible. The evidence for and against these things is very confusing, since it is colored by traditional beliefs and many people's desire that there should be some truth to the supernatural. If we are to get some firm conclusions out of this confusion, which of the following should we do?

(a) We could try to study such things as telepathy with laboratory methods, constructing cheat-proof tests of the skills of psychics and making careful and unbiased records of the results. Our standards should be the same as in any other science.

(b) We could rely on the best account of the world we have, which many people will take to be that of physical science, and we should reject all speculations that contradict it. Life is too short to investigate things that we know in advance are impossible.

(c) We could appreciate that psychics and mystics have insights that are very different from those of science, but just as valid. And their skills are not going to flourish under laboratory conditions. So we should welcome the richness of human life without trying to squeeze it all into one intellectual container.

Medicine   Medical science now has a large body of theories about the causes and cures of diseases. These theories tend to connect with one another and support one another, and they are taught and used by a medical profession which makes a lot of money out of its knowledge of them. On the other hand there is a very varied collection of alternative medical ideas, such as herbalism, homeopathy, and acupuncture. They sometimes call themselves "holistic" because they claim to treat the human organism, including both mind and body, as a whole living thing instead of as a collection of mechanical systems. The tension between medical science and alternative medicine can become quite bitter. In reaction to this we could adopt one of the following attitudes.

(a) We can try to study how effective particular alternative therapies are, apart from their mystical justifications. For example, we can run controlled studies comparing a group of people with some particular disease being treated by an alternative technique such as herbal medicine and another group being treated with standard medical methods.

(b) We can try to educate the public so that it is not taken in by unsubstantiated claims of people who know nothing about the workings of the body.

(c) We can try to appreciate holistic medicine on its own terms, taking it not as a substitute for scientific medicine but as a way of dealing with areas beyond the scope of science.

Psychotherapy People suffering from depression, anxiety, and other emotional troubles often get help from psychologists and psychotherapists. There are many rival schools of psychotherapy. Some schools believe that many emotional difficulties are basically disorders of brain chemistry and are best handled by medication. Psychoanalysis believes that most troubles of later life come from traumas in early childhood. Other therapies have developed ways in which people can talk through their difficulties until they find an attitude to life that works for them. Not only do these rival schools disagree about the reasons why people are unhappy; they disagree about what techniques will help people overcome their difficulties. Which of the following is the best reaction to these disagreements?

(a) We can gather data about the effectiveness of different therapies and compare them. We can also try to study the life histories of large numbers of people to try to see if they confirm or refute theories of the origins of psychological difficulties.

(b) We can try to construct a general theory of the human mind, drawing on everything we know about the brain and about such things as perception, memory, thought, and emotion. Then when we have a powerful enough theory we can try to apply it to the ways in which people's attitudes and emotions develop and can be changed.

(c) We can recognize that every person is unique and that every person has their own way of expressing universal desires to give and receive love. Because of this uniqueness each therapy is in its way true of some part of the infinite variety of human life.

Diagnosis

If you chose (a) most often, you are likely to be sympathetic to empiricism. If you chose (b) or (c) most often, you are likely to be hostile to empiricism. If you mostly chose (b) your attitude might be labeled "rationalist"; and if you mostly chose (c) your attitude might be labeled "mystical."

Warning These questions are supposed to help you find out how much the opinions you *now* hold fit into the pattern of empiricism. But studying philosophy should help you to examine and improve your opinions. So if your answers suggest that you are inclined to agree with empiricism, you should think hard about the criticisms of empiricism in Chapter 10. And in fact, thinking more about some of the implications of empiricism discussed in this chapter may shake your convictions. If on the other hand your answers suggest that you are inclined to disagree with empiricism, then you should use the present chapter to understand why many philosophers are inclined toward empiricism. When you understand their opinions you may have more sympathy for them.

9.2 The Appeal of Empiricism

Empiricism is really a family of theories about what evidence we can have for our beliefs and about the thoughts that we can think. There are many different empiricist theories, but they all have in common a vague theme, which might be expressed as "it all comes from experience." In fact empiricism emphasizes the role of a particular kind of experience, the experience of the world around us that we get by using our senses and trying not to let our beliefs influence what we think we perceive. This is the kind of experience that is found in experimental evidence for scientific theories, or in the data that a careful detective would use to discover the identity of a criminal. Empiricism says: good evidence for a belief always starts with (the right kind of) experience, and meaningful thought – as opposed to the meaningless gobbledegook that fills too much of our talk – is always about things we can experience.

There are many ways of filling in the details here. There are stronger ways and weaker ways. To see the difference consider the different things empiricists could say about evidence.

A *very* strong empiricism could say: to have a good reason to believe something you have to use your senses to make some observations that are conclusive evidence for it. The observations have to be things you could not doubt, and they have to make it impossible for the belief to be false. So in order to believe that extraterrestrials visit earth in flying saucers, a very strong empiricist would have to have observations of them that could not be rejected as hallucinations or dreams, and that could only be interpreted as extraterrestrials and not as earth people from the future or an elaborate hoax.

A rather weak empiricism could say: to have a good reason to believe something you have to have some evidence based on what people actually have perceived, such that, given that evidence and other things you firmly believe, it is very probable that the belief is true. So in order to believe that extraterrestrials visit earth in flying saucers, a rather weak empiricist would have to have some credible testimony from people who claim to have experienced them, and would have to have thought through some alternative explanations carefully enough to have rejected them.

There is room for a lot of middle-strength empiricisms between these two extremes. But why should anyone want to be an empiricist? Here are two features of empiricism that many people find attractive. (And some people find repulsive.)

◆ *Empiricism is hostile to speculation.* Empiricism says that you need evidence for your beliefs, and to get evidence you have to have experiences that support your beliefs. But we don't have this kind of evidence for many things which it might be nice to believe (reincarnation, say, or grand theories of history). So empiricism says we don't have good reason to believe them. Instead of speculating, we should just suspend judgment.

◆ *Empiricism is friendly to experimental science.* In some parts of science evidence is carefully gathered in controlled experiments and all conclusions are based on such evidence. For example, the less theoretical parts of biology, chemistry, or geology are like this. And this is, for empiricists, a model for all our beliefs.

Empiricism has a down to earth quality. It suggests limits to what we can understand, and urges a cautious evidence-based approach within these limits. That is its appeal. It is also the reason why some people dislike it, for it makes it unlikely that we can know anything about some topics which people have always thought it important to think about. Religious belief will be a problem for very strong empiricists, though a weaker empiricism can base religious belief on religious experience – for example, the sense of the divine presence that some people have. A very strong empiricism will doom all metaphysics, all attempts to discover general relations between what we think, what exists, and what is valuable. Some people find this prospect disappointing and depressing.

In fact, rather than get enthusiastic or depressed about empiricism, we should ask some sober questions. Is it true? Can it be defended? And since there are stronger and weaker empiricist theories, we should ask even more sober questions. How strong an empiricism could be true? What arguments are there to support (or attack) strong and weak empiricist theories?

9.3 Some Empiricist Views

Below are seven quotations from famous philosophers on the themes of empiricism. They were written at very different times, as empiricist ideas keep coming up in philosophy. Each is for or against some aspect of empiricism.

(1) *No one can learn or understand anything in the absence of sense, and when the mind is actively aware of anything it is necessarily aware of it along with an image. (Aristotle, De Anima ("On the Soul"), Book III, Chapter 8; fourth century BC)*

(2) *We clearly cannot obtain scientific knowledge by the act of perception. In fact it is obvious that even if it were possible to perceive that a triangle has its angles equal to two right angles we should still be looking for a proof. We would not have knowledge of it. . . . So if we were on the moon and saw the earth shutting off the sun's light, we would not know the cause of the eclipse. We would perceive the present fact of the eclipse, but not the reason for it. (Aristotle,* Posterior Analytics, *Book I, Chapter 30; fourth century* BC)

(3) *Our intellect understands material things by abstracting from perception, and through material things thus considered we acquire some knowledge of immaterial things, just as, on the contrary, angels know material things through the immaterial. (St Thomas Aquinas,* Summa Theologica, *I, Q 85, Art. 1; thirteenth century)*

(4) *I see no reason . . . to believe, that the soul thinks before the senses have furnished it with ideas to think on; and as those are increased, and retained, so it comes by exercise to improve its faculty of thinking . . . by compounding those ideas . . . (Locke,* An Essay concerning Human Understanding, *Book II, Chapter 1, Section 20; eighteenth century)*

(5) *The concept of truth was originated by the senses and the senses cannot be rebutted. The testimony that we must accept as most trustworthy is that which can spontaneously overcome falsehood with truth. What then can we pronounce more trustworthy than the senses? (Lucretius,* On the Nature of the Universe, *Book IV; first century* BC)

(6) *The senses . . . never give anything except examples. . . . Now all the examples which confirm a general truth . . . are not enough to show that it must always be true. . . . For example, the Greeks and Romans . . . noticed that before the end of twenty-four hours day changes into night and night into day. But we would be deceived if we believed that the same rule holds everywhere, for the contrary has been experienced in [the Arctic]. . . . So it would seem that necessary truths such as are found in pure mathematics . . . must have principles whose proof does not depend on examples and thus not on the senses, although without the senses it would never occur to us to think of them. . . . It is in this that human knowledge is different from that of animals. Animals . . . only guide themselves by examples. . . . But humans are capable of abstract reasoning. . . . This is why it is so easy for men to trap animals . . . (Leibniz,* New Essays; *seventeenth century)*

(7) *The best and safest method of philosophizing seems to be, first, to inquire diligently into the properties of things and to establish those properties by experiments, and to proceed later to hypotheses for the explanation of things themselves. . . . And if anyone offers conjectures about the truth of things from the mere possibility of hypotheses, I do not see by what stipulation anything certain can be determined in any science. . . . Hence I judged that one should abstain from contemplating hypotheses, as from improper argumentation . . . (Newton; seventeenth century)*

Some of these quotations support, and some oppose, empiricism. To be more precise, each of the quotations can be taken as describing a position that supports or opposes one of the three characteristics of empiricism listed below. Which quotations support, and which oppose, which of these three characteristics?

(a) *Evidence through perception*: knowledge is based on what we perceive through our senses.
(b) *Hostility to speculation*: when thinking gets too far from evidence gained through perception, we should distrust it.
(c) *Concepts from perception*: we think in terms of ideas that come from what we perceive.

Some of the quotations seem to support one characteristic of empiricism and oppose another. (This shows that philosophers who think for themselves are hard to pin down with simple labels like "empiricism.")

(i) Find a quotation which seems to support concepts from perception (c) but to oppose evidence through perception (a).
(ii) Find one which seems to support evidence through perception (a) and concepts from perception (c) but to oppose hostility to speculation (b).

9.4 The Idea Idea

In the seventeenth century a very simple form of empiricism developed, often called "British Empiricism" because the first great philosopher in this tradition was English, John Locke, and his ideas were developed further by a Scottish philosopher, David Hume, and an Irish philosopher, George Berkeley. It is one of the most influential philosophical movements of all time, and still affects our thinking about how we do and should reason.

To understand British Empiricism and the movements that follow on from it you have to grasp a single central picture of how we think. It describes how our thought begins with what we experience and then extends to things that we cannot experience. Best to begin with examples. Contrast the words – and what they mean – in the two lists below.

yellow	chair
green	lemon
round	iron
square	justice
high-pitched	America
low-pitched	energy
sweet	frying pan
sour	cruel

The words in the list on the right have very little in common. They are as varied as all the things we think about. The words in the list on the left are also very varied. But they do have something in common. They are all properties of things which are also qualities of our experience. A lemon can be yellow and you can see that it is yellow, and when you see that it is yellow you have an experience of yellowness. The lemon is also sour, and you can taste that it is sour, and when you taste that it is sour you have a sour taste in your mouth.

> According to empiricism all concepts come from what we experience.

Three things coincide here. First, properties of objects (objects can be yellow, round, or sour); second, our abilities to perceive (we can perceive that objects are yellow, round, or sour); third, the experience of perception (we can have yellow, round, or sour sensations.) Call concepts that combine these three features *experiential concepts*. (Locke called them "ideas of sensation," Hume called them "impressions." In British Empiricism they were generally called "ideas.")

How do you know that a lemon is yellow? By looking and seeing the yellow. Why do you understand what someone means when they say it is sour? Because you have experienced sourness. Suppose that this is the way we understand experiential concepts, the way we are able to think thoughts like "this is yellow," "that is high-pitched," "this is sour." Then we have the

◆ *first principle of empiricism*: we acquire experiential concepts by having experiences with those qualities.

How do you understand other concepts, like those on the right-hand list? If you ask someone what a lemon is, they might begin by saying: lemons are round along one axis and elliptical along the other, and yellow, and taste sour. Perhaps if someone said enough along those lines to someone who had no idea what a lemon was they might eventually have the same understanding of what a lemon is that we who eat, peel, and talk about lemons have. And most people get that understanding by contact with lemons: seeing, smelling, and tasting them. This suggests the

◆ *second principle of empiricism*: we acquire all other concepts by combining experiential concepts.

But this leaves something unexplained. How, exactly, do experiential concepts get combined to make other concepts? This is an important question, because if *all* concepts are acquired by combining experiential concepts, then words or concepts that we cannot define in terms of experience will be meaningless, just empty sounds. Depending on how an empiricist theory allows concepts to combine to make other concepts, it may find that concepts like that of *God*, or *justice*, or for that matter *kinetic energy*, turn out to be, according to the theory, meaningless.

9.5 Translation Exercises

Here is a description of a scene:

> *A chair lay on the floor. Beside the chair were the two cracked halves of a saucer, and around them a few drops of milk, which a black cat was eagerly lapping.*

And here is a translation of that description, which tries to use only experiential concepts. Notice that in the translation all concepts except experiential concepts are defined in terms of experiential concepts. (For it is often not easy to get an exact match between the meaning of a concept and a definition in terms of experiential concepts. So some concepts lose some of their meaning in translation. A better translation might keep more of their meaning, but it would be longer and more complicated.)

> *A brown object constructed of six long parts of square cross-section and a thin square part at right angles to the long parts was situated so that the square part was vertical. A short distance horizontally from the lower parts of the brown object were two smaller white objects each of which was shaped like a segment of a circle linked to an irregular edge. The irregular edges of the two complemented each other in shape. In several directions horizontally from the white objects were some even smaller white objects, which were liquid and smooth in shape. A larger black object with a furry exterior was near these smaller white objects and from one end of it a flat pink object was moving rapidly between them and that end of the black furry object, so that the number of small white objects outside the black furry object was decreasing.*

Which of these concepts found in the original has lost more of its meaning in the translation?

◆ chair
◆ saucer
◆ milk
◆ cat
◆ eagerly

Even this translation does not go as far as possible toward using only ideas that can be picked up in perception. Which concepts remaining in the translation are not really ideas that could be picked up by perception alone? Which of them could be translated by making the translation even longer and harder to understand, and which might be just impossible to translate into the language of perception?

Here is a description of another scene:

> *A red billiard ball rolled across a green cloth and collided with a white ball. The impact caused the white ball to leap off the table and fly into the air, striking a large arrogant man in the eye. He roared in pain and left the room in a very undignified manner.*

Make a translation of it into language that uses only experiential concepts, as far as possible. Do not expect perfection! What concepts in the original description are hardest to translate?

One way to do this is to spend five minutes writing out a draft translation, and then comparing it with another person's draft. Then combine the two, using the best suggestions in each.

9.6 Locke's "Way of Ideas"

The English philosopher John Locke (1632–1704) began the school of British Empiricism. He took the word "idea" from Descartes who had used it for anything one thinks. (Descartes speaks of "clear and distinct ideas," meaning roughly "clear and intelligible thoughts.") Descartes thought that many such ideas are innate, that we cannot get them from anything outside us. In fact, Descartes thought, the ideas that are most suited for scientific reasoning are the innate ones. For example, he wrote:

I find within myself two different ideas of the sun. One draws its origin from the senses. . . . By this idea the sun seems to me very small. The other is based on reasons found in astronomy, that is, on certain notions which were born with me or at any rate formed somehow by me. By this idea the sun seems to me several times bigger than the whole earth. Both ideas cannot resemble the sun that exists outside me, and reason makes me think that the idea which comes immediately from its appearance is the one that is least like it.

Locke opposed this. His picture of science, and all knowledge, was that it starts with the way things appear to the senses and then proceeds to more abstract and theoretical representations of things. And in particular he thought that there are no innate ideas. That is, there are no ideas (no thoughts or concepts) which are in the mind from birth. The mind acquires ideas in early life by perception and reflection. As he wrote,

Let us then suppose the mind to be, as we say, white paper, void of all characters, without any ideas. How comes it to be furnished? Whence comes it by that vast store, which the busy and boundless fancy of man has painted on it, with an almost endless variety? Whence has it all the materials of reason and knowledge? To this I answer in one word, from experience. In that, all our knowledge is founded . . .

Note that Locke is claiming two rather different things about the relation between ideas and experience. The first concerns the way human minds actually develop. He thinks that we start with no ideas and gain them from experience. The other concerns the basis of our knowledge. He thinks that everything we know is "founded" on experience. One thing this can be taken to mean is that if we do not have reasons based on experience for believing something, we cannot claim to know it. It can also be taken to mean that in science we should base our theories primarily on experience rather than on abstract reasoning. The first of these is a claim about what human psychology *is* like, and the second is a claim about how human beliefs *should* be organized. In the passage above, the first claim is most evident; in other writings, Locke and other empiricists argue equally forcefully for the second. It is characteristic of British Empiricism to argue for both of them, and to treat them as essentially the same.

Locke is arguing that we begin with perception and go on to more abstract thoughts. But what exactly is it that begins with perception? According to Locke and others influenced by him, perception gives us *ideas*, at first of simple qualities like "yellow" or "long" or "sour," which we combine to get other ideas such as "lemon" or "elephant" or "sun." It's the combining that is important here. Perception gives us some simple things and we combine them to get more complex things, and all thinking consists in the combining or recombining of these simple and complex things. Ideas are whatever these things are that get combined.

So whenever anyone thinks, for example, that elephants eat bananas, she has in her mind a complex idea made up from simple ideas of yellow and grey, of long and short and round, and many others. These are combined to give ideas of what elephants and bananas look like. Then they are further combined to give ideas of what elephants and bananas really are (since not everything that looks like an elephant really is one). Then they are combined yet further to give the idea that elephants eat bananas. It is not too hard to understand how the first stage of combination, to get ideas of complex appearances (like what an elephant looks like) might work. The second and third stages, which give the ideas of what things really are, and which give the actual thoughts we think, are more of a challenge. Empiricists give different and sometimes very difficult theories about how they go. (See Chapter 15, Section 7.)

9.7 Locke against Innate Ideas

John Locke began his *Essay concerning Human Understanding*, first published in 1689, with a series of arguments meant to show that people acquire all their ideas from experience. Here are five short passages in which Locke is arguing against innate ideas.

(A) *A child knows not that three and four are equal to seven, till he comes to be able to count to seven, and has got the name and idea of equality. . . . But neither does he then readily assent, because it is an innate truth, nor was his assent wanting till then because he wanted the use of reason. But the truth of it appears to him, as soon as he has settled in his mind the clear and distinct ideas that these names stand for. And then he knows the truth of that proposition [3 + 4 = 7] upon the same grounds, and by the same means, that he knew before that a rod and a cherry are not the same thing. (Book 1, Chapter 2, section 16)*

(B) *But alas, amongst children, idiots, savages, and the grossly illiterate what general maxims are to be found? What universal principles of knowledge? Their notions are few and narrow, borrowed only from those objects they have had most to do with, and which have made upon their senses the frequentest and strongest impressions. (Book 1, Chapter 2, section 27)*

(C) *If we will attentively consider new born children we shall have little reason to think that they bring many ideas into the world with them. For [besides] perhaps some faint ideas of hunger, and thirst, and warmth, and some pains, which they may have felt in the womb, there is not the least appearance of any settled ideas at all in them. (Book I, Chapter 4, section 2)*

(D) *. . . [there is a] great variety of opinions, concerning moral rules, which are to be found amongst men, according to the different sorts of happiness they have a prospect of, or propose to themselves. Which could not be, if practical principles were innate, and imprinted in our minds immediately by the hand of God. (Book I, Chapter 3, section 6)*

(E) *Suppose a man born blind, and now adult, and taught by his touch to distinguish between a cube and a sphere, and the blind man to be made to see . . . the blind man, at first sight, would not be able with certainty to say, which was the globe, which the cube, whilst he only saw them. (Book II, Chapter 9, section 8)*

One could object to these arguments in many ways. Here are eight possible objections. Which objections might be used against which of the five arguments (A) to (E) above? (Some objections may be relevant to more than one argument. And some may be relevant to none.)

(1) An idea can be in the mind and yet not be used until conditions are right.
(2) Sometimes an innate awareness of something can be blocked by something else a person has been taught.
(3) To show that some ideas are not innate is not to show that all ideas are not innate.
(4) You do not know what ideas someone has until you give that person the opportunity to express them.
(5) If we did not have innate ideas we would not know anything.
(6) The conditions under which an idea normally shows itself in human life may not show all the conditions under which it could occur.
(7) It may take time and practice to learn how to combine innate ideas with ideas that come from the senses.
(8) Illiterate people are as intelligent as highly educated people.

Considering all eight objections would take any person or any group quite a long time. The task could well be divided, with some people or groups relating the first four objections to the five quotations, and the other people or groups relating the second four objections to the same five quotations. Then going through the quotations one by one the whole class could survey the objections to them.

Locke has answers to some of these objections. Most of them are found in Book I of his *Essay*. But can you find answers to some of them?

In these arguments Locke makes several unstated assumptions about ideas. Here are three. Which one is made in which of the five arguments?

(i) Simple innate ideas would appear early in human development.
(ii) If an idea is innate then people will have innate knowledge of some facts about it.
(iii) If an idea is innate then all people everywhere will have it.

None of these assumptions is obviously true. Which of the eight objections above could be used to argue against which of these three assumptions?

9.8 Concepts, Beliefs, and Sensations

HARDER

The way we speak in everyday life is often influenced by philosophy. It is especially influenced by the philosophers of the past whose suggestions have had time to work their way into the language. Words like "matter," "form," "intention," "perception," and "will" come ultimately from the writings of philosophers, even though they are now learned by small children at the same time as they learn words like "cat" and "table." Two very important words coming from philosophy are "idea" and "concept." Everyday language took over the word "idea" from empiricism, and now we use "idea" to mean almost anything that comes into someone's mind. (For example: "She somehow has the idea that I am going to give her my house." "A sudden idea struck her: perhaps Henry didn't intend to give her his house.")

Philosophers do not now use the word "idea" as part of their theories, even if they are empiricists. (Though they may use the word in an ordinary way when giving examples.) The reason is that the concept of an idea lumps together too many different things. And philosophers have come to think that the differences between these things are very important. Three of them are beliefs, concepts, and sensations.

Suppose you are looking at a red rose. You have the *belief* that there is something red in front of you. And this belief involves the *concept* "red." You also have a red *sensation*. And these are different. For example, if you were blind but people had told you about colors you could have the belief that there were many red things in the world, in fact some right in front of you, without having any sensations of red. Or you might doubt whether the things you heard and read about colors were true, so although you had some sort of a concept of red you had very few beliefs about red. You neither believed that there were red things nor believed that there were not. Suppose now that your sight is restored by an operation and the first thing that is shown to you is a rose. You have a sensation of red but you do not know that that is what it is. You have the sensation of red but you do not connect it with your concept of red and it does not lead to any beliefs about red.

One basic difference between beliefs on the one hand and concepts and sensations on the other hand is that only beliefs can be true. If you believe there is a red rose in front of you then either there is, and your belief is true, or there is not, and your belief is false. If you have a sensation of red, that sensation is neither true nor false. And you can use your concept of red in many beliefs, some of which are true and some false. (Think of a blind person again. That person's concept of red – their grasp of what everyone else is talking about when they say "red" – may be rather different from the concept of red that someone who can see has. But it is not a false concept. Concepts cannot be false.)

Concepts are used to form beliefs. If you believe that the earth is round then you are combining your concepts of the earth and of roundness to make the belief. And, on the other hand, when you have or understand a concept there are usually some beliefs which are important signs that you have it. For example, if you have the concept of red then you believe that red is a color and that people who see red things usually have red sensations. Concepts occur in other states of mind besides belief. You can believe that an apple is red, but also hope that the sunset will be red, or want there to be enough red paint left to paint the kitchen wall. What all these states have in common is that they build on the person's having the concept red.

It is important not to confuse sensations, beliefs, and concepts. The definitions below bring out the ways they are different.

◆ *Sensations* occur when we perceive with the senses. They are the particular qualities of colors, sounds, smells, and so on that we must use to describe what our sensory experience is like.
◆ *Beliefs* occur whenever we think or remember. They can be true or false.
◆ *Concepts* are what is common to beliefs, desires, hopes, and other states. They cannot themselves be true or false, but having them is required for having beliefs.

"Concept" is also becoming a tangled word. People have begun recently to say "concept" when they mean "general or vague thought." For example: "He designed a car which runs on sea-water and solar energy, but it is still at the concept stage"; or: "Some people just don't have the concept that women are tired of being pushed around." "Concept" is picking up some of the ambiguities that "idea" had. It's so hard to be clear!

Here are five sentences, each containing a description of something that can be classified as a belief, a concept, or a sensation. Give these words the meanings described above. (Use the philosopher's, not the everyday, meaning of "concept.") In some of them you can find two or perhaps three. State the belief, or describe the concept, or identify the sensation, which corresponds to the word in italics in each sentence below.

(i) George had a sudden *conviction*: the reason his wine tasted funny was that his wife was trying to poison him.

(ii) Martha's grasp of science was fairly rudimentary. Her *understanding* of arsenic was that it was whatever was in the bottle labeled "arsenic."

(iii) George felt awful. The *taste* of the wine was bitter, almost poisonous.

(iv) As George fell to the floor his past life rushed before his mind. He *felt* a sudden regret. He had treated everyone he loved so badly.

(v) Martha felt suddenly elated, rich and free. She did not feel at all guilty, for her *idea* of justice was the biblical "an eye for an eye, a tooth for a tooth," and George had certainly done some terrible things to her.

Sometimes when we talk of "ideas" we mean beliefs, sometimes concepts, and sometimes (though less often) sensations. We say "I had an interesting idea last night: perhaps apes are descended from humans, rather than the other way around." Here "idea" refers to a belief (or perhaps a conjecture). But we also say "He has never been in love. He has no idea of what love really is." And here "idea" means "concept." And we say "The office has now been redecorated. As soon as a customer walks in he or she is struck with an over-powering visual idea of brightness and clarity."

So if you want not to confuse beliefs and concepts it is best not to talk of ideas. The distinction between beliefs and concepts is not clear in a lot of philosophy until fairly recently. (Reading Descartes, or the British Empiricists, or even Kant, a contemporary philosopher often feels that the lack of a distinction between concepts and beliefs is making it harder to understand what is being claimed and how an argument is supposed to work.)

Below are six uses of the word "idea." Which ones refer to beliefs and which to concepts? Some may be interpreted both ways. In that case describe the beliefs and the concepts that might be meant.

(a) Helena hasn't the slightest idea about music. She thinks a bassoon is a kind of foolish man.

(b) Les is the stupidest man I have ever met. His idea of a good time is getting drunk and then going hang-gliding.

(c) Ancient Chinese mathematicians had none of the ideas of the calculus, but they did have the idea of a linear transformation.

(d) What you have done is a completely new idea in dress design. No one has ever thought of a hem that is ankle-height at one leg and mid-thigh at the other; the impression it makes is overwhelmingly novel.

(e) The idea of infinite space is very hard to grasp. We naturally think things must have edges.

(f) I don't want to go on driving Marcus to the airport. I think he's getting ideas about me. Last time he asked me if I liked bald men.

HARDER

9.9 Ways of Defining Concepts

Empiricists claim that most concepts can be defined in terms of simple sensory concepts. The materials of our thinking are simple concepts we can get from experience, like *red*, *square*, *sour*, or *deep-sounding*, and then in terms of these we construct complex concepts like *elephant*, *city*, *justice*, or *reality*. But we don't literally construct concepts; we don't manufacture them by physically putting their components together. So how do we construct or define complex concepts out of simpler ones? Empiricists need a way in which this can happen that can start with concepts so simple that we can suppose that people can acquire them just by using their senses, and then go on to define most of the enormous range of concepts that we can have. It has to be able to define concepts like *elephant*, *justice*, and *electron* in terms of concepts like *grey*, *anger*, and *circular*.

(Empiricists refer to "most of" rather than "all of" the enormous range of human concepts, because they often claim that we fool ourselves when we think we understand some things. They are just pretend concepts, empty words. For example, an empiricist who cannot find a way of defining "fate" or "destiny" that fits all the things people say about them might reject these words, saying that they have no clear meaning to define.)

Here are three possible ways of defining complex concepts in terms of simpler ones.

Direct combination   If you think of ideas as simple bits of experience, then you can imagine them just being combined together, something like building a table by sticking four legs on a top, or budding a water molecule by attaching two hydrogen molecules to an oxygen molecule. So we could think of a complex concept as just being a combination of two simpler ones somehow stuck together. So the idea of an elephant would be, to a very crude first approximation: grey + big + four cylinders underneath + round bit in front + . . .

This is obviously not very plausible. The most obvious problems come from negation and generality. Negation is when one concept applies whenever another does not: non-red, uninteresting, undemocratic. Generality is when one concept applies to all or some of what another concept applies to: lover of someone, creator of everything. It is very hard to see how negative or general concepts can be got by sticking simpler concepts together. How can we get the concept "non-red" out of the concept "red" and similar concepts? We might try "green or pink or . . ."? But the list might be infinite, and even if it could be got down to a finite number we would still have used the concept of "or" and the same problems come back when we try to define "or." How can we get the concept "lover of someone" out of the concept "lover" and similar concepts? We might try "lover of George or lover of Helen or . . . ," but then we would have the same problems as with "non-red." It seems pretty clear that there is no general way around these problems. But to reject all concepts that involve negation or generality would be to impose a crippling limitation on our thought.

Logical combination   Combinations of concepts like "non-red" cannot be got by simply sticking their components together. So we might just accept that concepts typically have logical structure; they cannot be defined except by using "logical" words like "not" and "something." We would then accept a list of logical concept-making devices; it would include at least "and," "or," "if," "not," and "something." We would allow any complex concept to be defined in terms of simple concepts by using any combination of these devices. Then we would have no problems with really complicated concepts like:

"red and triangular if loved by someone and brown and square if not loved by anyone."

This is the line taken by many contemporary philosophers influenced by empiricism. It has clear advantages. One feature that some might see as a disadvantage is that it gives logic, abstract thought, an equal role with perception. That is, it accepts that the capacity to use "not," "and," "all" and similar concepts does not itself come from perception but is needed to make concepts out of perception. This is a major retreat from some of the original intentions of empiricism.

Psychological combination   Given some simple concepts, human minds will form complex concepts out of them. Which ones? Well, there may be no simple description of this: some may be formed very naturally and others, equally simple logically, may be very unnatural. Contrast the concept of an elephant with the concept of "grue," discussed in Box 10 in Chapter 5. Any child can easily get the idea of what an elephant is, from seeing elephants or pictures of elephants, or hearing them described. A definition that stated exactly what counts as an elephant, so that there would be absolutely nothing that satisfied the terms of the definition and was not an elephant, and absolutely all elephants satisfied the definition, would have to be really very complicated. Grue is much simpler to define, logically speaking. (Something is grue if and only if it is green and observed before time t or blue and observed after time t, for some given time t). But in spite of this short and simple definition the idea is one that the human mind has quite a lot of trouble grasping.

So whether people find a concept easy or hard to learn is not just a matter of whether it can be given a logically simple definition. As a result, discovering the ways in which human minds form complex concepts out of simple ones needs more than we can get from philosophy and logic alone. We also need psychology. We need to gather, analyze, and make theories about how people think and acquire ideas.

(Hume tried to describe laws for the "association of ideas," for the way having one idea in mind makes you have another. These were intended to be in part a contribution to such a study of how the mind collects simple ideas into complex ones. In fact, the British Empiricists were as much psychologists as philosophers, and many of their suggestions lie behind theories in modern psychology.)

9.10 Barriers to Concept Acquisition

Below are two lists: (i) is a list of concepts and of some people who might have difficulty acquiring the concept; and (ii) is a list of the problems that might arise. In most cases several problems will arise. So, in each of the seven cases, describe which of the four problems is the greatest obstacle to the person acquiring the concept. And for each of the problems try to find one case in which it would not play a significant role.

(I) Concepts and people

(a) Serafina is 10 years old and has been raised in a strict environment. No films, no television, no novels. Can she understand the idea of romantic love?

(b) Angelina is very musical and has been raised in a family of classical musicians. She has played in a string quartet since she was six. But she has never been allowed to listen to any jazz or popular music and in fact has never heard any wind instruments. She reads a book about jazz and wonders what a tenor saxophone sounds like. Can she have any concept of its sound?

(c) Cherubino is 10 years old and of average intelligence. He is good at arithmetic but knows no algebra. Can he understand the concepts of calculus?

(d) Gabriel is blind. He has read widely, through Braille and taped books, and knows from literature what people say about their reactions to colors and from science what properties of objects make them appear colored. Can he have the concept of red that sighted people have?

(c) Michael lives in England in the early nineteenth century. He has never been to school and cannot read or write. No one among his friends or family can read or write. Since the age of 6 he has worked in a factory from five in the morning till six in the evening. He is, however, extremely intelligent; he works out complicated arithmetic problems in his head and during the few hours between work and sleep he looks at the stars and wonders why they move in the patterns he observes. Can he have the concepts of mass and energy?

(f) Lucifer is a peasant working on the land of a very oppressive lord. The lord makes rules regulating every aspect of the peasants' lives. The peasants live in small family groups but all decisions about the family – who may marry whom, what occupation a child should have, and so on – are made by the master. Can Lucifer even understand what democracy is?

(g) Beatrice lives in a hunter-gatherer society in which diseases are thought to be caused by evil spirits. When someone falls ill ceremonies are performed to chase away the spirits, and sometimes the person recovers. Can Beatrice have the twentieth-century concept of a virus?

(II) Possible problems

(1) *Cognitive limitations* Human beings have limited powers of memory and reasoning. They cannot understand things that are too complicated for them, and they cannot follow chains of reasoning that involve too many steps. This is true for all of us. So the thinking that has to be gone through to acquire a concept must not be too complex.

(2) *Inadequate experience* Sometimes someone has not had the experiences that are needed in order to understand something. To contrast this factor with the others, understand "experience" in a narrow sense, so that only what you perceive with your own senses counts as experience.

(3) *Inadequate knowledge* Sometimes in order to understand a concept a person needs to understand a theory. Sometimes believing one thing prepares the way for understanding another. For example, in order to have the concept of a hominid (a prehuman ancestor of our species) you might have to understand the theory of evolution. (Note that in order to understand the concept the person does not have to believe the theory; understanding it is usually enough.)

(4) *Inadequate social environment* Sometimes in order to understand something a person has to be among others with a similar understanding. You can't understand some things all by yourself. You may need teachers, experts, friends.

More conclusions

Below are eight conclusions someone might draw from the examples in list (i) and the reasons in list (ii). Which ones are supported by which of the examples and reasons? Are any of them definitely not true?

(a) Each concept has a complicated combination of circumstances which must be satisfied if someone is to have it.
(b) All that is needed to have a concept is the right experience.
(c) Without the right experience it is impossible to understand a concept.
(d) People from different backgrounds cannot have the same concepts.
(c) Every person is stuck in a small range of concepts, from which they cannot escape.
(f) You can only think what others around you have taught you to think.
(g) People can never change their concepts.
(h) Different people can acquire the same concepts in very different ways.

9.11 Empirical Evidence

We often produce evidence to defend what we believe, or try to persuade other people to believe things. For example, if a prosecutor wants to convince a jury that an accused person committed a crime she may produce eye-witnesses who saw the person at the scene of the crime, or weapons or tools found in that person's house. Or if a team of scientists wants to convince other scientists that a theory is true they may produce laboratory results, observations using telescopes or microscopes, or the results of field studies, depending on what kind of theory it is. In all these cases people are trying to provide other people with undeniable facts from which they can reason to conclusions. The evidence does not always have its intended effect. People vary a lot in what they are prepared to believe and how they will think. But still, very often evidence can be produced for a theory or belief that will convince many reasonable people that it is true.

One of the most convincing and effective kinds of evidence is *empirical evidence*. One of the central sources of empirical evidence is experimental science. Empirical evidence is evidence obtained by careful and unbiased observation. Scientists working in subjects as varied as chemistry, biology, or economics perform experiments or make careful studies of the facts about their domains, and these provide them with the reasons for believing their theories. In performing experiments or collecting observable facts scientists are looking for facts that can be used to convince others that a theory is right, or to decide between competing theories. The aim is to make observations that people can agree on without having to decide which theory is true, which can then be used as a basis for reasoning that will wholly or partly settle the question. But science is only one source of empirical evidence. Most people spend most of their time looking and listening, so every person is gathering empirical evidence all the time. With a little care, this can be used to support or contradict a wide range of beliefs.

There are two separate aspects to empirical evidence. One is that it is obtained by observation, by use of the senses. The other is that it is neutral evidence; two people who hold different theories can both appreciate the force of the evidence. People who disagree about, for example, whether the earth is getting warmer or what the causes of unemployment are can agree about the changes in sea-water temperature at some location, or about how many people are unemployed at different places. They can agree about the observations while disagreeing about what theory explains them. (But the aim is to collect enough evidence, and to reason carefully enough from it, that disagreement is eventually minimized. That is the scientific ideal.)

It is easy to see why these two aspects go together. Most people have roughly the same senses and can use them in roughly the same way. And what you see or hear is in some ways independent of what you believe. So it is not surprising that people who disagree about the earth's climate or unemployment can agree about what they observe using a thermometer, or what data has been collected by government surveys. But this is only approximate: people do differ in what they perceive, and their perceptions are affected in some ways by what they believe. Two ways in which this happens are particularly important.

First, people who agree about what they perceive usually also share many commonsense beliefs, which most people in their society or in some cases most people everywhere share. So it is hard to find empirical evidence that is neutral about these commonsense beliefs. For example, people usually agree that someone who is screaming and writhing is likely to be in pain. That is common sense. But someone who had the mad delusion that everyone in the world was laughing at him, and that people who seem to be writhing in pain have just found another way of laughing, would not share this belief. Neither would someone who believed that there was no such thing as pain, as people are just robots without feelings. For reasons like this it is very hard to find empirical evidence against someone who has very unusual beliefs about other people's states of mind or who doubts that other people have states of mind.

Second, people usually use empirical evidence to convince other people in some particular group. Scientists try to convince other scientists in their field; prosecutors and defense lawyers try to convince juries. So the evidence is not usually just facts which anyone, whatever their beliefs, could understand and agree about. The evidence for a theory in economics may include complex statistics that most of us would find extremely confusing; the evidence for a theory in physics may include facts about experimental equipment whose very names mean nothing to most of us; the evidence presented to a middle-class jury to show that a defendant has a criminal personality might be understood in a completely different way by people from a different social class. As a result, we often treat as empirical evidence facts that many people could reasonably disagree with.

Empiricism stresses the importance of empirical evidence, since the aim of empiricism is to get reliable beliefs by basing them on what we can learn by using our senses. As a result, these two facts about empirical evidence present a problem for empiricism. They suggest that it will not be easy to give empirical evidence for many of our commonsense beliefs, and they suggest that what we often take as empirical evidence is not completely neutral or unbiased. These are not unsolvable problems for the use of empirical evidence in science or everyday life. But they are problems for empiricism as a philosophical program, which aims to construct a whole system of beliefs founded almost entirely on unbiased empirical evidence.

In response to this problem, empiricists often focus on a very special kind of empirical evidence. They want to base our beliefs on evidence that is absolutely neutral, evidence that no one could doubt, whatever beliefs they had. There are two obvious question to ask here. Is there any such evidence? If there is, can we really base all our beliefs on it?

The ideas of the British Empiricists were meant to be absolutely unbiased empirical evidence. An "idea" was supposed to be no more than pure sensory experience – just what a person senses without any taint of their beliefs. These would form the safest possible evidence for beliefs and theories, since they would not have any possibly false built-in assumptions. Later empiricist philosophers, such as Bertrand Russell, talked about "sense data," which were also meant to be just the information received by a person's senses, without assuming any theories about what in the world is causing them or even if there is a world at all.

This project of founding all our beliefs on completely safe evidence is discussed in the next chapter. Until then, there are two important points to make.

The search for certainty may lead to doubt.   Suppose you think that it is only reasonable to believe something when it can be based on completely safe evidence, ideas or sense data, and you appreciate how hard it may be to find enough completely safe evidence to make it reasonable to hold our commonsense beliefs and our complex theories. Then you may suspect, or fear, that some of these beliefs are not reasonable. Perhaps there is not sufficient justification for believing that there is a physical world around us, or that people have minds, or that physics is true. Perhaps some of these are just myths or illusions. Or so one might suspect if one made these strong empiricist assumptions.

Empirical evidence does not have to be completely safe.   Much of the evidence on which scientific theories rest is not completely neutral. It often involves assumptions about how experimental apparatus works, about the truth of other theories, and about what suggestions are too ridiculous to consider. Evidence for a complicated theory in physics will usually take it for granted, for example, that telescopes work by focusing light, that energy is conserved, and that scientific data is not produced by gremlins playing with the equipment.

And outside science, when we present empirical evidence we usually have a particular audience in mind, and choose evidence accordingly. When presenting evidence for a defendant's guilt a prosecutor will not normally need to rule out the possibility that the defendant was being controlled by Martians, or that all the witnesses were victims of a mass hallucination. So both in science and in everyday life the evidence we use has a limited target: it is meant to defend a particular conclusion to particular people with particular beliefs. It is not absolutely neutral. But that does not make empirical evidence pointless: giving empirical evidence is still one of the most powerful methods we have of discovering truths and refuting falsehoods. But, powerful as it is, it has limits.

9.12 Adequate Evidence?

Fitting evidence to belief

HARDER

Below are three lists. (A) is a list of beliefs and theories. (B) is a list of sources of empirical evidence. (C) is a list of assumptions that would be taken for granted in using evidence from (B) to support or refute a belief from (A). For example belief (i) from (A) is "You had four grandparents." One source of evidence for this is (f) from (B): "reports of what others have seen," since even if you never met all of your grandparents, or were sure that they were your grandparents, others who are older than you can give you information about the past. Sources (c) and (d), "studies of human behavior" and "studies of animal behavior," are also relevant, since they provide evidence that humans, like most other animals, always have two parents, and that nearly all humans have four distinct grandparents (but not always, since sometimes parents are cousins). Using source (f), "reports of what others have seen," to support the belief that you had four grandparents takes for granted assumption (1), "What people say is generally true." If one doubted this then empirical evidence of this kind would not have much force. Similarly, sources (c) and (d) take for granted other assumptions from (C).

(A) BELIEFS

(i)   You had four grandparents.
(ii) Red-haired people feel the same pain sensations as brown-haired people.
(iii) The phases of the moon are caused by herds of mice migrating across it and grazing on cheese.
(iv) The universe is more than a million years old.
(v)   Tuberculosis is caused by a micro-organism.
(vi) When you go to sleep the houses, trees, and people around you continue to exist.

(B) Sources of empirical evidence

(a) data collected with astronomical instruments such as optical telescopes and radio telescopes;
(b) data about the spread of disease from one person to another;
(c) studies of human behavior;
(d) studies of animal behavior;
(e) reports of what people feel when stimulated in various ways;
(f) reports of what others have seen.

(C) Assumptions

(1) What people say is generally true.
(2) When people give similar descriptions of experiences, the experiences themselves are similar.
(3) Physics is at least approximately true.
(4) Medical science is at least approximately true.
(5) Telescopes work by focusing light that comes from an object, presenting an accurate image of that object.
(6) Humans and other animals share many fundamental features.
(7) $2 + 3 = 5$
(8) Other people's memories are not delusions.

You can write the connections between beliefs, sources of empirical evidence, and assumptions in the table. (The row for (i) has already been filled in.)

Belief	Sources of empirical evidence	Assumptions
(i)	(f), (c), (d)	(1) for (f), (7) for (f), (4) for (c), (6) for (d)
(ii)		
(iii)		
(iv)		
(v)		
(vi)		

Limits to evidence

Empiricists would like to have empirical evidence that does more than just support a belief given certain assumptions. They would also like to be able to support the assumptions. But sometimes this turns out not to be so easy to do. Many problems arise. A rough classification of the problems puts them into three groups.

◆ *Circles* Sometimes it is hard to give empirical evidence for a belief because much of the evidence one can find assumes that the belief is true.
◆ *Hitting bottom* Sometimes it is hard to find empirical evidence for an assumption because if you did not assume it was true you would be in no position to search for evidence.
◆ *Lack of alternatives* Sometimes it is hard to find empirical evidence for an assumption because it is hard to think what other assumptions one might make in its place.

For example, to find evidence for assumption (1) in list (C) above, you would have to ignore everything you have been told and everything people now say to you. This would mean doubting just about everything you believe. So here we have Circles, and Hitting bottom.

To find evidence for assumption (5) (telescopes work by focusing light that comes from an object, presenting an accurate image of that object), you would have to consider whether physics gives a correct account of how lenses work, but in doing this you would not be able to use any of the physics which is based on this assumption. So here we have Circles, and Lack of alternatives.

To find evidence for assumption (2) (when people give similar descriptions of experiences the experiences themselves are similar), you would have to find a way of knowing what people's experiences are like without relying on their descriptions of their experiences. You would have to know, for example, what different people experience when they say "It looks red" or "It smells like lavender." So here we have Circles, and Lack of alternatives.

To find evidence for assumption (7) ($2 + 3 = 5$), you would have to check up on arithmetic without using it. You could not use any science that depends on mathematics, and you would have to be very careful with the results of counting. So here we have Hitting bottom, and Lack of alternatives.

The conclusion to draw from this is that when we use evidence to support a belief there are always other beliefs which we are taking for granted. You hold on to some things while moving others. It does *not* follow from this that some of these background assumptions can never be confirmed or refuted. For the three problems described here are obstacles and not insuperable barriers. For example, you could find alternative theories of light and lenses, if you were thoughtful and patient enough. And perhaps someday we will find a direct way of knowing about people's experiences. But to confirm or refute these background beliefs we would have to use yet other background beliefs. We are always finding new ways of getting and using empirical evidence. The process never

HARDER   stops.

Conclusions of This Chapter

♦ *Empiricism is a collection of attitudes about when a person is justified in holding a belief. The main attitudes are a hostility to speculation, a friendliness to scientific theories based on perception, and a suspicion of concepts that are not derived from experience. These attitudes are all different, and it is possible to have any one of them and not the others.*

♦ *British Empiricism centers on the concept of an idea, which applies to both beliefs and concepts. If this kind of empiricism is right, we get all our concepts by combining concepts we get from experience.*

♦ *Empirical evidence is important in science and in many other fields. But in science we do not usually require the evidence for a theory to be completely certain.*

♦ *A very strong empiricism, such as British Empiricism, will have difficulty explaining why beliefs such as the belief that there is a physical world around us which causes our sensations, or that people have minds which cause their behavior, are justified.*

Further Reading

British empiricists

Selections from Hume and Locke in Part I of John Cottingham (ed.), *Western Philosophy: An Anthology*. Blackwell, 1996.

David Hume, *An Inquiry concerning Human Understanding*, chapters 2 and 3 (also 7 and 12), in *Hume's Enquiries*, edited by A. Selby-Bigge. Oxford University Press, 1966.

John Locke, *An Essay on Human Nature*, Books I, II, edited by Peter Nidditch. Oxford University Press, 1975; see also Roger Woolhouse, *The Empiricists*. Oxford University Press, 1988.

Roger Woolhouse, "Locke," in *The Blackwell Companion to Philosophy*.

Empiricism

Chapters 2 and 5 of Adam Morton, *A Guide through the Theory of Knowledge*, third edition. Blackwell, 2002.

Chapter 10, sections A and B, of John Cottingham, *Rationalism*. Oxford University Press, 1988.

*Chapters 6 and 10 of Jonathan Dancy, *An Introduction to Contemporary Epistemology*. Basil Blackwell, 1988.

Electronic resources

Routledge Encyclopedia of Philosophy (available online at many universities): articles on Empiricism; Hume, David; Locke, John.

Stanford Encyclopedia of Philosophy (http://plato.stanford.edu/): Concepts; *Locke, John*; Perception; *Perception, epistemological problems of* (*italicized* items are available as this book goes to press; the others should be available soon).

10 Beyond Empiricism

Introduction

Outside ethics, an influential way of responding to changing evidence is described by empiricism. Empiricism tries to provide beliefs that are based in a reasonable way on evidence, while keeping the risk of error at a minimum. It does this by considering only evidence which concerns what we perceive and allowing only beliefs that use concepts based on perception.

Empiricism has difficulty explaining why many commonsense and scientific beliefs are reasonable. For example, it makes it hard to understand why it is reasonable to believe that other people have minds and experiences like yours. More powerful ways of basing beliefs on evidence are provided by the inference to the best explanation, the falsificational method, and the hypothetico-deductive method. These are all attempts to describe the kinds of reasoning used in science.

From the debate between utilitarianism and Kantian ethics, and from the problems of empiricism, we can see ways of responding to the false-belief trap of Part I.::::

Chapter Objectives

By the end of this chapter you should be able to answer the following questions:

❖ What is the difference between accuracy and informativeness?
❖ How does empiricism try to solve the other minds problem with the argument from analogy?
❖ What is folk psychology, and how does it give another solution to the other minds problem?
❖ What is the inference to the best explanation?
❖ How does Popper's criterion of falsification characterize scientific belief?

Definitions

The following words used in this chapter are defined in the list of definitions at the end of the book:

accuracy	falsificational strategy	hypothetico-deductive method
falsifiable	folk psychology	informativeness

10.1 Risk of What?

It is time to look back, both at the history of philosophy and at the ideas developed in this book. Part I began with a search for certainty about the world and about morals. In order to avoid the false-belief trap, the danger that we might be caught in a closed system of false beliefs, each supporting the others, philosophers have wanted to find ways of getting beliefs that minimized the risk of falsehood. Rationalists want to do this by basing our beliefs on our capacity for logical thought. Empiricists want to do this by basing our beliefs on perception. Each program runs into problems (described in Chapters 3, 5, 6, and 9). It is hard now to see how by basing our beliefs either on reason or on perception, or even by carefully combining the two, we will avoid all danger that some of our beliefs might be false.

But consider how different things must have seemed to philosophers in earlier times. In particular, consider philosophers in the early days of the scientific revolution, between the time of Galileo and the time of Hume. On the one hand they hoped that careful use of reasoning and evidence would give them something better than the commonsense and traditional beliefs of most people in their times. On the other hand they did not have very much to show as an example of what reason and evidence could supply. Science was for them a dream.

Things look different now. Science is not for us a dream but a central part of our lives. It gives us many of our beliefs. But it is different from the philosophers' dream in three ways.

First, we have a large body of scientific beliefs, which are based on evidence and form the background that allows more evidence to be discovered and evaluated. Partly because of the ideas of rationalist and empiricist philosophers, we have physics, chemistry, and biology. And as a result we have engineering, electronics, and medicine.

Second, we find that these beliefs are *not* certain. They are the latest in a succession of scientific accounts of the world, and we expect that they will be replaced by future scientific theories. (*Better* theories, say science-lovers. *Different* theories, say more skeptical souls.)

Third, we find that the methods that have given us science have left many of our beliefs unchanged. We cannot solve Descartes' problem of giving scientific reasons to show that there is a physical world around us and that other people have minds like our own. We cannot solve Hume's problem of showing how often induction will give us true conclusions. And we do not have a morality based on reason and evidence.

So, in retrospect, it seems that something is right and something is wrong with the original search for certainty. Even in its modified form, as a search for beliefs that are as certain as possible, it does not seem to fit what it is reasonable for human beings to want.

To begin thinking this out, concentrate on *risk*. In searching for a method for finding and testing beliefs, rationalism and empiricism both want to take as few risks as possible. But risks of what? Here are four possibilities:

(a) risk that the beliefs the method first gives us will be false;

but notice that this is not the same as:

(b) risk that the beliefs the method eventually leads us to will be false.

Another kind of risk is:

(c) risk that we may have false beliefs on any subject;

but notice that this is not the same as:

(d) risk that we may not have true beliefs on subjects of interest to us.

Rationalists and empiricists write as if they were trying to minimize (a)-type and (c)-type risk. They are terrified of falsehood, and they want their methods to be as *accurate* as possible. In fact, they ignore the differences between (a) and (b), and between (c) and (d), since their optimism leads them to think that on all topics they can get beliefs that are so clearly right that they will never need to be changed. This seems almost childishly optimistic to us now, especially with respect to moral beliefs.

The purpose of this chapter is to show the advantages of minimizing (b)-type and (d)-type type risk. That is, to show that besides wanting accurate beliefs we can also want *informative* ones, beliefs which now and in the future will give us information we need.

> If we want informative beliefs we may have to accept less accurate ones.

Most contemporary philosophers think that in order to get informative beliefs we have to take the risk of less accurate ones. This chapter gives some of the reasons why contemporary philosophers think this. It will concentrate on two weak points of the search for accuracy: our beliefs about other people's minds and the way scientific beliefs are continually changing. Moral beliefs will wait until the next chapter.

10.2 Accuracy versus Informativeness about Friendship

To strive for accuracy is to want to have as few false beliefs as possible. To strive for informativeness is to want to have as many true beliefs as possible. The contrast between them is clearest if we have a particular topic in mind. For example, suppose you have bought a guide book for a country that you will be visiting. You want to know whether it is a good guide. There are two ways in which it could be a good source of information. In the first place, it could have no mistakes in it. It won't tell you that the weather is always sunny when actually there are often blizzards and thunderstorms. That is accuracy. But an accurate book could still be a pretty poor guide if, although it told you nothing false, it didn't tell you the facts you wanted to know. Suppose you want to know what kind of weather is typical, whether it is safe to walk in the streets at night, and whether the water is drinkable, and the book just tells you the name of the president and the districts of the capital city. It could be accurate about all those things and yet be a pretty poor guide because it did not give you answers to the questions you were most concerned about. It could be accurate without being informative.

One source of information is more *accurate* than another on a given topic if whenever it tells you something about that topic it will be more often right than the other. And a source of information is more *informative* than another on a given topic if, whatever the facts are about that topic, it is more likely to tell you that they are that way. In effect, a more accurate method gives you fewer falsehoods (perhaps at the price of very few answers), and a more informative method gives you more truths (perhaps at the price of a few falsehoods).

Below, five people worry about what other people (or animals) think. Each uses a method to find out. Which methods are more accurate, and which are more informative?

❖ Art wants to know which of the people he treats as friends really like him. The method is to ask them "Do you like me?" and then to believe what they say.

❖ Bert wants to know which of the people he treats as friends really like him. His method is to subject a few of them to a long series of tests. For example, he pretends to disagree with them and sees how they react; he hides and listens to conversations between them and other people; and so on.

❖ Chris wants to know which of the people she knows but is not friends with might be friends. Her method with such a person is to find a friend of hers who is also a friend of that person, and then to ask her what she likes about him or her. If what the friend likes is what she likes about her friends, she believes that that person could be a friend of hers.

❖ Di wants to know which of the people she treats as friends really despise her. Her method is to assume that they do despise her unless they act in such a definitely friendly way as to disprove it.

❖ Ernie wants to know which human thoughts are shared by cats. The method is to look for a human-type thought which would make sense of each action that a cat performs. If such a thought is found then he supposes that that is what the cat is thinking.

Art's method is not very accurate. Someone who does not like him will very likely lie to him, so he will get a false belief about that person. If Art's friends really are friends it is likely to be fairly informative, since they will truly say "Yes, I like you." (But if he is surrounded by lying enemies it will be as uninformative as it is inaccurate.) Is Bert's method more accurate than Art's? Is it more informative?

Is Chris's method more or less accurate than Bert's? (That is, is it less or more likely to give false results?) Is it more or less informative?

Di's method is clearly not very accurate, unless she is surrounded by false friends. Under what conditions might it be informative?

Ernie's method is not extremely accurate. That is, he will surely end up with a fair number of false beliefs about cat thoughts. But how informative is it? (How many true beliefs will he get?)

Judging from these examples, when your aim is to know about other people's attitudes to you, what are the advantages and disadvantages of an accurate method? What are the advantages and disadvantages of an informative method?

10.3 Other Minds

Empiricism can run into trouble when it tries to give reasons for some of our most familiar beliefs. Consider our beliefs about other people's minds. We often have beliefs about people's moods and emotions, for example, that they are sad or angry. We have beliefs about what they think and want, for example, that they believe in God or want a cup of coffee. And behind all these we have very general beliefs about what it is to be a person: we believe that each person has their own mind with their own experience, and that much of what they do is because of what they believe and want and value. We think that people have minds. Most people think that many animals have minds – though they disagree about exactly which animals do – and that stones and trees do not have minds.

These certainly seem like reasonable beliefs. There does not seem to be much of a chance that they are wrong. It seems incredible that, for example, you might be the only person in the world with a mind or that people's actions are not the result of what they think and feel. But empiricism has trouble making a clear case why these are incredible possibilities. There are two reasons for this.

First, for empiricism a mind is first of all given by its ideas: images, auditory sensations, real or imagined smells, and so on. In terms of these we construct our more complex thoughts. So to know another person's mind you have to know what ideas that person is conscious of. But your evidence for this is very different from ideas. All you have to go on is their *behavior*: their actions and their involuntary movements. (Speech is just another piece of behavior. Facial expressions and eye movements are just behavior. Everything has to be interpreted.) So your evidence is made up of things like people hitting their thumbs with hammers and then jumping around with interesting sounds coming out of their mouths. This is very different from what we believe to be in their minds, namely pain, surprise, and anger.

Second, the kinds of reasoning empiricism allows are very limited. Empiricism allows reasoning that begins with empirical evidence and goes on to conclusions that go beyond the evidence as little as possible. Reasoning by simple induction is a good example of such reasoning. Suppose then that our evidence is that whenever a person hits their thumb with a hammer he or she jumps around and makes loud noises. The least speculative conclusion to draw is simply that when people hit their thumbs with hammers they jump around and make loud noises. To infer that they are in pain or that the noises have meanings related to that pain would be to go a long way beyond the evidence.

From the point of view of empiricism, then, there is a problem explaining why our beliefs about other people's minds are not wild speculation. It is called the *other minds problem*. You can feel the force of the other minds problem as long as you think that all your evidence about other people concerns just what they do, while what you want to know about them concerns what they think and feel.

> Empiricism generates the other minds problem, and tries to solve it with the argument from analogy. This is not a very convincing solution.

If you think this way, other people will seem very remote from you. And in some moods other people do seem very remote. While we usually find ourselves attributing states of mind to other people pretty automatically, every now and then, for example, when we are tired or depressed, it becomes more difficult to do this, and other people seem remote and robot-like. A kind of paranoia creeps over us. It is not too unusual for children to have fantasies that the people around them are robots, or are hiding important facts from them, or that their apparently loving parents are really indifferent to them. All this is evidence of the psychological power of the other minds problem.

Empiricists have an answer to the problem. It is the argument from analogy. It runs as follows. You know what ideas occur in your own mind, and you can observe your own behavior. As a result you can notice correlations between your own behavior and your own ideas. For example, you can notice a pattern of bringing a hammer down on your thumb, followed by the sensation of pain, followed by waving the thumb in the air and producing interesting language. So you can reason by simple induction to the conclusion that whenever you bring a hammer down on your thumb the first result is pain and the second result is a waving of the thumb and violent language. Then you can observe that other people sometimes hit their thumbs with hammers and then wave their thumbs in the air while cursing. So you extend your inductive generalization to conclude that in all people the pattern is: hammer on thumb, pain, cursing. So you have reason to believe that other people feel pain just as you do.

This is not a very convincing argument. If someone *really* believed that other people did not have experiences like their own they would not find their belief seriously challenged by it. Think first of the two stages of inductive reasoning. Each of them has problems. The first – to the conclusion that simple patterns connecting behavior and sensation are found in your own experience – needs there to be such patterns, without exceptions, in your own experience. But in fact such simple patterns are pretty rare. Sometimes the hammer hurts a lot and sometimes hardly at all. Sometimes you jump up and down and curse and sometimes you just hit the next nail extra hard. The second stage – from a generalization about one's own experience to a generalization about other people – is just as bad. It too is affected by the variability of behavior. And in addition it involves an enormous leap from one small class of events – your own behavior and sensations – to another very different class – those of someone else. What reason is there for believing that the same generalizations hold among these different events? It is like discovering, say, how far iron expands when heated, and then concluding that copper will expand by the same amount.

10.4 Testing the Argument from Analogy

The argument from analogy can be summarized as follows:

> **On many occasions I have had S in my mind followed by behavior B.**
> **Therefore S is always followed by behavior B.**
> **Therefore behavior B is always preceded by S.**
> **Often I observe that others exhibit behavior B.**
> **Therefore others have S when they exhibit behavior B.**

(S can be anything that a person can know is in their own mind, for example, a sensation, an emotion, or a thought.)

One question about the argument from analogy is: how much do we use reasoning like it in getting our conclusions about other people's minds? Each of the mini-stories below is relevant to this question. Consider two ways in which they could be relevant.

(a) Some show a situation in which we use something like the argument from analogy.
(b) Some show that we sometimes reason in ways that are very different from the argument from analogy.

Which of the following mini-stories are relevant in which ways?

(i)   You have made soup for a guest. The guest takes one sip and immediately her face puckers up. You think: "Oh oh. Too much salt."

(ii) You have two friends, George and Helen. George behaves in a very strange way to Helen. He waits for hours in places where Helen is likely to be, and then when she arrives he is rude and unpleasant to her. You have never behaved like this yourself, but you read in a psychology book that repressed love can reveal itself in aggressive behavior.

(iii) You are walking out of your front door and you see that your neighbor is sitting on his doorstep, weeping. You immediately think that something awful must have happened to someone he loves.

(iv) You have two friends, George and Helen. George behaves in a very strange way to Helen. He waits for hours in places where Helen is likely to be, and then when she arrives he is rude and unpleasant to her. You remember that once you were strongly attracted to someone without knowing it, and acted in a similar way.

Another question is how accurate or informative the argument from analogy is. Below are three new mini-stories. They can

(c)   Show that the argument from analogy can give false conclusions. (So it has problems about accuracy.)

(d)   Show that the argument from analogy can miss true conclusions. (So it has problems about informativeness.)

Which of the following mini-stories are relevant to (c) and which ones to (d)? To decide this you have to think what one person in the story would want to know about another person. Then you have to see what the argument from analogy would make them think was in the other person's mind. If what the argument from analogy suggests is false then it has a problem with accuracy.

If it gives no answer (especially when some other method would give a true answer) then it has a problem with informativeness.

(v)   You want your professor to give you an extension on an assignment. So you come to her with tears streaming down your face and looking as if you have not slept for days and explain that your parents and siblings have just been killed in a car crash. The professor is overcome with sympathy and gives you a month's extension.

(vi) Liz and Phil are very different. She is very interested in motorcycles. In fact she finds everything in life depressing except riding motorcycles. Phil is interested in nothing but violin music. One day Phil is walking to a concert when Liz stops her motorbike and waves at him. He is puzzled why she looks so happy.

(vii) You have a friend who is extremely musical. When he hears a note he knows immediately what note it is. When he hears music that is even slightly out of tune it hurts him. You and he are at a concert and the music sounds fine to you but he winces as if someone had stuck a pin into him.

10.5 Folk Psychology: the Argument from Explanation

Empiricism has problems explaining our belief that other people have minds, and our beliefs about what they are thinking and feeling in their minds. The difficulties come from a way of thinking in which you start from within your mind, assume that you understand what you are thinking and feeling, and then try to judge from other people's behavior if they are thinking and feeling similar things. But that first assumption, that it is clear to you what is in your own mind, may be a mistake. Your own behavior and your own thoughts and feelings may be in some ways as puzzling to you as those of others.

The basic fact is that all human behavior can be pretty mysterious. And trying to understand why people do things is a basic human aim, partly because we need to know what people are likely to do next, and partly because we need to know people's character and trustworthiness. (And partly just because otherwise we would be so puzzled by each other.) People's behavior is often mysterious to themselves, too. We lessen the mystery by learning to explain what people do. As children learn how to get along with others they learn a lot of rules, principles, and theories about how people work. They learn when people are likely to get angry, what kinds of things people are likely to notice or overlook, what kinds of things people try very hard to get, and so on. You wouldn't survive in kindergarten without knowing a lot of this. And as children learn these things, they find that they understand some of their own feelings and behavior.

An example. You are walking across the room with a coin in your hand, approaching a coffee machine. A friend is watching you; someone asks her "Why is that person walking across the room?" Your friend says "To get a coffee." And this prediction is based partly on knowing what people usually do and partly on knowing that you like coffee. If this explanation is doubted they may ask you "Why are you going over there?" And your reply is "I wanted a cup of coffee and I'm going to get it from the machine."

What your friend says about you in this example is the same as what you say about yourself. And the reasons you have for what you say are very similar to the reasons your friend has. You too know that the most likely reason why you are walking in the direction of the coffee machine, digging a coin out of your pocket, is that you want a cup of coffee. And you too have noticed that you often want a cup of coffee at that time of day. So when you are asked why you are walking across the room you may answer so quickly that you do not even notice what your reasons are. (It is true that you may have some information that your friend does not. You may be aware of sensations of thirst and caffeine withdrawal. But your friend may have some information that you do not have. Your regular craving for coffee at that time of day may be something which is obvious to your friends but something that you find it hard to acknowledge, perhaps because you do not want to admit how much coffee you drink.)

What examples like this suggest, together with facts about how children and adults ascribe states of mind to themselves and others, is that we make sense of what people do by comparing their actions to standard patterns we have learned. These standard patterns are like outlines of stories, for example, stories about how someone gets angry when they don't get what they want and then works off their anger on someone else. And they are also like rough theories, for example, the theory that people deceive themselves about many of their motives. Philosophers call this mixture of stories, theories, and rules *folk psychology*. People use folk psychology in everyday life to explain why other people do things. They also use it to explain why they themselves do things. In both cases we often do not notice that we are using folk psychology. We just say "He is angry at me because I took his parking space" or "I am upset because I didn't get the job I applied for," as if these things were perfectly obvious.

What does all this have to do with empiricism? Empiricism tries to explain our beliefs about other people's minds in terms of the evidence we can get from our senses, and that means our observations of their behavior plus our sensations of our own minds. But it turns out that it is very hard to justify these beliefs in terms of just this evidence. It isn't enough. And in everyday life we do not base our beliefs about other people just on this evidence. We also use folk psychology. We observe a person's behavior, interpret it in terms of folk psychology plus our own experience, and then use folk psychology to give the best explanation of the behavior. For example, in mini-story (vii) of the previous section you are at a concert with an extremely musical friend. The music sounds fine to you but he winces. You cannot tell from analogy with your own experience why he winces, but using folk psychology you can explain his behavior as the reaction to qualities of the music that you cannot hear. You can appeal to principles of folk psychology like "some people can hear things other people cannot" and "when people experience things that seem ugly to them they make faces." These may not be things you know from your own experience, but you can learn them from folk psychology, your culture's collected knowledge of our minds.

When we use folk psychology we explain people's actions in terms of their beliefs, desires, emotions, and other states of mind. We suppose that people really do have all these states of mind because we have no other way of explaining what they do. If we did not think that they cry because they are sad, get angry because they are frustrated, make friends because they want cooperation and affection, and so on, we would find their behavior completely mystifying. There are two sides to this. One side is that each of us draws on a fund of beliefs that we get from other people. The other side is that each of us, like the whole culture we draw on, holds many beliefs because they explain things that need explaining. This idea, that we are justified in believing things because they explain things that would otherwise be mysterious, is an important one. This chapter and the next will explore its power and its limitations.

10.6 Being Wrong about Yourself

If we use folk psychology instead of the argument from analogy we attribute to people the states of mind that make most sense of their behavior. You can think this way to attribute states to others, and you can also think this way to attribute states to yourself. Sometimes the explanation you get of someone's behavior is not the same as the reason they would give. (Sometimes the explanation someone else will give of your behavior is not the same as the reason you would give.) Can people be wrong about their own minds? (Can you be wrong about your own mind?)

Imagine a typical person and their typical best friend. Call the person P and the friend F. Some things about someone it is hard for even their best friend to know. And some things a person's best friend can know more easily than the person themselves can. And some things both a person and their best friend can easily be wrong about. Suppose that P and F each give answers to each of the questions below.

(a) Is P a generous person?
(b) Is what P feels toward some other person love or lust?
(c) Is P in pain at the moment?
(d) Is P's pain as bad as some other person's pain?
(e) Does P believe in God?
(f) Is P's claim to believe (or disbelieve) in God deep faith or social posturing?

For which of these would you:

(i)   trust what P says more than what F says?
(ii) trust what F says more than what P says?
(iii) trust neither what P says nor what F says?
(iv) trust either P or F depending on some other fact about them? (What other fact?)

When you consider the answers you and others have given to these questions, you may find that you agree on some and not on others. (The love/lust question seems to be a confusing one. It divides people who agree on the other questions. Why might this be?) You may well find that some of your disagreements come down to a competition between relying on the argument from analogy and relying on folk psychology. If you rely on the argument from analogy you think that people are generally right about their own experiences and behavior and project the connections between these onto others. If you rely on folk psychology (the argument from explanation) you think that the best way we have of knowing about someone's mind is by seeing what best explains what they do; and it is sometimes hard for someone to see the best explanations of their own actions.

10.7 The Inference to the Best Explanation

Empiricism embodies a low-risk strategy: stick to the perceptual data. It is low-risk in the sense that it avoids the danger of immediate false beliefs. But there is a price to pay for playing it so safe. The other minds problem suggests that by avoiding false beliefs so strenuously it gives a high risk of not giving us enough true beliefs to get on with our lives. Perhaps a strategy that accepted a greater danger that some of its results would be false would have a greater chance of giving some useful truths.

Crazy high-risk strategies are easy to think of. For example: believe whatever comes into your head, believe whatever your guru tells you, believe whatever gives you most spiritual consolation. But though these strategies may give you many beliefs, and many of them may guide you through life, there is not much chance that many of them will be true. The reward for accepting the possibility of some false beliefs was to be a greater chance of useful *true* beliefs. Non-crazy strategies that raise the chance of getting true useful beliefs are not that easy to describe.

One such strategy is the inference to the best explanation. It can be described as a simple rule for acquiring beliefs:

> **If you have a body of data which needs explanation, and a theory that (a) explains the data, and (b) explains it better than any alternative explanation, then you should believe the theory.**

Using folk psychology to explain our beliefs about minds is an instance of the inference to the best explanation, where the data is people's behavior and the theory is folk psychology. We need explanations of why people do the things they do, and the "theory" that people have beliefs, desires, and emotions allows us to make explanations of these things.

The inference to the best explanation is more powerful, but also more risky, than pure empiricism.

A similar case can be made for many of our beliefs. Each of us believes that there is a world of physical objects around us, which exist in space and persist through time and cause our perceptions of them. We have these beliefs because we are human beings to whom these beliefs come naturally, and because we grow up in contact with other human minds that communicate these beliefs to us.

But the reason it is not unreasonable to believe in a physical world is that it makes sense of our experience in a way that is completely necessary to us, and for which we have no substitute.

Science builds on our belief in a world of physical objects. It develops on that basis a whole set of beliefs about the structure of matter. We believe that material objects are made up of molecules, which are made up of atoms, which are made up of electrons, neutrons, and protons, which are made up of quarks. It is not easy to justify these beliefs in strict empiricist terms, beginning with perception and reasoning by simple induction alone. For one thing, to express these beliefs one has to use concepts like "energy," "electromagnetic field," and so on, which have no obvious definitions in terms of perception. Another, closely related, reason is that these beliefs seem to do a lot more than just sum up regularities in our experience. They also describe complex unobservable structures and events.

There are two important contrasts with pure empiricism here. First, the *concepts need not be empirical.* Empiricism requires that all the concepts that make up our beliefs should be defined in terms of experience. (See Section 9, and also Sections 8 and 10.) The inference to the best explanation, on the other hand, does not care where the concepts come from, as long as the explanation that uses them is a good one. They can come from experience, but they can also come from the society around us, from previous theories, or anywhere at all.

Secondly, *background beliefs matter.* That is, whether the inference to the best explanation supports a belief depends on what other beliefs you have. Suppose, for example, you have a better explanation of human behavior than folk psychology. Perhaps you can explain what people do in terms of what happens in their brains, without having to talk about beliefs, desires, and emotions. Or perhaps you can treat people as complex robots, following the commands of some computer program. If you have such a better explanation, or even if you just think you have, you do not need to believe in folk psychology. Background beliefs – the whole pattern of beliefs against which a particular belief makes sense – are also a source of the concepts used in explanations.

These two features of the inference to the best explanation – the freedom from empirical concepts and the importance of background beliefs – work together to allow really complicated beliefs, which go a long way beyond the empirical evidence. For example, consider theories about heat. They begin as simple commonsense beliefs about hot things and cold things, and how things get hotter or colder by contact with hot or cold things. Then physics uses this as a background in order to develop thermodynamics, a mathematical description of the difference between heat and temperature and of the way heat flows and distributes itself in physical systems. This uses commonsense concepts such as "heat" but mixes them together with concepts (such as "entropy") invented just for the theory. But this then combines with the theory that matter is made up of molecules, to give the theory that heat and temperature are consequences of the motion of the molecules of matter. Heat is the total kinetic energy of the molecules of a substance, and temperature is their average kinetic energy. By this time, the theory has got a long way from its commonsense origin, and a long way from empirical evidence – further than empiricism would allow.

The advantages of the inference to the best explanation are pretty clear. It allows us to justify beliefs involving much richer concepts than pure empiricism will allow us. And this makes it possible to justify beliefs about invisible causes of things we can perceive. If the world is a sufficiently complex place we will have to go beyond the resources of empiricism if we want to have beliefs about much of it.

The disadvantages are equally clear. It's riskier. There is the risk, as with inductive reasoning, of making the wrong predictions about future observations. And there are additional risks. Even if the predictions are true, the theory, for all its explanatory power, may be false. And it may be false in the most fundamental of ways: the concepts it uses may correspond to nothing in reality. In past ages people believed that fevers were caused by poisonous air, that demons caused madness, and that one person's curse can cause another person's bad luck. None of these is true, according to present-day beliefs. Fevers have different causes, bad luck has no cause, and there are no demons. But at least some such beliefs were the best explanations available at the time of various obvious phenomena. So perhaps "entropy" and "kinetic energy" are like "demon." We cannot be completely sure that they are not.

So false beliefs can be good explanations too, and sometimes they can give the best explanations available. Still, this does not show that it is not reasonable to hold a belief because of what it can explain. The job of explaining the world around you is like any other task: you have to use the best tools available. If you want to cut down a tree and a chainsaw is not available (perhaps because it has not been invented yet) then you will have to use an ax, or perhaps a sharpened flint; if you want to predict the phases of the moon and you don't have modern astronomy then a theory of the relation between the moon goddess and the spirit of the night may be your best tool. You have to use what you've got. But you ought to use the *best* of what you've got.

10.8 Explanation

The *inference to the best explanation* says:

> **If you have a body of data which needs explanation, and a theory that (a) explains the data, and (b) explains it better than any alternative explanation, then you should believe the theory.**

But what is an explanation? If you wonder why it is dark at night and someone tells you "because the sun gets tired of shining," that is not much of an explanation. Perhaps it is no explanation at all. At any rate, it is a very weak explanation, so it should be easy to find a better one.

In each of the five cases below there is some data and an explanation. Some of the explanations are terrible ones, while others do give acceptable reasons why the phenomena may have occurred.

(1) *The data*: **After being the dominant species on earth for millions of years, the dinosaurs became extinct in a relatively short space of time.**
An explanation: **Nothing lasts for ever. Every species, like every individual animal, has its time on earth which must eventually end.**

(2) *The data*: **There are eclipses of the sun. Sometimes in the day when the sun is above the horizon it becomes dark and all or part of the sun is no longer visible.**
An explanation: **The sun is a giant glowing flower in the sky. There is a dragon who longs for this flower and stretches out his tongue towards it. After completely or partially surrounding the flower its bitter taste repels the dragon who withdraws his tongue. But eventually the dragon forgets and tries again.**

(3) *The data*: **There are five continents (North America, South America, Eurasia, Australia, Antarctica).**
An explanation: **The human race is the dominant species on earth, and we have five senses (vision, hearing, touch, taste, smell). Moreover, there are five basic colors (red, yellow, blue, green, white.) And most animals have five limbs (front legs, back legs, tail). So most things come in fives.**

(4) *The data*: **The sun rises every morning in the east, and during the morning gets steadily higher in the sky and further to the south (in the northern hemisphere), then in the afternoon sinks towards the west.**
An explanation: **The shadow of the CN Tower in Toronto stretches to the west in the morning, shrinks and turns toward the north during the morning, and in the afternoon grows and turns to the east. Light travels from the sun to the tower in straight lines, so given these morning, noon, and afternoon, positions of the shadow, the sun has to follow its morning, noon, and afternoon motions.**

(5) *The data*: **Often when you turn up the hot water control in a shower there is at first a rush of cold water.**

An explanation: **When you turn up the hot water control a greater pressure of hot water enters the pipe leading to the shower head. The first effect of this pressure is to force colder water already in the pipe to rush out of the shower head.**

Classify the above explanations in order of value as explanations. Some may be terrible explanations or not be explanations at all. Some may explain the data but be very weak explanations, so that there could easily be a better explanation. Some may be good explanations, which you might consider believing. Mark your reactions with a tick in the table.

Example	Terrible	Weak	Good
1			
2			
3			
4			
5			

Compare your classifications with those of others. But do not discuss them yet.

There are several very different reasons why an explanation can be less than good.

(i)   The data it claims to explain may not be true.
(ii) The theories it appeals to may not be true.
(iii) It may not connect with important features of the data.
(iv) It may not give causes of the data.
(v)   There may be better explanations of the same data.
(vi) There can be no explanation of this data.

The first two of these reasons are rather different from the rest. The data or the theory could be false and still it could be that if they were true the theory would explain the data. The last three reasons are really reasons why one explanation is better or worse than another, as an explanation.

For each of the explanations (1 to 5) that you classified as "terrible" or "weak" in your table, mark on the table which of the six reasons, (i) to (vi) above, apply. (In some cases more than one reason may apply.) Write the appropriate number, (i) to (vi), beside the tick you have already put in the table.

Now compare your table with those of other people. When you disagree about the value of an explanation do you also disagree about which of the reasons (i) to (vi) apply?

10.9 Justifying Astrology

Here is a defense of astrology, appealing to the inference to the best explanation.

> **Astrology explains very many things. It explains why people have good and bad days, why some couples are good couples and others not, and what days are good and bad for romance. It explains why some people's investments succeed at some times while other people's fail. These are things that we obviously need explanations of. And science will not give us explanations of them. (Try using physics to explain why an apparently well-matched couple hate each other at first sight.) And in fact if you want guidance about when you should make business ventures, or how to avoid disasters in romance, there is no theory which gives you more advice than astrology. So it is the best tool for the job and we should accept it.**

Some might take this argument to show that there is something wrong with the inference to the best explanation. But is it a convincing argument? Think about the following reactions to it.

(a) The argument depends on a false assumption: astrology does not explain business and romantic success.
(b) The argument depends on a false assumption: astrology is not a reliable guide for business and romance.
(c) Even if astrology does explain success in business and romance it is not the best explanation of them. Other mystical theories are better.
(d) Even if astrology does explain success in business and romance it is not the best explanation of them. Only a scientific theory could be good enough.
(e) Some things do not have any explanations, because they are due to chance. So we should not accept any theory that claims to explain them.
(f) The argument is basically correct. We should accept astrology as an explanation of success and failure in romance and business.

When you have considered or discussed these you will be in a better position to judge how much the argument about astrology should make you doubt the value of the inference to the best explanation. Here are four possible conclusions. Each one is linked to one or more of the six reactions above. Which conclusions seem to be best supported?

(i) Reasoning by the inference to the best explanation requires us to understand what explanations are best. But this is often not something that we do know. (Link to (a), (b), (c). Do you know how well other explanations of success and failure work?)

(ii) The best explanation is the one that fits best with the rest of what we believe. So the inference to the best explanation will usually be very conservative, reinforcing whatever happens to be the orthodox point of view. (Link to (d), (f). Astrologers and scientists have different background beliefs.)

(iii) Reasoning by the inference to the best explanation is essentially speculative: it allows conclusions that the evidence does not really show to be true. (Link to (e), (f). Anything that allows astrology must be pretty permissive.)

(iv) There is a big difference between what it is useful to accept as a device to achieve some purpose, and what we really think is true. The best explanation is more likely to be a useful device than a description of the true facts. (Link to (b), (c), (e). People accept astrology because of their needs rather than because they have good evidence for it.)

10.10 Inference to the Best Explanation versus Simple Induction

HARDER

Reasoning by induction is meant to be cautious. It is intended not to take many risks of getting false conclusions. The inference to the best explanation, on the other hand, allows more risky conclusions if they provide a means of explaining things we want to explain. That is the general idea, anyway; but when you look at detailed cases the picture seems less simple. Consider the following.

(1) The world annual emissions of ozone-depleting gases (in thousands of tonnes) at five-year intervals over 40 years were (somewhat smoothed out) as follows

year	1955	1960	1965	1970	1975	1980	1985	1990	1995
amount	80	190	320	400	500	580	700	800	880

The pattern is roughly that every five years the amount of ozone-depleting gases emitted into the atmosphere increases by 95,000 tonnes. At this rate, by the year 2020 more than 1,400,000 tonnes of ozone-depleting gases will be emitted. But this is an absurd conclusion.

(2) Suppose that the following were the case. There is in many people a genetic predisposition to contract lung cancer. People with some inherited

characteristics are – on this hypothesis – more likely to get lung cancer than people without them. A side effect of this predisposition is a tendency to nicotine addiction. As a result, many of the same people smoke and get lung cancer. But – on this hypothesis – it is not because they smoke that they get lung cancer, any more than it is because women lack beards that they bear children. Rather, the same people have a tendency to both.

(3) A child, Archie, has a favorite toy. He is playing with this toy when he wishes that his cruel aunt would die. She dies almost immediately. Archie grows up to be a frustrated and bitter man. One day he finds his favorite toy in an old trunk. He immediately wishes his wife to die in a car crash, and she does. He then wishes for his mistress to die in a fire, and she does. And so on: over a period of several years Archie's woman-hating wishes made in the presence of the toy are followed by the deaths of the women concerned, though there is no apparent connection between the wishes and the deaths, or one death and another. (Based on Luis Buñuel's film *The Criminal Life of Archibaldo de la Cruz*.)

Suppose in each case the facts are as stated. (Actually, only (1) is factual. There is no reason to believe (2), and (3) is fiction.) Imagine someone given the data in each case (about ozone-depleting emissions, or the proportion of smokers who contract lung cancer, or the correlation between Archie's wishes and women's deaths). Suppose (a) that this person reasons in accordance with simple inductive reasoning, and (b) that this person reasons in accordance with the inference to the best explanation. What conclusions will they come to in each case? In which cases will each kind of reasoning give a believable conclusion?

In thinking about this you can use the following descriptions of the two kinds of reasoning.

♦ *Simple induction*: When a pattern is repeated in many instances in the data and there are no exceptions to it, conclude that the pattern will be found in all future data.
♦ *Inference to the best explanation*: When a theory explains all the available data and explains it better than any available alternative theory, conclude that the theory is true.

You may also want to consider what conclusions someone reasoning about the data in the three cases would come to if they used a method even more cautious than simple induction, for example:

♦ *Minimal induction*: If your evidence is that a certain number of things of one kind have a particular property, and you know of nothing of that kind that does not have that property, then conclude that the next object you find of that kind will probably have that property.

Which of the following conclusions are supported by your reflection on these examples?

(a) Seeing patterns in the data is not the same as seeing why those patterns occur.
(b) We cannot decide what method to use in understanding the world without some idea about what the world is like.
(c) Knowing the reasons why a pattern is found can lead one to see why it may *not* continue.
(d) All science is fantasy.
(e) Sometimes we are convinced there is an explanation for a pattern in the data even though we have no idea what it is.
(f) Every theory will be refuted sooner or later.
(g) Looking for explanations can sometimes lead us to postulate false connections.
(h) Most data is unreliable.
(i) Greenhouse gases cause lung cancer.

HARDER

10.11 Perception and Belief

HARDER

Empiricism claims that all our beliefs are based on perception. (All our justifiable beliefs, that is. Superstition, fantasy, or delusion may not be based on anything.) Moreover, it claims that the relation between perception and our beliefs about the world around us is a one-way influence: perception shapes our beliefs but is not shaped by them. Empiricists would like this to be so because they want perception to function as a source of certainty: you can be sure of what you perceive even if you are wrong about everything else.

But can perception be so independent of belief? There are good reasons for thinking that it cannot be. (Or, more

> Our beliefs can make us trust or distrust our perceptions.

carefully, that not enough perception can be independent of belief to serve as a foundation for our beliefs about the world.) Consider first all the obvious ways in which perception is unreliable. There are dramatic failures of perception: illusions, hallucinations, dreams, and so on. And there are also much subtler but much more ordinary facts. Think of all the stray flashes and reflections that glasses or contact lenses or even natural corneas produce; think of the hums and throbbings that human ears produce (especially if they haven't been cleaned recently). In all these cases our senses produce data which are not accurate reports of the world. In the everyday cases we are rarely misled; we automatically discount things that we know mean nothing. (And some people have hallucinations that they learn to ignore.) All these are relevant in two ways. They are examples of perception which cannot give certainty because it is obviously unreliable. And they are examples of how our beliefs influence the way we react to perception: we ignore our senses when we know that the belief they suggest is not true.

Empiricists have an answer to this. If perception is to be a foundation for belief it will have to provide data for inductive reasoning. That means looking for general patterns in perceived data. So we can employ a short cut which says: ignore small exceptions to very general patterns. That way you don't end up with beliefs like: no elephants can fly except those that I was seeing on Thursday night.

Allow this answer: it opens the door to more drastic thoughts. We can reject perceptions because they don't fit into the general patterns we are looking for. But there are many other reasons for rejecting perceptions. Suppose, for example, that you are walking with a friend in a large stone building. You seem to hear voices nearby though you can see no one. After a little thought you realize that this is due to an echo: your own words are coming back to you with a small time delay. So you ignore these sounds. In this example you have applied your knowledge of the way sound waves are transmitted and reflected to guide your reactions to your own perceptions. You are correcting perception by using some fairly abstract beliefs – the kind of beliefs that empiricists want to base on perception.

This way of correcting perception is very common. One important instance of it concerns scientific observations made with instruments such as microscopes and telescopes. To interpret what one sees with a microscope or telescope one has to apply a theory of optics. In fact, an important moment in the history of science was when Descartes first explained how a telescope works, and at the same time showed the similarities between a telescope and an eye. Once Descartes had done this, people had much better reasons to trust the observations that Galileo and others following him had made with telescopes. It was much more plausible after Descartes' explanation that things Galileo had seen through his telescope – sunspots, for example, or the moons of Jupiter – were real things and not just illusions produced by the mysterious device.

One can imagine that very abstract beliefs, a long way removed from the observations they ultimately explain, could affect our trust in our perceptions. Suppose, for example, that we learned that the conditions on a planet as it enters the gravitational field of a black hole exactly reproduce the contents of a typical human dream. This might combine with other discoveries to give us a kind of faith in dreams: we might conclude that they give true information about events on far-away planets. Far-away planets are a far-out possibility, but it shows how radically our theories could affect our attitude to our perceptions.

Our beliefs can make us trust or distrust our perceptions. They can influence perception in subtler ways, too. One example of this occurred when early scientists discovered that with microscopes they could see things too small to be seen with the naked eye. Among the first things they examined were human sperm. These scientists believed in a biological theory according to which the mother only provides a warm and nutritious environment in which the potential human, the sperm, can develop. (Had no one noticed that boys often look like their mothers?) When they drew what they saw when they looked at sperm through microscopes they drew little elongated men. (Sometimes with beards.) These were careful and honest scientists doing their best to describe what they saw. But what they saw was shaped by what they believed, by the theories they accepted.

Perception is theory-laden: we use our beliefs to interpret what we perceive.

Now consider a very ordinary scientific situation. Someone is recording the result of an experiment. Her notes begin like this: "We dripped 20 ml of sulphuric acid into a suspension of frog DNA and a nutrient medium . . ." That is her report of what she observes. But note the words she uses – "sulphuric acid," "suspension," "DNA." These are obviously not words for concepts she could have got straight from perception. They are words which describe her perceptions *as shaped by the theories in terms of which she interprets them.* All scientific observations are like this: in order to test or find evidence for some theories we presuppose others, which give us the concepts we need to describe what we perceive. Or, as many philosophers put it, *all perception is theory-laden.*

Does this mean that theories are not based on evidence obtained ultimately from perception? Not at all. What it means is that our theories help to get, evaluate, and interpret what we perceive. Without a rich and powerful background of theories and other beliefs we would not be able to make the subtle and discriminating observations we need to serve as evidence for further theories. (There is a different project, of making one's perceptions as independent as possible of one's beliefs. It is the project of an impressionist painter, for example. But it is not the same as the project of making scientific observations.)

Look at Figure 10.1. How would a medieval peasant describe this scene? How would a child psychologist describe it? How would a modern scientist describe it? What would each one notice that the others would miss?

Figure 10.1

Box 17 **Telescopes and Illusions**

In one scene of Bertolt Brecht's play *The Life of Galileo*, Galileo is defending his claim that other planets besides the earth have moons, before a young prince, in the presence of a philosopher and a mathematician. Through a telescope he has observed the moons of Jupiter (which he called "the Medicean stars"). No one had ever used a telescope for astronomy before.

> **Philosopher:** And disregarding whether such stars are possible, which the mathematician seems to doubt, may I as a modest philosopher ask the question: are such stars necessary?...
>
> ...
>
> **Galileo:** But your majesty can perceive these impossible and unnecessary stars through this telescope.
> **Mathematician:** One could try to answer that: your tube, showing something which cannot exist, cannot be a very reliable tube, can it?
> **Galileo:** What do you mean by that?
> **Mathematician:** It would be very helpful, Mr Galileo, if you could tell us your grounds for assuming that in the highest spheres of the unchangeable heavens there can be stars freely floating around.
> **Philosopher:** Your grounds, Mr Galileo, your grounds.
> **Galileo:** My grounds? When one look at the stars themselves and at my notes shows the phenomenon. Sir, this dispute is becoming ridiculous.
> **Mathematician:** If I could be sure that you would not get even more agitated, I might say that what is in your tube and what is in the sky might be two different things.

Galileo is the hero of this play, and one is meant to sympathize with his frustration at the intellectual conservatism of his opponents. But one can also see that the philosopher and the mathematician have a point. Unless we have some beliefs that explain why what Galileo sees with his "tube" is really there, we could well suspect that it was making some kind of illusion. (The gap was filled by Descartes a generation later, when he explained the optics of the telescope and showed how it resembles the eye, so reasons for mistrusting telescopes would be reasons for mistrusting eyes.)

HARDER

10.12 Falsification

To retreat from empiricism is not to retreat from empirical evidence. Since the inference to the best explanation brings a greater risk of false belief, it is important to have ways of limiting this risk, reducing the chance that a belief, while providing a good explanation of some accepted data, is false. A firm connection with empirical evidence is one way of limiting the risk. Ways of keeping this connection without slipping back into a narrow empiricism have been found by a number of twentieth-century philosophers. This section discusses the ideas of one of them, Karl Popper (1902–1994).

Popper's views have had a particularly vivid impact on the way scientists think of their activities. In opposition to earlier philosophers who had emphasized the way evidence supports theories, Popper argued that the most important procedures in science are those that *refute* theories. Popper's central claim is that while we can never show beyond all doubt that a scientific theory is true, we can often show that it is false. For if a theory has true observational consequences, that does not show that it has to be true. But if it has false observational consequences then it has to be false. So with a single observation we can refute a theory. Theories can be *falsified*, refuted by empirical evidence.

Popper used the idea of falsification to describe the line between truly scientific theories and other theories which pretend to the authority of science but do not have the same intellectual qualities. (Popper was thinking of things like astrology, some forms of alternative medicine, psychoanalysis, and the Marxist theory of history.) According to Popper, these pseudoscientific doctrines never allow themselves to be falsified. Whatever evidence you produce against them they always will have a way out, a way of evading the force of the evidence against them. Real science, in contrast, always allows ways in which the right experiment or the right calculation could show that a theory is wrong. So according to Popper, scientists must not only be careful and patient; they must also be brave.

Critics of Popper point out difficulties with the claim that all scientific theories can be definitively falsified. The biggest problem is that in deducing an observable consequence from a theory we usually use not just that theory but also many other "background" theories. For example, suppose the theory is that the earth is flat, and the observable consequence is that if you sail due west for long enough you will sail over the edge of the world or bump into the wall of the sky. This consequence also depends on many other assumptions, for example, that the direction "due west" represents a straight line on the surface of the earth. As a result, if we observe sailors sailing due west and not falling off the edge of the earth we may still defend the flat earth theory by claiming that they had sailed a curved route avoiding the ends of the earth. And this feature is true of more respectable theories too. Since most consequences follow from the combination of a large number of theories, an observably false consequence shows just that something is wrong with the combination, not that any particular theory has to be false. (One consequence of this fact is that experimentalists need a detailed understanding of scientific theory. For in order to test a conjecture you have to apply other theories, often in ingenious and unexpected ways, to set up a situation in which, if the conjecture is right, some predicted result will be observed.)

So the simple idea that scientific theories can be falsified, and nonscientific theories cannot be, is too simple. But Popper's general idea is still appealing.

There does seem to be a slippery quality to pseudoscience: you never know whether there is anything that would make the people who hold a pseudoscientific theory accept that the theory had been refuted. So we can state something rather more vague than Popper's original idea. We can say that being scientific means accepting the need to test theories as well as to make them, in fact to search for experiments that might find errors in your theories.

Consider the eight beliefs listed below. Think of them all as "theories." For each of them, think of what someone who believed the theory would accept as evidence that their belief might be false. (Think of possible evidence against the belief, and then think of the reply that someone who held the belief could use to argue that their belief was not really challenged by the evidence.) Think also whether the belief in question could be part of science. Classify each of the beliefs as: (a) falsifiable or unfalsifiable (that is, whether there could be evidence suggesting strongly it was false, or not), and (b) scientific or not (that is, whether or not the belief could be part of the system of beliefs of scientists). You can sum up your responses by circling the "Yes" or the "No" response to each of the two questions after each belief.

(i) **Human beings have beliefs, desires, and emotions, and perform most of their actions as a result of these.**
Falsifiable? Yes No   **Scientific?** Yes No

(ii) **Diseases are caused by people's emotions and attitudes, so that a cure can be achieved by thinking the right thoughts and feeling the right emotions.**
Falsifiable? Yes No   **Scientific?** Yes No

(iii) **The earth is part of the solar system, which is a very small part of the entire universe.**
Falsifiable? Yes No   **Scientific?** Yes No

(iv) **The universe was made by God.**
Falsifiable? Yes No   **Scientific?** Yes No

(v) **All humans are morally equal.**
Falsifiable? Yes No   **Scientific?** Yes No

(vi) **Energy is always conserved; that is, in any physical process the total amount of all forms of energy at the end of the process is the same as at the beginning.**
Falsifiable? Yes No   **Scientific?** Yes No

(vii) Psychological disturbances are caused by events in early childhood.
Falsifiable? Yes No   Scientific? Yes No

(viii) People's lives are shaped by the astrological sign under which they were born.
Falsifiable? Yes No   Scientific? Yes No

Compare your responses with those of others. If one person has marked a belief as falsifiable and another has not, then the first should describe empirical evidence which would show the belief to be false.

The idea of falsification complements the inference to the best explanation. It suggests that we should simultaneously accept beliefs when they have the power to explain empirical data, and search for data to refute the beliefs that we have accepted. In this way we will end up with complex and powerful beliefs while giving ourselves a chance to root out the ones that are false. (We thus have some assurance that we are not caught in the false-belief trap of Chapter 1. See Chapter 11, Section 6.) This can be summed up as the *falsification strategy*:

(a) Accept beliefs when they provide the best explanation of which you are confident.
(b) Reject beliefs when they conflict with empirical evidence.
(c) Search for ways of finding empirical evidence that might conflict with your beliefs, including those beliefs that seem most certain.

The importance of (c) must be emphasized. The scientific spirit, according to Popper, involves actively looking for ways in which even our most cherished beliefs can be refuted. This can take the form of inventing new experimental apparatus, inventing new experiments, or thinking of new connections between our beliefs.

How general is this strategy? Could we apply it to all our beliefs? Popper meant falsification to be a way of telling scientific from unscientific belief, not of telling good from bad belief. But some philosophers think we should try to base all our beliefs on science. And some others think that it is not an accurate picture even of science. These are difficult and controversial questions. Your answers to the questions earlier in this section – about which beliefs are falsifiable and which could be part of science – should be relevant to them. Classify your answers according to the following system. (The labels are meant just as labels; they don't mean much.)

◆ If you thought that four or more of these were both falsifiable and part of science you are a *wide scientist*. (That is, you think that science can potentially include many or even all our beliefs.)

◆ If you thought that fewer than four of these were both falsifiable and part of science you are a *narrow scientist*. (That is, you think that science has important characteristics that many of our beliefs could not share.)

◆ If you thought that five or more of these are not falsifiable you are a *nonscientist*. (That is, you think there is nothing very special about science.)

Now consider the following questions. They are too general and vague to have definite Yes or No answers. But they represent positions that most people will feel intuitively they want to support or disagree with. Wide scientists, narrow scientists, and nonscientists are likely to have different views on them, so it is best to consider them in groups that contain at least one of each. Think of examples!

(1) Science relies on nonscientific beliefs. If scientists did not have a background of beliefs which we hold for nonscientific reasons we would not be able to function as scientists.

(2) Science has the power to govern all our beliefs. Eventually, everything we believe could be shaped by scientific theories based on experimental evidence.

(3) Science and nonscience are fundamentally different. Only confusion can come from trying to combine them.

(4) Science only pretends to be different from the rest of what we believe. Really, it all comes down in the end to faith.

The aim of thinking about these should not be to find out which ones are right. Instead, it should be to discover what other questions should be asked and what ideas should be clarified, in response to the issues they raise.

10.13 The Hypothetico–deductive Method

The falsificational strategy can be put in a wider context. It is one particular form of a picture of science that has been developed by a number of twentieth-century philosophers. The hypothetico-deductive method is part of a picture of science due to many philosophers. Prominent among them are Rudolf Carnap (1891–1968), W. V. Quine (1905–2001), and C. G. Hempel (1905–1997), as well as Karl Popper. All of these philosophers describe how there are safeguards against the risks of theorizing built into standard scientific procedures. The result is a delicate but powerful combination of gamble-seeking and risk-avoiding factors. This powerful and delicate process is one of the glories of our culture. Let us see in more detail how it works.

HARDER

Here is a simplified imaginary story about the life cycle of a scientific theory. We begin not from nothing but with theories that have been accepted, each as a way of explaining some data. Consider one in particular. Suppose it explains how heat flows from one object to another. Call it the "old heat theory." Typically, there will be things a theory does not explain very well. They are often called "anomalies." Perhaps the old heat theory does not explain such things as why hitting a metal object with a hammer makes it hotter. People try to find a way of tinkering with the theory to make it handle the anomalies, but they do not succeed.

Then someone has a pretty wild idea about how to explain them. She may get this idea not from any careful reasoning process but from her imagination. Perhaps she is at a party and sees people meeting one another and getting into "heated" conversation and, inspired by social excitement and alcohol, she thinks: impact makes heat because it stirs things about. The next day she tells her colleagues that she can explain the anomalies that baffle the old heat theory: when objects impact on one another they move other objects within one another, and this makes heat. Her colleagues laugh at her, but, undeterred, she goes away and formulates a more careful version. Bulk matter is made of smaller particles of matter – molecules – and heat is a result of their motion. She presents this to other scientists who try to refute the idea by drawing false predictions from it. If her theory were true, some point out, it would not be just metals that get hot when they are banged together. They perform experiments with wood on wood and with colliding currents of water, and to their surprise they find that heat is produced by these kinds of impact.

> Science involves a delicate balance of taking and minimizing risks. It tries for the advantages of free conjecture and the safety of careful testing.

Other, more complicated and more ingenious attempts are made to refute the theory. Some of them require exact numerical predictions from it, so the scientist has to refine her theory to make it have these predictions. Eventually, she can formulate it so that it can pass most of the tests other scientists can devise. By now many other scientists have come to believe her theory. It gets written down in textbooks as the "new heat theory" and taught to students.

There are some facts that the new heat theory cannot explain, though. And there are some difficulties relating it to other theories that are generally accepted. It has its own anomalies. Then one day another young scientist has a bright idea . . .

The whole process can be represented as a diagram (Figure 10.2). The general features of this account would be accepted by many philosophers of science. The most important ones are these:

◆ Theories result from *conjecture*. This need not be a careful or deliberate process, but it is prompted by the anomalies produced by previous theories and requires an expert knowledge of the previous theories. The attractiveness of a conjecture is not a reason to believe it.

◆ A conjecture is subjected to *tests*. These consist in comparing it with existing theories and trying to draw false predictions from it. In the process of testing a conjecture it may be formulated in more exact terms.

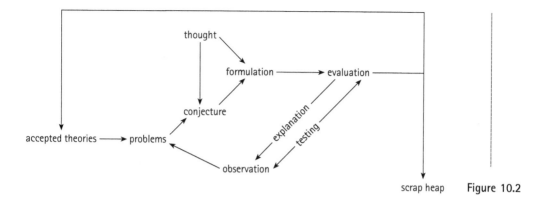

thought

formulation ⟶ evaluation

conjecture

accepted theories ⟶ problems

explanation

testing

observation

scrap heap   Figure 10.2

♦ A new theory is accepted only if it explains the anomalies of the old theory it would replace, and does not create very similar anomalies of its own.
♦ Science needs theoreticians who think up conjectures, and experimentalists who test them. Each is a very specialized skill.

> The hypothetico-deductive method reconciles risk and confidence, inspiration and carefulness, and to some extent empiricism and rationalism. But it is not skeptical or individualistic.

The belief-forming strategy that this describes is known as the *hypothetico-deductive method*. The name comes from the fact that it combines hypothesizing, when conjectures are formed, and deduction, when a conjecture is tested by deducing consequences from it. The most striking quality of the hypothetico-deductive method is the way it reconciles apparent opposites. The riskiness of freely formed conjectures is reconciled with the need for beliefs we can safely trust. The risk inherent in conjectures is tamed in three ways: by carefully testing them, by comparing them with a background of accepted theories, and by the fact that a conjecture has to do better than a previously accepted and relatively successful theory. And the free-ranging concept-creating imagination is, by the same devices, reconciled with careful, methodical attention to empirical detail.

The hypothetico-deductive method also to some extent reconciles the basic motivations of empiricism and rationalism. No theory is accepted except after it has been tested against empirical findings. But creating theories is sometimes a matter of imagination and mathematics, in isolation from the details of experiments. On the other hand, the method breaks with some basic assumptions of both rationalism and empiricism. For it does not accept what in Part 1 was called the "ground-clearing assumption" (see Chapter 3, Section 1). It assumes that every theory is evaluated in a context in which a number of other theories have already been accepted. (Some of these theories may be moral theories. The method allows that your values may influence your beliefs.) And it describes a process that is not very individualistic: science seems an inherently social matter if it involves a cooperation between such different skills as those of theoreticians, experimentalists, and those who incorporate new theories into the structure of older ones.

What the hypothetico-deductive method takes from empiricism is the desire for an accurate way of acquiring beliefs. But it sees that accuracy has to be balanced against informativeness. We have to find a compromise between two kinds of risk rather than decide how much of just one kind to accept. (See Sections 1 and 2 of this chapter.) And in fact there are several ways in which science can be seen as a search for both informativeness and accuracy. For one thing, it involves a subtle interaction between one component, experimentation, which is by itself quite accurate but of limited informativeness, and another component, theorizing, which is by itself potentially informative but presents a danger of inaccuracy. Moreover, one by-product of theorizing is the likelihood that some theories will concern things (such as the aether of nineteenth-century electromagnetic theory, or the crystal spheres of medieval astronomy) which correspond to nothing in reality. But the combination of many true beliefs and some beliefs which correspond to no objective facts is exactly what one would expect from a method which occasionally produces informative but inaccurate results. To have a chance of discovering the truth about a wide range of facts one has to accept the probability that one will also acquire some beliefs that correspond to

HARDER nothing in heaven or earth.

10.14 A Test Case: Continental Drift

HARDER The geological theory of continental drift provides a good example of many of the points made in this chapter. Earth scientists now believe that the continents are attached to plates of rock that float on layers of softer rock. As a result, the position of the continents relative to one another changes. They move very slowly and it takes millions of years for major changes to occur, but given millions of years, the way the continents are distributed over the surface of the earth can undergo major changes. In fact, according to the theory, continents can split, so that continents that are now a long way from one another were once joined together.

Here are the facts that are usually used as evidence for the theory of continental drift.

The shape of the continents   The western coastline of Africa and the eastern coastline of South America fit together in an obvious way. (The fit is even better if you look at the continental shelves rather than the present-day coastlines.) And this kind of fitting is found in a number of parts of the earth, where coastlines separated by an ocean have complementary shapes. We can find a complicated sequence of movements of the continents, from an original situation in which they were all clustered together, ending up with their present locations, which accounts for all these matching shapes. (At one stage of these motions Scotland and Nova Scotia were connected. But South Wales and New South Wales are always far apart!)

Unusual rock formations   When the shapes of two continents fit and this can be accounted for by this sequence of movements, we often find that there are similar rock formations in corresponding areas of the two continents. Sometimes these rock formations are very unusual, not found elsewhere on earth.

The distribution of species   Similar animal and plant species are often found in regions of continents that were, according to the theory, once near each other. More significantly, where the theory claims that, in the past, continents were separated at some point in time, the fossils of species from that period are often very different. Thus the theory claims that North and South America were separated at one time, and the fossils of animals in North and South America before they were joined are very different. (Much more different than they are now.)

The height of land   The distribution of the earth's surface between the depths of the oceans and the tops of the mountains is not random. Most of the earth's surface clusters around two heights, one of them at about sea level and the other about 5 kilometers below sea level. This would make sense if the surface of the earth consists of flat plates – the continents – floating on a basis of different, denser, material.

Which of these facts supports which of the following aspects of the theory of continental drift? (Some of them may support no aspect of the theory.)

(1) Continents do not have fixed locations on the earth's surface, but move.
(2) Continents that were once near together are now far apart.
(3) Continents that were once far apart are now near together.
(4) Continents are the portions of large plates which are above sea level; the whole plates float on larger bodies of different material.

Which of the following are serious objections to the theory? Which ones would scientists take seriously?

(a) The ways opposite edges of continents seem to fit might be just coincidence.
(b) Fossils may not represent ancient species. They may be fakes, or the result of some quite different process.
(c) The distribution of heights of land is consistent with many different theories about the structure of the earth.

(d) The theory does not say what makes the continents move, and it does not describe any forces powerful enough to break up continents and rearrange them.

(e) With enough ingenuity any shapes of continents could be fitted into some story involving the breaking up and rearranging of earlier continents. So the actual shapes of the continents do not provide any evidence for the theory.

Which of the following are alternative explanations of the data? What advantages and disadvantages do they have over the theory of continental drift?

(i) God created the earth with its continents just as they are. He also created all the species of animals and geological formations. We cannot expect to understand all the patterns in His creation.

(ii) A random process will often give the illusion of a pattern. If you toss a coin ten times you will very likely see some simple pattern in the results, like "two heads followed by three tails then three heads followed by two tails" or "head, head, tail, tail, head, head, head, tail, tail, tail." But these patterns mean nothing since they are produced by chance. Similarly, the distribution of coastlines, geological features, species, and heights of land is sure to fit some pattern if we look hard enough, but in fact the real explanation is that all these things result from random processes.

(iii) The continents have always been where they are. But between them there have been bridges of land, regions connecting the continents as Central America now connects North and South America. These rise and fall so that they are sometimes above sea level and sometimes below it. Animals and plants can move across land bridges.

What experiments or further facts could help decide between any of these alternatives and the theory of continental drift?

The theory of continental drift resulted largely from the work of Alfred Wegener, a German scientist who worked in the 1910s and 1920s. Wegener's training was in astronomy, and much of his research was in geography and meteorology. He lacked the expertise in geology to put his case in a way that would convince geologists. And in fact it was not until the 1960s that the idea of continental drift became generally accepted among earth scientists. The most serious objection was that Wegener had not explained what forces could make the continents move. His first suggestion was that the movements of the continents are the result of forces in the earth much like tides in the oceans. Geologists found it quite easy to show that these forces do not exist. It was not until scientists began to understand convection currents in the earth's mantle (below the continents) that they saw how rising currents could inject rock between the continents, forcing them to move.

From the history of the theory of continental drift we can see the following features of scientific theories and scientific reasoning:

◆ Scientists can have good reasons to doubt something that turns out later to be accepted as the truth.
◆ Scientists can have good reasons to accept a theory that turns out later to be wrong.
◆ In deciding whether to accept a theory, one very important factor is whether besides predicting the observed data the theory explains how it could have been produced.
◆ The early formulation of a theory may have to be changed before it can be accepted.
◆ A theory may be reformulated because of experiments or arguments suggested by its earlier formulation.

Which of these features strengthen the claim that scientific reasoning can give us a true account of the world, and which of them weaken it?

HARDER

Conclusions of This Chapter

◆ *Empiricist philosophies have problems about our beliefs about our own and other people's minds. An alternative way of explaining these beliefs is as an inference to the best explanation.*
◆ *The inference to the best explanation is a fairly risky way of acquiring beliefs. It pays for a greater chance of true beliefs by taking a greater risk of false ones. A more careful way of acquiring beliefs is the hypothetico-deductive method.*
◆ *The hypothetico-deductive method reconciles some of the basic ideas of empiricism and rationalism. No theory is accepted except after it has been tested against empirical evidence, but creating theories is sometimes a matter of imagination and mathematics rather than direct reflection on the evidence.*
◆ *Wanting accurate beliefs, which are unlikely to contain falsehoods, is not the same as wanting informative beliefs, which are likely to contain important truths. If we want informative beliefs we may have to accept less accurate ones.*

Further Reading

On other minds

Selection from John Stuart Mill in Part III of John Cottingham (ed.), *Western Philosophy: An Anthology*. Blackwell, 1996.

Chapter 8 of Adam Morton, A *Guide through the Theory of Knowledge*, third edition. Blackwell, 2002.

Chapter 4 of Paul Churchland, *Matter and Consciousness*. MIT Press, 1984.

*Chapter 5 of Jonathan Dancy, *An Introduction to Contemporary Epistemology*. Blackwell, 1988.

On falsification

Selection from Popper's *Conjectures and Refutations* in Part VI of John Cottingham (ed.), *Western Philosophy: An Anthology*. Blackwell, 1996.

David Miller (ed.), *A Pocket Popper*. Fontana, 1988.

*Karl Popper, *The Logic of Scientific Discovery*, third edition. Hutchinson, 1972.

A. F. Chalmers, *What Is This Thing Called Science?* Open University Press, 1982.

On the inference to the best explanation

Chapter 8 of Willard Quine and Joseph Ullian, *The Web of Belief*. Random House, 1978.

Chapter 4 of Adam Morton, *A Guide through the Theory of Knowledge*, third edition, Blackwell, 2002.

*Peter Lipton, *The Inference to the Best Explanation*. Routledge, 1991.

*Chapters 9 and 10 of Donald Gillies, *Philosophy of Science in the 20th Century*. Blackwell, 1993.

On the hypothetico-deductive method

C. G. Hempel, *Philosophy of Natural Science*. Prentice-Hall, 1966.

N. R. Hanson, *Patterns of Discovery*. Cambridge University Press, 1958.

Donald Gillies, *Philosophy of Science in the 20th Century*. Blackwell, 1993.

Other topics

*Colin Howson and Peter Urbach, *Scientific Reasoning: The Bayesian Approach*. Open Court, 1989.

*Thomas Kuhn, *The Structure of Scientific Revolutions*, third edition. University of Chicago Press, 1996.

Electronic resources

Routledge Encyclopedia of Philosophy (available online at many universities): articles on Falsification; Folk psychology; Inference to the Best Explanation; Other minds; Popper, Karl; Scientific method.

Stanford Encyclopedia of Philosophy (http://plato.stanford.edu/): Folk psychology as a theory; Other minds (articles listed here are not yet available as this book goes to press; they should be available soon).

11 Objectivity

Introduction

Empiricism tries to provide beliefs that are based in a reasonable way on evidence, while keeping the risk of error at a minimum. It does this by considering only evidence which concerns what we perceive and allowing only beliefs that use concepts based on perception.

Empiricism has difficulty explaining why many commonsense and scientific beliefs are reasonable. For example, it makes it hard to understand why it is reasonable to believe that other people have minds and experiences like yours. More powerful ways of basing beliefs on evidence are provided by the inference to the best explanation, the falsificational method, and the hypothetico-deductive method. These are all attempts to describe the kinds of reasoning used in science.

From the debate between utilitarianism and Kantian ethics, and from the problems of empiricism, we can see ways of responding to the false–belief trap of Part I. For we can see how we can sift through our moral and scientific beliefs, finding new ways of testing and connecting them, so that we have a hope of eventually rejecting the ones that are false.

Chapter Objectives

By the end of this chapter you should be able to answer the following questions.

◆ *What is fallibilism, and how does it allow truth in science and ethics?*
◆ *How can background beliefs influence the force of evidence?*
◆ *How can background beliefs be changed by evidence, in both science and ethics?*
◆ *Why do some background beliefs make evidence powerless?*
◆ *What is reflective equilibrium between judgments and principles?*
◆ *What similarities are there between changes in scientific and moral beliefs?*

Definitions

The following words used in this chapter are defined in the list of definitions at the end of the book:

background beliefs   *moral status*   *reflective equilibrium*
fallibilism

11.1 Escape from the Cave

In his dialogue *The Republic*, Plato describes the situation of some imaginary people who are chained in a dark cave.

> Conceive them as having their legs and necks fettered from childhood, so that they remain in the same spot, able to look forward only, and prevented by the fetters from turning their heads. Picture further the light from a fire burning higher up and at a distance behind them, and between the fire and the prisoners and above them a road along which a low wall has been built. . . . See also, then, men carrying past the wall implements of all kinds that rise above the wall, and human images and shapes of animals as well, wrought in stone and wood and every material, some of these bearers presumably speaking and others silent. (Book VII, 514–15)

All that these people can see, as long as they are chained, are shadows on the wall in front of them, which they mistake for real things. They do not even know what a real thing is.

Plato means this as an allegory of the human condition. We are trapped in our own primitive ways of thinking, which allow us only to see shadows of reality. Those shadows are not completely unreal. They are the distant effects of the sun outside, which they resemble. But observing them, we cannot see the real nature of the sun and the outside world unless we ignore our natural tendencies and turn away from the shadows. Unless we do this, if Plato is to be believed, we are doomed to remain in something like the false-belief trap of Chapter 1, eternally prisoners of what we believe and feel.

The trap applies to all sorts of beliefs. Beliefs about the causes of events in our everyday lives (diseases, the weather, the fates of individual people), beliefs about the nature of the universe (the structure of matter, the laws of physics, the origin of space and time), and beliefs about right and wrong (how to treat one another in personal relations, how to make good political systems). In all these cases we can ask whether the beliefs that we inherit from our society, and the beliefs that come naturally to us as human beings, might have the effect of trapping us in primitive ways of thinking, cutting us off from better ways of understanding the world and better ways of living our lives.

In the previous two chapters we have seen two ways out of the cave. Or at any rate, two ways which philosophers have defended as ways of achieving objective knowledge: ways of getting beliefs that correspond to the way the world actually is, rather than the way we happen to think. Empiricists (Chapter 9) think that we can ignore most of our traditional beliefs, and build a system of knowledge just on reasoning from pure perceptions. To stay with Plato's metaphor, this amounts to looking at the shadows on the wall and refusing to interpret them as people, animals, and things, instead saying: "They are shadows, and we must try to discover the laws of shadow." Advocates of the falsificational strategy (Chapter 10, Section 12) or the hypothetico-deductive method (Chapter 10, Section 13) propose a rather different way out. They suggest taking our traditional beliefs and filtering them, slowly testing them against reasoning and observation while developing new extensions and alternatives to them. The hope is that in this way we will have a rich enough variety of beliefs to make sense of the world, while being critical enough that falsehoods among our beliefs will eventually be eliminated. In Plato's terms, this amounts to continuing to observe the shadows while also thinking about the nature of light and shadow, hoping that eventually we will learn which shadows tell us about real things and which are just illusions.

Three basic factors are vital here, whether one is considering the physical world or moral life: the purposes of our investigations, the role we give to experience, and the role we give to background beliefs. Since each of these will play a part in the rest of the chapter it will help to say something about each one now.

Purposes   We have reasons for trying to get new beliefs. There are different destinations outside the cave we might want to find ways to. We might want the ultimate truth about the origin of the universe, or we might want practical information about how to make machines and cure diseases. We might want to understand the ultimate purposes of human life, or we might want guidance about how to make a society that works. And running through all of these is the contrast between accuracy and informativeness: do we want to avoid falsehood or to seek usable truth?

Experience   We learn things by using our senses, from carefully arranged experiments and general experience in life. Most of the beliefs we get in this way are shaped also by other things we believe, and these may include beliefs that we will later want to reconsider. (See Chapter 10, Section 11.) So there is a fundamental decision. Are we going to make use only of experiences that we can be sure are not infected by beliefs that we may later reject? Are we to take the shadows not only as shadows but also as the images they seem to be?

Background beliefs   We understand our experience in terms of our beliefs. (For example, we divide our experiences into perception and hallucination on the basis of our beliefs about what could exist: we think there are no tiny pink flying elephants, so when you seem to see one hovering over your desk you suppose you must be dreaming or hallucinating.) So we experience the world only against a background of beliefs about what kind of a place it is. We also need the beliefs we already have in order to tell what new ideas are worth considering, and what would follow if they were true. But some of these background beliefs will later get rejected as our beliefs develop. So we have a more general form of the fundamental decision about experience. How much use are we going to make of beliefs we may later reject? Are we going to take the play of shadows even partly seriously, or are we going to ignore it completely and by sheer force of will turn our attention in a different direction?

This chapter will end with two claims. Call them *limited optimism* and *fallibilism*. Limited optimism claims that we can put together the methods described in several chapters of this book to give us some confidence that we can find true beliefs and eliminate false ones. There is a path out of the cave. This limited optimism applies to both ethics and science. Ideas like it are the reason that contemporary philosophers are usually rather less skeptical than philosophers in the past have sometimes been. Fallibilism claims that we have to accept that any of our beliefs could be false. None of them is totally secure. Fallibilism and limited optimism sound like opposites. But the most surprising claim is that they are not opposites; in fact they support one another.

Although many, perhaps most, contemporary philosophers accept limited optimism and fallibilism, many would not. And even among philosophers who would accept them, the details are controversial. So you may find yourself agreeing or disagreeing, or accepting some details and rejecting others. But in thinking out your attitudes to these claims you should find many of the themes of the first two parts of this book coming together.

11.2 Background Beliefs: First Test Case – Probability

We depend on background beliefs whenever we find evidence for a theory, a prediction, or any other belief. But these background beliefs can themselves be tested. That is one of the reasons for limited optimism. The way in which background beliefs can be tested is shown clearly when they are beliefs about probability, as in the example in this section. The example does not require that you know any probability theory. (But if you do you will be able to check some of the details for yourself.)

You take a coin and you toss it four times. It comes down heads each time. How likely is it that when it is tossed a fifth time it will land heads again? Here are two general answers:

(a) Heads and tails are equally likely each time the coin is tossed. And each toss has no influence on the next. So there is a fifty-fifty chance that it will be heads on the fifth time.
(b) The fact that the coin came down heads five times in a row suggests that it is not a fair coin, but has a bias toward heads. So it is more likely to land heads than tails on the fifth (or any) throw.

(You may think of a third answer: tails are more likely after a run of heads. If you think that, you might like to (re)read Box 12, "The Gambler's Fallacy," in Chapter 6.)

In contrasting these answers, note that (a) and (b) make different assumptions about the coin: (a) assumes that it is a fair coin, and (b) suggests that it is biased. Note also that both answers can explain the fact that it has come down heads four times in a row: (a) explains it by saying that the run of heads was just one of the many things that could happen when a fair coin is tossed; (b) explains it by saying that the run of heads was the most likely result of a biased coin. So how could a person who believed (a) and a person who believed (b) settle their difference?

Imagine a discussion between *Fair*, who thinks the coin has equal chances of coming down heads or tails, and *Biased*, who thinks the coin is more likely to come down heads. In fact, imagine two discussions. Both start the same way. The first discussion runs as follows. They have just seen the coin land heads four times in a row.

> **Biased:** There, just as I suspected, the coin is biased.
> **Fair:** No, a fair coin can easily give a run of heads. But it won't last for ever.
> **Biased:** What would it take to convince you? It could come down heads a hundred times and you could still call it a very unusual fluke. Do you admit that it is even a little bit probable that the coin is biased?
> **Fair:** ★ Yes, there is a very small chance it is biased, but I don't think it is.
> **Biased:** And if it were biased then these four heads in a row would be less of a surprise, and a hundred heads in a row would be less of a miracle.
> **Fair:** Yes, supposing it to be biased would make what we have just seen less surprising. Not enough to overcome my conviction that it is a fair coin, though. If it came down heads a hundred times in a row then I would have to suppose that, unlikely as it seemed at first, the coin is after all biased.
> **Biased:** So we know how to proceed: we should toss the coin a few more times.
> **Fair:** OK, as long as if it comes down both heads and tails from now on you'll admit it might be a fair coin.

The crucial point in this dialogue came at ★, where Fair admitted that there is a very small chance the coin is biased. Fair need not have admitted this, for her honest opinion might have been that the coin could not have been biased. In that case the dialogue could have gone as follows:

> **Biased:** There, just as I suspected, the coin is biased.
> **Fair:** No, a fair coin can easily give a run of heads. But it won't last for ever.
> **Biased:** What would it take to convince you? It could come down heads a hundred times and you could still call it a very unusual fluke. Do you admit that it is even a little bit probable that the coin is biased?

Fair: ★ No, I know it's a fair coin. It was made by the coin-making machines in the mint, and they were designed by my uncle and he assured me that they never produce biased coins. But keep my family out of this.

Biased: So if we tossed the coin a hundred times more and it came down heads every time you would still think it was fair.

Fair: Well, since I know the coin is fair I'm sure that it will not come down heads a hundred times more. But if it did, I'd just say it was one of those one-in-a-billion occurrences.

What Fair says in this second dialogue is perfectly reasonable, given what she believes. And what she says in the first dialogue is also reasonable, given the different beliefs she has there. Whether Fair should reject, consider, or accept that the coin is biased depends on how likely she considers the hypothesis before seeing the coin tossed. If Fair is completely convinced that the coin is fair then no series of heads can shift her opinion. But the more she thinks that it could possibly be, the more easily is her opinion shifted by the evidence. That is, the more that she thinks it is possible that the coin could be biased, the more sensitive are her beliefs about the probability of heads on the next toss to the number of heads that have already appeared. Suppose that she can reject, consider, or accept that heads are more likely than tails on the next toss. Which of these should she do, given her beliefs and the evidence as described in the table below? (The table uses the numbers 4, 8, and 100 to make the example definite, but there is no significance to the exact numbers.)

If Fair believes that the hypothesis that the coin is biased is	And the number of successive heads is		
	4	8	100
Impossible	reject	reject	reject
Barely possible	reject	consider	accept
Possible	consider	accept	accept

Fair's belief about whether it is possible that the coin is biased is a good example of a background belief. It is a belief she may hardly know she has, since she may just think "the coin is fair." But while thinking the coin is fair she must either think that it could not be biased, or that it could be. (Just as you probably think there is no life on Mars. But you may think that it is not impossible for there to be life on Mars: evidence could convince you that your belief is false.) And her particular background belief – exactly how possible she thinks it is that the coin is biased – will determine how she changes her beliefs about how likely heads are on the next toss. This illustrates three general points about background beliefs.

Background beliefs influence the force of evidence. If Fair believes that the coin could not be biased, then a hundred heads in a row will not change her conviction that heads and tails are equally likely next time. If she thinks "I don't think it is biased, but it could be," then enough heads will change her belief. If she thinks "I don't think it is biased, but it could easily be," then a shorter run of heads will change her belief.

> Background beliefs can determine whether evidence has small, great, or no influence on a belief.

Background beliefs are changed by evidence. Although background beliefs influence the way evidence supports or refutes other beliefs, they are themselves changed by evidence. As long as Fair thinks it is possible that the coin could be biased, as more and more heads appear she will think it is more and more likely that it actually is biased, until eventually she changes her background belief and decides that it is biased.

Some background beliefs make evidence powerless. If Fair thinks that the coin could not possibly be biased, then a hundred heads will not convince her. In fact, no number of heads will convince her. So the belief that the coin could not possibly be biased makes it impossible for this kind of evidence to change her beliefs about how likely another head is. But as long as she thinks there is even a very small possibility, enough evidence will eventually change her mind. So in a way it is better for her to leave open a very small possibility that the coin might be biased. If we can have beliefs about which of the things that we do not think true could be true, and which are more likely than others, then we have a better chance that as more evidence comes in it will direct our beliefs toward the truth.

Suppose that, after Fair and Biased have tossed the coin four times and it has come down heads four times, they continue to toss the coin. They toss it four more times, and it comes down tails two times and heads two times. Then they toss it four more times and it comes down heads once and tails three times. What should Biased believe now? Fill in the table with Biased's attitude (accept, consider, reject) to the hypothesis that the coin is fair, given each of the three chunks of evidence. Compare your table with that of others.

If Biased believes that the hypothesis that the coin is fair is	And the pattern of heads and tails is		
	hhhh	hhhhthht	hhhhthhttht
Impossible			
Barely possible			
Possible			

Which two of the following conclusions are *not* supported by the examples in this section?

(a) Some background beliefs allow evidence to support only a few theories, while others allow evidence to support many different theories.
(b) Any background belief is consistent with any theory.
(c) Evidence can change background beliefs.
(d) Given enough evidence, a theory can be supported whatever the background beliefs.

HARDER

Box 18 Bayes' Theorem

A central theorem of probability theory, Bayes' theorem, can be used to describe the way evidence supports a theory. It uses the concept of prior probability, written $P(p)$, representing how probable it is that p is true, and conditional probability, written $P(p,q)$, representing how probable p is on the assumption that q is true. Then Bayes' theorem asserts that given a hypothesis H and evidence e, $P(H,e) = P(e,H) \times P(H)/P(e)$. Three consequences of this theorem interest philosophers.

(i) The probability of a hypothesis, given evidence, is increased if the hypothesis makes the evidence likely. So we can calculate, for example, how likely it is that a coin is biased, given a run of heads, by seeing how probable some particular degree of bias would make that run of heads.

(ii) Prior probabilities can change. If we accept a piece of evidence and replace all our prior probabilities with their probabilities conditional on that evidence, then we can use these new prior probabilities to consider new evidence.

(iii) The probability of a hypothesis, given evidence, depends on the prior probability of the hypothesis. In particular, a hypothesis that has prior probability of zero has zero probability conditional on any evidence.

These three points are very similar to the three conclusions about background beliefs described above. There is an influential movement of philosophers and statisticians who think that the resemblance is a very deep one, and that we can use Bayes' theorem to describe how evidence should influence our beliefs. This is the *Bayesian* theory of evidence.

HARDER

11.3 Background Beliefs: Second Test Case – Moral Status

We don't usually worry about how we treat stones or toothbrushes. We do not avoid hurting them, or feel concern about their well-being, nor are we obliged

to keep any promises we might make to them. We do not think that our relations with them are a matter of morality. On the other hand, our relations with our friends and family are matters of moral concern: we think it would be wrong to hurt them or do things that are not in their best interests, and we feel we have a duty to keep our promises to them. We take our friends and family to be *moral agents* in a way that stones or toothbrushes cannot be. And since they are moral agents, not only do we have duties to them but they have duties to us. We expect them to keep their promises too.

A moral agent is something whose well-being is a matter of moral concern, which others have moral obligations to, and which has moral obligations to others.

But what things are moral agents? There are many possible beliefs about this. At one extreme, imagine an adult male member of a small tribe in a slave-owning culture. He treats other adult males of his tribe with great respect. He is concerned for their interests and expects them to be concerned with his. But women and children in his tribe are a different matter. He cares about them in much the way he does about his property. He wants them to get what is good for them, but this good is determined by his wishes rather than theirs. Then there are slaves, who are just like animals, to be exploited entirely for his own benefit. And as for members of other tribes, they have no value at all and any way of treating them is acceptable. For him, only adult males of his tribe are moral agents.

At the other extreme, compare a member of our society who has a well-developed liberal conscience. He or she wants to be completely free not only of sexism and racism, but also of speciesism, agism, and various other "isms." So he or she treats members of other races, social groups, and genders with the same consideration as they treat their close friends. Moreover, they take the well-being of some animals, for example, whales and apes, as being as important as that of human beings. So all humans and many animals are morally equal. All are moral agents.

There has been an evolution in human moral beliefs from tribalism toward liberalism. Whether or not the liberal described above has satisfactory moral views, as our cultures have developed they have tended to enlarge the class of moral agents. More and more people are thought of as having rights and being morally important. In fact, most modern people think that all humans have moral rights. How did we come to think this?

> As moral ideas have developed, we have come to accept a wider class of people as full moral agents.

One factor that has led most modern societies to think that all human beings are moral agents – that all human beings have the same rights – is evidence about human capacities. In a traditional society people have traditional roles, which determine their lives from childhood. Girls are raised to be wives and mothers, children of farm workers are raised to be farm workers, sons of rich or powerful people are raised to be able to make decisions and influence events themselves. It is not hard for people in such a society to believe that some people are just naturally very different from others. Since there are very few examples of intellectually accomplished females or of socially powerful peasants in this kind of society, it is not unreasonable for people to think that there is some natural reason why gender and social class are signs of differences in basic human capacities. And in particular, people will tend to think that they are signs of differences in the capacities that are important to morality, such as keeping promises, resisting impulses, or thinking through difficult social problems. (For example, in the eighteenth century Rousseau wrote that uneducated people were "stupid and unimaginative," and slightly later Gibbon wrote that a peasant was "superior but little to his fellow labourer the ox in the exercise of his mental faculties.") When these differences of gender and class become combined with differences of race, the attitudes become even more entrenched.

The picture changes when more evidence appears. In a modern world very different societies come into contact with one another. And economic development forces people into very different ways of life. Agricultural workers move to cities, women get jobs in factories. One result is that people discover that they can live very different lives from the ones that tradition had assigned to them. Sometimes they like these lives and sometimes they hate them, but the important point is that they discover they are capable of living them. As a result, the belief that different people are intrinsically different begins to weaken.

People in modern cultures are usually not convinced that there are morally relevant differences between genders, classes, and races. This is not to say that we think that everyone is identical. But we think that within any group there is a great variation in abilities. And, most important, we think that the differences rarely or never concern the features on which moral respect is based. We take all human beings to be moral agents.

This is a moral belief that is based on factual evidence. The evidence is quite indirect: a lot of it concerns features like intelligence or artistic ability, which are of little relevance to a person's moral status. But once we come to think that there are not very many general differences between rich and poor, or male and female, we come to doubt the particular differences in terms of which different moral treatment is based. This evidence is not the only factor here. There is also the influence of moral philosophy, for example, Kant's view that no person should ever be treated as a means to an end, or the utilitarian view that a social policy should create the maximum happiness for all people. And there is the influence of religions such as Christianity.

As a culture's moral beliefs develop, then factual evidence, traditional moral beliefs, and moral arguments combine and interact with one another. Each of these is necessary for the others to have their full effect. In particular, factual evidence can only lead to new moral beliefs if it is interpreted through older moral beliefs. For example, if you do not believe that anyone has any rights then evidence about the equality of human beings will not lead you to think that all people have equal rights. And if you do not believe that the capacity to make and keep promises is a sign of moral worth, then you will not be impressed by evidence that badly educated people can make and keep promises.

This shows that background beliefs operate in moral thinking as well as in science. Evidence about what is needed in order to take part in society or to live a valuable life needs to be interpreted against a background of moral beliefs, which connect it with the values of a culture. To get a better grasp on how this can happen, imagine a tribal society of the kind described at the beginning of this section. Take these as background beliefs, and see how factual evidence can begin the slow process of enlarging the class of people who are counted as full moral agents. Below are five possible items of evidence. Think of them as coming in the order they are listed, but over a very long period of time, perhaps hundreds of years.

(1) Faced with common enemies, the tribe makes a peace treaty with a rival tribe. To the surprise of both sides the terms of the treaty are honored, and members of each tribe find that they can make deals with members of the other.
(2) The hereditary leadership of the tribe passes first to a senile old man, with the intellectual capacity of a 5-year-old, and then to a psychopath, who is intelligent but has no sense of honor or responsibility.
(3) After the senile and psychopathic leaders, a third man rules wisely and successfully. After his death it is revealed that all his decisions were made by his wife.
(4) Fantasy fiction develops in the culture. Stories are written in which some of the participants are neither male nor female. Some of them are holy children, 3-year-old geniuses. Other stories feature extraterrestrials or talking animals. Many of these creatures, though not adult male humans, participate in moral life. They make promises, show concern for others, and help people make hard choices.
(5) Biology develops in the culture. As the nature and origins of humans and other animals become better understood, the differences between humans and other animals seem less significant than the differences between higher and lower animals.

In response to these developments (and others) the beliefs of the tribe change. Which of the following beliefs could be responses to which development?

(i) Moral agency is a matter of what kind of a mind one has. Bodily features are less important than mental attributes in determining whether somebody is worthy of respect.
(ii) Not all adult males have all the qualities we expect of moral agents.
(iii) Membership of a tribe is irrelevant to moral status. Members of all tribes can be honorable or dishonorable, guilty or innocent.

(iv) Some animals could be moral agents.

(v)   There are moral agents among all kinds of human beings.

In each case, the change of belief would depend on some background belief. Of the five traditional beliefs below, which ones are necessary for acquiring which of the five beliefs above? That is, for each of the five new beliefs, (i) to (v) above, find one of the traditional beliefs, (a) to (e) below, such that members of the tribe who did not have that traditional belief would not acquire that new belief in response to the evidence.

(a) Someone who can make wise decisions must be taken seriously.

(b) The capacity to make and keep promises is a sign of being worthy of moral respect.

(c) People we can imagine taking as moral equals we can actually take as moral equals.

(d) Someone without any sense of responsibility is not worthy of full moral respect.

(e) What matters for whether something is a moral agent is how it could fit into a system of moral rules.

You may find you think that the tribe made a mistake at one stage. That is, when they concluded that some animals could be moral agents. In that case, you probably have background beliefs that make this conclusion too unlikely for the evidence to support it. Here are some possible reasons for thinking that nonhuman animals can *not* be moral agents.

(1) Moral agency depends on having an immortal soul, and only humans have immortal souls.

(2) No nonhuman animal could ever be intelligent enough to understand and keep promises, or to help humans make hard choices.

(3) In the end, we have to decide who and what we count as a moral equal, and since it is we humans who are deciding we can always decide that all animals are always less important than all humans.

Which of these best fits your beliefs? Could there be evidence for or against any of them?

11.4 Reflective Equilibrium

In his book *Fact, Fiction, and Forecast*, the philosopher Nelson Goodman discusses how we can justify rules for inductive reasoning (such as the rule of simple induction, discussed in Chapter 5). He compares rules for inductive reasoning to rules for deduction. (See Chapter 5 on deductive reasoning.) He says:

the rules themselves must eventually be justified. The validity of a deduction depends not upon conformity to any purely arbitrary rules we may contrive, but upon conformity to valid rules. . . . But how is the validity of rules to be determined? Here again we encounter philosophers who insist that these rules follow from some self-evident axiom, and others who try to show that the rules are grounded in the very nature of the human mind. I think the answer is much nearer the surface. Principles of deductive inference are justified by their conformity with accepted deductive practice. Their validity depends upon accordance with the particular deductive inferences we actually make and sanction. If a rule yields unacceptable inferences, we drop it as invalid.

This looks flagrantly circular. I have said that deductive inferences are justified by their conformity to valid general rules, and that general rules are justified by their conformity to valid inferences. But this circle is a virtuous one. The point is that rules and particular inferences alike are justified by being brought into agreement with each other. A rule is amended if it yields an inference we are unwilling to accept; an inference is rejected if it violates a rule we are unwilling to amend. The process of justification is the delicate one of making mutual adjustments between rules and accepted inferences; and in the agreement that is achieved lies the only justification needed for either.

All this applies equally well to induction. . . .

One of the philosophers who have found this passage suggestive is the American moral philosopher John Rawls. In his book *A Theory of Justice*, he describes the "original position," which is a neutral standpoint from which thoughtful people could decide what principles they wanted to live their social lives by. He says:

In searching for the most favored description of this situation we work from both ends. We begin by describing it so that it represents generally shared and preferably weak conditions. We then see if these conditions are strong enough to yield a significant set of principles. If not, we look for further premises equally reasonable. But if so, and these principles match our reasoned convictions of justice, then so far well and good. But presumably there will be discrepancies. In this case we have a choice. We can either modify the account of the original situation or we can revise our existing judgements, for even the judgements we take provisionally as fixed points are liable to revision. By going back and forth, sometimes altering the [principles], at others withdrawing our judgements and conforming them to principle, I assume that eventually we shall find a description . . . that both expresses reasonable conditions and yields principles which match our considered judgements duly pruned and adjusted. This state of affairs I refer to as reflective equilibrium.

One thing Rawls is saying here is that we have judgments on whether a particular situation is just, and we have general principles about justice. We defend or criticize each of these by comparison with the other, changing a general principle if it conflicts with many judgments about particular cases and changing a judgment about a particular case if it conflicts with general principles. For example, if you believe the general principle that it is unfair ever to treat one person differently from another you may find that this principle conflicts with the judgment that it is fair to give people in wheelchairs special access to buildings. And enough conflicts like this can make you modify the general principle. In the same way, your judgment that some person is paid a fair wage may conflict with your general principle that people should be paid the same wage for the same work. And then you may change your judgment on the particular case. Eventually, Rawls hopes, by adjusting both judgments and principles we will get a set of beliefs about justice (or other moral concepts) which is in harmony with itself. This is reflective equilibrium.

> Reflective equilibrium occurs when our judgments about particular cases are consistent with our general moral principles.

Rawls' picture of morality has connections with some ideas of Kant's. (See Chapter 8.) Kant, in his *Foundations of the Metaphysics of Morals*, imagines that besides being members of real human communities, with their particular moral conventions and their particular power relations, we are also members of what he calls "the realm of ends." This is the imaginary world of perfect morality, where the rules are universal principles applying in the same way to everyone at all times. Moreover, these principles are the ones that people have decided on in order to regulate their lives. Here is the way Kant puts it:

A rational being belongs to the realm of ends as a member when he makes universal laws in it while also himself being subject to these laws. He belongs to it as sovereign when he, as legislating, is subject to the will of no other. . . .

Morality, therefore, consists in the relation of every action to that legislation through which alone a realm of ends is possible. This legislation, however, must be found in every rational being. It must be able to arise from his will, whose principle is to take no action according to any maxim [rule] which would be inconsistent with its being a universal law . . .

The main idea here can be expressed as follows:

In the world of ideal morality everyone would both make and obey all the rules. So to act morally is to act in the way you would if you were obeying rules that you had made yourself but that could apply to everyone else too. Whenever you act morally, you are finding a rule to follow, which is a rule that could apply to everyone at all times.

There are obvious resemblances between Goodman's picture of justifying beliefs about logic, and Rawls' picture of justifying beliefs about ethics. And there are less obvious resemblances between Rawls' picture and Kant's. For Kant is saying: to find the true moral principles, you try to think your way toward understanding what an ideal moral community would be like. And in an ideal moral community there would be no conflict between the general principles people took to rule their lives (the "universal laws") and their judgments about particular cases. There would be reflective equilibrium. You can think of Rawls as taking an idea from Goodman and using it to express and develop one of Kant's fundamental suggestions.

Goodman's basic formula is:

A rule is amended if it yields an inference we are unwilling to accept; an inference is rejected if it violates a rule we are unwilling to amend.

Rawls comes close to this formula when he discusses how moral principles and judgments about particular moral situations are to be harmonized. He is confident that:

> by going back and forth, sometimes altering the [principles], at others withdrawing our judgements and conforming them to principle, . . . eventually we shall find a description . . . that . . . yields principles which match our considered judgements.

This statement of Rawls' is very much like Goodman's formula. We could paraphrase Rawls as saying:

A principle is amended if it yields a judgment we are unwilling to accept; a judgment is rejected if it violates a principle we are unwilling to amend.

Kant, in the passage quoted above, is describing the search for general moral principles. (Very general ones, universal in fact: they should apply to all people and for that matter to all creatures that can think out intelligently how they should act.) He says in effect that we should accept principles which we could use as such universal rules. Most of our everyday rules cannot function for this purpose. For example, the rule "Always answer people's questions fully and honestly" might seem like generally good advice, but it could give bad results if, say, a depressed person who is considering suicide asks you exactly what you think of them and of their prospects of happiness. Perhaps then you should try to find a way of being honest which allows you to hold back some of what you believe. Similarly for most moral principles. They take a lot of modification before they could be applied universally. So we have to do a lot of testing of them against possible situations before we get anything like universal principles. And this is the core of Rawls' "reflective equilibrium."

For example, we might start with the principle "Do not kill." Then we might confront it with facts and situations like the following:

(i) A maniac is about to bomb a nursery and the only way to stop him is to shoot him.

(ii) In wartime it is often necessary to kill to defend your country.

(iii) We kill animals in order to eat them.

(iv) We often do not do everything we could to help people in danger of death (for example, people starving in far away countries), and thus we perform actions (for example, refusing to give them aid) that we know will kill them.

There are many responses to these. Some are:

(a) We should be pacifists.

(b) We should be vegetarians.

(c) We should not kill unless our lives are threatened.

(d) We should minimize loss of life.

(e) We should try to distribute life expectancy with absolute equality throughout everyone in the world.

(f) We should not kill those to whom we have close ties.

Each of these changes the original moral principle "Do not kill" in response to less general judgments. For each of the responses (a)–(f) identify the situation among (i)–(iv) which it might be a response to, and state the moral judgment that the situation suggests. You may find that it is a moral judgment that you would not make yourself. Then consider what alternatives to the response might also either accommodate the force of the moral judgment or find a way of rejecting it.

Kant in fact thought that some moral rules much like those given by common sense would serve as universal principles. The examples he gives suggest that he thought that "Never lie" and "Never kill" could be rules that all thinking beings everywhere could follow. You don't have to agree with him about this to see the power of the idea of moral rules which we agree to because we think that they could be principles we would choose to live our lives by. But once you see the difference between this powerful idea and Kant's particular examples you see some disturbing possibilities. For example:

◆ There may be several competing ways of modifying our original principles so they can be absolutely general rules.

◆ Moral principles that could apply at all times and places might be extremely different from the commonsense morality that we learn from our culture.

In another way, these possibilities are exciting rather than disturbing. For they suggest that Kant's idea, developed in Rawls' way, does more than give a rubber stamp of approval to conventional morality. It suggests ways in which we might filter through our moral beliefs and discover which ones survive under the pressure of comparison with principles, judgments, and newly discovered situations. This resembles Popper's suggestion (discussed in Chapter 10, Section 12) that we can filter through scientific beliefs, comparing them with empirical evidence and rejecting the ones that we discover to be faulty.

11.5 How Ethics Is Like Science

Later on in this section there is a dialogue on the topic of how science and ethics resemble (and don't resemble) each other. To set up your reactions to the dialogue here is a questionnaire. It is meant to focus your attention on the idea of moral progress, the idea that over the centuries people can get better ideas about how to manage their lives. Mark your reaction by drawing a ring round (a), (b) or (c).

(1) In this century in Western countries, ideas about the place of women in society have changed drastically. It is no longer customary to think that women should focus their lives on taking care of men and raising children. Equality of pay and opportunity between women and men seems to many people now to be a basic human right.

Is this attitude to equality between the sexes (a) better than, (b) worse than, or (c) simply different from, a traditional attitude to the role of women?

(2) Punishments for crimes are generally less drastic than they were in previous centuries. In many criminal justice systems the emphasis is on preventing a criminal reoffending, rather than punishing him or her for the sake of punishment. Capital punishment, while still fairly common, is now often thought to require justification: for example, it has to be shown that executing murderers deters others from murder, in order to make it acceptable to take their lives as punishment.

Is this modern attitude to punishment (a) better than, (b) worse than, or (c) simply different from, a traditional one in which severe penalties are justified simply because they are responses to acts which are wrong?

(3) Many centuries ago, slavery was a central part of the economy of many societies. In Europe and America slavery was abolished within the past two hundred years. Now slavery is very rare throughout the world and most societies consider slavery to be morally wrong. Yet in most societies many people work for very low wages, and institutions with some resemblances to slavery – such as the use of prisoners as workers, or long-term work contracts which are very hard to get out of – are found in many places.

Is the abolition of slavery (a) an achievement of a basic human right, (b) a loss of a valuable economic device, or (c) an irrelevance in terms of the actual conditions of oppressed people?

(4) In most societies throughout most of history, sexual matters have been governed by strict moral codes. These usually restricted sex to marriage and outlawed homosexuality. Nowadays, many people live by much more permissive and less definite rules. Many people govern their sexual lives by an intention to respect other people and not to hurt them, but do not subscribe to any simple list of acceptable and unacceptable sexual practices. And very many people live their lives by much more traditional and restrictive rules.

Which of the following seems to you nearest to the truth about modern sexual permissiveness? (a) It opens up valuable possibilities to people that were pointlessly closed to them in the past; (b) it creates dangerous situations in which people will inevitably suffer; or (c) it doesn't change anything: hypocrisy will always be with us and sex and heartbreak are inevitably linked.

(5) Not long ago, most people had responsibilities only to those in their family or workplace or community. They knew very little about what was happening beyond these limits, and did not feel they had obligations toward people with whom they had no close social ties. Recently, however, the world has become smaller and more closely knit. People know about famines, disasters, and injustices happening far away and have attitudes to them. Many people think they have an obligation to do something to relieve the suffering or improve the situation of faraway people they have no social or economic links with.

Which of the following comes nearest to expressing your attitude to this widened sense of responsibility? (a) It recognizes obligations that people always had but did not appreciate the importance of; (b) it distracts people from the more important obligations they have to their families and their communities; or (c) it is appropriate to a more closely knit world, just as the older attitude was appropriate to a world of more isolated communities.

Classification Your answers to these questions suggest general attitudes to moral progress. They probably put you into one of three classes which we could label "optimist," "pessimist," or "cautious."

Optimists about moral progress think that as we consider more varied cases and develop our moral principles to handle them, we get nearer and nearer to a moral system that is really adequate for human life. Optimists often think we are getting nearer to reflective equilibrium. You are an optimist if you gave three or more (a) answers.

Pessimists about moral progress fear that in trying to improve our moral ideas we may often make them worse, either by creating situations in which people suffer or by deviating from an absolute moral standard. You are a pessimist if you gave three or more (b) answers.

Those who are cautious about moral progress suspect that all moralities have their advantages and disadvantages, which are very hard to compare. They tend to think that morality does not improve; it just changes. You are cautious if you gave three or more (c) answers.

Your answers may have a more complex pattern that does not put you simply into one of these three classes. You can probably still use the labels to describe your attitude to moral progress. For example, if you gave two (a)s, one (b), and two (c)s, you are a cautious optimist. You may find it helpful to think why you react differently to some of the cases than you do to others.

You may find that you are confident in your answers to some of these questions and very uncertain about others. In particular, you may find (5) or (4) puzzling. You may feel you don't know which answer is nearest your own attitude to the issues in them. This may be because you feel that one or both of them describes a moral problem that we do not have a satisfactory solution to. Then you should ask yourself: is this because we should do more thinking and experimenting about these topics, or because the problems are fundamentally insoluble?

The dialogue

Two students, Alfa and Beth, have been taking their first philosophy course. In fact, they have been studying from this book. They are discussing the effect the course is having on them.

Alfa: This course is making me think differently about a lot of things. The most surprising side to it all is that it is making me consider beliefs I didn't know I had. For example, I suppose I must always have thought that ethics was completely different from science. When I was a child I thought that my parents, or God, knew what was right and wrong. What they thought made things right and wrong. Then when I was passing through periods of doubt about religion, or rebellion against authority, I thought that people just make these things up, and really they can make them up any way they want. But now I am beginning to doubt this.

Beth: Well, I still think we make up our morals. Morality is very different from science, anyway. After all, science is about this world around us. You can see and touch it. And different people can all see and touch it, and make experiments. Then they can discuss it; they can knock holes in each other's theories. That's what falsification is all about. You don't get anything like that for right and wrong.

Alfa: You've just missed the big point. You don't see why the method of falsification is so different from empiricism. It doesn't say "Ignore all your previous beliefs and just look at the observable facts." It says "Use your previous beliefs, but test them, compare them with new ones, and if they are false you'll eventually find out." That's exactly what reflective equilibrium says about ethics, too. Add to that the fact that science is based on falsification, and not on empiricism, and you get the conclusion that science and ethics work in basically the same way. I don't know if I love or hate that conclusion, but it really blows my mind.

Beth: I just don't believe that reflective equilibrium is like scientific method. There aren't people making theories and other people doing experiments.

Alfa: Yes there are. There are philosophers and novelists and people who write advice columns in magazines. They're the theory-makers. And then there are the people who actually try to follow the ideas of these people. They're doing experiments with their lives.

Beth: ★ It seems a pretty strained analogy to me. I don't see anything corresponding to empirical evidence. The point about using your senses to learn about the world is that they are actually connected to the world. You see things because they're there.

Alfa: Think of the analogy this way. Someone has a moral theory which says "This is a good way to live," and then other people try living that way. Then they may find it works, or they may find it is awful. Often something sounds great until you actually try it. Complete sexual freedom, for example, but that's just my opinion. The point is, you can't tell till you try, and that's the dialogue of a scientific experiment.

Beth: Seems a pretty incompetent experiment to me. No control groups, no double blind method. But I've just thought of a different problem. There's an aim to science, to discover the truth about nature. But you're testing moral theories, if you really insist on calling them that, against the ways people find it pleasant or painful. That's a completely different kind of aim. People could be as happy as pigs in clover, though their values were completely false.

Alfa: ☆ No, no: you're missing something else too. That's what it is for a moral theory to be true. The true morality is the one that works socially, the one that can be at the heart of a functioning society of all sorts of people. Including rebellious skeptical people doubting everything they're taught.

Beth: You might as well say "The truth about witches and demons and little green men from outer space is whatever works for the people who believe in them." ✦

Alfa: Well, just suppose for a minute that there is a reflective equilibrium in morals, a theory about right, wrong, justice, blame, and all that, which is the best fit we can get between our background of moral beliefs and our feelings about particular situations. Suppose it. Just give it to me for the sake of argument. ✧ Then supposing this exists, think of how we could find out what it's like. We'd have to take some risks of getting it wrong, in order to have a good chance of discovering anything worthwhile. In fact, we would have to balance between accuracy and informativeness. Just like in science. And the resemblance goes deeper yet. We could try to use utilitarianism to find the best moral theory. We could try to see all the consequences of all the acts we might perform and see how much pleasure or pain each consequence would have. This would resemble using empiricism to find out the truth about nature. Both are strategies which are high on accuracy and low on informativeness. And both proceed very slowly, needing a lot of evidence before they come up with any answers. And both ignore the whole background of our commonsense beliefs.

Beth: Hold on a minute. Utilitarianism and empiricism are completely different things. You could be a utilitarian in ethics without being an empiricist about knowledge. Or the other way around.

Alfa: Sure, I'm not denying that. But there are resemblances between them. Here's another. They're both based on things you can experience immediately, in ways that they suppose to be independent of your beliefs. Pleasure and pain for utilitarians, and sense perception for empiricists.

Beth: I suppose any two things are alike if you look hard enough. But the more I think about utilitarianism and empiricism the less I like either of them. So I don't really care if they're similar.

Alfa: But the best alternatives to both of them are similar, too. Kantian ethics is the natural competitor to utilitarianism, and if you develop it so as to take out its crazier aspects you end up with reflective equilibrium. Or something like it. And that expresses a pretty similar attitude to falsification in science.

Beth: Though you'll admit they're completely independent. Neither implies the other. But look, why don't you just tell me why you're digging out these similarities. What's underneath them?

Alfa: It's easy. When I began this course I thought that either we had to accept the beliefs we learn from our culture or we had to try to make completely new and trustworthy beliefs from scratch. I thought this for beliefs about the physical world, beliefs about religion, beliefs about morals, everything. But now I see that there is a third alternative. We can accept the beliefs we need to get on with science or moral life, but proceed in a questioning, testing, way, so that we eventually filter out the ones that are wrong. That is practical and reasonable and critical all at once: between skepticism and complacency.

Beth: Perhaps you have something there. But none of that can hide the fact that morality could be an illusion. The world of science could be an illusion too, though somehow I find that harder to believe.

Chapter 11

The questionnaire at the beginning of this section led to a classification of answers as those of optimists, pessimists, and those who are cautious about moral progress. Is Alfa an optimist, a pessimist, or cautious? What is Beth at the beginning of the dialogue? What is Beth at the end?

By the end of the dialogue, Alfa and Beth have come to agree on some things. Beth grudgingly accepts Alfa's assertion that "We can accept the beliefs we need to get on with science or moral life, but proceed in a questioning, testing, way, so that we eventually filter out the ones that are wrong." But Beth also says that "none of that can hide the fact that morality could be an illusion." Can Beth say both these things? Can we allow the possibility of moral progress and also the possibility that morality is an illusion? Suppose that Alfa were to press Beth on this point, trying to get Beth to say that since we can filter out "wrong" moral beliefs, morality cannot be an illusion. Which of the following would be good replies for Beth to make?

◆ In science too we filter out wrong beliefs. But all of scientific belief just might be an illusion.
◆ There is nothing in morality that corresponds to the link empirical evidence makes between science and reality.
◆ Moral beliefs are based on tradition, while science is based on evidence alone.
◆ It might turn out that only a fool takes morality seriously, while you're a fool if you don't take science seriously.

Which of the sentences below states a conclusion of the dialogue, something that Alfa and Beth have given good reasons for believing?

◆ Empiricism has similarities to utilitarianism.
◆ Empiricism has dissimilarities to utilitarianism.
◆ Reflective equilibrium in ethics is like falsification in science.
◆ There are experiments in ethics.

At the point marked ✧ Alfa makes an assumption, which Beth does not challenge, although Beth probably does not actually agree with it. At the very end, Beth admits that perhaps Alfa is right in thinking that there is a middle position "between skepticism and complacency." Suppose that Beth had remembered letting Alfa get away with the assumption at ✧. Which one of the following would then be the best thing for Beth to say at the very end?

◆ No, I don't agree at all about this middle position. It all depends on an assumption you never justified.
◆ Both morality and science are illusions.
◆ We should agree that if there were a reflective equilibrium in ethics then ethics would be like science.
◆ If morality is like science then science is based on an illusion.

At ✦ Beth says that what Alfa says about ethics would also be true about demons, witches, or little green men from outer space. Alfa does not reply directly to this. But Beth returns to the issue at the very end of the dialogue. Which of the following would be a good reply for Alfa to make to what Beth says at ✦?

◆ Yes. If we could find opinions about demons, witches, or extraterrestrials which stood up to all the evidence and criticism we threw at them, they would be as certain as our opinions about science.

◆ No. There's a big difference. There are no demons, witches, or little green men from outer space, but there are ways in which people can live well together.

◆ Witches, demons, and extraterrestrials have nothing to do with ethics or science.

◆ Ethics is like the supernatural in that you can't be certain about it. That's why it's quite different from science.

Beth's speech at ★ describes a difference between science and ethics. Alfa does not respond to this point. Could Beth have pushed the point a bit harder, and resisted some of the things Alfa subsequently says?

Alfa's speech at ☆ states a rather bold theory of what morality is about. Does anyone who accepts Alfa's conclusions at the end of the dialogue have to agree with this theory?

11.6 Fallibilism

Some of the central problems of Western philosophy are about skepticism. Are there good reasons to think that the beliefs we normally take for granted are true? Is there any way of ruling out all the strange but possible ways in which reality might be very different from how we think it is? These are questions that apply with equal force to science, to everyday life, and to ethics. But by now we have met a number of ideas that, taken together, give solutions to many of these problems. The philosophical position these ideas add up to is often called *fallibilism*.

According to fallibilism, nearly everything we believe could be false, and yet there is a difference between the beliefs we have good reasons to hold and the ones we do not. In other words, the reasons that make some beliefs rational or justified and other beliefs irrational do not prevent some of the justified, rational beliefs from turning out to be false.

Fallibilism is most powerful when combined with what in Section 1 of this chapter was called *limited optimism*. That position claims that by reasoning, considering evidence, and filtering through our beliefs looking for contradictions and conflicts with empirical evidence, we can find some true beliefs and eliminate many false ones. The optimism is very limited: it claims that in this way we can *eventually* move toward truth and away from falsehood. We may never get to a position where all our beliefs are true, and whenever we change our beliefs we may add some new falsehoods. But in the long run many falsehoods get filtered out. That is why limited optimism is consistent with fallibilism.

Fallibilism holds that any of our beliefs could be false. Limited optimism holds that we can discover truths. These support one another.

In fact, limited optimism and fallibilism support one another. Fallibilism provides the assurance that anything can be tested, since anything could be false, which allows the profound and wide-ranging testing that limited optimism builds on. And limited optimism provides the assurance that fallibilism is not just pointing to an abstract possibility: we can actually discover that any belief could be false.

If falsification and limited optimism are right, we can hope to find ways of testing beliefs that now we have to take for granted. One example is the belief that different people have the same experiences in the same situation, that colors look the same and pain feels the same to one person as to another. We use this belief as a background belief in testing other beliefs. But we do not know how to test it. Yet it is possible that as we change and expand our beliefs we will find a way of testing this belief and comparing it with alternatives. And then we might have a way of seeing how similar the experience of animals of different species is. Another example is our beliefs in the assumptions of logic and mathematics. We need these beliefs and they seem obviously true, but we have no idea how we would begin to test them. We do not know how to describe alternatives to compare them with, or how we would go about making the comparisons. We can have a limited optimism that fallibilism can apply here: as our knowledge develops we may find ways of putting even these things in doubt. The more we know the more we can test.

Part I of this book began with problems of skepticism. At the end of Part I it seemed that the answer to skepticism was "be content with a lot less than certainty, learn to live with doubt." In Part II we have seen that this is only part of the answer. For we can *use* our capacity to doubt as a tool for discovering truths. If we put as much value on discovering truth as on avoiding falsehood, and if we realize that we may have to believe many false things on the way to learning a few true things, this acceptance of doubt becomes a much more positive factor. It points to new and currently unimaginable changes in our beliefs in the future.

There is a price for accepting this solution to skepticism. It shows up with both science and ethics. Suppose, for example, that after a lot of reflection you decide that a certain moral rule is right. Perhaps you decide that people should never have any secrets from their friends and family. You come to this conclusion after considering many real and imaginary examples and think out carefully the consequences of this rule and various alternatives. So, having decided that it is right, you use it to suggest to others what they ought to do, and to criticize their behavior. These suggestions and the criticism are sincere; they come from your honest and thought-out opinion about what is right. But you have to admit that a bit more thinking, or some situation you hadn't taken account of, might change your opinion. So you have to say: this is what I really and honestly think you ought to do, but perhaps tomorrow my advice will be different. Is that really moral conviction?

A similar problem arises with fallibilism about science. We have many opinions that are based on solid scientific evidence. For example, we think that influenza (flu) is caused by a virus. In fact it seems too weak to call this just an opinion. We take it that we know that influenza is caused by a virus. But we have to admit that new evidence could come in tomorrow showing that some, many, or even all cases of influenza are caused by something completely different. So we have to say: this is what I know, but it might turn out to be wrong. Is that really knowledge?

Fallibilists want to say: you can have deep moral convictions while admitting that they may change, and you can have knowledge while admitting you might be wrong. If that sounds strange, they say, it is a strangeness we just have to get used to. But this is something they have to argue for. The solution to skepticism has made new problems.

Philosophy is usually like this. When we solve problems we make new ones. But that is one of philosophy's advantages, not one of its defects.

Box 19 Boats versus Houses

Philosophers from Descartes on have used house metaphors. Our beliefs need a solid *foundation* and skepticism finds ways of *undermining* them. From a solid foundation, whether given by reason or empirical evidence, one *builds* upwards to get ever more elaborate structures of belief: scientific castles. One striking metaphor by a modern philosopher that contrasts with this is *Neurath's boat*. Otto Neurath was an Austrian philosopher who wrote in the 1920s and 1930s. He was a member of the "Vienna Circle" of logical positivists. He wrote:

We are like sailors who have to rebuild their ship on the open sea, without ever being able to bring it to a port and construct it again from the best materials.

The idea is that sailors in a damaged boat in the open sea have to repair one part at a time, always keeping the whole boat afloat, until they have eventually got a boat that will float better and withstand fiercer storms. If they started to rebuild their boat from the bottom up in the middle of the ocean they would drown. Similarly, we have a set of beliefs that we need to keep in working order in order to live our everyday lives and carry out scientific research. We want to improve it, but we have to do so without destroying it. So we have to carefully examine one belief at a time, leaving the others in place.

Conclusions to This Chapter

◆ *In science, ethics, and everyday life, the way we react to evidence is shaped by our background beliefs. But background beliefs can themselves change in response to evidence.*

◆ *One important way in which our moral beliefs can change, in philosophy and in everyday life, is by moving toward reflective equilibrium. That is, there are always conflicts between, on the one hand, our general ideas about right and wrong, duty, human rights, and so on, and on the other the reactions we have to particular situations. These conflicts can be reduced by modifying both the general ideas and the particular reactions.*

◆ *Reflective equilibrium resembles Popper's ideas of falsification, or the hypothetico-deductive method, in suggesting that we can filter through our beliefs, in ethics, science, and everyday life, finding the ones that do not stand up to criticism. Unlike the ground-clearing assumption of rationalism and empiricism, this filtering happens slowly, while we acquire new beliefs rather than in preparation for them.*

◆ *Fallibilism, which holds that any of our beliefs could turn out to be false, and limited optimism, which holds that we can filter through our beliefs finding the faulty ones, support one another. Fallibilism gives us the confidence to test anything, and limited optimism suggests that we can eventually discover when our beliefs are false.*

Further Reading

Rawls and Goodman

Chapters 1, 2, and 3 of John Rawls, A *Theory of Justice*. Harvard University Press, 1971.
Chapter 1 of Nelson Goodman, *Fact, Fiction, and Forecast*, fourth edition. Harvard University Press, 1983.

Fallibilism

Chapter 3 of Martin Hollis, *Invitation to Philosophy*. Blackwell, 1985.
Chapter 5, section F, of John Cottingham, *Rationalism*. Oxford University Press, 1988.
Chapter 5 of Adam Morton, *A Guide through the Theory of Knowledge*, third edition. Blackwell, 2002.
*Chapter 10 of Donald Gillies, *Philosophy of Science in the 20th Century*. Blackwell, 1993.

Electronic resources

Routledge Encyclopedia of Philosophy (available online at many universities): articles on Fallibilism; Moral justification; Induction, epistemic issues in; Rawls, John.
Stanford Encyclopedia of Philosophy (http://plato.stanford.edu/): Animals, moral status of; Bayes' Theorem; *Epistemology, Bayesian*; Reflective equilibrium (*italicized* items are available as this book goes to press; the others should be available soon).

Postcard History of Philosophy II

Some ancient Greek philosophers thought that perception cannot give us important knowledge of the world. Other Greek philosophers, such as Aristotle, disagreed and emphasized perception as well as reason. Aristotle argued that we should not expect to achieve certainty on all topics. Aristotle also described ways in which a person's life could achieve happiness. Some later Greek philosophers such as Epicurus, interpreted happiness as an intelligent search for pleasure.

Although Aristotle's science was rejected during the early years of the scientific revolution, and rationalist thinkers also reject the role he gave to perception, a picture of knowledge that emphasizes perception was given by empiricism, which was first suggested by Francis Bacon but most clearly thought out by *Locke* and philosophers influenced by him, such as *Berkeley* and *Hume*. According to empiricism, perception not only gives us our basic evidence but also provides the concepts in terms of which we think.

A moral philosophy that fits the empiricist picture of how we think was provided by utilitarianism. The first explicit utilitarian ethics was that of *Bentham*, whose basic idea was that the right action is the one that produces the greatest amount of happiness for the greatest number of people. *Mill* developed Bentham's ideas, trying to avoid some of their undesirable consequences.

Kant produced a theory of knowledge that combines empiricism and rationalism. According to Kant, we have to make some assumptions that, although they are not provable by reason, are necessary in order to make sense of our experience. Later philosophers have usually accepted that we have to make some arbitrary assumptions in order to get started with interpreting evidence and evaluating theories. If this idea is combined with the need to test even these arbitrary assumptions the result is the hypothetico-deductive method described by twentieth-century philosophers of science such as *Popper, Quine,* and *Hempel*.

In ethics too, Kant points to twentieth-century views. He emphasized the importance of moral rules that we could use as general principles governing all human conduct. Later thinkers have usually not agreed that this would result in a single set of rules, which should be obeyed under all circumstances. But modern moral philosophers such as *Rawls* have described how the search for general principles can result in a reflective equilibrium, a balance between our feelings about particular cases and the general principles we accept, which is in some ways like the hypothetico-deductive method in science.

Part III   Reality

Here is an outline of the sequence of topics in Part III. At the beginning of each chapter the thread of prose will reappear in a way that shows the connection of the chapter with the whole of Part III.

Is science *the* way to understand reality, or just one way among many? Are there other pictures of reality that are as good or better? Physical science is sometimes used to support materialism, which claims that everything is physical. In contrast, idealism claims that everything is mental. If materialism is true then our minds are physical. One theory which disagrees with this is dualism, which says that minds are not part of the physical world.

If materialism is true, morality might be an illusion. Some philosophers have tried to show how moral principles could be true even if everything is physical. One influential approach is to study contracts that people in a society could make with one another for mutual benefit.

If materialism is true, many other features of our lives could be illusions. The example of colors shows many of the problems that also arise with our conviction that we make free decisions and our conviction that we are the same persons throughout our lives.

Idealism is the opposite of materialism. Arguments for idealism that were used by Berkeley in the eighteenth century are still influential in the form of verificationism and instrumentalism. The conflict between instrumentalism and realism about science is part of much larger questions about how our thinking relates to the world.

Introduction: Pictures of Reality

Part III of this book is about general pictures of reality that philosophers have defended. In particular, it is about the problems that have arisen in philosophy from the influence of physical science. Does science show that many of our beliefs are false, and that many of the ways we think are illusions? Is science *the* way to understand reality, or just one way among many?

Suppose someone says to you "In my hand I have five grains of sand. They look small but each of them is bigger than our whole galaxy. In fact, one of them contains our whole galaxy. And as I shift them around, I make things happen in our galaxy millions of years ago." You can be pretty sure that if what this person says is right, just about everything you believe is wrong. What this person says contradicts most of what you believe because it contradicts a *picture of reality* that you have. A picture of reality is a very general framework that helps you fit together all your more detailed beliefs. Your picture of reality tells you that small things, like grains of sand, cannot contain big things, like galaxies. And it tells you that what happens at one time, like moving those grains now, cannot have effects at an earlier time. You may not know you have this picture of reality, but it shapes the things you believe. It gives background beliefs without which you would not be able to think or consider evidence.

The commonsense picture   The central concept of the commonsense picture of reality is that of a *thing*. Things have locations in *space*, and *properties* such as color and shape. When you perceive a thing you have an experience which reflects the properties of the thing: when you touch a hot stove your hand feels hot, when you see a full moon you see a round shape. Changes in an object have *causes*: they are the effects of earlier changes in other objects. The relation between causes and effects is closely connected with the existence of *laws of nature*, which are general facts about the patterns of changes that happen to *kinds* or *species* of things.

The scientific picture   The picture of the world given by contemporary science is different from this everyday picture in several ways. Scientific theories usually involve what we might call *constitutive principles*, which say what the *parts* and *structure* of things are. Cells have cell walls and nuclei, molecules are composed of atoms, which are composed of electrons, photons, and neutrons, and so on. And scientific theories also involve more basic *laws of nature*, such as: energy is conserved, or entropy (physical disorder) increases. Now the distinctive thing about scientific theories is the lack of a direct connection between the constitutive principles and the laws of nature. For the laws of nature discovered by physics are not about fundamental particles in particular, or any objects in particular. They are about very abstract properties which just about anything can have, such as the energy and entropy of an individual thing or physical system.

Because the laws of nature postulated by scientific theories tend to be so abstract and general, they need not have much connection with common sense. For example, Einstein's theories of relativity replace the time and space of common sense with a strange and complicated structure which is easier to grasp with mathematics than with visual imagination. The commonsense idea that objects exist in space and endure through time is replaced with the idea that time and space form a four-dimensional "continuum." How we divide the continuum up between time and space is to some extent arbitrary. Another theory, quantum mechanics, the physics of subatomic particles, gives fundamental laws governing the locations and other properties of particles. But these laws do not predict what particles will do. Instead, they state probability distributions. For example, they give a probability for an atom's emitting a photon of light, and a probability for its not emitting it, and, according to quantum mechanics, there is no way of telling for sure if the photon will be emitted or not. As Einstein said, it is as if God is throwing dice.

Since the world described by science is so different from the world of common sense, it is not surprising that science has an explanation of why the world *seems* to fit the commonsense picture. The explanation describes how we perceive the world. Properties of objects produce sensations which our brains interpret in order to give us our beliefs. This interpretation can be very inaccurate, and this is why, according to science, we have the commonsense beliefs we do.

But if this is true, a lot of what we take to be obvious features of the world are really illusions. Can this really be? Part III explores the question.

Further Reading

About metaphysics

Simon Blackburn, "Metaphysics," in *The Blackwell Companion to Philosophy.*

About modern science

Richard Feynman, *Six Easy Pieces.* Addison-Wesley, 1995.
Paul Davies and J. R. Brown (eds), *The Ghost in the Atom.* Cambridge University Press, 1986.
Freeman Dyson, *Infinite in all Directions.* Harper and Row, 1988.

About relativity

Jeremy Bernstein, *Einstein.* Fontana, 1973.
Albert Einstein, *Relativity,* 15th edition. Methuen, 1954.

About Quantum mechanics

Robert Gilmore, *Alice in Quantum Land.* Sigma Science, 1994.
J. C. Polkinghorne, *The Quantum World.* Longman, 1984.
*R. I. G. Hughes, *The Structure and Interpretation of Quantum Mechanics.* Harvard University Press, 1989.

12 Materialism and Dualism

Introduction

Is science *the* way to understand reality, or just one way among many? Are there other pictures of reality that are as good or better? Physical science is sometimes used to support materialism, which claims that everything is physical. In contrast, idealism claims that everything is mental. If materialism is true then our minds are physical. One theory which disagrees with this is dualism, which says that minds are not part of the physical world.

If materialism is true, morality might be an illusion. Some philosophers have tried to show how moral principles could be true even if everything is physical. One influential approach is to study contracts that people in a society could make with one another for mutual benefit.

If materialism is true, many other features of our lives could be illusions. . . .

Chapter Objectives

By the end of this chapter you should be able to answer the following questions.

◆ *What are materialism, naturalism, idealism, and dualism?*
◆ *Why is it hard to understand how our thoughts and feelings could be produced by our brains?*
◆ *Why do materialist philosophies of mind suggest that people can be wrong about their own minds?*

Definitions

The following words used in this chapter are defined in the list of definitions at the end of the book:

dualism	*identity theory*	*vitalism*
eliminative materialism	*materialism*	
idealism	*naturalism*	

12.1 Materialism, Naturalism, Idealism

Some people believe in ghosts, and some do not. There can be good reasons for both belief and disbelief in ghosts. Think of the evidence there could be *against* the existence of ghosts. There could be direct evidence. For example you could read many books on parapsychology, attend séances, talk to people who claim to have seen ghosts, and so on, and as a result come to the conclusion that whenever someone claims to have seen a ghost there is an equally good purely physical alternative explanation. But most people who do not believe in ghosts do not have this kind of reason. Their disbelief is more likely to be on metaphysical grounds. They don't think that ghosts are the kind of thing that really exists. And one reason for thinking that ghosts are not the kind of thing that really exists is *materialism*.

> Materialism says that everything is material. It claims to give a framework into which we can put all our theories about particular aspects of the world.

Materialism is the belief that everything is made of matter. Both "matter" and "made of" are slightly unclear concepts. (Modern physics suggests we should say "matter/energy" instead of matter.) So it is clearer to describe materialism as the belief that there is a single set of laws of nature that governs the behavior of all the things we normally call "material" – mountains, chairs, planets, oceans, electrons, pencils – and that this same single set of laws governs the behavior of everything. Everything including everybody! (So everything that exists is like material things in two ways: the same laws of nature apply, and everything interacts with matter in the way matter does.) If materialism is true then we have a reason for thinking that there are no ghosts. For, according to the usual concept of ghosts, they are not made of flesh and blood, or any other kind of matter, and do not interact with matter in the way physical things do. (They pass through walls, disappear unpredictably, and have no weight.)

Ghosts are not the issue here. Materialism is. It has many hard-to-believe consequences. If materialism is true then your mind, if it exists, must be material. So why should anyone be a materialist? Metaphysical beliefs such as materialism are parts of general pictures of reality (see the Introduction to Part III). We believe in pictures of reality because they claim to make sense of our more detailed theories. For example, materialism explains why physics can be successfully applied in such a wide variety of areas, and why theories that appeal to nonmaterial forces have usually turned out to be wrong.

(We sometimes use the word "materialism" to mean something different. We call someone a materialist if they value material possessions such as money and property above spiritual possessions such as love, happiness, and the respect of others. This is only very loosely connected with the materialism we are concerned with here. You can think that everything is material and still value love; you can even think that everything is spiritual and still value money.)

Box 20 **Epicureanism**

In the third century BC the Greek philosopher *Epicurus* taught his students theories about life and the universe which are still influential. Epicurus argued for a materialist view of the universe, according to which everything in the world is made of material atoms. This theory was invented by an earlier Greek philosopher, *Democritus*. Epicurus used his materialism as a basis for a philosophy of life. This philosophy was hedonistic in that it made pleasure the central good in life. But it emphasized the pain that comes from greed or excess. So Epicurus valued a calm thoughtful life. Since the soul is material it does not survive death and therefore, according to Epicurus, there is no reason to fear death. There is nothing bad that can happen to us after death, since we will not exist. Much of what we now know about the Epicurean philosophy comes through a long poem written two hundred years later by *Lucretius*, a Roman follower of Epicurus.

Materialism is not the only possibility here. There are other metaphysical beliefs that could make sense of our collection of partial theories of reality. A milder alternative to materialism is *naturalism*, the belief that everything that exists forms a unified whole, governed by the same laws. So naturalists expect the behavior of living beings to be explained by the same principles as the behavior of nonliving beings. (And they disbelieve *vitalism*, the view that living things are fundamentally different from nonliving things.) And naturalists, like materialists, expect that human beings are part of the natural world, to be understood with the same theories and techniques.

Or one could believe the exact opposite. *Idealism* says that everything that exists is not material but mental. So idealists too think that there is a unity to nature. But idealists usually think that this unity is not to be found in the terms of the sciences of matter, such as physics and chemistry. If we are to see how everything is one, we have first to think of it all as the expression of mind.

Idealism should be taken seriously. But consider first materialism, to see whether it passes some very simple tests. If materialism is to be an adequate metaphysics it has to make sense of other things that we believe, two in particular. It has to make sense of what we believe about our own minds. And it has to make sense of the difference between right and wrong.

12.2 Materialisms

We sometimes make a simple contrast between materialism and idealism because we see it as part of a conflict between science and religion. Since the days of Galileo in the sixteenth century some scientists, theologians, and philosophers have feared or hoped that if science can explain many events in terms of physical laws then we will not need to understand the world in terms of God. But before the sixteenth century people did not see a science/religion conflict; and recent physical science is in some ways less threatening to religion. (As physics has developed, energy rather than matter has become the central concept.) Moreover, many famous scientists, notably Newton, have had firm religious convictions, and many religious thinkers have not been idealists. There are many possibilities here.

To see some of the ways we could think about these things first consider the four possibilities below.

(1) Some nineteenth-century spiritualists believed that ghosts and spirits were made of a kind of gaseous matter, called ectoplasm. They thought it could be seen and photographed. They wondered whether it had any weight. (Sometimes dying people were weighed to see if they lost any weight as their spirits left their bodies.) Suppose they were right, and that every person has a soul which is made of a kind of perceptible matter, which is different from matter in the person's body or in the rest of the nonliving world.

(2) Some religions believe that after death people live on in another physical world. They have real bodies and feel real sensations and pain, and eat real food. But this other world is not part of the universe we live in. Suppose this is right, and there is another universe, made of the same kind of stuff as this one but not connected to it.

(3) Many people believe in telepathy, and think of it as a physical force. They think that something like radio waves can travel from one person's brain to another, carrying that person's thoughts. Suppose that this sometimes happens, so that our minds can contact each other over a distance by an invisible physical means.

(4) Some scientists studying psychic phenomena think that human beings have a capacity to predict random events. In some studies, people asked to guess what sides dice would fall or what random numbers a computer would generate got more correct answers than they would by chance. Suppose that this is true, so that we have better than chance knowledge of random aspects of the future.

Possibilities (1)–(2) are not easy to fit into a simple materialism-idealism contrast. Here are five general positions:

Physicalism: All events occur in accordance with the laws of physics.
Materialism: Everything is made of matter.
Vitalism: Living things obey different laws from nonliving things.
Naturalism: Everything forms one connected whole, since the laws of nature link everything to everything else.

***Spiritualism*: There is a dimension to reality that is independent of everything physical.**

- Could someone believe both (1) and materialism? What would they have to mean by "matter"?
- Could someone believe both (2) and naturalism? What would they have to mean by "connected"?
- Could someone believe both (2) and spiritualism? What would they have to mean by "independent"?
- Could someone believe both (3) and physicalism? What would they have to mean by "physics"?
- Could someone use (4) to support vitalism? How might they connect them?
- Could someone use (3) to oppose vitalism? How might they connect them?

Physicalism, materialism, and naturalism are all similar positions. And vitalism and spiritualism are similar. But all five positions are distinct from one another. For example, someone might believe in vitalism and materialism. They might use (1) to support this combination of views. How might the connection work? (Think: kinds of matter.) Or someone might believe in spiritualism and physicalism, and use (3) to support this combination. How might this connection work? (Think: kinds of force and energy.)

An interesting possibility is to use (4) to connect vitalism and naturalism. How might this connection work? (Think: patterns amid randomness.)

12.3 Are You a Materialist or an Idealist?

Choose one answer to each of the following questions (before looking at the scoring method below). Then use the scoring method to classify your metaphysical tendencies.

(1) Telepathy would occur when one person could receive another person's thoughts, without speech or electronics. On present evidence is telepathy (a) impossible, (b) unlikely, (c) possible, or (d) actual?
(2) Suppose that there were firm evidence of telepathy. Would this mean that physics ought to be (a) abandoned, (b) supplemented with a very different discipline, (c) expanded, (d) left as it is?
(3) Suppose there were statistical evidence that the positions of the planets influence human fate. Would this be because of (a) an accident, (b) unknown causal processes, (c) something beyond our understanding, or (d) the truth of astrology?
(4) That human beings can survive death is (a) likely, (b) possible, (c) unlikely, (d) impossible.
(5) That today's physics may someday be seen as wildly inaccurate myth is (a) impossible, (b) unlikely, (c) possible, (d) probable.

(6) Where are rainbows: (a) in the sky, (b) in people's minds, (c) in raindrops, or (d) nowhere?

(7) Numbers are (a) fictions, (b) marks on paper, (c) ideas in our minds, (d) objects independent of us.

(8) Compare democracy (in politics) and energy (in science): (a) energy and democracy are both just concepts we use to describe our experiences; (b) both energy and democracy are dubious concepts; (c) energy is a useful concept and democracy a dubious one; (d) energy is real and democracy is just an idea.

(9) A factor in many diseases is "stress," which in part depends on a person's experiences and emotions. The suggestion that stress might one day be understood in purely physical terms is (a) likely, (b) possible, (c) improbable, (d) impossible.

(10) Brain chemistry seems to be connected with some severe mental disorders. The possibility that a person's personality might be completely explicable in terms of their brain chemistry is (a) crazy, (b) far-fetched, (c) likely, (d) probable.

(11) People who believe that they are biological organisms governed by biological principles are likely to treat other people in a way that is (a) more understanding than, (b) different from, (c) the same as, (d) less understanding than those who believe that humans are exceptions to the principles governing other animals' behavior.

Scoring system: for odd-numbered questions, give answers a, b, c, d the points 4, 3, 2, 1 respectively. For even-numbered questions give answers a, b, c, d the points 1, 2, 3, 4 respectively. Then add up your score.

◆ Total of 35 to 44: you are a materialist. You accept science roughly as it is, and interpret it as requiring everything to be explained in terms of interactions of matter and energy.

◆ Total of 27 to 34: you are a naturalist. You think science is a large part of the truth, but it may have to be revised in fundamental ways.

◆ Total of 19 to 26: you are a semi-idealist. You think that science is a useful but potentially misleading tool.

◆ Total of 11 to 18: you are an idealist. You think that science is at best a partial guide to the truth, and that not everything about humans and other thinking creatures can be described by it.

12.4 Dualism

The question is whether materialism, or any similar position, can give an adequate philosophy of mind. Begin with an extreme antimaterialist position, *dualism.* Dualism is the view that mind and matter are very profoundly different – so different that understanding one of them leaves basic facts about the other unexplained. (So "spiritualism" in Section 12.2 is a form of dualism.) In particular, no amount of knowledge of the human brain or the rest of the human body will give a full understanding of the human mind.

Dualism is sometimes expressed as saying that mind and matter are different *substances.* "Substances" here does not mean chemical substances, like hydrogen or sulphuric acid. It means "basic constituent of reality." So dualism is the view that mind and matter are as different as things can get.

An analogy may help. Consider on the one hand physical objects, like cars and planets, and on the other hand events, like wars and football games and collisions. Clearly, both objects and events exist. And clearly, objects and events are different. Cars and collisions are completely different sorts of things. You can't imagine discovering that events were really things, or vice versa. Dualism says that mind and matter are as different as objects and events. In fact, many dualists think that mind is even more different from matter than this. For events and objects can only exist together, but some dualists think minds could exist without matter.

Why might one believe in dualism? It is not hard to find reasons why someone might *want* dualism to be true. For example, you might want to be able to believe in immortality, and you might think that since after people die their bodies soon cease to exist, there is no chance of a human mind's surviving death unless it is very different from its body. Or you might think that morality is impossible unless people have free will, which is impossible if they are parts of the material universe. Or you might have disgust or contempt for the body, seeing it as the source of lust and sin, and thus want our minds to be very different from it. But reasons for wanting something to be true are not reasons for believing that it actually is true.

There might be scientific evidence for dualism. Attempts to understand the mind in terms of the brain might fail so completely that everyone acknowledged that we have to consider some completely different possibility. Or there might be religious grounds for believing in dualism. Some religious authority in which you have faith might assure you that mind and matter are profoundly different.

Suppose you have neither of these reasons for believing in dualism. It still might be that much more ordinary facts about mind and matter support dualism. Some philosophers have thought that they could make arguments based on everyday hard-to-deny observations that would show how different mind and body must be. The most famous such argument is that of Descartes.

Descartes bases his argument on an undoubted fact: that it is very hard to imagine how a material structure such as a brain can produce thinking and feeling. Now at first sight this seems just to show that materialism is hard to believe, not that it is false. (Compare: it is hard to believe that the universe is billions of years old, and will continue for billions of years after human life has ceased on earth. But the difficulty of believing this does not show that it is false.) Descartes, however, finds an ingenious way of bridging the gap.

To begin, he assumes that he can imagine that his body and the whole physical world do not exist. (See the discussion of Descartes' rationalism in Chapter 3, Section 5.) And he takes himself to have shown that he cannot imagine that he, his mind, does not exist. (That is the famous "cogito" argument, discussed in Chapter 3, Section 11.) So there is one very basic difference between his mind and his body: he can imagine away his body but he cannot imagine away his mind. But if two things are different in any respect at all they cannot be the same. So his mind is not the same as his body.

Here are two ways of summarizing the argument:

(a) I can imagine that my body does not exist.
I cannot imagine that my mind does not exist.
Therefore my mind is not my body.

(b) I can imagine that my mind exists but my body does not exist.
Anything that I can imagine is possible.
Therefore it is possible for my mind to exist without my body.
Therefore my mind is not my body.

Whether or not you are convinced by these arguments, you have to be impressed by the cleverness of them. Let me discuss each of them in turn.

The idea of (a) is to find a difference between mind and body, to show that they must be different. Logically speaking, this is an instance of *Leibniz's law*, which states that if any objects are such that one of them has some property that the other does not have then they must be different objects. (Consider two identical twins. Why are they not the same person? Because they were born at different times, even if only minutes apart; because they are always located at different places; because they see and experience different things. Any one of these differences will establish that they are two different persons.) So to show that mind and body are different objects you need to show that one of them has some property that the other does not. That property is that I can imagine its nonexistence. My body has this property and my mind does not.

One might challenge this argument by denying that you can really imagine that your body does not exist. Or one might challenge the assumption that you cannot imagine that your mind does not exist. (After all, you can imagine that your parents never met. And in that case you – and presumably your mind – would not have existed. So in that way you are imagining your mind is not existing at this very moment.) But the general strategy of the argument does not depend on these particular assumptions. The idea behind the argument can work with other assumptions, which might be more believable. For example, consider a particular idea or sensation in your mind, say a headache. You can know that it is a pain, and what sort of a pain it is, just by introspection – that is, just by your capacity to look into your own mind. You can know what it feels like. Now contrast this with any aspect of your brain or its functioning. (Call any fact about a brain at a particular time a brain state. More about brain states soon.) You cannot know what sort of a brain state it is by introspection. So we can make the following argument; call it the *transparency argument*:

I can know the nature of this pain just by introspection.
I cannot know the nature of any brain state just by introspection.
Therefore this pain is not any brain state.
(Ideas are transparent to introspection, physical things are not; therefore ideas are not physical things.)

The section below on materialism discusses ways in which the premises of this argument can be challenged. But the validity of the argument itself can also be challenged. That is, you can make parallel arguments from obviously true premises to obviously false conclusions, in the way described in Chapter 5, Section 5. For example:

Lois Lane loves Superman.
Lois Lane does not love Clark Kent.
Therefore Superman is not Clark Kent.

But Superman *is* Clark Kent. (It may bother you that Lois Lane and Clark Kent / Superman do not really exist. If that bothers you, reword the example with any pair of names referring to the same thing. For example, you could use the names "Mark Twain" and "Samuel Clemens," since Samuel Clemens wrote his books, such as *Huckleberry Finn*, under the name "Mark Twain." So we might consider someone, call her Jane, who admires Mark Twain but does not know that he is also Samuel Clemens, and argue that since Jane admires Mark Twain and Jane does not admire Samuel Clemens, therefore Mark Twain is not Samuel Clemens.)

What is going on here? The reason that we can say that Lois Lane loves Superman while denying that she loves Clark Kent is that when we are talking about Lois Lane's emotions we talk about her ideas of Clark Kent and Superman. And her ideas are of two different people. But this is not a difference between Clark Kent and Superman; it is a difference between Lois Lane's ideas of them. Or, another way of making the point, Lois Lane in a way *does* love Clark Kent. She just does not know that Clark Kent is the person she loves.

(The general topic of why Leibniz's law seems to go haywire in some cases is called *intensionality*. It is a controversial topic. But this much is clear: when words like "believes," "imagines," "wants," "knows" are involved, Leibniz's law does not apply smoothly. It only applies in a straightforward way with objective nonpsychological properties of things like their colors, locations, causes, and effects.)

This leaves (b), the second version of the argument. ("I can imagine my mind existing without my body; therefore it is possible for my mind to exist without my body." It is stated more fully above.) The most worrying step in this argument is from "I can imagine my mind existing without my body" to "It is possible for my mind to exist without my body." For many things seem imaginable which may not be possible. You can imagine living for ever, but that does not show that it is possible for you to live for ever. The fact that you can imagine existing without your body may show something profound about the mind, but it does not seem to give an easy argument that it is different from the body.

This does not show that dualism is false. It does not even show that Descartes was wrong to try to argue for it in terms of our different powers of thinking about mind and body. For the most basic fact about our minds, which makes them seem different from everything else in the universe, is that we see them from the inside, either just by being ourselves or by having sympathy for others and imagining what it is like to be inside their lives. So any philosophy must account for the fact that minds are capable of being seen from the inside – that there is a subjective as well as an objective side to existence. Does this mean that mind has to be different from matter? Perhaps not, but in trying to drive the wedge between them just here, Descartes was drawing attention to a very central and profound point.

Box 21 Dualism and Religion

Since immortality forms part of much religious belief, one might expect that many religions insist on a difference between mind and body. In fact, though, not many religions have as part of their beliefs a dualism as strong as that of Descartes. For example, many Catholic and some Jewish thinkers argue that immortality requires the resurrection of the body. This is because, they argue, if we are to exist as the same separate individuals we are in this life we need the particular bodies we have in this life. Some forms of naturalism, if not wholehearted materialism, are certainly compatible with the general outline of Jewish, Christian, and Islamic belief.

12.5 Leibniz on the Unimaginability of Materialism

The philosopher, mathematician, and scientist Gottfried Wilhelm Leibniz (1643–1716) anticipated modern logic, invented calculus – at the same time as Newton did – and constructed a subtle metaphysical system. In this quotation he is trying to show how hard it is to imagine the mind as a physical system.

> *If we imagine there is a machine whose structure makes it think, sense, and have perceptions, we could conceive it enlarged, keeping the same proportions, so that we could enter it, as one enters into a mill. So, when we inspect its interior, we will only find parts that push one another, and we will never find anything to explain a perception.* (Monadology, 17)

Another way of putting what Leibniz is saying would be like this:

> *Suppose there could be a machine that could think. Then we could make a version of it big enough to go into, and walk around. But looking around in it we would only find the parts and see them working. We wouldn't ever see any thoughts or images. So it would always seem incredible to us that what we were seeing were thoughts and perceptions occurring.*

The image of walking around in a giant thinking machine, or shrinking in size and traveling into a human brain, brings out dramatically how hard it is to imagine how a physical system could produce thoughts and feelings. But this may be a problem with our powers of imagination rather than with physical systems. To sharpen your ideas about this, consider the following questions about Leibniz's point.

Would it make any difference if the "mill' were a giant computer? Then you wouldn't see many moving parts, but there would be electrical currents and magnetic fields. (The tour might be dangerous.) Would it be any easier to imagine how these might be thoughts and perceptions?

The second sentence in the original quotation reads "So, when we inspect its interior . . . we will never find anything to explain a perception." Is this true? Might we be able to *explain* why the machine had thoughts and perceptions without actually observing the thoughts and perceptions. Would this affect the point Leibniz is really trying to make?

Suppose that inside the machine there were screens on which images of the world around it were projected. Would you be able to say you were observing the machine's perceptions?

Suppose that scientists were able to construct miniaturized machines which could travel around inside your brain and radio their observations back to a control center outside. (Suppose that they enter via the bloodstream and can travel into the fluid cavities also.) Would any amount of observation tell the scientists what you were thinking and feeling? Would any amount of observation tell them what it is like for you to think your thoughts and feel your emotions?

Suppose that you could go through *everything* that was happening in the giant machine and know that it was not a thought. Would this show that either the machine did not have thoughts or that its thoughts were not anything physical? Consider an altered version of the transparency argument for dualism described in the previous section. That argument went:

> **I can know the nature of this pain just by introspection.**
> **I cannot know the nature of any brain state just by introspection.**
> **Therefore this pain is not any brain state.**

The new argument runs:

> **I can know the physical state of the machine by inspecting it.**
> **I cannot know the mental state of the machine by inspecting it.**
> **Therefore the physical state of the machine is not the same as its mental state.**

Is this argument more convincing than the original transparency argument?

12.6 Crude and Subtle Materialisms

Most materialist philosophies of mind rest not on abstract metaphysical arguments but on empirical evidence. (The evidence has to be interpreted, though, and the interpretation is sometimes pretty devious or elaborate.) The basic evidence concerns *correlations* between facts about people's minds and facts about their bodies, particularly their brains. There is now a lot of evidence that when anything happens in a person's mind there is a corresponding event in the person's brain. (What makes the two correspond? Here is one way of putting it: if a different event had occurred in the person's mind, it would have been because there was some difference in what happened in the brain.)

The evidence is of two kinds. The older evidence comes from damage to people's brains. Strokes and gunshot wounds, especially, can damage very particular areas of the brain. And people who have such damage often exhibit very particular problems with their psychological functioning. More recent evidence goes the other way: one studies what is happening in the brain when a person is performing a very specific task, like imagining a scene or doing arithmetic or speaking. (Recent technology allows us to do this, for example, by using radioactive tracers to find out where brain metabolism is more or less active at a particular time.)

> Mental events are correlated with brain events. Materialists explain this by saying that they are the same things.

Both kinds of evidence point to the same conclusion: there are specific areas of the brain, and specific pathways between areas of the brain, which are correlated with specific mental capacities. For example, vision is associated with the back of the cerebral cortex: damage there impairs capacities to see and imagine, and seeing and imagining are accompanied by brain activity in that region. It is important to note that the correlations are between areas of the brain and general mental capacities, not particular states of mind. No one has ever found a region of the brain which is active whenever a person thinks it would be nice to have a cheese and pickle sandwich, or one which is correlated with believing in God.

A very simple response to these correlations between the mental and the physical might be just to say: the mental is physical. That is the response of *crude materialism*. Crude materialism says that everything mental – thoughts, sensations, emotions, and everything else that is "in" the mind – is physical. As the eighteenth-century French philosopher d'Holbach said, "the brain secretes thoughts like the liver secretes bile."

It is hard to believe this. If thoughts and emotions are material they must, for example, have weight, and be made of specific chemicals. Could we really weigh my belief that London is further north than Beijing? Does it weigh more or less than your belief that New York is to the east of San Francisco? Could we mix together in a test tube your desire for a ham sandwich, my suspicion that it is wrong to eat meat, and a bit of sulphuric acid (to get a thought resolving the conflict between desire and principle, perhaps)? It is hard to take these possibilities seriously.

Many more sophisticated materialisms are carefully stated so that they don't have any of these ridiculous consequences. The most influential such theory of recent times is the *identity theory*. It asks: what happens when you think, imagine, dream, or anything else mental? And it answers: what is happening is that something is going on in your brain. To put this more carefully we have to talk in terms of brain states or brain events, and states of mind or mental events. A brain state is just the way a brain is at a particular time, or some aspect of the way a brain is. And a state of mind is just (part of) the way a mind is at a particular time. For example, you might be sitting in the dark imagining your mother's kitchen. The state of mind is your imagining the scene, and the brain state is what is happening in your visual cortex at that time. Then the identity theory says: this state of mind is the same as this brain state. (They're identical.) And in general the identity theory says that every state of mind is a brain state.

(Sometimes this is expressed in terms of events: every mental event is a brain event. There are advantages and disadvantages of each version of the theory.)

Saying that states of mind are brain states does not tell us what beliefs, desires, and sensations are. The identity theory goes with a simple and radical line: these things do not exist. You think, you dream, you are in pain, but there is no such thing as your thought, your dream, or your pain. Thoughts, dreams, and pains are just fictions we invent in order to describe how we are thinking, dreaming, and hurting. They do not exist any more than Hamlet and Santa Claus do, and saying "My pain is worse than yesterday" no more means that there is something, a pain, which is worse than it was yesterday than saying "She did it for my sake" means that there is something, a sake, which is mine and for which she did it. Instead they just mean that I am hurting more than I did yesterday and that her motive was to help me.

(Here is another way of putting the point. We should avoid nouns when talking about mind, and use verbs instead. So instead of saying that someone *has* a pain we should say that they *pain*, and instead of saying that someone is throwing a tantrum we should say that they are tantruming. In this way we don't seem to suggest that pains and tantrums are things.)

Why should we believe the identity theory? Its defenders claim that we should believe it for the same kinds of reason that we believe scientific theories. It explains how the mind causes the body to move and the body causes the mind to perceive. Motion and perception are then no longer mysteries. The explanation is similar to the way that we can explain how heat causes motion and motion causes heat by saying that heat is a kind of motion, the motion of all the molecules in the hot substance. Belief that states of mind are identical to brain states is the result of an inference to the best explanation.

Here is a very natural objection to the identity theory. We can observe states of the brain, for example, by recording electrical activity. And we can experience states of mind, for example, by being angry or by believing. But when we do this we see how different they are: no pattern of electrical activity can look like how being angry feels. Defenders of the identity theory have a reply to this. One thing can seem very different when aspects of it are experienced. Clark Kent does not appear to fly through the air; the kinetic energy of molecules does not seem to be hot. But in fact Clark Kent does fly through the air and rescue people; the kinetic energy of molecules is heat: we just do not realize that these things have these properties until we know their true identities.

This objection does not in the end refute the theory. But it does point to a worrying difference between the identity theory and other cases in science where one thing is identified with another. When we know that heat is the motion of an object's molecules we can explain why hot objects feel hot. The molecules of a hot stove transmit their motion to the nerves of your hand when you touch it. But when we know that, say, vision is the activation of the visual cortex, we do not seem to understand why vision has the mental properties that it does. For example, it is not clear how we can explain the difference in sensation between a sight and a sound by identifying the sight as the activity of the visual cortex and the sound as the activity of the auditory cortex. Would understanding enough about these parts of the brain allow one to tell a blind person what the color purple looks like, or tell a deaf person what an oboe sounds like? Perhaps this can be done, but defenders of the identity theory have not shown how.

12.7 Lucretius on Mind and Body

Here is a quotation from the ancient Roman philosopher Lucretius:

Mind and spirit are both composed of matter. We see mind and spirit propelling the limbs, rousing the body from sleep, changing the expression of the face and guiding and steering the whole person. All these activities clearly involve touch, and touch in turn involves matter. How then can we deny that mind and spirit are material? You see the mind sharing in what happens to the body. When the impact of a spear tears bones and sinews, even if it does not penetrate the heart, it is followed by faintness and a tendency to fall, and later, on the ground, the person's mind is in turmoil and they try occasionally to stand up again. The substance of the mind must therefore be material, since it is affected by the impact of material weapons.

There are two arguments for materialism in this quotation. Which of the following seem to fit what Lucretius is saying?

(a) **The mind touches the body.**
Therefore the mind is material.
(b) **Material causes have effects on the mind.**
Therefore the mind is material.
(c) **The mind causes effects in the material world.**
Therefore the mind is material.
(d) **Weapons can pierce the mind.**
Therefore the mind is material.

Which of the following would be a serious objection to Lucretius' arguments?

◆ Material causes can have nonmaterial effects.
◆ Nonmaterial causes can have material affects.
◆ Touch involves something nonmaterial.
◆ Weapons cannot hurt the spirit.

Here are two made-up quotations from two imaginary Roman philosophers. Which one makes a point that Lucretius might feel troubled by?

Moronus: The course of a battle is determined by the Gods. Mars can stir one man's heart to courage and Venus can whisper distraction in another man's ear. So whether you suffer the pain of being pierced by a spear or the pleasures of victory depends on the decisions of the Gods. And the Gods are spirits, not matter. So matter does not determine what happens in our minds.

Acerclunis: The heat and light of the sun travel across space and warm the earth. The colors of objects travel through the air and make us see. Light is not matter, colors are not matter. Throughout nature things that are not material affect things that are. So it is with our minds: they are not material but they cause the motions of our material limbs.

12.8 Antidepressants, Psychosomatic Medicine, and the Mind–Body Problem

Below there are two arguments. One is an argument for materialism and one is an argument for dualism. Neither is completely convincing, but each brings out reasons people have for thinking in materialist or dualist terms. Below the arguments there are four considerations that could strengthen or block the arguments. And below them there are four alternative conclusions, positions rather less extreme than either materialism or dualism, which might also be related to the two arguments.

An argument for materialism **Depression is a state of mind. But depression can often be relieved by antidepressant drugs. These drugs must affect our bodies, and in fact we know quite a lot about how they affect the brain. So changes in the brain can cause changes in the mind. So the mind is an aspect of the brain.**

An argument for dualism **The diseases people develop and their chances of recovering from them are related to their personalities. Some types of personality are more likely to develop heart disease or back pain. And patients with cancer tend to respond better to treatment if they can maintain an optimistic, combative attitude. Sometimes they are taught to visualize their disease as an enemy and to imagine fighting it. This fosters states of mind that hinder the progress of the disease. So we need to affect the mind in order to affect the body: our minds are distinct factors controlling our bodies.**

Since neither of the two arguments is completely convincing as it stands, each might make a stronger case if it could use some further assumptions. On the other hand, making some assumptions might make each argument weaker: the conclusion of the argument would be less likely to be true if the assumption were true. Which of the following considerations strengthens or weakens which of the two arguments? (It is not relevant whether they are true or false. But *if* each one were assumed to be true, and included in one of the arguments, would the result be a stronger or a weaker support for the argument's conclusion?)

(a) Mood and personality are states of the brain.
(b) The effects got by visualization and the like cannot be obtained by physical means.
(c) The effects of antidepressants cannot be obtained by therapies based on talking and thinking.
(d) There are physical mechanisms linking personality to disease.

Fall-back positions

Often, when philosophers want to defend a position they find that the arguments they can offer are not strong enough to show that the position must be true. And other philosophers often have strong counterarguments. Then a *fall-back* position is likely to appear. That is, the philosopher will say: "OK, I still believe it, but if I can't convince you, I can at least defend this weaker claim." The weaker claim is the fall-back position. For example, one person might be arguing that everyone who drives a BMW is rich. Another person might object with all sorts of possible situations in which someone could be very poor and still own a BMW. Then the first person may say "At any rate, most of the people you and I are ever going to meet who own BMWs will be rich." Even that fall-back position may not be true, but it is easier to defend.

Here are some positions that materialists and dualists might fall back to, if they despair of being able to convince each other of their full-strength original positions.

(i)   Very detailed aspects of the mind can be affected by changes in the brain.
(ii) Everything in mind and brain is mirrored by something in the other.
(iii) Everything that happens in the mind is caused by something that happens in the brain.
(iv) Mind and brain are fated to run in parallel, never interacting but always reflecting one another's changes.

Suppose a materialist were to fall back to (i). Would this be an easier or a harder conclusion to defend with the argument about antidepressant drugs?

Suppose a dualist were to fall back to (ii). Would this be an easier or a harder conclusion to defend with the argument about disease and personality?

Suppose a materialist were to fall back to (iii). Would this make it easier to defend materialism against (b)?

Suppose a dualist were to fall back to (iv). Would this make it easier to defend dualism against (d)?

12.9 Materialism and Self-knowledge

Materialism is opposed to dualism, since it claims that there is only one basic kind of thing – material things. It has no room for fundamental two-part divisions like that between mind and body. Arguments for dualism are often based on pure logic plus obvious facts about human experience. (Or at any rate what are claimed to be obvious facts.) Arguments for materialism, on the other hand, usually depend on scientific discoveries that were not at all obvious before modern times. The last section mentioned discoveries about how mind and brain are correlated. Another group of discoveries concerns gaps in people's knowledge of themselves.

How wrong can we be about ourselves? One of the striking developments in the twentieth century was the erosion of people's confidence in their self-knowledge. The work of Sigmund Freud, the founder of psychoanalysis, provides one example of this. Although most people do not believe everything that psychoanalysis claims, almost everyone accepts that repression and self-deception are real. We believe now that people often hide their real desires and beliefs and feelings, even from themselves, so that they do not act on them directly and are not aware that they have them.

Another example of how we have come to doubt self-knowledge is provided by recent cognitive and social psychology. A large number of experiments show pretty clearly that even when people are aware of their beliefs and desires, they are very often wrong about which ones lie behind their actions. Even when people know *what* they are thinking and doing, they are wrong about *why* they are thinking and doing it. A typical (but imaginary) experiment of this kind might divide a sample of teenagers into two groups. Group A is simply asked to arrange a list of rock bands in order of desirability (which bands would you go 100 miles to hear, which ones would you go 1 mile to hear, and so on.) People in group B are first given tapes by bands on the list, and then asked to arrange the list in order of desirability. Then people in both groups are asked why they ranked the bands the way they did, and in addition the people in group B are asked whether their rankings were affected by the fact that they had been given tapes of some bands. The result is that the two groups produce very different rankings of the rock bands but very similar explanations of their reasons. For people in group B deny that being given the tapes affected their judgments, though it is clear by comparing them with group A that it did. (So a person is given a tape by the Digitals but not given one by the Analogs, and rates the Digitals high and the Analogs low, though people who have not been given tapes rate them in the reverse order.)

Materialists usually welcome these discoveries, and dualists usually find them disturbing. The reason is that if the mind is like any other part of nature then we ought to be able to study it and learn surprising new things about it. What people say about it should be corrected by scientific experiments and scientific theories. Science should even be able to correct what a person says about their own mind. To make this vivid, suppose there were a machine that allowed medical scientists to "see" the activity of your whole brain. Imagine electrodes attached to your scalp and sensors picking up activity within the brain, and so on, all feeding into a computer which then can show on its screen the activity of any region or cross-section of your brain. Call this a "brainoscope."

Could a scientist examining your brain with a brainoscope correct what you say about yourself? Suppose that you say that you are in pain, or longing for a cheese and pickle sandwich, or that you prefer the Digitals to the Analogs because their songs have better lyrics. Could the brainoscope tell whether you were telling the truth, lying, or deceiving yourself? If crude materialism were true, then it probably could. Your pains and your beliefs would show up on the screen as clearly as the firings of the nerve cells and the synthesis of brain chemicals.

Assume that crude materialism is false, and that the identity theory is true. Then it is less clear when the brainoscope will be able to correct what you say about yourself. Although the identity theory denies that pains and beliefs exist, it does say that people are in states of pain and belief, and that these states are states of the brain. So by observing the brain it should be possible to "see" what state of mind you are in. But in fact things are not so simple on the identity theory. Suppose that a person is longing for a cheese and pickle sandwich, and at the same time the brainoscope reveals a flurry of intense activity in the brain. The identity theory suggests that the flurry of brain activity is the longing for the sandwich. But that does not mean that by observing the brain activity anyone could know that the person was longing for a cheese and pickle sandwich. It might be that the most anyone could say would be "this person is undergoing a vivid imaginative experience."

So we should make a distinction between two kinds of identity theory. A *strong identity theory* says that each state of mind is identical with a state of the brain, which determines its mental characteristics. So according to a strong identity theory, knowing enough about a brain state should tell you exactly what kind of state of mind it is. So a perfect brainoscope should be able to tell you what someone is thinking and feeling. And this information might correct what people themselves say about their thoughts and feelings. On the other hand, a *weak identity theory* says simply that each state of mind is identical with a state of the brain, without specifying whether knowing anything about that state of the brain will tell us anything about the state of the mind. Thus a weak identity theory will not predict that any brainoscope or other technological device could correct people's opinions about their own minds.

The contrasts between crude materialism and the two kinds of identity theory can be summed up in a table. In the table, "technological correction" means "whether technology such as a brainoscope could correct what people say about their own minds."

	There are thoughts and feelings	People think and feel	Technological correction
Crude materialism	Yes	Yes	Yes
Strong identity theory	No	Yes	Yes
Weak identity theory	No	Yes	No

12.10 Technology versus Introspection

If there is a close connection between the mind and the brain then knowledge of the brain should give us information about the mind. But we have a completely different source of information about our minds, namely introspection. That is, each person is able to say many things about what they feel, what they think, and what they would do under various circumstances. Psychologists have many theories about how these kinds of self-knowledge work, and indeed about how much of this is knowledge at all, rather than self-illusion.

Introspection and information about the brain can conflict. And there are conflicts between them that have not happened yet because our technology is not advanced enough. Use your imagination to put yourself in the five situations below. In each of them, information got through technology conflicts with information from what someone believes about their own mind. When you have understood the situation and the conflict between the two sources of information, ask yourself which source you trust in that case. Draw a ring round (a), (b), (c), or (d) to mark your choice.

(1) You have been having trouble sleeping and you go to your doctor who takes a blood sample. The lab results come back in a week and the doctor tells you "You have been sleeping badly because you are depressed. Your blood contains typical by-products of the brain chemistry of depression. I am going to prescribe you an antidepressant drug." You answer "But I'm not feeling at all depressed. Often I'm quite cheerful. There must be some other cause."

   Is what the doctor says (a) very likely true, (b) possibly true, (c) probably false, or (d) certainly false?

(2) You go to a very advanced dating agency. People you might date are brought into a laboratory with you and you talk to them while your brain waves are being recorded. A computer then analyses the data. An hour later the scientist comes back with a printout and reading from it tells you "When

you were talking to the thirteenth possible date your brain waves showed that you were already deeply in love, after five minutes' acquaintance." You reply "That's crazy. I felt no love for that person at all. In fact all that time I wanted to run out of the room."

Is what the scientist says (a) very likely true, (b) possibly true, (c) probably false, or (d) certainly false?

(3) You go for root canal work to a very progressive dentist who promises you that you will feel no pain at all. While your teeth are being drilled sensors attached to your skin, spine, and skull record tiny changes in electrical conductivity. The dentist promises you a thousand dollars for every three seconds of real pain. Afterwards you say sincerely to the dentist "That was the worst experience of my life: undiluted agony. The only consolation is that you owe me about a million dollars." "No," the dentist replies. "You don't know what real pain is. According to my apparatus, during the whole operation you never experienced anything more than moderate discomfort."

Is what the dentist says (a) very likely true, (b) possibly true, (c) probably false, or (d) certainly false?

(4) You take part in a psychological experiment to study the effects of advertising on people's thoughts. You are shown some standard television advertisements, and then you are injected with a radioactive chemical that is used in some kinds of brain activity. By mapping the patterns of radiation around you the psychologists can then study your reactions to the advertisements. The psychologist tells you "When you were watching that shampoo advertisement you were thinking about sex." You reply "No I wasn't. I was planning a skiing trip with my best friend."

Is what the psychologist says (a) very likely true, (b) possibly true, (c) probably false, or (d) certainly false?

(5) You go to have your eyes examined and the optician uses a new technique which monitors the chemical reactions in the retinas of your eyes as light is shone on them. The optician says to you "You are a very unusual case. When you look at red things you have the color experience that most people have when they look at green things." You say "How could you know what my experience is like?"

Is what the optician says (a) very likely true, (b) possibly true, (c) probably false, or (d) certainly false?

Different people will react in different ways to these five cases. People will generally agree about in which cases the technological answer is more likely to be right and in which cases it is more likely to be wrong, even if they disagree about exactly how plausible the technological answer is in each case.

Check to see if the order of plausibility shown in your reactions is the same as other people's.

There is very likely a correlation between the degree of faith you have in the technological answer and your classification on the "materialist to idealist" range of the questionnaire in Section 12.3. What is this correlation? What reasons are there for it?

On which of the following topics is technology least likely to be able to correct what people say? And on which is it most likely to be able to correct us?

◆ pleasure and pain
◆ thoughts
◆ the quality of experience (like what colors look like and sounds sound like)
◆ moods (like depression)
◆ emotions (like love)

What types of technology are most likely to be able to correct what people say about their own minds?

12.11 Eliminative Materialism

The plausibility of a materialist philosophy of mind depends in part on how it relates everyday self-knowledge to scientific theory and observation. Given that we now think that people can be very wrong about some aspects of their own minds, the important thing is not whether a materialist theory allows that scientific evidence can overrule what people say about themselves, but on *what* topics it allows people to be overruled. So a theory can plausibly allow that scientific evidence can overrule people about the causes of their opinions and actions (remember the experiment about the teenagers and the rock bands). But it must be more careful in saying that someone can be wrong about whether they are in pain. (Not that people's beliefs about what they are experiencing are completely beyond scientific correction. A hypochondriac may think he is in intense pain when really he is just rather uncomfortable. And scientific evidence may help convince him of this.)

So far, we have considered individual people's beliefs about their own minds. What about a whole society's shared beliefs about what minds are and how they work? Can scientific evidence correct that? Folk psychology is the body of beliefs that people in a culture use to explain, predict, and coordinate their actions. (Folk psychology was discussed in Chapter 10, Section 5.) How correctable could folk psychology be? Compare it to our nonscientific beliefs about the physical world. Call that "folk physics." Folk physics is the body of beliefs about how things will move and influence one another. In terms of it we understand how balls will move when we throw them, what will happen when one snooker ball hits another, and so on. You don't have to go to school to know these things. And they are generally accurate. If they were not we wouldn't be able to play ball games or succeed at many practical activities.

But folk physics is not completely accurate. Most people have false beliefs about, for example, what paths falling objects will take. Most people believe that if you are walking past a hole in the ground and want to drop a ball down it while still walking, you should let go of it when you are directly above it. But this is false: you should let go before you are above the hole so that it can follow a curved path down. Might folk psychology also be partly false?

No doubt folk psychology does contain some falsehoods. One school of contemporary philosophers believes something much more drastic, though. According to *eliminative materialism*, folk psychology is riddled with false-hoods, so much so that we should not even bother trying to reconcile its concepts – belief, desire, memory, imagination, etc. – with what we have learned about the brain. Instead we should just forget about them, for serious purposes anyway, and just use brain concepts. Different eliminative materialists have different diagnoses about what is wrong with folk psychology. Some are in effect disagreeing with the picture of subjectivity (see Part II) that they think is part of it. More recent eliminative materialists tend to focus on the concepts of belief and desire (and other "propositional attitudes," concepts which describe thoughts that one could express in language). What they argue is that when we describe what we think and what we want we are telling comforting or socially useful stories about ourselves much more than we are describing real causes of our behavior. The real causes lie in our brains, and there may be no way of describing them by using the words folk psychology gives us.

> Eliminative materialism claims that the concepts of folk psychology are like "witchcraft" or "luck." For serious purposes we should ignore them.

Eliminative materialism represents an even greater break with common sense than identity theory does. For not only does it deny that beliefs and desires (and so on) exist, it also denies that we believe and desire. Or, more cautiously, it denies that we can use these concepts any more seriously than we can use, say, the concept of a witch or the concept of good and bad luck. (When a series of good things happens to someone we say "your luck is holding out." But sophisticated people don't really believe that being lucky or unlucky is an objective property of people, or that some things bring good or bad luck.) Yet in another way eliminative materialism is more like common sense (and indeed more like Cartesian dualism) than the identity theory is. That is, it does not allow scientific evidence to contradict what people say about themselves. For what scientific evidence does is to reject the whole apparatus of folk psychology, according to eliminative materialism. It does not support some of what one says in terms of folk psychology as true and reject some as false. (Can physics show that someone is lucky or unlucky? No. What thinking about physics tells you is: don't think that way.)

To sum this up, here is the table of Section 9, expanded somewhat:

	There are thoughts and feelings	People think and feel	Technological correction
Cartesian dualism	Yes	Yes	No
Crude materialism	Yes	Yes	Yes
Strong identity theory	No	Yes	Yes
Weak identity theory	No	Yes	No
Eliminative materialism	No	No	No

12.12 Five Typical Quotations

Below are five quotations from philosophers discussing the relation between mind and brain. One is a dualist, one an identity theorist, one an eliminative materialist. Which is which? How would you describe the views of the two remaining ones, which do not fit perfectly under any of these labels?

(1) *I am not arguing that the after-image is a brain process, but that the experience of having an after-image is a brain process. It is the* experience *that is reported in the introspective report. Similarly, if it is objected that the after-image is yellow-orange, my reply is that it is the experience of seeing yellowy-orange that is being described, and this experience is not a yellowy-orange something. . . . There is in a sense no such thing as an after-image or a sense-datum, though there is such a thing as the experience of having an image. . . . Trees and wallpaper can be green, but not the experience of seeing or imagining a tree or wallpaper.*

(2) *If we approach* Homo sapiens *from the perspective of natural history and the physical sciences, we can tell a coherent story of his constitution, development, and behavioral capacities which encompasses particle physics, atomic and molecular theory, organic chemistry, evolutionary theory, biology, physiology, and materialistic neuroscience. That story, though still radically incomplete, is already extremely powerful, outperforming FP [folk psychology] at many points even in its own domain. And it is deliberately and self-consciously coherent with the rest of our developing world picture.*

(3) *Psychical events themselves are never public and never can be made so. That, for example, I now remember having dreamed of a Siamese cat last night is something which I can publish by means of perceptually public words, spoken or written. Other persons are then informed of it. But to be informed that I remember having so dreamed is one thing, and to remember having so dreamed is altogether another thing, and one inherently private.*

(4) *The first observation I make at this point is that there is a great difference between the mind and the body, inasmuch as the body is by its very nature always divisible, while the mind is utterly indivisible. For when I consider the mind, or myself in so far as I am merely a thinking thing, I am unable to distinguish any parts within myself; I understand myself to be something quite single and complete. Although the whole mind seems to be united to the whole body, I recognize that if a foot or arm or any other part of the body is cut off, nothing has thereby been taken away from the mind.*

(5) *. . . a physiologist might attach his apparatus to my brain, mutter about electrical discharges and chemical transformations, check his graphs and pointer readings, and then say: "You've been making a joke." Even if a physiologist could do this, while I should be both mystified and impressed by the way he found out, I should not be surprised by what he told me. After all, it was I who was making the joke. But what is crucial here is that if he wants me to improve my jokes he must talk about the theory and practice of humor, and not about his findings concerning my brain cells. Those, we must never forget, are parts of another science.*

Conclusions of This Chapter

◆ *The most persuasive arguments for materialism about mind and body are based on the fact that what happens in our minds is caused to a large extent by what happens in our bodies.*
◆ *The most persuasive arguments for dualism about mind and body are based on the fact that knowing facts about someone's brain (or about the rest of someone's body) does not allow you to know what it is like to be that person.*
◆ *There are stronger and weaker versions of materialism. A stronger version will allow that science can correct what people say about their own minds. In some cases this is not as implausible as it might at first seem.*
◆ *One of the strongest forms of materialism is eliminative materialism, which claims that our commonsense way of talking about mind is so confused that we should not try to relate it to the science of the brain but just abandon it. But, surprisingly, eliminative materialism does not allow scientific results to show that commonsense beliefs about mind are false.*

Further Reading

Classic texts

Selections from Descartes, Spinoza, and Malebranche in Part III of John Cottingham (ed.), *Western Philosophy: An Anthology.* Blackwell, 1996.
René Descartes, *Meditations*, especially Meditation 2, in *Descartes: Philosophical Writings*, translated and edited by Elizabeth Anscombe and Peter Geach. Nelson, 1954.
Gilbert Ryle, *The Concept of Mind.* Hutchinson, 1949, especially chapter 1.

Modern works

Chapters 1 to 5 of Peter Smith and O. R. Jones, *The Philosophy of Mind.* Cambridge University Press, 1986.

Chapters 7 and 8 of Paul Churchland, *Matter and Consciousness.* MIT Press, 1984.

*Chapters 4 and 5 of Paul Churchland, *Scientific Realism and the Plasticity of Mind.* Cambridge University Press, 1979.

Electronic resources

Routledge Encyclopedia of Philosophy (available online at many universities): articles on Eliminativism; Introspection, epistemology of; Materialism in the philosophy of mind; Mind, identity theories of.

Stanford Encyclopedia of Philosophy (http://plato.stanford.edu/): Identity theory of mind; Lucretius; Materialism; Materialism, eliminative; Self-knowledge (articles listed here are not yet available as this book goes to press; they should be available soon).

13   Morality for Naturalists

Introduction

Physical science is sometimes used to support materialism, which claims that everything is physical. In contrast, idealism claims that everything is mental. If materialism is true then our minds are physical. One theory which disagrees with this is dualism, which says that minds are not part of the physical world.

If materialism is true, morality might be an illusion. Some philosophers have tried to show how moral principles could be true even if everything is physical. One influential approach is to study contracts that people in a society could make with one another for mutual benefit.

If materialism is true, many other features of our lives could be illusions. The example of colors shows many of the problems that also arise with our conviction that we make free decisions and our conviction that we are the same persons throughout our lives. . . .

Chapter Objectives

By the end of this chapter you should be able to answer the following questions.

◆ *Why do some philosophers think that morality requires a God, and why do other philosophers disagree?*
◆ *Why do attempts to make a moral system that does not involve anything supernatural often use the idea of a social contract?*
◆ *What is the prisoner's dilemma, and what does it say about the possibility of cooperating for the common good?*
◆ *What is an implicit contract, and how does it relate to the ideal of a good society?*

Definitions

The following words used in this chapter are defined in the list of definitions at the end of the book:

implicit contract   prisoner's dilemma   state of nature

13.1 God and Morality

Consider this quotation from the nineteenth-century Danish philosopher Søren Kierkegaard.

> (1) *If a human being did not have an eternal consciousness, if underlying everything there were only a wild fermenting power that writhing in dark passions produced everything, be it significant or insignificant, if a vast never-appeased emptiness hid beneath everything, what would life be then but despair? If such were the situation, if there were no sacred bond that knit humankind together, if one generation succeeded another like the singing of birds in the forest, . . . how empty and devoid of consolation life would be!*

Kierkegaard is expressing the feeling that if naturalism is true, if there is nothing beyond nature, then there is a great gap in our lives. Life is meaningless. Human relations are shallow and pointless (there is no 'sacred bond'). And there is no real difference between right and wrong. People often think also that if there is a God who has a purpose for human life and who decides what is right and wrong for us, then there is not this gap in our lives. (Kierkegaard expresses this as our having an "eternal consciousness," by which he means an awareness of something beyond space and time and the physical universe.)

Is this true? Let us sidestep the problem of whether there is a God. Instead, ask whether the existence of a God would make our lives meaningful and make morality objective. It might seem obvious that it would. But this seemingly obvious idea faces some problems, which we might call the "Euthyphro problem," the "Vonnegut problem," and the "Abraham and Isaac" problem. Consider the ideas behind some more quotations.

> (2) *I will call no being good, who is not what I mean when I apply that epithet to my fellow creatures, and if such a being can sentence me to hell for not so calling him, to hell I will go.* (John Stuart Mill)

> (3) **Socrates:** *Then what are we to say about the holy, Euthyphro? According to your argument, is it not loved by all the gods?*
> **Euthyphro:** *Yes.*
> **Socrates:** *Because it is holy, or for some other reason?*
> **Euthyphro:** *No, for that reason.*
> **Socrates:** *And so it is loved because it is holy; it is not holy because it is loved.*
> (Plato, Euthyphro)

The Mill quote suggests that the commands of a god would not make an act right unless that god were good. No problem, you may say, God obviously is good. But then consider the Plato quote. If we think that God is good (and that is why we should obey him) then "good" must mean something more than just "liked by God." If you already know what is good then you will be able to say that God is good. But if you are in doubt about what is good then you first need some assurance about God before you can use his commands to determine what is right.

And then there is the "Vonnegut problem." In *The Sirens of Titan*, the novelist Kurt Vonnegut tells a story about the last surviving human being. After the painful extinction of the entire human race he meets a robot, who explains to him that he broke down while carrying a message from one galaxy to another. He then caused life to evolve on earth just so that millions of years later a cataclysmic war would result in this man standing before him with, in his pocket, the small piece of metal he needs to repair himself. Then he can continue on his way. "What," asks the man, "is the message you are carrying?" The robot searches and finds it. The message says "Hello." All the history and the suffering of the human race were for that.

The Vonnegut problem is that a purpose and an intelligence behind human life would not make it meaningful, or underwrite morality, unless that purpose was a good one. So we must be able to think that God's purposes are ones we would think of as good. They must not treat human beings as incidental tools, as in Vonnegut's story, or as objects of amusement, as in some ancient myths. Can we think of God as having good purposes? According to most religious thinkers, we cannot understand God's purposes. If we could understand them, God would be like just another person, with no more authority than one of us. But if we cannot understand God's purposes, how can we think of them as good?

Suppose we just accept on faith that God's purposes are good. Then we run into the "Abraham and Isaac" problem. In the Bible (Genesis 22: 1–3) God commands Abraham to sacrifice to him his son Isaac. Abraham agrees, with a heavy heart. He leads his son to Mount Moriah to be sacrificed, but just as he raises the knife God tells him that the whole thing was just a test, and that instead he should sacrifice a ram. At the beginning of his *Fear and Trembling*, Kierkegaard retells the story in several different ways. One of them runs as follows.

> (4) *It was early in the morning, and everything in Abraham's house was ready for the journey. . . . They rode along in harmony, Abraham and Isaac, until they came to Mount Moriah. Abraham made everything ready for the sacrifice, calmly and gently, but when he turned away and drew the knife, Isaac saw that Abraham's left hand was clenched in despair, that a shudder went through his whole body – but Abraham drew the knife.*
>
> *Then they returned home again, and Sarah hurried to meet them, but Abraham had lost the faith. Not a word is ever said of this, in the world, and Isaac never talked to anyone about what he had seen, and Abraham did not suspect that anyone had seen it.*

Here Kierkegaard is suggesting that what God asked of Abraham was something that ordinary human morality cannot approve of. If a human master asked this of his human servant we would consider him a tyrant. Kierkegaard does not conclude that God is a tyrant. Instead, he says:

> *(5) Now we are face to face with the paradox. Either the single individual as the single individual can stand in an absolute relation to the absolute, and consequently the ethical is not the highest, or Abraham is lost: he is neither a tragic hero nor an esthetic hero.*

By this Kierkegaard means that if there is a God whose existence gives meaning to our lives, then to the extent that he is beyond our understanding his commands will sometimes not command what we would think of as right. He will be "beyond" human morality. (An "absolute relation to the absolute" means something like "being in a position where you can understand the ultimate truth." A "tragic hero" is someone who tries to do what is right and fails, an "esthetic hero" is someone who tries to do what is right and succeeds.)

There are many similarities and contrasts between what Kierkegaard, Mill, Plato, and Vonnegut are saying.

Kierkegaard is not just talking about morality. He thinks that without an "eternal consciousness" our lives are poorer in other ways too. But it is hard to be certain exactly what he is saying. Assume that we can take "eternal consciousness" to mean "belief in God." Then we could take quotation (1) to be arguing for any of the following conclusions.

(a) There would be no meaning in life if God did not exist.
(b) We could find no meaning in life if we did not believe that God existed.
(c) If naturalism is true then humans must be unhappy.

Conclusions (a) and (b) are different. How could each be true even if the other was false? Conclusion (c) does not refer to God or to the meaning of life. Whether we should take the quote along the lines of (c) or of (a) and (b) depends on what we think Kierkegaard means by "what would life then be but despair?" What meanings can we give it to make (c) the conclusion; and what meanings make (a) or (b) the conclusion?

The quotation from Mill is not saying quite the same thing as the quotation from Plato. Which of the following seem to be something that Mill is saying in (2) but Plato is not saying in (3)?

(a) Whether God's commands are right is something that must be judged by human reason.
(b) God commands what is right because it is right.
(c) A bad God would command bad things.

Kierkegaard's meaning in (5) is not easy to grasp. It helps to think of him as struggling with the same problem that Vonnegut is raising in *The Sirens of Titan*, and which Mill is raising in (2). If God is beyond human understanding, how can his actions and his commands make moral sense to us? How can we take the meaning of our lives from something we cannot understand?

Thoughtful religious people have to find answers to these questions. Bearing in mind the way Kierkegaard is alluding to the story of Abraham and Isaac in (5), which of the following seems to be nearest to his answers to these questions?

(a) If we could understand God's motives then we could rise above morality and be gods.
(b) Since we cannot understand God's motives his existence does not give meaning to our lives.
(c) Morality is either second-best or pointless.

The issues that are troubling Kierkegaard, Mill, Plato, and Vonnegut are deep and difficult ones. How is your morality affected by your beliefs about the nature of reality: should it make a difference to your morality whether or not you think this physical universe is all there is, or whether or not you think there is a God? Can materialists make a morality?

13.2 The Moralist's Nightmare

You are a stamp collector. You have seen a stamp that you really want, advertised in a stamp collectors' magazine. You phone the number in the ad and reach an agreement with the person who has the stamp. She will put the stamp in the mail immediately and you will put cash for the agreed amount in the mail. You want the stamp more than you will miss the money, and she wants the money more than she will miss the stamp, so you should both gain. But then you think: "She sounds like a trusting sort of person. If I don't send the money I'll get the stamp for nothing."

In this case it looks as if cheating – going back on a promise or on an expectation you led someone else to have – will pay off. (Assume that there's no way she will be able to catch up with you and make you pay or suffer.) It is pretty clear that cheating, and other forms of bad behavior, often pay. In the short term, and just for the cheater, that is. Philosophers thinking about morality often find this a troubling likelihood. Sometimes they try to argue that in some way bad behavior does not pay. For example, Plato in the *Republic* argued that the price for unjust actions is having an unjust soul. He argued that this is not a price anyone would pay if they really understood what it involved. And there is something to this: many forms of cruelty or callousness would involve being the kind of person most of us would not want to be. So the temptation to these forms of bad behavior diminishes when we see the cost to our personalities. But it is hard to believe that this is a full or devastating reply. Surely there remain many forms

The moralist's nightmare is that it may be stupid to be good: bad people can exploit good ones. But this misses the fact that when immoral people interact with one another they often come out less well than when moral people interact with other moral people.

of behavior that are morally wrong but that need not turn you into someone you would hate to be. And suppose you are someone who would like to be selfish, cruel, or whatever: in terms of your own depraved desires doesn't bad behavior very definitely pay off?

This is the moralist's nightmare. It may be stupid to be good. Bad people may have better lives. To put the worry more carefully, distinguish between rationality and morality. Rationality is doing what achieves your desires most efficiently. (That is, what gives the greatest probability of satisfying the greatest number of your desires to the greatest degree. See "Risk and Decision-making" in Chapter 7, Section 12.) Morality, whatever it is, involves keeping promises most of the time, and not inflicting pain and death on others without some very special justification. Then the nightmare thought is: being moral may often not be rational. Breaking promises or inflicting suffering on others may often give the greatest chance of getting what you want.

The moralist's nightmare is one reason why people sometimes think that God is needed to back up morality. If there is a God who will punish you if you don't keep your promises and who will reward you if you do, then it is no longer stupid to keep them. Being good pays, if there are rewards and punishments. This does not give a reason for thinking that there is a God. But it does give a reason why someone might think that if there is not a God, morality is pointless. Or, as the nineteenth-century Russian writer Fyodor Dostoyevski put it, "If God does not exist, all is permitted."

There is a catch here, something the nightmare misses. It can be illustrated with the example of the stamp–money exchange. The thought that if you don't send the money you can get the stamp for nothing assumes that the other person will send the stamp. But suppose she is thinking along the same lines as you. She will think: you will either send the money or you will not. If you send it then she will be better off if she doesn't send the stamp. If you do not send it then she will again be better off if she does not send the stamp. In the one case she will have gained by cheating you, and in the other she will have gained by avoiding being cheated by you. So, if that is the way she operates, she will not send the stamp. And you won't send the money. So you will not do business, and since you wanted the stamp and she wanted the money you will both be worse off than if you had been honorable, trustworthy, and trusting.

There are two important points this brings out. Call them the comparison point and the paradoxical result. The comparison point is just this. When moral and immoral people interact, the immoral people often do better. But that is only one of three possibilities. What happens when moral people interact with other moral people, or when immoral people interact with other immoral people? One important question is whether immoral people do better interacting with other immoral people than moral people do interacting with other moral people. It is far from obvious that they do. Think of the stamp example. If both people try to cheat the other then neither the stamp nor the money is sent, and both are worse off than if they had been able to do business. The marketplace only functions under certain conditions, and one of them is a confidence that contracts will be honored.

The paradoxical result is that sometimes rational people acting to get the best results for themselves will fail because they are being rational. The stamp example again. Suppose for simplicity that all the two people care about is the stamp and the money. Then the reasoning that leads to trying to cheat one another seems fine. But it backfires: by being individually rational they prevent a result that would benefit both of them.

These points take some of the terror out of the nightmare. It's not so stupid to be moral, if immoral people lose the benefits of cooperative activity. If moral people can work markets and other social exchanges based on trust, while immoral people cannot, then there is a high price to pay for immorality.

To say this is not to prove that morality pays. There is a lot more to be said: for, against, and in clarification. But it does open up a new way of seeing the issues. The first philosopher to see the issues in this way was Thomas Hobbes.

13.3 Hobbes on the State of Nature

The seventeenth-century English philosopher Thomas Hobbes tried to imagine what life would be like if there were really no constraints, moral, social, or political, on people's treatment of one another. He tried to imagine what he calls the "state of nature." The essence of the situation is not just that there are a number of immoral people around, but that every person, whatever her character, can have no expectations of anyone else's behavior besides that everyone will maximize their own individual interest. There is no mechanism for enforcing agreements, and no reliable way of getting back at people who have mistreated you. Hobbes describes this situation as the "war . . . of every man against every man" and says of it:

> There is no place for industry; because the fruit thereof is uncertain: and consequently no culture of the earth; no navigation, nor use of the commodities that may be imported by sea; no commodious building; no instruments of moving, and removing, such things as require much force; no knowledge of the face of the earth; no account of time; no arts; no letters; no society; and which is worst of all, continual fear, and danger of violent death; and the life of man, solitary, poor, nasty, brutish, and short.

Note here the emphasis Hobbes places on the bad effects of uncertainty. Because people in the state of nature can have no confidence about the future, industry is impossible and life is filled with fear. Note also that Hobbes is not claiming that life anywhere is or was ever quite like this. Rather, this is what life would be like if society had no power to limit people's actions and each person acted in a purely self-interested way. Life is so bad in the state of nature that the only reasonable response is to escape it – that is, to try to achieve "peace," the absence of the war of every person against every other. Hobbes, in fact, thinks that it is a law of human nature that people will try to escape the state of nature, a consequence of the more fundamental law that people will do what they can to get what they want. To quote Hobbes again:

> [In the state of nature] every man has a right to every thing; even to one another's body. And therefore, as long as this natural right of every man to every thing endureth, there can be no security to any man, how strong or wise soever he be, of living out the time, which nature ordinarily alloweth men to live. And consequently it is a precept, or general rule of reason, that every man ought to endeavour peace, as far as he has hope of obtaining it; and when he cannot obtain it, that he may seek, and use, all helps, and advantages of war. The first branch of which rule, containeth the first, and fundamental law of nature; which is, to seek peace, and follow it. The second, the sum of the right of nature; which is, by all means we can, to defend ourselves.
>
> From this fundamental law of nature . . . is derived this second law; that a man be willing, when others are so too, . . . to lay down this right to all things; and be contented with so much liberty against other men, as he would allow other men against himself . . . This is that law of the Gospel; whatsoever you require that others should do to you, that do ye to them.

Hobbes is claiming something extremely interesting here. He is appealing to principles of human nature which would be accepted by a materialist. (And Hobbes' philosophy of human nature was materialist.) He claims that from these he can deduce the necessity of behaving morally, in fact in accordance with principles that are often given a supernatural foundation. His argument can be summarized in crude outline as follows:

The state of nature is bad for everyone.
Therefore it is rational to escape it.
The only escape consists in following general rules that give all people the same rights.
Therefore it is rational to follow such rules, if others agree to.

The really fundamental concept Hobbes is introducing here is that of negotiation. People in the state of nature will find things so bad that they will be forced to negotiate a contract restraining one another's actions. And since this contract gives them the only way to peace, they should keep it. Thus we can add some more details and expand the argument as follows:

The state of nature is bad for everyone.
Therefore it is rational to negotiate a way out of it.
The result of this negotiation will be general rules that give all people rights.
Therefore it is rational to comply with the agreed contract, and treat all people as if they had such rights.

Is this a good argument? It is certainly an interesting and suggestive argument. But there are several difficulties with it. Does the result of the negotiation have to be a set of general rules giving everyone the same rights? Even if it is rational to make such a contract why is it rational to keep it? And why do facts about what it would be rational to agree to if you were in the state of nature determine what you should agree to here and now? These are questions that we will return to.

Hobbes thought of the state of nature not just as the absence of moral constraints on people's behavior, but also as the absence of government. And he thought of the agreement between people that would escape the state of nature as establishing the authority of government. And he saw this as a solution to the second question raised above: even if it is rational to make such an agreement, why is it rational to keep it?

To sympathize with Hobbes' reasoning here think yet again of the stamps for money example. The two people would like to be able to make the sale work. Both will gain if they can. One way in which this can happen is if they change the situation so that it is in the interests of both of them to keep their promises. For example, they could each deposit a sum of money that they would lose if the promised money or stamp did not arrive. Or they could approach a third person and authorize him to do something bad to either of them if they do not keep their word. It seems a bit absurd to go to all this trouble just to allow a stamp to be sold, but if there were such a device that would ensure that all contracts are kept then it would be very desirable. In fact, it would be rational to specify it in the contract by which we escape from the state of nature. For then the contract will be self-enforcing. And, according to Hobbes, there is such a device. It is the authority of government.

What Hobbes actually says is this:

> *The only way to erect such a common power, as may be able to . . . secure them in such sort, as that . . . they may nourish themselves and live contentedly; is, to confer all their power and strength upon one man, or upon one assembly of men, that may reduce all their wills . . . to one will. This is more than consent, or concord; it is a real unity of them all in one and the same person, made by covenant of every man with every man, in such a manner, as if every man should say to every man, I authorize and give up my right of governing myself, to this man, or to this assembly of men, on this condition, that thou give up thy right to him, and authorize all his actions in like manner.*

The way to get a self-enforcing contract between people in the state of nature is to institute a government with great, in fact absolute, authority. And the authority of the government derives from its function as a guarantor that contracts will be kept and rights respected. Note how striking a doctrine this must have been in Hobbes' day, when the authority of government was usually thought to derive from God, who established kings to rule over their subjects.

This is a direct justification of political authority, and indirectly a justification of moral behavior. It says, in effect, keeping promises and respecting rights

---

Box 22 **Thomas Hobbes**

Hobbes (1588–1679) was one of the first thinkers to take the physics of Galileo as suggesting a materialistic metaphysics. And as one of the founders of modern political thought he anticipated the conclusions of twentieth-century game theory. His life and thought turn on themes of anarchy and order. He lived through the English civil war, being on the Royalist side. There seems to be an aversion to disorder shown both in his arguments for absolute political authority and in his love of rigorous reasoning. He came on Euclidean geometry at a fairly late age and was fascinated by its capacity to derive unobvious conclusions inescapably from obvious axioms. His most famous work, *Leviathan*, supports order in both senses. It uses a method of deductive reasoning modeled on geometry to argue from materialistic premises to the justification of political authority.

---

is not rational in the state of nature, but we can make such behavior rational by setting up a system of political authority that will punish people who trample on promises and rights.

In anarchic conditions, handing total power over to a single political authority could well be the easiest, perhaps the only, way to order and peace. Most people do not live in completely anarchic conditions. Does Hobbes' argument show that they ought to establish an absolute political authority (or "Leviathan") and use it to enforce their morality? Hobbes' political theory helps show what a basic and important question this is.

13.4 A Restaurant Dilemma

You are one of a party of three people having lunch in a restaurant. You have agreed that you will split the bill equally; each of you will pay one-third of it.

Chez Babette	
Main course	
Beefsteak with fresh vegetables	$25.00
Beefburger	$5.00
Drinks	
House wine, red or white	$15.00 per half litre
Beer or juice	$2.00 per glass
Dessert	
Death by chocolate	$8
Vanilla ice cream	$2

As you can see from the menu, an expensive meal will cost $48 and a cheaper meal around $9. You would rather not pay that much, since you are trying to save money, but you do like good food. If you were on your own you would order a cheaper meal. You know that the other two also want to save money but also like good food. In order to save time, each of you will write down an order and give it to the waiter without the others seeing it. And also to save time, each of you will pay one-third of the total bill. Do you order an expensive meal or a cheap one?

It is best to begin thinking through this question by simulating the situation. Groups of three should discuss the advantages and disadvantages of ordering a cheap or an expensive meal, but should not reveal what choices they are going to make. Then they should write their choices on a piece of paper. (Simply "Expensive meal" or "Cheap meal" will be enough.) Finally, the decisions on the papers are read out. Each person will get the meal he or she wrote on their paper. Each will pay one-third of the total cost of the meals.

Did you get the meal you most wanted? Did you pay what you wanted for it?

Repeat the process. Order a meal again. Again, you don't know what other people are ordering, though you do know what they ordered last time. Are the results the same or different? What reasons can you or others give for changing your choice from the first trial to the second? If you did not change your choice, why do these reasons not influence you?

How does each of the following labels apply to people's choices in this situation?

◆ self-interested
◆ altruistic
◆ taking advantage
◆ sharing
◆ trust
◆ greed

This restaurant problem resembles the stamp and money example of Section 2 in certain respects. Which of the following is true?

(a) In both situations, trusting people lose out.
(b) In both situations, there is an opportunity to take advantage of another person.
(c) In both situations, if each person goes for their best personal gain all lose out.
(d) In both situations, it pays to trust others.
(e) In both situations, greed is self-defeating.
(f) In both situations, greed overcomes trust.

13.5 The Prisoner's Dilemma

The stamp and money example of Section 2 illustrates a very common pattern in interactions between two or more people. It is called the prisoner's dilemma. The name comes from another example with the same pattern. In this example, two prisoners – call them Adam and Beatrice – are being interrogated in separate cells. The police suspect them of jointly committing some crime. But they do not have any evidence they are willing to use in court. So they want one or both of the prisoners to confess. Beating does not work, so they try persuasion. To Adam they say: "If you confess, implicating Beatrice, but she does not confess, then you will go free but she will be given ten years' hard labor. If she confesses but you do not then she will go free but you will get ten years. If neither of you confess then we will find some excuse for giving both of you a year in prison. And if both of you confess then you will both get five years' hard labor." They describe the same consequences to Beatrice, and although they do not allow the two to communicate, they make sure that each knows that the other knows all these consequences.

Adam and Beatrice can then reason in the way that the two people in the stamp example did. Adam can think: either Beatrice will confess or she will not. Either way I am better off if I confess. And Beatrice can see that whatever Adam does, she will be better off if she confesses. So they will both confess. The result will be that each of them will get five years' hard labor. But if they had both not confessed they would have got only one year in prison each. This is the same paradoxical conclusion as in the stamp example: when each person reasons toward their individual good the result is that both are worse off.

The prisoner's dilemma is part of game theory, a central tool of modern economics. Game theory studies strategic choice. That is, choice between actions when the outcomes of actions depend on what choices other people have made. It makes an enormous difference whether the outcomes of your choice depend on what other people choose, because what those other people choose may depend on what they think you will do. (And this is a fact of vital importance to ethics.) To see how this matters compare two situations. First, suppose you are walking up a road and there is a runaway truck rolling down it. You have to decide which side of the road the truck is likely to roll down and get to the other. Either you guess right or you do not. Contrast this with what happens when you meet someone in a narrow alley. Each of you wants to walk on the side that the other is not walking on. It doesn't matter what each chooses as long as they are different. So if you think the other is going to one side you'll go to the other. That's simple, so consider something more complicated. If you think the other person thinks you will go to one side you will decide to go to that side, since it means they will go to the other. Now consider something really complicated. Suppose you think the other person thinks that you think that they will go to one side! Then – if you are paying a lot of attention – you will go to the other side, because the other person will go to the side they think you expect them to.

Strategic choice can get very complicated. In real life, people meeting in an alley often settle it with a glance at each other's faces. In real life, people in prisoner's dilemma situations find it a bit more difficult. The prisoner's dilemma is an example of difficult strategic choice. When considering strategic choices it is important to be explicit about the options open to each person, and the consequences or pay-offs for them of each option given each choice of each other person. One way of doing this is with a pay-off matrix. The pay-off matrix for the story of the two prisoners might look like the following:

		Beatrice	
		Confess	Not confess
Adam	Confess	−5, −5	0, −10
	Not confess	−10, 0	−1, −1

(The pairs (−5, −5 etc.) represent the gain to Adam and Beatrice respectively from the corresponding combination of actions.)

Any two-person interaction in which the matrix has the following general form is known as a prisoner's dilemma, or PD.

		B	
		Option 1	Option 2
A	Option 1	second worst, second worst	best, worst
	Option 2	worst, best	second best, second best

(So that if, for example, A chooses option 1 and B chooses option 2, then A will get the best outcome and B will get the worst outcome.) Note that there are two ways of writing down the pay-offs. We can use positive or negative pay-off numbers (called utilities), as in the first matrix above. Or we can describe the people's preferences, as in the second matrix. (Write out the stamp example in terms of utilities. Then rewrite it in terms of preferences, so it is clear that it fits the pattern for a PD.) In any PD each person will be able to reason that they should go for option 1 whatever the other person does. So they will end up with what is for both of them second worst.

One important class of situations that are essentially the same as PDs is that of free rider problems. Suppose that four people are pushing a cart along a muddy road. It takes three to keep it moving. Any one of them can think: "If the other three are going to push then I can ride, which is better for me; and if the other three are not going to push then I am wasting my energy pushing. So I should ride." But each person can think this way, so each person is likely to ride, and the cart will stop, which is what no one wants.

Perhaps someone inclined to let the three others push him along can be coerced or threatened into cooperation. But imagine a public transit system where it is easy to beat the fare by jumping over a barrier or by some other means. Thousands of people use the system. Each person knows that if they avoid paying their fare the system will continue to operate and they will get a free ride. But if many people get free rides then the system will fail and no one will ride. But each person can think: "If others pay then I'm better off not paying, and if others don't pay the system will fail and I'm a fool to pay; either way I'm better off not paying." So people will not pay, and the system will fail, and everyone will be worse off.

It is clear how free rider problems capture some of the obstacles to setting up the cooperative action we need in order to achieve public aims. Free rider problems are like PDs in that there is an action which each person is best off performing, whatever the other people do, but if everyone does this "best" action, everyone is worse off than they would have been if everyone had acted more cooperatively. Free rider problems have added complications because there are more than two people involved, though.

13.6 Hobbes and the Prisoner's Dilemma

Which of the following are PDs? (It will help to write out the matrix of four possibilities and the four pay-offs for each person.)

(a) A and B can each go to the theater or to a party. Each wants to be with the other. But A prefers theater to party, and prefers theater alone to party with B. On the other hand, B prefers party to theater and prefers theater with A to party alone. (The two options for each are: Party, Theater. What will happen?)

(b) A and B are industrialists whose factories pollute the air that both breathe. Each one prefers breathing polluted air to going bankrupt. If only one installs pollution control equipment that one's costs rise and she is put out of business by the other, with the result that air quality comes down to acceptable levels. If both install the equipment then their profits diminish, but not drastically. If neither instals the equipment then each breathes foul air: each of them thinks this is worse than diminished profits. (The two actions are: Install, Not install. What will happen?)

Consider the postage stamp dilemma (A sends/does not send money, B sends/not does send stamp):

(i)   Which of the four outcomes corresponds to Hobbes' state of nature?
(ii) Why is it "worse" for both people? (Worse than what?)
(iii) What is the "best" outcome? (For whom? Why?)
(iv) If the two people were able to negotiate an agreement, which some third person would then be able to enforce, what combination of actions would be agreed? Why?
(v)   If there were no third person to enforce the agreement then any of the outcomes in the following list might happen. Under which circumstances would each of these be likely?

- ◆ The two people might be unable to cooperate and no sale would take place.
- ◆ One person would exploit the other (so the stamp is sent but not paid for, or paid for but not sent).
- ◆ The two people might cooperate in order to gain the trust of the other in future dealings.
- ◆ The two people might negotiate an agreement and stick to it even though it could not be enforced.

Consider the Hobbesian argument:

In the state of nature it is rational to want peace.
Peace can be obtained by bargaining (negotiation).
Bargaining will only succeed if people abide by the bargain.
Therefore it is rational to abide by the bargain that would bring peace.

Suppose you are in the state of nature. Which of the following points might prevent you from being convinced by this argument? (Imagine you are (a) a powerful lord, or (b) a peasant, or (c) cleverer than other people.)

(i)   I can gain more by war than by peace.
(ii) I can gain most by pretending to abide by the contract.
(iii) In a fair contract I might have to give up some of what I have gained.
(iv) I can get peace by intimidation rather than by bargaining.

Suppose you are not in the state of nature. Which of these same points might then prevent you from being convinced by the argument? (Imagine you are one of the same three kinds of people.)

Suppose that the state of nature is a PD, as described in the previous section, and that "option 1" is "remain in the state of nature" and "option 2" is "negotiate your way to peace." That is:

	B	
	Nature	Peace
A Nature	second worst, second worst	best, worst
A Peace	worst, best	second best, second best

How do points (i) and (iii) in the "state of nature" case above relate to this description of the situation?

13.7 Implicit Contracts

HARDER

Consider the theater/party example of the previous section. A and B can each go to the theater or to a party. Each wants to be with the other. But A prefers theater to party and prefers theater alone to party with B. On the other hand, B prefers party to theater and prefers theater with A to party alone. Each of them knows these facts about the preferences of the other. The pay-off matrix for the two agents is as follows:

	B	
	Theater	Party
A Theater	(best, second)	(second, third)
A Party	(worst, worst)	(third, best)

That is, if both go to the theater A gets both of his desires but B's less important desire is thwarted. If they both go to the party then B gets both of her desires, but A's most important desire is thwarted. If they separate, A to party and B to theater, then neither satisfies either of their desires. And if they separate, A to theater and B to party, then A's most important desire is satisfied and only B's less important desire is satisfied.

What will they do? There is a line of reasoning that they will almost certainly follow. It can be described in two ways. One way runs: B knows that if she does not go to the theater with A he will go alone, since where he goes is more important to him than whether he goes with her. But she would rather go to the theater with B than go to the party alone. So she will go to the theater, as he will, achieving his first choice and her second.

A more formal way of putting the same reasoning is like this: when B considers her options without making assumptions about what A will do, neither option is obviously best. It all depends on what A chooses. (Neither option is dominant.) But when A considers his options he will see that if B chooses Theater he is best off choosing Theater too (best rather than worst outcome), and if B chooses Party he is still best off choosing Theater (second rather than third best outcome). So he will choose Theater. But B can figure this out, so she will consider what is best for her given that A will choose Theater. Then it is a choice between the second and the third best outcomes for her, and she will naturally go for the second best, which happens when she chooses Theater.

Imagine A and B thinking this out, without talking to one another. They will have arrived at an agreed pattern of action by considering each other's preferences and the ways each of them can reason. It is a kind of silent negotiation. Call this implicit bargaining.

Is it a fair contract? Intuitively, it is not a clear case. On the one hand A has used a kind of a threat: "If you don't come to the theater with me I'll go alone." And that does not seem fair. On the other hand, it seems right that A's genuinely different preferences should be reflected in the contract. So let us not conclude that it is a fair or an unfair contract. But do note that contracting can be implicit in people's recognition of each other's preferences and reasoning, that an implicit, unspoken, contract can be fair or unfair, and that it is not obvious what makes an implicit contract fair or unfair.

Now consider the industrialists and pollution controls example of the previous section. The pay-off matrix in that case is:

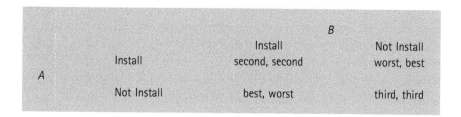

		B	
		Install	Not Install
A	Install	second, second	worst, best
	Not Install	best, worst	third, third

You should be able to see both that this has the general structure of a PD, and that each agent will have a strong argument for Not Installing. The result will be that neither will install and both will have to live in barely breathable air. If each had found some way to think of Install as the best option they would have found their way to an outcome they both prefer, in which they both Install. (But it is important to see the reasons against Installing in the situation as described. To install with no assurance that the other will is to risk bankruptcy.)

One way in which the two industrialists could resolve the problem would be to negotiate with a third person or agency, as a result of which they would sign an enforceable contract that both would install the pollution control equipment. The contract would be enforceable in that if one person did not keep their side of the contract there would be definite penalties to pay. Then the situation would no longer be represented by the pay-off matrix above. For the consequence to each industrialist if she chose to Not Install while the other chose Install would not be that she flourished and the other went bankrupt, but rather that she paid a crippling penalty.

Suppose that two people find themselves interacting on a number of occasions on a number of topics, and that many of these interactions take the general appearance of the PD. Suppose, moreover, that they fall into the pattern of choosing the cooperative option with respect to each other. (Perhaps they choose it for dealing with each other, though they fail to cooperate when up against other people.) Then they can be seen as behaving as if there is an implicit contract between them, to choose options so that in general although neither of them will very often get her first choice, they will very rarely get their worst or near-to-worst choice. It is as if they had signed an enforceable contract to cooperate for mutual benefit. Each one knows that if they do not cooperate now, the other will not cooperate in the future, and the result will be that both will get their worst or next-to-worst choice. That is not worth a chance of getting their best choice now, so each acts as if there were some rule forcing them to cooperate.

Many philosophers and political theorists have seen human social relations as governed by an implicit contract. We refrain from doing various harmful things to each other because of an implicit understanding that we will refrain from harm in order to cooperate for the good of all. Certainly, people do generally act as if they were bound by such an understanding.

It is important to see that the reasons why people might want to adhere to such an implicit contract are stronger than just the simple idea that by cooperating people can get results that individuals alone cannot. (A hundred people can build a fort against invaders; a thousand people can build an economy.) The idea that many can do what one cannot corresponds in the simplest cases to interactions with pay-off matrices like the following:

		B	
		Cooperate	Don't cooperate
	Cooperate	best, best	middle, middle
A			
	Don't cooperate	middle, middle	worst, worst

Or perhaps somewhat more subtly to the following (which introduces a small free-riding possibility):

		B	
		Cooperate	Don't cooperate
	Cooperate	best, best	third, second
A			
	Don't cooperate	second, third	worst, worst

In either of these, the two people are better off if they cooperate. But there is no rational motive for not cooperating. The special feature of the PD is that there is ample rational motive not to cooperate. And yet people are better off if they all cooperate than if they all defect from cooperation. So they have a strong motive to enter into some sort of a contract with one another. And if in spite of the reasons for defecting they do cooperate with one another, it is very natural to say that there must be something like a contract governing their behavior.

HARDER

13.8 Imaginary Social Contracts

(1) Imagine a society in which the men protect the women from men and other wild animals, and in return the women are kind to children and men, and accept the men's decisions on important matters. Under what conditions might this be an implicit contract? Under what conditions might it be a fair contract?

(2) Imagine a country in which the government pays for the education of scientists and doctors, because it needs them for its economic development. Under what conditions have students accepting this free education entered into an implicit contract which requires them not to leave that country and get better wages elsewhere?

(3) Imagine a society in which highly paid executives say to low-paid workers: "Our pay is part of a fair contract, because it allows us to run businesses efficiently so that we are all better off than we would otherwise be." Under what conditions can this be fair?

Which of the factors below could be relevant to determining whether there was a fair contract in which of the above three cases? (That is, relevant to whether it is a contract, and to whether it is a fair one.)

(i)   whether there were alternatives that would have been better for everyone;
(ii)   whether there were alternatives that would have been better for just one group of people;
(iii)   whether the consequences of not acting in this way would really be catastrophic;
(iv)   whether the roles assigned to the people are chosen by them;
(v)   whether the relevant choices are made freely;
(vi)   whether the roles are assigned to the people for some reason or arbitrarily;
(vii)   whether the people understand the consequences of their actions;
(viii)   whether the situation violates some human right.

Which of the three cases (1)–(3) is most controversial? Do your opinions about whether there is a fair contract in that case differ because you disagree about whether one of (i)–(viii) is satisfied, or for some other reasons?

Suppose that (v) or (viii) are important factors in determining the fairness of a contract. How might each of them be an obstacle to the project of making a moral system that has no need for anything outside the natural world?

13.9 Morals in Nature? Rousseau, Hegel, Marx

HARDER

We have now seen the basic materials out of which a naturalistic ethics might be constructed: the benefits of cooperation, strategic choice and PD or free rider situations, implicit contracts. How can all the bits be put together?

The pieces we have assembled can fit together into a straightforward, plausible, objective ethics, which one could believe in without having to believe in anything beyond the natural world. God is not required. Nothing is required that a hard-core materialist could not believe. (And this may matter even to people who are not materialists, if they need to be able to defend a morality to materialists.) They can do this if certain conditions are met. The conditions would be, roughly, that there is a unique and obvious pattern of cooperative action which it is in everyone's interest to see generally followed. For if there were such a unique pattern, then acting in accordance with it would be to act in a way that benefits everyone else while at the same time supporting something that is in one's own interests. It would be the sort of thing that people might agree to as a contract designed to obtain mutual benefit. That sounds a lot like morality. And it would require nothing that a naturalist, or even a hard-core materialist, could not believe in.

It is worth stating more carefully the conditions under which this could be true. For it is unlikely that this ideally simple picture can be quite right. And the ideas of several philosophers are relevant to seeing why.

An objective naturalistic ethics would be possible under the following conditions. To state them we have to consider a number of people, think of them as all the people in a society, or even all the people on earth, who have open to them a number of options. Each option specifies how that person lives their life. For example, Option 2 might be, in part: "Keep all your promises and be kind to everyone." Option 365 might be: "Be nice to other people in your tribe and go out of your way to do harm to everyone else." Option 35 might be: "Always try to get as much money for yourself as you can." The important things are not so much these options as combinations of them. One combination might be: person One chooses Option 365, and person Two chooses Option 35, . . . and person Three Billion and Six chooses Option 2. The combinations are really just squares in a gigantic pay-off matrix, so for each such combination there is a pay-off for each person. And there is one very special combination of options which has the following three features:

(a) If many people deviate from it then everyone suffers. That is, if many people fail to act in accordance with it, everyone does less well than they would have if everyone had acted in accordance with it.
(b) Of all the combinations satisfying (a) it is best for everyone.
(c) There is a description of it that everyone can understand.

Call any such pattern of action an *ideal contract*. Note that (a) gives the ideal contract a kind of self-enforcing quality. If numbers of people break the contract then they will suffer by doing so. Nevertheless, there can be a PD-like quality too, in that individuals or even small numbers of people breaking the contract may gain by doing so. Thus people may have a motive for making the contract into an explicit and enforced one, for example, by setting up a political system.

Why is this not the answer to moral skepticism? Why does it not show that believing in right and wrong is no more of a problem than believing in stars and electrons and the rate of inflation? The problem is that it is hard to believe that there is a unique combination of actions satisfying these conditions. To see why, imagine people in a Hobbesian state of nature. They realize that their condition is pretty awful and decide to formulate a social contract. They have no experience of complex social institutions, and their contract will have to be enforceable among people used to the war of all against all. So they decide to have a single powerful moral and political authority which enforces an easily stated moral code (no lying, no killing, no messing with someone else's property). This proves to be a definite improvement in their lives. Commerce begins, people can make long-term plans, relations between people contain a larger element of trust.

A later generation of people in this post-contract society comes to think that the contract is too simple and too restrictive. They change the moral code so that some of the rules allow exceptions. (You can avoid telling the full truth to avoid causing someone great distress, perhaps.) And they begin to separate moral from political obligation. (Some infractions of the code bring no formal punishment, but people visibly disapprove.) This makes a different social contract, which allows a yet later generation to think of yet different improvements. And so on.

Now connect this story with the idea of an ideal social contract. Among the combinations of options available to people in the state of nature are those that, say, define a representative multiparty democracy plus an independent central bank, or an ethos of the realization of human potential. But these are not options that are really open to people in the state of nature. For they are not capable of imagining them. So condition (c) rules them out. But they are – let us suppose, at any rate – better for almost everyone. There is thus a tension between condition (b) and condition (c). Not all the options and combinations of options that are abstract possibilities for people are ones that they can describe to themselves.

There are two closely connected points here. Call them the Hegel point and the Rousseau point.

The Hegel point is that membership in a society changes people's capacity to imagine the options that are open to them. There is a historical dimension to this. In a hunter-gatherer society you cannot imagine capitalism. Both G. W. F. Hegel (1770–1831) and his follower Karl Marx (1818–1883) thought of history as a linear progression. There is a main track of historical evolution, and societies on it evolve toward the ultimate in human social possibilities. According to Hegel, European society of his time was unique in that it understood the principles by which societies evolve, so that it was the ultimate social possibility. So people living in the modern age, according to Hegel, do understand the options open to them well enough that what they understand as the most profitable combination of different people's actions is the ideal social contract. Marx, on the other hand, thought that in modern industrial society we can see an alternative to our present conventions that improves on them. So this alternative, communism, is the ideal social contract.

Perhaps the moral common sense of the twentieth century, plus representative democracy and lightly regulated capitalism, are the ideal social contract. Or perhaps modern people can see the one final improvement that modern life demands. Perhaps. It seems equally likely both that there is no ultimately best combination of human actions and that there is often no simple comparison of such combinations. For condition (b) requires that the ideal social contract be better for everyone. But what is best for men may not be best for women, what is best for women may not be best for children, what is best for the rich may not be best for the poor, and so on. This complication becomes more worrying when we take account of the Rousseau point.

The Rousseau point is that what people want depends on their social training. Being a member of a society changes one essentially. (Our awareness of how profoundly people are affected by membership in a society dates from the Swiss-French philosopher Jean-Jacques Rousseau, 1712–1778.) So the grandchildren of the original imaginary state of nature contract-makers will be very different creatures from their grandparents, in what they want as well as in what they can imagine. This puts another obstacle in the way of considering all the combinations of actions open to people, and the pay-offs to them of each combination. Given a certain reference point, the actual combination of their actual actions, people can imagine what they would want in some "nearby" easily imagined combinations. But more remote ones are inaccessible to them. For the people who might choose those different combinations of actions, those remote ways of life, are really different people.

Put the Hegel point and the Rousseau point together and you get real problems with the idea that there is a single implicit social contract that defines what is right and what is wrong. For there just is no contract that will work for all times and all places. Still, at any particular time and place there will usually be social contracts that will be in people's general interest. In fact,

> ### Box 23 **Jean–Jacques Rousseau**
>
> Rousseau, who was born in 1712 in Switzerland, anticipated many of the ideas
> of Romanticism and twentieth-century thought, and his writings were part of
> the inspiration for both the French and American revolutions. He had very little
> education, and left home at the age of 16 to seek his fortune. He was protected
> by an older woman, Madame de Warens, who helped him to educate himself.
> He tried to become a composer and had one opera performed. But he was most
> successful as a writer on political and moral topics. His most famous work, *The
> Social Contract*, appeared in 1762. He lived for several years with a woman by
> whom he had five children, whom he sent to orphanages. In the rest of his life he
> wandered around Europe, spending some time in England with Hume. He thought
> that Hume, and almost everyone else, was persecuting him, and his last writings
> show a mixture of deep insight and psychological strangeness. He died in 1778.

there will usually be two kinds of potential contract. On the one hand there
are "practical" contracts defining the existing situation: the set of rules that
people generally follow and that it would be in almost everyone's interest to
follow more consistently. And on the other hand there are "idealistic" contracts
defining possible social situations which, with a bit more imagination and
smoother coordination of our actions, would make better lives for almost all
of us.

(To bring out the contrast between practical and idealistic contracts, think
of the institution of punishment. Imagine a traditional society in which many
forms of stealing and dishonesty are punished harshly, few excuses allowed.
These practices maintain private property and allow enough trust for commerce.
A practical contract is the understanding between people that they will not
steal or cheat, and if anyone does they will make sure that person is punished.
But an idealistic contract would allow, say, that some people steal because they
are psychologically disturbed, and that in some cases punishment does more
harm than good. If people could act in accordance with the idealistic contract,
commerce would work just as well, without an unnecessarily harsh punitive
system. But people pointing this out run the risk of undermining the actual
understanding on which a delicate social harmony rests.)

HARDER

13.10 Real States of Nature

The state of nature is an imaginary place. No real people have ever lived there.
But some situations approximate to it, in various different ways. Consider four
real types of human interaction:

(a) relations between nations;

(b) relations between business corporations;

(c) relations between people under conditions of murderous civil war, for example, Bosnia in 1993–5;

(d) emotional relations between student age people in your society.

And consider four characteristics of the state of nature:

(i) Agents maximize their purely individual interests.

(ii) There is no mechanism for enforcing contracts.

(iii) There is no reason to trust in another's goodwill.

(iv) There is no incentive to go for a mutually acceptable solution.

Which of (a)–(d) exhibit which of (i)–(iv), and to what degree?

One worry about social contract theories of morality is that they may have very little consideration for the interests of vulnerable, disabled, faraway, or nonhuman individuals. For if what is right is what would come out of a fair bargain between individuals, then what bargaining power would individuals have who have few contributions to make? One extreme case is that of animals. Are the relations between humans and animals fair?

Let one group represent humans proposing to domesticate a species, for example cattle, represented by another group. What can the humans offer the cattle in exchange for domestication? (Protection against predators, food in winter . . . What else?) What is asked of the cattle in exchange? (Milk, slaughter of some, restrictions on mating, slaughter of calves to permit milking . . . What else?) The "humans" should formulate an explicit offer to make to the "cattle." The "cattle" should consider it, and then either accept it or reject it. If they reject it they should formulate a counteroffer for the "humans" to consider. And so on until an agreement is made that is acceptable to both groups. Is an agreement ever reached?

Which of the following factors make it hard to arrive at a fair bargain in the "cattle" case?

(i) The two parties have too few interests in common.

(ii) The two parties cannot communicate.

(iii) The two parties do not have any way of enforcing a contract.

(iv) The two parties have no affection for one another.

Which of these factors (i) to (iv) would make it difficult to determine a fair contract between, on the one hand, the working and earning people in a society, and on the other hand any of the following?

(a) children

(b) retired people

(c) disabled people

(d) starving people in another country

(Any of these groups could have been used instead of the "cattle" of the negotiation above.)

13.11 Moral Motivation: Decency, Villainy, and Hypocrisy

The prospects for a naturalistic ethics seem tantalizing. On the one hand we have the PD and free rider situations. These show how the benefits of cooperative behavior can only be achieved if people accept constraints on their self-interested behavior. On the other hand the prospects for defining a social contract that defines morality do not seem very good. Ignore the exact definition of morality for a while, and characterize moral, or perhaps less grandly, simply decent behavior as behavior that tends toward achievable cooperation for mutual benefit. Why should someone be decent?

The central worry for naturalists here is still the basic fact that noncooperation often pays. More specifically, it is pretend cooperation that often pays. When there is an understanding between people that they will cooperate in a certain way, the course of action that maximizes an individual's chances of getting what she wants is often to give the impression of cooperating while waiting until the right moment to defect. That was the weakest point of Hobbes' argument: while it is rational in the state of nature to make a social contract, it is not so clearly rational to keep the contract once it is made. There is another side to the story, though. It has two parts.

First, remember that the context for action usually involves many people, sometimes thousands. So we must not consider just simple two-person PD situations, but larger n-person free rider situations. Many of them have characteristic (a) of the ideal social contract. That is, if many people act uncooperatively then everyone will suffer. (One person can gain by lying about vital matters, but if this becomes common no one is able to believe anyone else.) As a result, it is in everyone's interest that most people act decently. Everyone should, if they are rational, want there to be a lot of decency around. So they should not want their own actions to undercut it. So the really subtle and effective villain should be on the border between real decency and hypocrisy, upholding standards that they intend sometimes to break. Thus everyone, even the villains, should want most of their actions to be decent.

To be a good hypocrite you have to understand the principles you are pretending to adhere to. But in a complex society the rules that constitute decent behavior are often very subtle and hard to state. Consider promising, for example. It is not easy to say exactly what counts as keeping or breaking a promise. And in fact, in terms of what was said in the last section about the way coordinations evolve as society evolves, this makes a lot of sense. The better combinations of the actions open to us are very likely to be subtle and hard to state. So in order to gain the benefits of cooperation, a person will have to find ways of making these subtle patterns of action come easily and naturally. And there is a simple and natural way of doing this: become a member of a community, grow up in it and internalize its standards. Then you will know many of these benefit-bringing rules without having to put them in words, in the way that you know the rules of your community's language without being able to state them.

But this presents the self-centered villain with a problem. The best way to get the benefits of cooperation is to learn the rules. And the best way of doing this is to be a real member of a community. And this has its price – the "Rousseau point" of Section 9 – for when you become a member of a community your desires change. You find yourself actually caring for others. (You will care for those near to you in the community, at any rate. Unless you are a saint or a psychopath you are likely to feel less strongly about other people who are more socially remote from you.)

The crucial point here is that consistent and effective hypocrisy – faking decency – may be beyond the powers of normal human beings. A more efficient strategy for a selfish person to maximize the satisfaction of her desires may be to transform herself into a not-so-selfish person. Then she can really take part in social cooperation and really get the benefits. And the benefits will include satisfaction of (some of) the original selfish desires.

And what happens when this transformed person finds herself in the interrogation room, being offered the opportunity of getting her freedom by betraying her friend in the next cell? She is unable to take the opportunity. And the repressed egotist within her curses the transformation. But under most conditions the egotist would have gained most by undergoing the transformation. The transformation is a strategy to deal with a risky world, and like all such strategies it can sometimes fail.

13.12 Morals within Nature?

Can there be a morality worth the name that makes no appeal to anything beyond the natural world? Many philosophers have thought that there can be, and many philosophers have disagreed with them. (And many have tried to duck the question.) This chapter has tried to explain one way in which philosophers have tried to think of a naturalistic morality: as an implicit contract which people in a society make for their mutual benefit. In what ways and to what extent can this idea work? Here are three reactions you might have after working through the chapter.

(1) Morality without religion is a farce. There is no basis for morality within nature alone.

(2) Morality without religion is different from morality with religion. There can be a real morality whose basis lies within nature, but it will be different from one based on the supernatural.

(3) Religion is completely irrelevant to morality. You can have exactly the same beliefs about right and wrong whatever you believe about the relation between the natural and the supernatural.

All three of these can be defended intelligently. To see in which direction your own thinking tends, see how you put together your reactions to the different sections of this chapter. Below are conclusions one might reasonably draw from each section, except the first. (The first is omitted because it sets up the issues for the whole chapter.) You may have to go back and look quickly at each section to remind yourself of what was in it and what reactions it provoked. And you may find that later sections have changed the reactions you had to a section when you first worked through it.

Section 2: The moralist's nightmare

(a) People who behave morally gain from it.
(b) If everyone behaved morally everyone would be better off than everyone would if everyone behaved immorally.
(c) People who behave immorally can take advantage of those who behave morally.

Section 3: Hobbes on the state of nature

(a) A system of rewards and punishments is the only alternative to anarchy.
(b) It is in people's interests to set up rules by which to live.
(c) One way out of the state of nature is to make a social contract and stick to it.

Section 4: The prisoner's dilemma

(a) Sometimes individuals acting in their own individual interest will frustrate each other.
(b) Sometimes people's actions need to be coordinated by some factor external to them.
(c) Sometimes one person can take advantage of the cooperative actions of others.

Section 5: Hobbes and the prisoner's dilemma

(a) It is sometimes in people's interests to have cooperation imposed on them.
(b) Pretending to be moral is often the best strategy.
(c) It is often hard to get people to accept a mutually acceptable solution.

Section 6: Implicit contracts

(a) People often bargain without knowing that is what they are doing.
(b) People act as if there were contracts between them, even when there is no explicit contract.
(c) People can easily enter into unfair social arrangements without realizing it.

Section 7: Imaginary social contracts

(a) People often accept unfair societies.
(b) Everyone's accepting something does not mean that it is fair.
(c) The circumstances in which a social contract is first made can affect whether it is seen as fair.

Section 8: Morals in nature? Rousseau, Hegel, Marx

(a) There is no social contract that is right for all times and places.
(b) What social contracts people can imagine depends on the society they are in.
(c) What people want depends on the society they are in.

Section 9: Real states of nature

(a) Individuals without power cannot negotiate a social contract that protects their interests.
(b) People may not accept a fair solution because it would threaten their interests.
(c) People may not agree about what is a fair social contract.

Section 10: Moral motivation: decency, villainy, and hypocrisy

(a) It is sometimes in your interest to turn yourself into a less selfish person.
(b) Noncooperation often has real benefits.
(c) Even immoral people should want others to be moral.

Matching reactions and conclusions

Which of these conclusions supports which of the reactions (1), (2), (3)? It is worth going through the whole list and thinking out for yourself the relation between each of the three conclusions that could be drawn from each section and each of (1), (2), (3). But as a short cut consider that the early sections of the chapter, Sections 2 to 4, support (3). The later sections raise doubts that allow more room for (1) or (2). In particular, consider (b) of Section 5, (c) of Section 6, (b) of Section 7, (a) of Section 8, and (a) of Section 9. Which of these give some support to (1) and which to (2)?

One conclusion that several sections suggest is that a naturalistic moral theory must consider not only what social contracts people might accept, explicitly or implicitly, but also what would make a social contract fair. Can fairness be defined without appealing to anything outside the natural world? Which section conclusions show the importance of this question?

Conclusions of This Chapter

◆ *Everyone is likely to suffer if everyone acts immorally. Therefore it is in everyone's interest that there be some sort of a contract between people to act in accordance with some moral system. This is one way in which a moral theory can give reasons for morality without appealing to anything supernatural.*

◆ *There are situations in which people who act only for their immediate individual interest will be unable to cooperate with each other for mutual gain. An important example of this is the prisoner's dilemma.*

◆ *One class of problems about social contract theories of morality comes from the lack of protection such a contract might afford to people who have very little bargaining power. Another comes from the fact that people have limited imagination and limited understanding of what they might want in different social situations, so that any contract actual people will make will reflect their actual situation rather than a moral ideal.*

◆ *Individual rationality – doing the most intelligent thing in your own interest – may be better satisfied not by always cooperating with others but by pretending to cooperate. On the other hand, pretending can be hard, and one of the best ways of learning how to pretend is to take very seriously the values of your culture.*

Further Reading

Hobbes and Rousseau

Selections from Hobbes and Rousseau in Part IX of John Cottingham (ed.), *Western Philosophy: An Anthology*. Blackwell, 1996.

Thomas Hobbes, *Leviathan*, Part II, edited by Michael Oakeshott. Blackwell, 1946.

Jean-Jacques Rousseau, *The Social Contract*, in *The Social Contract and Discourses*, translated and edited by G. D. H. Cole. Dent (Everyman), 1966.

Chapters 24 (on Hobbes) and 29 (on Rousseau) of George Sabine and Thomas Thorson, *A History of Political Theory*, fourth edition. Dryden Press, 1973.

Tom Sorrell, "Hobbes," in *The Blackwell Companion to Philosophy*.

*David Gauthier, *The Logic of Leviathan*. Oxford University Press, 1969.

*Gregory Kavka, *Hobbesian Moral and Political Theory*. Princeton University Press, 1986.

Social contracts

Chapter 8 of Martin Hollis, *Invitation to Philosophy*. Blackwell, 1985.

Chapters 5 and 10 of Peter Singer, *Practical Ethics*, second edition. Cambridge University Press, 1993.

*David Gauthier (ed.), *Morality and Rational Self-interest*. Prentice-Hall, 1970.

Naturalism and ethics

Chapter 15 of Robert M. Martin, *There Are Two Errors in the the Title of this Book*. Broadview, 1992.

Chapters 9 and 13 of Gilbert Harman, *The Nature of Morality*. Oxford University Press, 1977.

Chapters 3, 8, and 10 of J. L. Mackie, *Ethics: Inventing Right and Wrong*. Penguin, 1977.

On the prisoner's dilemma

Garret Hardin and John Boden, *Managing the Commons*. W. H. Freeman, 1977.

*Part II of Shaun Hargreaves Heap, Martin Hollis, Bruce Lyons, Robert Sugden, and Albert Weale, *The Theory of Choice*. Blackwell, 1992.

*David Gauthier, *Morals by Agreement*. Oxford University Press, 1985.

Electronic resources

Routledge Encyclopedia of Philosophy (available online at many universities): articles on Hobbes, Thomas; Naturalism in ethics; Rational choice theory; Rousseau, Jean-Jacques.

Stanford Encyclopedia of Philosophy (http://plato.stanford.edu/): *Contractarianism*; Free rider problem; Game theory and ethics; *Hegel, Georg Wilhelm Friedrich*; Hobbes, Thomas: Moral and political philosophy; Marx, Karl; *Prisoner's dilemma* (*italicized* items are available as this book goes to press; the others should be available soon).

14 Deep Illusions

Introduction

If materialism is true, morality might be an illusion. Some philosophers have tried to show how moral principles could be true even if everything is physical. One influential approach is to study contracts that people in a society could make with one another for mutual benefit.

If materialism is true, many other features of our lives could be illusions. The example of colors shows many of the problems that also arise with our conviction that we make free decisions and our conviction that we are the same persons throughout our lives.

Idealism is the opposite of materialism. Arguments for idealism that were used by Berkeley in the eighteenth century are still influential in the form of verificationism and instrumentalism. The conflict between instrumentalism and realism about science is part of much larger questions about how our thinking relates to the world.

Chapter Objectives

By the end of this chapter you should be able to answer the following questions.

◆ *How does modern science suggest that some aspects of the world may be illusory?*
◆ *What are the compatibilist and libertarian positions on free will?*
◆ *What is the difference between determinism and fatalism?*
◆ *What are the problems in assuming that persons can continue as the same persons through time?*

Definitions

The following words used in this chapter are defined in the list of definitions at the end of the book:

compatibilism   *incompatibilism*   *secondary quality*
determinism   *libertarianism*
fatalism   *primary quality*

14.1 Primary and Secondary Qualities

There are scientific books about the properties of uranium. There are scientific books about elephants. That is because there are general scientific laws about things composed of uranium or things which are elephants. But there are no scientific books about red things or green things. That is because there are no general scientific laws about red things or green things. For that matter, there are no nonscientific books about red things or green things either. There are books like *Fried Green Tomatoes* and *How Green Was My Valley*, but you do not find books with titles like *Green Things and How To Use Them* or *Purple Objects of the World*. For green things come in all shapes and sizes, and have many different properties. The most obvious thing they all have in common is that they look green to human beings. And that is not a very basic natural fact about them.

From the early days of science, scientists and philosophers have wondered how to fit tastes, colors, smells, and other perceptual qualities of things into a picture of the world based on the basic ideas of physics, such as shape, motion, and energy. Here is a quotation from Galileo, writing in 1623 and expressing a rather drastic view:

> But I cannot believe that there exists in external bodies anything, other than their size, shape, or motion . . . which could excite in us our tastes, sounds, and odors. The latter . . . I believe to be nothing but mere names. (Galileo Galilei, Il Saggitore)

Primary qualities are basic physical properties of objects. They cause us to attribute to objects secondary qualities, such as colors and smells.

Galileo is arguing that the real properties of physical objects are the ones that physics describes. These properties cause human beings to have sensations of taste, sound, and smell, so that they think, mistakenly, that tastes, sounds, and odors are real properties of the objects. (Galileo thinks that physics uses only spatial properties of objects: size, shape, motion. We would not think this now.) This is an early version of the distinction between *primary* and *secondary* qualities. To put it very roughly: primary qualities are properties that objects really have because of their physical nature, while secondary qualities are properties that we attribute to objects because of the effects of their primary qualities. It is important to see that there are many different things this can mean. Here are three:

First version, properties versus powers　Primary qualities are basic physical properties of objects, while secondary qualities are powers that objects have as a result of their primary qualities. For example, red is the power to reflect long wavelength light.

Second version, nonrelational versus relational　Primary qualities are physical properties that objects have in isolation, while secondary qualities are properties that objects have in relation to observers. For example, an object is red if it will seem red to a normal observer under standard conditions.

Third version, real versus illusory Primary qualities are real properties of objects, secondary qualities are purely subjective. Objects are not really red, but people sometimes have red sensations from looking at objects.

Galileo was defending the third version. Most philosophers who have defended a primary–secondary quality distinction have defended the first or the second version. And the most frequent example is not taste, sound, or odor, but color. For on the subject of color there is a very striking contrast between the picture of the world we get from science and the way it normally seems to us. The world seems a bright and dappled place, filled with objects of many different colors. That is one source of its beauty. Moreover, an object's color seems a real property of it, like its size or weight. Objects can change in color – they can fade or be painted. But so too can they change in size or weight. And yet when we think of the world scientifically, all this disappears: objects are complexes of material particles that are too small to have any colors at all. (What color is an electron? No color.) And color does not come in at all when we use scientific theories to explain what objects do. (At any rate when we use physics and chemistry. Color plays a role in biology.) The world of science seems colorless. As the German poet Goethe said, "Grey, my friend is all theory, Green the golden tree of life." (This might be a reason for rejecting the scientific picture of the world. Idealists like Berkeley would think so. See Chapter 15, Section 3.)

Rather than say that colors are simply illusions, philosophers usually think of them as real, but not basic properties of objects. To see what this means, consider how, according to contemporary science, colors are produced. Suppose that white light strikes an object and reflects off it toward a person's eyes. The person will see the object as colored; which color the person sees the object as having will depend on the wavelengths of the light reflected. Very crudely, long wavelengths make the object look red, and as the wavelength gets shorter the object will be yellow, green, and eventually blue. (The whole story is actually much more complicated than this.) Moreover, we are beginning to understand how the eye and the brain translate light of different wavelengths into color sensations. So we understand in scientific terms roughly what happens when, for example, red objects reflect long wavelength light toward people, who then see them as red. So "red" does relate to the basic physical properties of objects, in two ways. First, there is the way objects reflect light of different wavelengths. Second, there is the way this reflected light causes people to see the objects as colored. And these two ways correspond to the first and second versions of the primary–secondary quality distinction described above.

Color is an important example for philosophy because it is something that seems very real to us but that does not fit easily into the scientific picture of the world. This is not to say that it does not fit in at all. It can fit in by being defined in terms of scientific concepts – that is, the first version of the primary–secondary quality distinction above – or by being defined as a property not of the world alone but of the way we perceive it – that is the second version of the distinction. But it is also possible that – as in the third version of the distinction – colors do not fit in because there really are no such properties. Color would then be like luck or fate or magic, according to the scientific picture of the world. If the world is the kind of place that most of us think it is, then luck or fate or magic are not real. Sometimes lucky things happen to people, for example, but there is not any property that some people have that makes them lucky. And there are not things you can do that will give you good luck. Perhaps colors are like luck, fate, and magic, ways we can describe our experiences which do not correspond to anything in reality. Perhaps if naturalism is true many of the ways we describe the world, ways we care deeply about, are like this: deep illusions.

This chapter will discuss color, free will, personal identity, and the meaning of life. In all these cases some philosophers have argued that the scientific picture of reality leaves no room for something that is vital to our lives. And in all these cases other philosophers have argued the opposite, that things we care about can find a place in the world as described by science.

14.2 Hard Questions about Color

Below there are three questions about color. There are intelligent reasons for answering both Yes and No to each of them. First think what your answers to the questions are. (Do others agree with you?)

(1) Suppose the human visual system changes one night, and the next morning grass looks to everyone the way blood used to. And blood looks to everyone the way grass used to. And so on. Is grass now red?

(2) Suppose there are extraterrestrials for whom what we call red is three separate colors. We have no names for these colors and we have trouble understanding which things get classified as which kind of red for the extraterrestrials. Could they be seeing colors that we cannot see?

(3) Are roses red in the dark?

Now recall the three versions of the primary–secondary quality distinction:

First version, properties versus powers   Primary qualities are basic physical properties of objects, while secondary qualities are powers that objects have as a result of their primary qualities. For example, red is the power to reflect long wavelength light.

Second version, nonrelational versus relational   Primary qualities are physical properties that objects have in isolation, while secondary qualities are properties that objects have in relation to observers. For example, an object is red if it will seem red to a normal observer under standard conditions.

Third version, real versus illusory   Primary qualities are real properties of objects, secondary qualities are purely subjective. Objects are not really red; but people sometimes have red sensations from looking at objects.

(a) Suppose you answer No to question (1) above. Which of these three versions should you agree with? (b) Suppose you answer No to question (2) above. Which of these three versions should you agree with? (c) Suppose you answer No to question (3) above. Which of these three versions should you agree with?

Which of the following reasons for giving a No answer to question (3) could someone give while still believing most of what contemporary people normally believe?

(i)   Roses become purple when light is not shining on them.
(ii)   In the dark, roses are not reflecting long wavelength light at any person's eyes.
(iii)   In order to know what color roses are in the dark we would have to look, but we couldn't do that while it was still dark.

Which of the following reasons for giving a Yes answer to question (1) could someone give while still believing everything that twentieth-century people normally believe (except perhaps about color)?

(i)   Everyone would say "Grass looks red now."
(ii)   Grass would now have the same capacities to give us color sensations that blood used to.
(iii)   The perceptions we would now have would show that our earlier perceptions were illusions.

Which of the following reasons for giving a Yes answer to question (2) could someone give while still believing everything that contemporary people normally believe (except perhaps about color)?

(i)   Extraterrestrials are sure to have a much better understanding of the universe than humans.
(ii)   As long as there are properties that they are responding to, it does not matter whether we can understand them.
(iii)   Any subset of the range of shades that we call "red" might as well be called a color.

14.3 Color as Illusory

The Galileo quote fits the third version of the primary–secondary quality distinction. ("Secondary qualities are illusions.") But Galileo is discussing tastes, sounds, and odors rather than colors. What kind of a case can be made for taking colors to be illusions? Here is an argument for saying that objects are not colored.

> **A bush on the side of a hill may look bluish-green when seen from far away, as part of the hillside. When you get nearer to it, it seems yellow-green. Then when you focus on individual leaves and berries they seem many different greens and reds and yellows. Then when you examine an individual leaf through a microscope, different cells and parts of cells seem different colors. Only the chlorophyll is green. Then if you look at parts of cells through an electron microscope you see no colors at all. So objects are not really colored independently of how we look at them.**

Here are some objections to this argument:

(i) The color of an object is not the color it seems to have looked at any which way, but the color it seems to have when looked at under good white light from about three feet away.

(ii) A race-track may look like a dot when seen from miles away, like an oval when seen from a hundred yards away, and like an irregular jagged shape when seen from very close up. So shapes are just the same as colors in this respect; how they seem depends on how we are looking at them.

(iii) The hillside is blue; the leaf is green; the berries are red; the chlorophyll is green; the molecules are no color at all. They're all different.

(iv) Whole objects are not colored but tiny spots on their surfaces are.

Which of these are powerful objections to the argument that someone using the argument would feel they had to find a reply to?
 Here are three replies to objection (ii), the race-track example:

(a) Yes, shapes are illusions too.

(b) We can measure shapes, but we cannot measure the colors of objects, and the argument shows why.

(c) All the shapes an object seems to have, from different distances and directions, are similar and related, while the colors it has vary wildly.

Which of these are replies that someone using the argument would be forced to make, and which are simply replies they might choose to make? . . . Which of these replies says something true?

Now here are three replies to objection (iii):

(a) A hillside cannot be blue if it is made up of green and red parts.
(b) The smallest parts of an object, its molecules and atoms, have no colors, so color is not a real property of the whole object.
(c) The individual leaves will seem different colors when seen from different distances.

Which of these express in a different way the same ideas that are found in the argument, and which of them say something beyond what is found in the argument? . . . Which of these replies says something true?

14.4 Free Will

Color is just an example. There are many other aspects of the world that science or simply careful thought might show to be illusions. One of these is human freedom. When people think about what it is like to make decisions, or to perform deliberate actions, they often have an overwhelming sense of their own freedom. It is very hard to put this impression into words coherently, but for many people it is a striking and vivid fact about their own mental lives, as striking and vivid as the colors of objects around them. And just as a naturalist view of the world threatens the colors, it threatens the sense of freedom.

The sense of freedom can be illustrated with some examples. Suppose that you are facing a hard decision. You have been offered a high-paying and interesting job, but to take it you would have to drop out of university. You want the job and you also want to study and get a degree. You think about it for days and you do not find any conclusive reasons for either choice. Both desires are strong and you cannot say which is stronger. The day comes when you have to accept or reject the job. You think about it one last time and you suddenly find your mind clear: you will stay at university and get a very similar job in a few years' time.

The important point about the decision in this example is that the reasons for taking the job and the reasons for staying in university were equally strong. You would not have been crazy to have made the opposite decision. In fact, you could easily have made the opposite decision. But you did not act randomly either. Your action was guided by the facts, but it was you who chose it. It was a free decision.

Or suppose that you are an artist painting a picture. You look at the canvas with your brush in your hand and you are about to put a spot of white paint to represent a highlight in the hair of your model. Suddenly you stop, put down the brush, pick up another one and paint the highlight yellow instead. When other people admire the picture and comment on the original colors you say: "I don't know why I did it that way; the idea suddenly came to me." Your actions were guided by the aim of producing an interesting portrait, but you chose your own way of doing this. They were free acts.

The threat to freedom comes from *determinism*. Determinism is the idea that everything that happens is completely determined by what happens earlier. Given earlier events, later events could not have been different. The universe develops in time like the working of a perfectly programmed machine, so that once it is started there is only one course it can take. Physics is sometimes supposed to support a deterministic view of the world. In fact, one particular central theory in physics, "classical mechanics," based on the work of the seventeenth-century English physicist and mathematician Isaac Newton, is generally deterministic: the state of a system at an earlier time, plus the laws of mechanics, fix its state at later times. This led the nineteenth-century French physicist and mathematician Pierre Laplace to write that:

> An intelligence knowing all the forces acting in nature at a given instant, as well as the momentary positions of all things in the universe, would be able to comprehend in one single formula the motions of the largest bodies as well as the lightest atoms in the world, provided that its intellect were sufficiently powerful to subject all data to analysis; to it nothing would be uncertain, the future as well as the past would be present to its eyes.

Determinism is the idea that everything that happens is completely determined by what happens earlier. It can seem to threaten our freedom to choose our actions.

Human beings are included in this claim. If the behavior of everything in the world could in principle be calculated in advance, then so could the behavior of human bodies. But where does this leave our thought that *we* determine our actions. Imagine someone making a difficult decision. She thinks out her options and ponders what their results would be, and how much she likes these results. She tries to think of new options. She takes long walks, trying to sort out all her thoughts. Finally an answer just comes to her. It feels as if it appeared from nowhere, but she knows that all her ruminating has made this possible. Her decision is to do something that at first had seemed very undesirable. But as she thought about it, not only have hidden advantages to this course of action appeared, but also her desires have changed. When she sees more clearly the consequences of some of her options she ceases to want them. Could all this thinking and agonizing, all this reforming of her beliefs and her desires, be the result of a mechanical process?

If it were the result of a mechanical process then someone with enough information could have predicted it. So someone could have known in advance what decision she would make. And, even more unsettling, she herself could have known in advance what decision she was going to make. If only she had had enough information about herself, about her body and her brain, and enough calculating power, she could have spared herself all the thinking and agonizing.

Now of course she could never know enough about herself, and the calculations would be too hard for any human being to carry them out. But it seems – to many people – that she would face deeper problems than that. Decision-making is not something that could be got down to a set of rules whose results could be predicted in advance. It involves choices made creatively by people and not mechanically by their situations. *When you act freely you could have acted otherwise.*

One reason for taking the threat seriously is the link between human freedom and moral responsibility. If people's actions are *not* free, we do not praise or blame them. The link between praise or blame and freedom can get very complicated. But consider a very simple example. You are walking in your sleep and meet a burglar who takes you for a ghost and runs away in terror. He falls down a flight of stairs and dies. You are not praised for defending the house against burglary nor blamed for the burglar's death. In some way it wasn't *your* action. You did not *choose* it.

So our sense that there is freedom inside us is as threatened as our sense that there are colors outside us. And the same general strategies are available. Colors could be *powers* of physical objects, *relations* between physical objects and human observers, or *illusions* produced in humans by physical objects. Consider the analogs of these positions in the case of freedom.

Compatibilism: freedom as a power   A number of philosophers have argued for the position that freedom is compatible with determinism. We can be free even if we are determined. Among our powers as physical systems is the power to act freely. To see the motive for this, consider cases where someone is *not* acting freely. Suppose, for example, you are in a crowd on the platform of a subway station and someone behind you pushes you. You bump uncontrollably into the person in front of you who is pushed over the edge in front of the approaching train. Your pushing the person in front of you is not a free act (and you would not be morally or legally blamed for it), for its cause was the push you received from behind. Suppose, on the other hand, you see an enemy on the platform in front of you, decide that in the crowd and the confusion you can get away with the crime, and push him over the edge. That is a free act, and you are responsible for the consequences. The difference is that the cause of the action was now *in you*. You pushed yourself. So we can make a first crude definition:

> Compatibilism says that freedom is compatible with determinism – we can have both.

Compatibilism   **A person's act is free if it is caused by a decision which is caused by the person's own beliefs and desires.**

Hume was one of the first philosophers to suggest this kind of compatibilism. At the end of an argument that human actions are as regular and law-governed as events in the physical world he claimed that:

> *By liberty, then, we can only mean* a power of acting or not acting, according to the determinations of the will; *that is, if we choose to remain at rest, we may; if we choose to move, we also may.* (Enquiry, *section 7, part 1*)

There are many natural objections to this account. Suppose that before you get to the subway someone kidnaps you and by a combination of drugs and hypnotism puts you in a strange state where you are convinced that all people with red hair are evil and should be destroyed. You see a red-headed person on the platform and push her in front of a train. As soon as you have done the deed you snap out of this state and are amazed and horrified at what you have done. Was this a free act? It seems that the person who kidnapped you and tampered with your mind was controlling you as surely as if they had pushed you. Instead of pushing you they are pushing your beliefs and desires, which then push you. So the bare fact that your action was caused (even by way of a decision) by your beliefs and desires does not seem to make the act a freely chosen one. It matters what caused the beliefs and desires.

Examples like this are probably fatal to a very simple compatibilism like Hume's. But there are more subtle versions, and they can cope with more challenging counterexamples. One of the things you come to appreciate when you study what is written on this topic is the survival power of compatibilism: the general idea that we can be at the same time free and determined is very hard to refute. Here is a quotation from the twentieth-century philosopher Mary Midgley, describing a compatibilist position:

> *Does conduct cease to be free merely by being predictable? It is not obvious why it should, provided that the prediction rests on the right sort of grounds – namely, on there being good reason to act.*

Compatibilism tries to define freedom in terms of determinism. Suppose that this cannot be done. Suppose that however hard we try to find a place for free choice in a deterministic world, we fail. Then we might conclude that there is no such place, that the opposite of compatibilism, *incompatibilism*, is true.

Incompatibilism **If determinism is true then no human actions are free.**

Note the "if". An incompatibilist can reason in two opposite ways. The first runs:

> **If determinism is true then no human actions are free.**
> **Determinism is true.**
> **Therefore no human actions are free.**

Call this position *hard determinism*. (Compatibilism is sometimes called *soft* determinism.) But an incompatibilist can also argue:

If determinism is true then no human actions are free.
Some human actions are free.
Therefore determinism is not true.

Call this *libertarianism*. Which argument an incompatibilist chooses, whether it is hard determinism or libertarianism that is chosen, depends on which the incompatibilist thinks is more believable: that everything is determined, or that there are free actions.

From this perspective we may consider rejecting not just determinism but also materialism. For it has seemed to some philosophers that even if the physical world is not completely deterministic, there is no real place in it for spontaneous choice. This is because the obvious alternative to determinism in physical terms is randomness, as in the fall of a die or radioactive decay. But our choices are not random. We create our choices for good reasons, but freely. So, it has seemed to some philosophers, the only way to find a place for freedom is to place it outside the operation of physical cause and effect altogether.

14.5 Freedom and Responsibility

In the examples below, five people perform five acts. In each of them you should consider whether the act that the person performs is free. Count in how many cases you find the act free, and in how many not free. An act is free if it is the person's own deliberate action and they could have acted otherwise, and it is not free if it is the result of forces over which the person had no control. (See the previous section.) You should also consider whether the person should be blamed for the action (held responsible for it). And it may be helpful to consider whether anyone else is (also or instead) to blame.

(a) Alice meets Bertie and soon falls in love with him. She does not realize that Bertie is only after her father's fortune, which she will inherit. Bertie persuades Alice to poison her father and to give the fortune to a charity which actually helps just his bank account.

   The act is Alice's poisoning her father. Is it a free act? Is Alice to blame for it? Is anyone else to blame?

(b) Andrew goes to a party and gets very drunk. He refuses an offer of a ride home and drives, insisting that his girlfriend come with him. On the way he is crossing a narrow bridge when the car slides on a patch of ice. Andrew tries very hard to control the car but cannot and the car falls into the river below. His girlfriend is drowned.

   The act is Andrew's driving the car into the river. Is it a free act? Is Andrew to blame for it? Is anyone else to blame?

(c) Anneka has a very unhappy childhood. She is frequently beaten for no reason by her cruel mother. Twenty years later she has a daughter and to her horror finds herself repeating her mother's behavior. She feels a strong impulse to strike her child for trivial reasons. Usually, she can resist the impulse but on one occasion she does not, and hits her child with a heavy iron pot when the child interrupts a radio program she is listening to.

The act is Anneka's hitting her child with the pot. Is it a free act? Is Anneka to blame? Is anyone else to blame?

(d) Ambrose is walking down the street when an old woman sitting on the kerb asks him for money. He refuses her, rudely. She curses him, saying "Everything will go wrong for you. You will hurt those you love most." In the following years the old woman's curse comes true. For each person Ambrose becomes close to he says or does some wounding act which causes that person to hate him. Finally, he meets and loves Beatrice and they are going to get married. The day before the wedding she describes the wedding dress to him and he says "Don't wear that; it will emphasize your dreadful overweight figure." She does not turn up for the wedding and Ambrose learns she has got on a plane for Tokyo. "Why did I say that stupid thing?" he asks himself. "That curse will haunt me for ever."

The act is Ambrose's insulting Beatrice. Is it a free act? Is Ambrose to blame? Is anyone else to blame?

(e) Astrid is a very law-abiding person. She is walking downtown with her little sister when a man jumps out of a car and puts a gun to her sister's head. He commands Astrid to drive the car to a bank while he holds it up, and then to drive away down the highway. They come to a police roadblock and he tells her to drive through it, or he will shoot the sister. She drives through the roadblock, killing a police officer.

The act is Astrid's running down the police officer. Is it a free act? Is Astrid to blame? Is anyone else to blame?

If you thought that the act was free in three or more cases, then you are inclined to a strong belief in free will. You should find compatibilist or libertarian views attractive. You should ask yourself what kinds of compulsion would in your opinion make an action not free.

If you thought that the act was not free in three or more cases, then you are inclined to be skeptical about free will. You should find determinist views attractive. You should ask yourself whether this makes you doubt that people can be held responsible for their actions.

If you thought that the person was not to blame in three or more cases, then you tend not to hold people responsible for their acts. This may make you attracted to determinist views. You should ask yourself in what cases you would hold a person responsible for their action, and how they differ from these five cases.

If you thought that the person was to blame in three or more cases, then you tend to hold people responsible for most of their acts. This may make you attracted to libertarian or compatibilist views. You should ask yourself what kinds of compulsion would in your opinion make a person not responsible for their action.

If you thought in three or more cases that the act was not free but the person was responsible, then you are inclined to compatibilism. You should think about different kinds of compatibilism discussed in the next section.

If you thought in three or more cases that the act was free but the person was not responsible, then you are inclined to see no connection between freedom and responsibility. This is a rather unusual position. You should think what factors besides freedom do enter into making a person not responsible for their actions.

You should now discuss with others of opposite views to find what it is you really disagree about. (Determinists with libertarians; compatibilists with incompatibilists.) You may come to one of the following conclusions. (Or you may come to quite different conclusions, or you may conclude that some of the following are wrong.)

(1) The idea of a free action is too vague to allow any definite conclusions.
(2) The differences are basically religious. If you believe that God punishes people for freely chosen evil actions then you have to believe that some actions are free.
(3) There are many very different reasons for which people can be blamed or excused from blame.
(4) Before we can resolve issues about free action we have to resolve many other questions about how human actions are caused.

14.6 Freedom as a Secondary Quality

In Section 14.4 a compatibilist theory of the relation between free will and determinism was described. It was

Compatibilism: freedom as a power **A person's act is free if it is caused by a decision that is caused by the person's own beliefs and desires.**

This was an analog of the first version of the distinction between primary and secondary qualities. Here are the three versions again.

First version, properties versus powers Primary qualities are basic physical properties of objects, while secondary qualities are powers that objects have as a result of their primary qualities. For example, red is the power to reflect long wavelength light.

Second version, nonrelational versus relational   Primary qualities are physical properties that objects have in isolation, while secondary qualities are properties that objects have in relation to observers. For example, an object is red if it will seem red to a normal observer under standard conditions.

Third version, real versus illusory   Primary qualities are real properties of objects, secondary qualities are purely subjective. Objects are not really red; but people sometimes have red sensations from looking at objects.

The second and third versions also have analogs in theories of the relation between free action and determinism. Philosophers have defended positions like all three below.

(i) People have the impression of acting freely but there is no real fact about them that corresponds to this spontaneity.
(ii) A free action is an action that normal thoughtful people would consider to be free.
(iii) A free action is one that is produced by the mind in a way that is free from the determination of the body.

 Two of the positions (i)–(iii) are analogs of the second and third versions of the primary–secondary quality distinction. Which ones are analogs of which version, and which is an analog of neither version? To think this through, pay attention to the key words in the second and third versions of the distinction:

From the second version	*properties that objects have in relation to observers*
	standard conditions
From the third version	*real properties*
	purely subjective

Compare these with the key words in each of the three positions:

From (i)	*impression*
	real fact
From (ii)	*normal thoughtful people*
	consider to be
From (iii)	*produced by the mind*
	determination

First look for corresponding key terms and then look for analogs between the versions of the primary–secondary quality distinction and the three positions.

One of (i), (ii), (iii) is a kind of compatibilism, in that it leaves open the possibility that we can be both free and determined. One of them is a kind of hard determinism, in that it sees no room in the world for freedom. And one of them is a kind of libertarianism, in that it sees the possibility of freedom in an escape from physical causes. Which is which?

Below are three arguments. One of them is an argument for (i) and one of them is an argument for (iii). One of them is an argument *against* (ii). Which is which?

(a) Different societies have different ideas about when we can praise or blame people. For example, we now acknowledge many kinds of psychological excuses which would not have been admitted in the past, deriving from facts about people's childhood or the conditions under which they committed a crime. And we do not now allow provocation as an excuse for rape, or the rage of a deceived husband as an excuse for killing his wife and her lover, as has been the case in some past times and places. So people's opinions about whether someone could have acted otherwise are likely to be shaped by the assumptions of their societies. Therefore people's opinions about freedom need not correspond to what actions actually are free.

(b) Everything in nature is either determined, like the motion of the planets, or random, like the fall of a die or radioactive decay. But randomness is not freedom any more than determination is. So there is no room for freedom in nature.

(c) Everything in the physical world is either determined, like the motion of the planets, or random, like the fall of a die or radioactive decay. But randomness is not freedom any more than determination is. We create our choices for good reasons, but freely. So, since there is no room for freedom in the purely physical world, freedom must lie outside the purely physical world.

In each case, look for the conclusion (preceded by "so" or "therefore"). Which conclusion is most like (i)? Which is most like (iii)? Which is most like the denial of (ii)? Again, looking at key words may help. Pay attention to *people's opinions* in (a), *in nature* in (b), and *outside the purely physical world* in (c). Compare them to *real fact* in (i), *people would consider* in (ii), and *free from the determination of the body* in (iii).

Arguments (b) and (c) begin with the same assumptions and end up with different conclusions. How can this be?

Argument (a) begins with facts about blame and ends with a conclusion about freedom. Is the way in which it gets from blame to freedom convincing?

Box 24 **Chaos and Determinism**

Determinists, libertarians, compatibilists, and incompatibilists all usually assume that if a decision is determined then someone with enough information could have predicted it. This is probably false. For determinism does not entail predictability. There are many physical systems whose later states are determined by their earlier ones, but in such a way that no attainable amount of information about their earlier states will be enough to predict their later states. These are *chaotic* systems. Probably most physical systems are chaotic. In a typical chaotic system, although the connection between earlier and later states is deterministic, the connection is so delicate that the slightest error in describing an earlier state can lead to an enormous error in predicting a later state. So suppose that the earlier state is described with a single real number, specified as an infinite decimal. Then to know what the state will be at some later time you would have to know *all* the digits of that decimal, not just the first few million of them. Otherwise your prediction might be out by an enormous error. But obviously even an ideal calculator cannot handle infinite amounts of information. So the prediction of chaotic systems is really impossible.

Are human beings chaotic systems? The human nervous system probably is. Does this make room for freedom? That is very hard to tell. Certainly, it helps us to see how there are many more possibilities within the physical world than simple predictability and simple randomness. And it undercuts somewhat the original fear of determinism; the idea that a deterministic world is like a large soulless piece of clockwork. There is room for a lot of wild, unpredictable, chaotic things within determinism.

14.7 Fatalism versus Determinism

The fear of determinism is sometimes really a fear of predictability. It is also sometimes a fear of *fatalism*. Fatalism is not the same as determinism. Fatalism says that if something will happen it will happen whatever actions we perform. If you are fated to die in a car crash on next August 14 then you will, even if you lock yourself in a mine a mile below the ground or go up in a space shuttle five miles above it. Fate will find a way of keeping its appointment with you.

Fatalism is not only not the same as determinism, it is inconsistent with it. For determinism says that the future is shaped by the past, the past makes the future be as it will be. But fatalism says that the future, or at any rate some versions of it, will be as it will be *whatever the past*. So determinism asserts causal connections between past and future and fatalism denies them.

There are very few reasons for believing in fatalism. That is just as well, for if fatalism were true our lives would be pretty meaningless. (And so by confusing fatalism with determinism, people sometimes conclude that if determinism were true our lives would be meaningless.) To put the point more explicitly: if fatalism were true many of the qualities which we think our lives possess, and which we value them for, would be illusions. For example, we value accomplishment. This is a feature someone's life has if they have long-term aims which are achieved *as a result of* their efforts. We value love, which involves, among other things, people being able to shape their lives around a mutually defined pattern. And we value humor, which requires that we be able to see ourselves as trying for aims that are in a particular way incongruous with the things we actually can accomplish. None of these could be real features of lives if fatalism were true.

Which of the quotations (i)–(v) below are expressions of fatalism, and which of determinism? To decide, apply the following test:

> **Freedom** claims that if you had acted differently the future would have been different. **Determinism** replies: but you could not have acted differently. **Fatalism** replies: but even if you had acted differently the future would have been the same.

(i) *If God sees and cannot be deceived, whatever his providence foresees must inevitably follow. Therefore if from eternity He knows in advance not only the people's actions but also their intentions, then there can be no free will. (Boethius, fifth century)*

(ii) *The whole course of a man's life . . . is necessarily predetermined as the course of a clock. (Schopenhauer, nineteenth century)*

(iii) *I necessarily have the passion for writing this, and you have the passion for condemning me; both are equally fools, equally the toy of destiny. (Voltaire, eighteenth century)*

(iv) *Man's life is a line that nature commands him to describe upon the surface of the earth, without his ever being able to swerve from it, even for an instant. (Baron d'Holbach, eighteenth century)*

(v) *We can easily imagine a race of men whose knowledge of the future is comparable to our knowledge of the past, but for whom the past is shrouded in darkness and mystery. Such men would . . . think of the past as somewhat mysterious and filled with alternative "possibilities." They would regard with the profoundest skepticism any philosophical argument purporting to show them that they cannot do anything about the past, though it would seem entirely natural for them to think of the future this way. (Richard Taylor, twentieth century)*

You may find that you disagree about whether (iii) describes fatalism or determinism. It is ambiguous, because the words "necessarily" and "destiny" are unclear. Replace these words with words that make it an expression of fatalism, and with words that make it an expression of determinism.

Quotation (v) suggests an argument for fatalism that runs as follows:

We cannot change the past, but the past is no different from the future. Therefore we cannot change the future.

The most dubious premise is "the past is not different from the future." To challenge this, criticize the assumption that "we can easily imagine a race whose knowledge of the future is comparable to our knowledge of the past." Could it really be easy to imagine this?

14.8 Identity through Time

You are the same person you were yesterday. Yet you are not the same as you were yesterday. You have different memories; your hair is longer or shorter; many of the cells in your body have died and some of them – not all! – have been replaced with new ones. So how can you be the same person?

Consider a wooden ship, made of ribs and planks and spars. She sails out for trading or battle and returns damaged. Planks and spars are replaced. This happens several times and eventually some ribs and other structural parts must be replaced. Eventually, over a period of many years, every bit of the boat has been replaced.

Is it the same boat at the end of all this? If all the parts of the boat were replaced at once, we might hesitate. But with a slow continuous process of replacement it seems pretty clear that we would at any rate speak of it as the same boat, which has been slowly renewed.

Now a twist to the tale. There is a shed beside the dock where the boat is repaired. And in the shed someone has been storing all the planks, ribs, spars, and other bits that were taken off the boat to be replaced. This person has a sudden idea of putting them all together to make a boat. Now there is a very battered and sea-worn boat in the next dock. Paradoxically, although it has been newly put together it looks much older than the other, and in fact all its parts are older.

Which boat is now the original boat? We have a boat which is made of all the parts of the original boat, and we have a boat which over the years we have treated as the original boat, and which slowly developed out of it. Each has a strong case. And if the other did not exist, each would have an undisputed claim to be the original boat.

One conclusion emerges clearly out of this case. The boat is not just the collection of its parts. For while the parts were being replaced, the boat remained the same boat even though at the end of the story it has none of the original parts. The original parts, accumulating in a shed, could have been used to build an inn. Then the collection of original parts would make up the inn, not the boat at the later time.

Living bodies are like boats; they stay the same even though their parts change. After a few months your body changes almost all its cells (and possibly all its carbon and nitrogen molecules). But it is the same living human body. So your body is not the same as the collection of all its cells. What makes it the same human body through all the changes of size and functioning is hard to say. (And there are harder cases than human bodies. Think of animals like butter-flies or frogs that go through metamorphoses, having very different bodily forms at different times.) One way of describing it is that the same metabolism goes on functioning, maintains its functioning while changing many of its parts and even changing its size and shape. As long as it maintains a continuous metabolism we consider it the same living body.

There is another complication about identity through time that affects both complex man-made things and living creatures. Both can split and fuse. A single-celled animal can divide into two daughter cells. Each inherits the genes and carries on the metabolic processes of the original cell. Similarly, a boat could with some ingenuity be taken apart and made into two boats (even two boats of almost the same dimensions as the original, with a lot of luck and ingenuity). Each daughter boat or daughter cell has as good a claim as the other to be the original. And two boats could be taken apart and put together as one boat, looking much like either one of them. The important example of fusion of living creatures is that of the ovum and sperm of two animals when they mate. Ovum and sperm are each a living cell, and they combine to form another living cell, the fertilized ovum, which inherits genes from each.

All these things can happen to human beings as well as to boats and cells. People not only change the cells in their bodies, but can also gain and lose whole limbs and organs. Many people have kidneys or hearts that were trans-planted into them when their own organs failed. You can imagine someone so badly injured in an accident that most of her limbs and organs had to be replaced with transplants. We would then consider her the same person, even though most of her body was different. We can imagine a macabre experiment much like the boat example above, in which most of the limbs and organs from one person are transplanted to another, and those from that second person transplanted to the first. Which person then is which?

In the case of the two boats, where one was made of all the parts taken from an original boat, which had been replaced one by one over a period of time, it is hard to find anything in nature that makes one boat rather than the other the same as the original. It seems to be just a matter of the way we speak: we *call* one boat the same boat as the original, just for convenience. So there seems to be a real possibility that identity over time, what makes something the same thing at earlier and later times, may be like color or free will, something that is determined as much by the way we think and talk about it as by objective natural facts. Nature may be made of events occurring at different locations

HARDER

Box 25 **Identity as a Relation**

Relations are properties that hold between two or more things. Northwardness is a relation; it holds between Ottawa and Washington; Beijing and Canton; London and Paris. Bigger-than is a relation; it holds between the average elephant and the average mouse, and between the average star and the average planet. Identity can also be seen as a relation – a very special relation, because it holds between a thing and itself. We usually describe the same thing in two ways when we talk about identity. So, for example, we say that the person who burgled George's apartment is the person who painted Mary's portrait. If this is true then the relation of identity holds between one person – the burglar – and that same person – the painter.

Identity has some special features as a relation. First of all it is *transitive*. Suppose that identity holds between one thing and a second thing and between that second thing and a third thing. Then it holds between the first thing and the third thing. If the burglar is the painter and the painter is the priest then the burglar is the priest. There are many other transitive relations. For example, bigger-than. If the elephant is bigger than the cat and the cat is bigger than the mouse then the elephant is bigger than the mouse. Contrast this with fatherhood. If Adam is the father of Bill and Bill is the father of Carol, it does not follow that Adam is the father of Carol.

Identity is also *symmetrical*. If it holds between one thing and a second it will hold between the second and the first. If the burglar is the priest then the priest is the burglar. There are many other symmetrical relations too, for example, sisterhood. If Nicole is a sister of Janine then Janine is a sister of Nicole.

Identity is also *reflexive*. It holds between everything and itself. The burglar is the burglar. There are many other symmetrical relations, for example, being as nice as. All people are as nice as themselves.

There are relations besides identity that have all three characteristics – transitivity, symmetry, and reflexity. But any relation that has all three characteristics is in a general way like identity. It will divide things up into a number of classes so that anything in any class will have the relation to everything else in the class. For example, the relation of having the same temperature as (being just as hot as) is transitive, reflexive, and symmetrical. And it divides the world into a number of classes, in each of which are things of the same temperature. Any such relation is called an *equivalence relation*. Identity is the smallest equivalence relation: it divides the world into classes each containing just one object.

HARDER

in time and space, which we humans imagine together into continuing things. This is a fairly disturbing possibility. It becomes even more disturbing when you realize that we ourselves are among the things which, if this were right, are knitted together out of our imagination.

14.9 Personal Identity: Problem Cases

People are living creatures, like frogs and butterflies and single-celled animals, though vastly more complex. But we cannot do anything like saving cells discarded from a person's body and putting them together to make a person. (Not yet, anyway.) So you might think that there are not going to be serious difficulties about whether a person at one time is the same person as a person at an earlier time. But this is wrong. There are deep and important problems about what makes a person the same person over time. Consider four cases.

The aging monster   A young man takes an active part in civil unrest in his country. Before he is nineteen he has killed a number of innocent children and other noncombatants belonging to another group in his society, and has been involved in torturing and executing captives. For the next sixty years he lives an uneventful life as a carpenter, raises a family, and is eventually known as a gentle grandfatherly figure full of calm and wise advice. He does not remember much about his early life, and when he thinks back he has trouble separating real memories from stories others have told. He does not feel any identification with the young terrorist who aged into him. However, the country enters a phase of recrimination and guilt-finding about the past, and he is identified as someone who once took part in atrocities. There are calls for his punishment, even for his execution.

The case for condemning him is clear: he is the living human being who committed the atrocities. One of the possible arguments for not condemning him focuses on his lack of memory and identification with the person who committed the atrocities. They were committed sixty years ago by one person, full of hasty passions and a stupid desire to impress, and now we have another person, who cannot remember much from those days and who can find in himself none of the emotions and drives that led to the crimes. In punishing the old man how are we punishing the young man? Are they not in some way different persons even if they are supported by (different stages of) the same human body?

The changing husband   A woman marries a charming, intelligent, considerate young man. For twenty years they live happily together; then he has a car crash. When weeks later he emerges from hospital he seems completely different. He is short-tempered and inconsiderate, and given to unpredictable violent rages. In her despair she says "That is not the man I married."

The amnesiac wife   A woman lives the first twenty-five years of her life in one village. She marries and has a child. One day while out gathering berries she falls over a cliff and is severely concussed. She wanders into a village a few miles away. She has no memory of her previous life. She can speak but can say nothing of her past, not even her name. She builds up a new life and a new identity in this second village, marries, and again has a child. Her first husband finds her, but she does not recognize him and calls for her second husband to protect her against him. The first husband returns home saddened, considering himself a widower and his child motherless.

Problems about heaven   If there is a God as conceived of by Christianity then He can cause you to live again after your death. That is, He can make there be someone, perhaps with a living human body and perhaps not, who is you. But He can also do something different. He can make a copy of you. That is, he can make someone who has all your memories and emotions and who thinks that they are you. Yet this person is not you, but a duplicate. (God could make several, even hundreds, of these duplicates. They couldn't all be you.) Now what is the difference between the two cases? In both cases someone exists who thinks they are you and has all your memories. What is different about the case in which it is really you? Perhaps the best God can do is to make a duplicate that has the illusion of being you. If so, immortality would be an illusion.

In each case there is a question about whether a person at an earlier time is the same person at a later time. Think what the answers would be in each case if we assume each of the following simple theories. For each theory you may find it helpful to note whether it gives what you consider a possible answer, or an obviously wrong answer, or no answer at all.

(i)   If it is the same body, it is the same person.
(ii) If everyone thinks it is the same person, then it is.
(iii) If someone can remember a person's experiences, then they are that same person.

Probably, you will find that all three of these theories are too crude: the factors that determine whether a person at a later time is the same person as one at an earlier time are not fully captured by any of them. Which of the following factors are relevant?

(a) It is often hard to tell what is the same body at a different time.
(b) There are real memories and fake memories.
(c) There are hidden facts that people usually do not know, which make a big difference to identity.
(d) Neither body nor memory is soul.
(e) Memories fade over time.

14.10 Personal Identity: Theories

With such puzzling and troubling cases to think out, it would be good to have a helpful theory of personal identity. The theory should resolve our difficulties about difficult cases of personal identity by relating them to facts about things we feel less confused about. There are two main kinds of theory of personal identity.

Psychological theories The original psychological theory was defended by John Locke, who argued that a person at an earlier time is the same as a person at a later time if the later person remembers all the experiences of the earlier one. This is asking a lot. You may remember most of the experiences you had yesterday, but by tomorrow you will have forgotten some of yesterday's experiences, and by next year you might not be able to remember anything about yesterday. A more plausible definition would be based on chains of remembering: today you can remember most of yesterday's experiences, and tomorrow you will remember most of today's, and the day after that most of tomorrow's, and so on. So in 365 days' time there will be a chain of remembering leading back to yesterday, and indeed leading back to your fifth birthday, which you may now have no memory of at all.

In fact, it seems too restrictive to make the definition just in terms of memory. Say that a person at an earlier time is *psychologically continuous* with a person at a later time if from that later person there is a chain of linked memories and emotions and plans and character going back to the earlier time. Then we can speculate that psychological continuity is required for personal identity. If this speculation is right, then the amnesiac wife is clearly not the same person before and after her amnesia. The altered husband and the aging monster may or may not be, depending on the details of the case and exactly how we define psychological continuity. And on this account people with severe Alzheimer's will not be the same people they were before their dementia. The important thing is that a psychological theory opens up the possibility of non-identity in these cases. It allows that perhaps the later person is not the same as the earlier one.

(But the problems about heaven are still very puzzling, from the point of view of a psychological theory. The theory seems at first to make immortality easy. All God has to do is to recreate your memories and other states of mind. But then the theory seems to have made it so easy that it's impossible. For God can make sixteen duplicates of you with your memories and emotions and perspectives, and they cannot all be you.)

Bodily theories You are a human being, and a human being is a living organism of a particular species, *Homo sapiens*. So there is an obvious appeal to defining personal identity in terms of the identity of a living human body, using the same criteria for people that we would use for butterflies or elephants. The theory is very simple: a person at an earlier time is the same person as one at a later time if both are the same living human body. According to this theory, the aging monster, the altered husband, and the amnesiac wife are all the same person later as earlier. As for the problems about heaven, someone who believes in a bodily theory is likely to hold that immortality is possible only if God can recreate not only *a* body but *the very same body* you had in life.

It is hard to decide between psychological and bodily theories of personal identity. In everyday life we use both, and do not anticipate that they may pull in different directions. Here are two arguments, one *against* each theory.

Against psychological theories   Suppose that you have been convicted of a crime and you will soon be sentenced to one of two punishments. Either you will simply be painlessly killed. Or you will first be given a drug that induces total amnesia and then tortured slowly to death over a period of twenty-four hours. Which punishment do you hope for and which one do you dread, for your own sake alone? Most people imagining the situation find that they hope for a speedy death. But if the psychological theory were true it would not be you who would be tortured, so although you might think that it would be awful that this was going to happen to someone, your reaction would not really be dread for your own future. So, according to this argument, most people implicitly believe in a conception of personal identity that is not purely psychological.

Against bodily theories   Organ transplants are quite common now. Skin grafts are very common, as are cornea and kidney transplants. Heart transplants are far from unknown. It is not at all obvious that a person has the same body after such a transplant. Not all of the body is the same, at any rate. Moreover, a total body transplant is possible. Suppose that two identical twins, Fiordilighi and Dorabella, are walking down the road when a drunken farmer driving a combine harvester runs them down. They are rushed to hospital where it is discovered that Fiordilighi's body is beyond repair, except for her head, and Dorabella's body is hardly damaged, except for her head, which is totally destroyed. So the surgeons do the obvious and attach Fiordilighi's head to Dorabella's body. (The transplant is likely to be successful because they are identical twins.) The result is that Fiordilighi has had a body transplant: she lives on thanks to Dorabella's body.

Notice, however, that not all of Fiordilighi's body has been replaced. She still has her original head. And the reason for this is clear. The head contains the brain, and brain transplants do make us worry about identity. And the reason for this is clear too: we think there is a close connection between the brain and the mind. By transferring Fiordilighi's brain to Dorabella's body

---

Box 26 **Prudence and Altruism**

Suppose that personal identity is an illusion. Then what is real is not whole persons continuing through their life but *person stages*: people at particular moments. You today, me this week, the president at 12.32 pm. A person stage at a later time is a separate thing, even if we think of it as part of the same person. Then a difficult question arises: why should anyone care about "their" future person stages. If you know your body will be alive in fifty years' time and needing a pension, why should you contribute to it now? Why should your present person stages slave for the benefit of your later ones? One answer to the question is that the reasons are moral ones: you should care about future person stages associated with your future body just because you have an obligation not to let them suffer. But this obligation would be the same as your obligation to any other person stages. There's nothing special about the fact that they are associated with the future of your present body. So, on this point of view, prudence (being good to your future self) is just a special case of altruism (being good to others).

---

we ensure that Fiordilighi's memories and attitudes are preserved. So in the different importance we attach to different parts of the body we reveal, according to this argument, an implicit belief in a conception of personal identity that is not purely bodily.

14.11 The Meanings of Lives

Assuming that fatalism is not true, we can suppose that our lives really do feature accomplishment, love, and comedy. They really are successful, affectionate, and funny. Contrast this with, say, luck. Lives are not really lucky, in any deep sense. If someone has a repeated series of misfortunes, this is not because they have some quality of bad luck that could be brought on by walking under a ladder or being cursed. Such a varied pattern of events will usually have no common cause, and their all coming together in that one person's life is just an effect of randomness. Luck is an illusion: lucky and unlucky things happen to people but there are not lucky and unlucky people, and your luck cannot get better or worse. In fact, the opposite of luck, the random nature of many of the most important factors in our lives, is a very real feature of them. At any rate, this is so according to the scientific view of the world, and indeed the opinions of most modern people.

Human lives can have many fine qualities, and many awful ones. Some of these qualities we care deeply about. It really matters to us whether our lives have these qualities. Take a *meaning of life* to be any quality of human life such that:

It is a quality of whole human lives, not just of particular moments in them.
We care about whether our lives have it.
We shape ourselves by it: when we can choose which desires to have or which desires to satisfy we go for the ones that will result in our lives having it.

Might some of the meanings that we want life to have be illusions, as colors or freedom or personal identity might be? Might it be an illusion that there are any meanings to human life?

Suppose you see human beings as natural organisms in a natural world. Then you may think that the qualities of human lives have to be explained in natural terms. Nothing supernatural is allowed. Then you can still see human life as meaningful. But naturalism will affect *which* meanings you will think it has. Luck will no longer be a real meaning of life. Accomplishment can still be, and love. And humorousness, the fact that a lot of what happens to us is inherently ridiculous, may become a more central meaning. These – accomplishment, love, and humorousness – are real properties of our lives, even though they result from the way we live our physical lives in a physical world. Moreover, they are properties that we can deliberately describe and value. And that means that they figure in another even more basic meaning of life, the way we humans can look at our lives and recognize some aspects of them as important. Call this *satisfaction*. This is something very few other creatures could even begin to share.

For many people these meanings of life – accomplishment, love, humorousness, satisfaction – will not be enough. In fact, they can seem pointless or hollow if they are not accompanied by some deeper meaning. For many people this will be a reason for feeling dissatisfied with the scientific picture of the world. It makes their lives feel meaningless. But it is not easy to say what deeper meaning is left out. One meaning that lives will not have in a purely natural world is something we might call *transcendental approval*. Suppose that there is a God, or something else real and very fundamental to the universe, which sees your life and can think of it: "That's good; I approve of it; it has meaning from my point of view." Then your whole life has a quality that as a small child you may have wanted your parents to give it by loving you. That is, the meanings of your life are also meanings from a much larger perspective than yours. That larger perspective might be given by fame or history. But those still are human perspectives. The perspective of God, or some other fundamental aspect of reality, is larger yet, and is not merely human. If the meanings we humans can find in our lives were endorsed by this larger perspective, we could be sure that we were not just attaching importance to them out of vanity, or as an escape from despair.

There is another reason we could want the meanings we give our lives to be endorsed from a larger perspective. That is, as a protection against our natural tendency to find meaning in things. People see faces in clouds, hear tunes in dripping taps, and find unlikely coincidences everywhere. We are good at finding patterns, and when we can relate these patterns to our lives we find them very satisfying. So even if our lives were completely pointless, and those meanings we attached most importance to were illusions, we would still tend to *think* that human life was significant and important. That's just the way we are, just as we tend to think that we are free and that the moments of our lives can be knitted together to give us identities through time. It is like the false-belief trap of Chapter 1: we interpret the evidence so as to safeguard what we want to believe. If we could know that our lives were valued by something that was not subject to the human tendency to see a point to human life, we would know that we were not in such a trap. In valuing our lives for their accomplishments, loves, and humorousness we would not simply be performing another piece of typical meaningless human behavior.

But these larger than human perspectives may not be available. They may not exist; or we may not be able to know whether they really endorse the meanings we find for our little lives. Does this matter? Does lack of transcendental approval mean that our lives do not have accomplishment, love, humorousness, and satisfaction? Does it mean that we should not find it important that our lives have these qualities? If it does, then life in a purely natural universe is pretty bleak.

Below, (a) to (d) lists some qualities that a life could have. You should consider whether each one is a good candidate for being a meaning for life – that is, something that someone could care about deeply enough to make their life feel worthwhile.

(a) *Accomplishment*   People have plans and sometimes they achieve what they want.
(b) *Pleasure*   Some sensations are such that we find that we cannot help wanting them.
(c) *Transcendental approval*   Something fundamental to the universe is capable of loving us.
(d) *Existential courage*   People can face the fact that life lacks transcendental approval, and take pride in the fact that they do not let this realization undermine their capacity to live their lives.

Here are two lives, described as they might seem from the inside.

Zero   Early in life, Zero forms a number of ambitions. He wants to become rich, be extremely successful as a musician, and have four children. These are

Figure 14.1 Calvin and Hobbes © Watterson. Reprinted with permission of Universal Press Syndicate. All rights reserved.

partially satisfied. Zero never becomes very rich, and he has real but limited accomplishments as a musician, and although he has only one child he marries a woman he loves deeply and whose three children by a previous marriage become very attached to him. But when he looks back on his life he feels a sour sense of frustration.

Yvonne   Early in life, Yvonne forms a number of ambitions. She wants to become rich, make some important contributions to science, and have four children. These are not satisfied to any great extent. She never becomes very rich, and her original and valuable contributions to science are ignored by other scientists. She has four children: three of them die in childhood and the fourth spends most of his life in prison for fraud. Throughout these difficulties she is sustained by her faith that God is guiding her life.

Which of the four meanings could each of these lives have to Zero and Yvonne? Which of these meanings could make their lives feel worthwhile to them? Indicate your answers by putting ticks in the first four rows of the table. (The last two rows are used later.)

	Accomplishment	Pleasure	Transcendental approval	Existential courage
Applies to Zero's life				
Applies to Yvonne's life				
Could make Zero accept his life				
Could make Yvonne accept her life				
Could block Zero's acceptance				
Could block Yvonne's acceptance				

Zero and Yvonne do not know all the facts about their own lives. Consider each of the following possibilities.

(1) There is no God.
(2) Zero and Yvonne are about to achieve some of their long-held ambitions when a comet strikes the earth and wipes out all life.
(3) Zero and Yvonne have been in a virtual reality apparatus all their lives. None of the episodes or accomplishments in their lives is real, though they have had all the sensations and emotions of real lives.
(4) Zero has suffered from depression all his life, produced by abnormal brain chemistry, which makes him disappointed with situations that would satisfy others.
(5) Yvonne has been taking a mood-improving drug all her life, which makes her satisfied with situations that would disappoint others.

Which of these possibilities are such that if Zero or Yvonne knew about them it would prevent one of the meanings from making them feel their lives were worthwhile? Indicate your answer by putting numbers 1 to 5 in the fifth and sixth rows of the table. For example, if you think that if Zero knew possibility (1) it would prevent him from feeling that pleasure made his life worthwhile, put a 1 in the row "Could block Zero's acceptance" in the Pleasure column.

The deepest contrast is between transcendental approval and existential courage. A sense of either of these can shape your life and allow you to feel that it is a unity, one life, through crises and disasters. But they are opposed to one another: it is hard to shape your life by both. Which one you can *take* as a meaning for your life depends on the kind of a place you take the world to be, and which one can actually *be* part of the meaning of your life depends on the kind of place the world actually is. Opposed though they are, they are also surprisingly similar. Each gives a person a way of looking at their life as a whole and fitting the parts into a pattern, which they can see with satisfaction. It is almost as if existential courage says: there is no god, but if there were a god who wanted people to stand on their own feet and make their own lives, then she would approve of me. Does that attitude make sense?

Conclusions of This Chapter

◆ *Colors can be taken to be physical properties of objects, concerned with how they reflect light to our eyes. Or they can be taken to be properties of our experiences of objects, concerned with the sensations we have when we see the objects. It is hard to make colors both of these at the same time.*

◆ *Human freedom can be taken to be a physical property of our bodies and brains, even if determinism is true. This is compatibilism, and it can be defended more strongly than it might at first seem. The opposite view, that free action requires us to act independently of the laws of nature, forces us to believe that our actions are not free, or that the physical world is not deterministic, or that our minds are not part of the physical world.*

◆ *What makes a person the same person at one time and at a later time is not determined by the parts of the person's body being the same. But it is also not obvious that memories and other facts about a person's mind are enough to determine whether that person is the same at an earlier or later time. So there is a philosophical problem in defining personal identity in such a way that it does not turn out to be an illusion.*

◆ *The qualities we want our lives to have and which would give them meaning are also hard to understand as physical properties in a physical world. Thus they can be seen as a kind of illusion. But they do not seem more illusory than colors or freedom.*

Further Reading

On color

*C. L. Hardin, *Color for Philosophers*. Hackett, 1988.
*David R. Hilbert, *Color and Color Perception*. CSLI Lecture Notes, no. 9, 1987.

On freedom

Selections from Augustine, Hobbes, Laplace, and Sartre in Part IV(b) of John Cottingham (ed.), *Western Philosophy: An Anthology*. Blackwell, 1996.
Chapter 4 of Richard Taylor, *Metaphysics*. Prentice-Hall, 1963.
Gary Watson (ed.), *Free Will*. Oxford University Press, 1982.
D. C. Dennett, *Elbow Room*. Oxford University Press, 1984.

On personal identity

Selection from Parfit in Part IV(a) of John Cottingham (ed.), *Western Philosophy: An Anthology*. Blackwell, 1996.
John Perry, *A Dialogue on Personal Identity and Immortality*. Hackett, 1978.
John Perry (ed.), *Personal Identity*. University of California Press, 1975.
Harold Noonan, *Personal Identity*. Routledge, 1989.

On the meaning of life

Thomas Nagel, *What Does It All Mean?* Oxford University Press, 1987.
E. D. Klemke (ed.), *The Meaning of Life*. Oxford University Press, 1981.

Electronic resources

Routledge Encyclopedia of Philosophy (available online at many universities): articles on Free will; Life, meaning of; Personal identity; Primary–secondary distinction; Secondary qualities.
Stanford Encyclopedia of Philosophy (http://plato.stanford.edu/): *Color*; Determinism; Freedom; *Free will, Incompatibilism*; *Personal identity* (*italicized* items are available as this book goes to press; the others should be available soon).

15 Realism

Introduction

If materialism is true, morality might be all illusion. Some philosophers have tried to show how moral principles could be true even if everything is physical. One influential approach is to study contracts that people in a society could make with one another for mutual benefit.

If materialism is true, many other features of our lives could be illusions. The example of colors shows many of the problems that also arise with our conviction that we make free decisions and our conviction that we are the same persons throughout our lives.

Idealism is the opposite of materialism. Arguments for idealism that were used by Berkeley in the eighteenth century are still influential in the form of verificationism and instrumentalism. The conflict between instrumentalism and realism about science is part of much larger questions about how our thinking relates to the world.

Chapter Objectives

By the end of this chapter you should be able to answer the following questions.

◆ *What are the main conflicts between the scientific picture and the everyday picture of the world?*
◆ *How does Berkeley defend the idealist claim that to be is to be perceived?*
◆ *What basic fact about language do Berkeley's arguments ignore?*
◆ *What are verificationism and logical positivism, and how have they evolved into an instrumentalist philosophy of science?*
◆ *What is scientific realism, and how can it be defended?*

Definitions

The following words used in this chapter are defined in the list of definitions at the end of the book:

idealism	*logical positivism*	*verificationism*
instrumentalism	*realism*	

15.1 Science versus the Everyday World

If we take physical science as our main guide we will suspect that a number of familiar features of the world may be illusions. That was the theme of the previous chapter. Color, free will, the difference between right and wrong, the idea that people and objects continue being the same things through stretches of time: all of these may be features of the way we think which correspond to nothing in reality. All of them may be, or some of them may be, or none of them may be. The important point is not that science shows any of them to be illusions, but that thinking about science raises serious doubts about all of them, which can be very hard to refute convincingly.

But if these familiar qualities of the world might be illusions, what is real? The world of physics, according to some scientifically minded philosophers. Reality consists of the space-time continuum plus the fundamental particles and the forces by which they interact. Contrast the everyday and the scientific pictures of reality (see the Introduction to Part III). According to the everyday picture, the world has people who have minds and make free decisions, and physical objects that have colors and smells. Both people and physical objects exist in space and continue through time. The scientific picture is very different. According to it the world is made of fundamental particles: electrons, photons, mesons, and others. They can have energy and mass and various other properties that have no analogs in our everyday experience. And they exist in a four-dimensional space–time continuum that cannot be broken down into separate space and time. Which of these is right? Here are four possible answers, with a very rough argument for each of them.

(1) *The scientific picture is real and the everyday picture is an illusion.* Argument: The most reliable beliefs we have are our scientific ones. And there is more precise evidence for them than for anything else we believe. So in the end, when there is a conflict between science and common sense it has to be common sense that gives way.

(2) *The everyday picture is real and the scientific picture is an illusion.* Argument: The evidence we have for scientific beliefs comes from everyday experience. Scientists study experimental apparatus and living animals; they discuss each other's beliefs and hopes. So if they did not accept that there are everyday things in an everyday world of physical objects and minds, they would be taking away the basis on which all their beliefs rest. So in any conflict between common sense and science it has to be science that gives way.

(3) *Both are real (i): reductionism.* Argument: We can explain the everyday picture in terms of the scientific picture. Everyday things like tables and chairs and living bodies are collections of billions of fundamental particles. Colors are the powers things have to reflect light (photons) of various

wavelengths, and so on for the other everyday properties of things. So the everyday picture is real because the scientific picture is real.

(4) *Both are real (ii): incomparability.* Argument: We can think in everyday concepts or we can think in terms of scientific concepts. But reality isn't concepts; it's just what it is. So any system of concepts that serves some purpose is worth using, but it isn't better than any other. So both are real, or both are illusions: whichever you want to say, they're both the same.

Most people thinking about these positions, and evaluating these arguments, will decide that they agree with none of them. They are too simple to do justice to some very subtle and difficult questions. But most people will conclude that they have more sympathy for some of these positions than others. If you have sympathy for (1) or (3) then you tend toward *scientific realism.* You think that what science says is often literally true, and that the things it describes really exist. If you have sympathy for (2) or (4) then you tend toward *instrumentalism* about science. You think that science is a device for helping us live in the everyday world.

The rest of this chapter will not try to decide whether the everyday picture or the scientific picture is right. Instead, it will focus on the debate between realism and instrumentalism about science. Understanding that will be one step on the way to seeing how to decide what is the best way to describe reality.

15.2 Counting Objects

One place where conflicts between the scientific picture and the commonsense picture of the world arise is with questions about what objects there are. Is the world made up of everyday things like chairs and tables and mountains, or scientific things like electrons and photons? Or both? Or neither? These questions can be made less vague by approaching them in terms of counting. How many objects, real existing objects, are there in a room or a box? To see how this works, consider the following dialogue.

Ontie and Monty are having the kind of conversation only philosophers can have:

Ontie: Look Monty, I've got this nice little wooden box, and there are lots of marbles and shells in it.
Monty: It's a pretty box, and those things in it are really interesting colors. How many are there?
Ontie: How many whats?
Monty: You know, things, in the box, like.
Ontie: You're so inarticulate. I figure 2,047, all told.

Monty: That's impossible. Look, I'll count: five marbles and six shells. That makes 11.

Ontie: But you asked me how many things, and then I said "all told," though you weren't listening, as usual.

Monty: But there isn't anything there, except the five marbles and six shells.

Ontie: Sure there is, if only you could think as well as look. There are five marbles and six shells, and that makes 11, as even you know. And then there are 36 marshells so that makes 47. (I suppose I'd better explain, a marshell is what you get when you combine one marble and one shell.) But that's only the beginning. There are also 120 marmarshells. (A marmarshell is what you get when you combine two marbles and a shell.) So that brings us to 167. And so on, with all the different kinds of thing in the box. I thought it out and I got 2,047. I don't imagine you'd follow if I did the arithmetic.

Monty: You know I didn't mean crazy made-up silly things, but real things, like marbles and shells.

Ontie: That just shows the shallowness of your mind. Just because marbles and shells are the only things there that you have names for, you think that that's all there is. Well, you might have just had the word "marshell," and then you'd be complaining if I was counting shells.

There are many things to reflect on here, besides Monty's patience with Ontie. How many things *are* there in the box, after all? (Let's confine ourselves to things not much smaller than a shell or a marble, so we don't have to count molecules.) Here are some possible *answers*:

(a) 11
(b) 2,047
(c) millions
(d) infinitely many (or: however many you want)
(e) zero

Which of these is "the truth"? Below are six considerations (i) to (vi) that may help you decide. And below them there are three large positions (A) to (C) that may lie behind your reactions. After all of these there is a suggestion of one way of relating the answers (a) to (e), the considerations, and the positions.

All the following *considerations* might support one or another of these five answers.

(i)   Most things are made up of thousands of parts. So, for example, if we take a marble we can also take away a molecule from its surface, leaving a smaller marble. But that smaller marble was really there inside the larger marble all along.

(ii) There's no point to counting things unless you know first what kinds of things you're counting. And what kinds of things you are counting depends on the language you are speaking, indeed the conversation you are having.

(iii) The only real things are in one place, like tables and tigers and stars, not scattered around in different places like a marble in one place plus a shell somewhere else.

(iv) We often count things we have no names for. You might wake up in the middle of the night and look out of your window and see strange things like nothing you have ever seen before. You might say: "I have no idea what they are, but there are eight of them."

(v) The parts of many real things are scattered. For example, a galaxy is made up of many stars, with a lot of empty space between them. And the atoms that make up an object like a marble are really quite scattered, with a lot of empty space between them.

(vi) The divisions we make between one thing and another are completely artificial. We just make them for our convenience. So they don't tell us anything about reality.

These considerations are relevant also to some much larger *positions*.

(A) There are many, many objects in the world. We give some of them every-day names and some of them scientific names, but there are many more than we will ever be able to name.

(B) No one answer to what there is in the world is right. First we have to choose a way of thinking, and then we can say what there is in the world according to that way of thinking. (For example, the scientific way or the commonsense way.)

(C) The real world is the world as we see and touch and count it. Everything else is just a story we make up.

One way of relating answers, considerations, and positions is as follows:

◆ First, of course, you must read the dialogue – slowly enough to appreciate what both Monty and Ontie are trying to say.

◆ Then each person should read through the answers (a)–(e) and think out their own reaction to each, though they do not need to express it. But the whole class should go through the list of questions and find one objection to each answer. These should be written down, on the board, for example.

◆ Next, links between the objections that have just been written down and the considerations (i)–(vi) should be explored. Which of the objections assume which of these considerations? If some considerations have not been mentioned at the end of this discussion, think what further objections to which answers they might motivate.

◆ Now each person or group should state which of the answers he or she, after considering the links with the objections, is inclined to support, and which of the links to the objections seems most important.

◆ At the final stage, read and consider the positions (A)–(C). Then each person in a group or in the whole class should say which of the positions each other person is most likely to believe, given what they said about the answers and the objections. Are these guesses right?

Position (A) is a *realist* position. It takes all the objects that science or any other technique can find as real. (B) is an *idealist* position. It takes objects to be creations of our minds to some extent. (C) is an *instrumentalist* position. It takes science to be a creation of our minds, an instrument for living our lives in the real everyday world.

15.3 Berkeley's Idealism

The Irish philosopher George Berkeley, writing in the early eighteenth century, has two important places in the history of philosophy. The first is as the scourge of physical science. He saw that the emerging physics of Newton and his followers suggested a view of the universe which is in some ways rather different from common sense, and which challenges a literal traditional Christianity. The aspect of Newtonian physics that particularly worried him was the way it explained natural events in terms of matter. (Newton's physics adds mass to the more spatial primary properties discussed by Galileo and Descartes.) In response to this he raised serious doubts about whether the idea of matter makes any sense. He argued that physicists were basing their theories on something which could not possibly exist.

As part of his attack on matter Berkeley gained his second important place, as the inventor of modern idealism, the doctrine that objects only exist when they are connected with a mind in some way, by being perceived or thought about. His main idea is that materialists get things backwards. They think that material objects exist and then we have a problem of explaining in terms of them how our minds can be part of the material world. But the truth, according to Berkeley, is the other way round, physical things are not independent of our minds, and the basic facts we should start from are facts about our own experiences. It is in terms of these that we should explain how the objects around us exist.

Berkeley said that "To be is to be perceived." This is typical of idealism, which claims that we should explain the physical world in terms of minds.

Berkeley's idealism is summed up in his slogan "To be is to be perceived." If no minds at all existed then nothing would exist. It is for making clear and challenging arguments for this implausible conclusion that Berkeley is most important.

Berkeley's arguments are clearly set out in his *Three Dialogues between Hylas and Philonous*. Philonous is a defender of Berkeley's position. (The name means "lover of mind.") And Hylas is a defender of the standard scientific doctrine of the day. (The name means "materialist," but although Hylas believes in matter his view is not as strong as the materialism discussed in Chapter 12.)

One way Berkeley defends his idealism is by arguing that there is no distinction between primary and secondary qualities (see Chapter 14, Section 1). Features of the everyday picture of reality, such as colors and smells, are just as real as features of the scientific picture, such as shapes and weights. For all of them are as much in our minds as they are "out there" in the world. In fact, according to Berkeley there are no important differences between secondary qualities such as colors and purely subjective qualities like pains. We do not take pains to be in objects but in our bodies or our minds. So why should we take colors or shapes to be in objects? Whether you experience pain from an object will depend on your relation to the object. But so will your perception of colors and of shapes. In the case of colors this takes the form of the *argument from microscopes*. To quote from Berkeley:

Philonous: . . . *are then the beautiful red and purple we see on yonder clouds really in them? Or do you imagine they have in themselves any other form than that of a dark mist or vapor?*

Hylas: . . . *those colors are not really in the clouds as they seem to be at this distance. They are only apparent colors.*

Philonous: *"Apparent" you call them? How shall we distinguish these apparent colors from real?*

Hylas: *Very easily. Those are to be thought apparent which, appearing only at a distance, vanish upon a nearer approach.*

. . .

Philonous: *But a microscope often discovers colors in an object different from those perceived by the unassisted sight. And, in case we had microscopes magnifying to any assigned degree, it is certain that no object whatsoever, viewed through them, would appear in the same color which it exhibits to the naked eye.*

Colors are not really in objects, Berkeley is arguing, because any object can be taken to be many colors depending on how we see it, for example, how close to it we get. (The argument from microscopes is discussed in Chapter 14, Section 3.) Berkeley says the same of shapes and sizes and speeds. An object that seems small to you might seem enormous to a dust mite. An object that seems spherical if you examine it carelessly will on closer examination turn out to have many small bumps, depressions, and corners. (Berkeley uses different examples.)

All properties of objects, according to Berkeley, are really only qualities of our perception. (They are "ideas" in his terminology. See Chapter 9, Section 2.) What about the objects themselves? Are they not totally independent of whether we see or think of them? Berkeley's arguments to show that objects are not independent of minds are more abstract. The central argument runs as follows. Call it *the unperceived tree argument*:

> **Hylas:** ... *What more easy than to conceive a tree or house existing by itself, independent of, and unperceived by, any mind whatsoever?* ...
>
> **Philonous:** *How say you, Hylas, can you see a thing which is at the same time unseen?*
>
> **Hylas:** *No, that were a contradiction.*
>
> **Philonous:** *Is it not as great a contradiction to talk of conceiving a thing which is unconceived?*
>
> . . .
>
> **Philonous:** *How then came you to say you conceived a house or tree existing independent and out of all minds whatsoever?*
>
> **Hylas:** *That was I own an oversight. . . . As I was thinking of a tree in a solitary place where no one was present to see it, methought that was to conceive a tree as existing unperceived or unthought of, not considering that I myself conceived it all the while.*

This is an important argument. One way of understanding it is to take the idealist, Philonous, to be challenging the materialist, Hylas, to produce an example of something which exists but is neither perceived nor thought of. Suppose Hylas tries to oblige. The example he produces *will* have been perceived or thought of, by Hylas himself. So no one can ever come up with an example of something that has no connection with our minds! And the best explanation of why no one can find any examples of such things is that they don't exist. So everything is related to our minds.

One way of laying out the unperceived tree argument is as follows (for brevity, "unperceived" in this argument means "not perceived and not thought of"):

If you give an example of anything it cannot be unperceived.
Therefore you cannot give any example of anything unperceived.
Therefore you cannot show that there is anything unperceived.

The most that this argument could show is that no one can show that there is anything unperceived, not that there is not anything unperceived. But there is a good deal of overlap between this argument and the following argument, which seems to be implicit in Berkeley though he does not state it in these terms. (The relation between the two arguments is discussed in Section 5 below.) Call it the *reasons for belief argument*.

The only reason for believing that something exists is that it is perceived.
Therefore the only things we have reason to believe exist are perceived things.
Therefore we have reason to believe that only perceived things exist.

The conclusions of all three of these arguments – the argument from microscopes, the unperceived tree argument, and the reasons for belief argument – are surprising. Yet it is not so easy to say what is wrong with them. When people first meet Berkeley's ideas they often think he is saying: "There are only ideas in our minds; there are no physical objects." But he is not saying this. Instead he is saying: "There are physical objects; they are ideas in our minds." So there are stones and electrons and planets, but they do not exist independently of our minds: if there were no minds there would be no stones and electrons and planets.

One objection to Berkeley's claims might be: there were planets and stars before there were human beings, and there will be planets and stars after the human race has died out, so these things cannot depend on human minds. Another objection might be: two people can look at the same thing, an elephant, for example; but on Berkeley's theory each person is seeing a different thing, the idea of the elephant in their own mind. Berkeley has an answer to these objections. His answer is God. God is a mind and God existed before there were any stars or planets. So "To be is to be perceived" does not mean "To be is to be perceived by a human mind." Moreover, when two people see an elephant, although there are two ideas of the elephant in the two people's minds they are both copies of the idea of the elephant in God's mind, and this is the single true elephant they are both seeing. So if Berkeley is right, as long as we believe that there are objects around us that different people can see, and which would exist even if all human minds ceased to notice them, we must believe in God.

Figure 15.1 Calvin and Hobbes © Watterson. Reprinted with permission of Universal Press Syndicate. All rights reserved.

15.4 A Puzzle about Pain: the Locations of Qualities

When you touch a hot stove you pull back your hand and say the stove is hot. You may experience pain as well as heat. But you don't say that the stove hurts. Your hand hurts. Shouldn't you either say your hand is hot and hurts, or the stove is hot and hurts? Why do we treat heat and pain differently?

Perhaps the reason that we say that the heat, unlike the pain, is in the stove is that your hand feels hottest near the stove. But:

(i)   We say that a flower smells, even though the smell may be strongest at some distance from the flower.

Perhaps the reason that we say that the pain, unlike the heat, is in the hand is that the hand is being damaged. But:

(ii) People having heart attacks often say they feel pain in their arms, though the damage is in the heart.

Perhaps the reason that we say that the heat, unlike the pain, is in the stove is that heat is the molecules of the stove moving. But:

(iii) If a violin is played we say the music, and not the violin, is high or low, or clear or muffled, though the molecules of the violin's strings and body are moving.

Perhaps the reason that we say that the pain, unlike the heat, is in the hand is that the pain is coming from nerve endings within the hand. But:

(iv) People who have had a limb amputated often experience a "phantom limb." They feel pain as if it is in the limb that is not there.

When a person perceives a quality like heat or pain or a smell or a musical sound we can attribute the quality to many different things. Sometimes we say the quality is "in" the object that is its source, as with heat. Sometimes we say that it is in something abstract such as music. Sometimes we say it is in the environment, as when we say that the air smells though the smell comes from a particular flower. And sometimes we say that it is in the body of the person perceiving it, as when pain is in a person's hand. It is hard to explain why we put qualities in different things at different times.

All of the following factors might be relevant to explaining why we say that the heat is in the stove but the pain is in the hand. Which ones are most important?

(a) Two people can both feel that something is hot.
(b) Heat can move from one object to another.
(c) Heat is a form of energy.
(d) Heat can be perceived in more than one way.
(e) The fact that something is hot explains other things about it.

Berkeley thought that there was no real difference between heat and pain, both are as much "in" a person as they are in an object. Do any of these factors suggest a way in which Berkeley might be wrong? If not, does this suggest that Berkeley might be right?

15.5 Apples, Surprises, Scopes, and Existence

Berkeley's arguments for idealism raise many interesting problems. This section is concerned with the "reasons for belief" argument and the "unperceived tree" argument. Some problems with them are easiest to see with different, but parallel, examples, where there is no difficult philosophical question at issue.

Here are two little dialogues. In each of these one person, the one whose speech is put in *italics*, is making a rather implausible argument.

(1) "I want an apple."

"Here's an apple. I climbed halfway up the tree to get it."

"No, I don't want that one, I want one from right up at the top."

"But you can't see any of those apples, so you can't want to have one of them."

(2) *"Nothing you can say tomorrow will surprise me."*

"No one can anticipate everything. I'm sure I can think of lots of things you won't expect."

"Give me just one example."

"Well, I might tell you that you have just been elected Pope."

"That won't surprise me, since you've just told me you might say that."

Here are two arguments that might be found in the italicized strands of the dialogues.

If you cannot see an apple you cannot want it.
Therefore you cannot want an apple you cannot see.
Therefore you cannot want to have an apple you cannot see.

If you give me an example today it cannot surprise me tomorrow.
Therefore you cannot give me an example today of something that will surprise me tomorrow.
Therefore you cannot show me today that anything will surprise me tomorrow.

The final conclusions of both these arguments are obviously false. Where have they gone wrong? In both cases the premise might be challenged. (You could want an apple someone had told you about. You could forget by tomorrow an example given to you today.) But ignore that; accept the premises for the sake of argument. The final conclusions still do not follow. The premises could be true and the final conclusions false.

Consider first the first argument. What has gone wrong is that the first of its two conclusions is ambiguous. It can mean two things, and one of them follows from the premise and the other does not. And only the one that does not follow from the premise leads to the final conclusion. So you can only get to the final conclusion by switching meanings at the first conclusion. To see this, consider the first conclusion:

You cannot want an apple you cannot see.

Here are some things it can mean:

(i) If you cannot see an apple you cannot want that apple.
(ii) You cannot want that you get an apple which you cannot now see.

(iii) You cannot want a particular unseen apple.

(iv) You cannot want to have some unseen apple or other.

Which of these mean the same? Which of these follow from the premise "If you cannot see an apple you cannot want it"? Which of these lead to the conclusion "You cannot want to have an apple you cannot see"?

(It is hard to express the difference between meanings like these ones in ordinary English. Philosophers often express the difference in rather unnatural language by saying that if you want a particular apple then *there is an apple such that you want that you have it*, while if you want some apple or other then *you want that there is an apple such that you have it*. This is a *scope distinction*. Because we say that in the first, "have" is *within* the scope of "there is," while in the second, "there is" is within the scope of "have.")

Now consider the second of the two arguments above. ("If you give me an example today it cannot surprise me tomorrow. Therefore you cannot show me today that anything will surprise me tomorrow.") It also gets from a possibly true premise to a certainly false final conclusion by going through an ambiguous middle step. The middle step, the first conclusion, is

You cannot give me an example today of something that will surprise me tomorrow.

Again, here are some possible meanings this can have.

(i) If you give an example today then that example cannot surprise me tomorrow.
(ii) You cannot today give an example of a kind of situation which would surprise me tomorrow.
(iii) You cannot describe any particular situation today which will then surprise me tomorrow.
(iv) You cannot describe today how some situation could surprise me tomorrow.

Which of these follow from the premise "If you give me an example today it cannot surprise me tomorrow"? Which of them leads to the final conclusion "You cannot show me today that anything will surprise me tomorrow"?

Now look again at Berkeley's "reasons for belief" and "unperceived tree" arguments.

The only reason for believing that something exists is that it is perceived.
Therefore the only things we have reason to believe exist are perceived things.
Therefore we have reason to believe that only perceived things exist.

If you give an example of anything it cannot be unperceived.
Therefore you cannot give any example of anything unperceived.
Therefore you cannot show that there is anything unperceived.

The problems with these arguments are very similar to the problems with the two arguments discussed earlier in this section. Express the first conclusion of each of them – "The only things we have reason to believe exist are perceived things," "You cannot give any example of anything unperceived" – in two ways, so as to bring out how it is ambiguous.

15.6 Verificationism

Berkeley's ideas are good survivors. They keep on coming back in new and different forms. For example, in the nineteenth century the German philosopher Hegel described a form of idealism in which the history of the human mind plays the role that God plays in Berkeley's philosophy. In the twentieth century Berkeley's largest influence has been through the idea of *content*.

The content of a belief is everything that would have to be stated to fully describe or express the belief. Thus if you believe that there are apples at the top of the tree, the content of your belief cannot be given just by the words "apple in tree." For the belief includes the idea of existence ("there is") too. And to describe what it is that you are believing we would have to describe what you thought an apple and a tree is, and what you mean by "at the top of."

Empiricism suggests that the contents of beliefs are the ideas that come from perception and which are combined to make the belief. (See Chapter 9, Section 4, "The Idea Idea.") But most philosophers now think that it is extremely doubtful that the contents of complex beliefs can be expressed just as combinations of ideas derived from perception. We can think a wider range of thoughts than empiricism would suggest. But that is not to say that anything that can come into someone's mind or out of their mouth can represent a real belief, something that could actually turn out to be true or false. Some things people say, and some thoughts that they can think, are simply nonsense, whether or not the people realize it. Sometimes people think they have a belief with a real content when really they are just spouting words. For example, suppose someone is listening to other people talk and one of them says about a car, "That is a really wonderful car, such a venerable machine; when it was stolen she must have been apoplectic." The person listening has never heard the words "venerable" or "apoplectic" before but supposes that "venerable" must mean something like "wonderful," and "apoplectic" must mean something like "sad." So next day, when he is talking to his friends about a skiing trip, he says: "It was completely venerable; we had such a great time, and when I had to leave I felt quite apopleptical." He clearly is misusing one word and not even remembering the other correctly. ("Venerable" means "worthy of veneration because of dignity or age," so it must have been an antique car; "apoplectic" means "resembling having a stroke," and sometimes we use it to suggest that someone is so angry that they could have a stroke.) But, more importantly, he does not really have any definite meaning at all in mind; he is just making social noises.

Berkeley argued that scientists who make theories about matter are not expressing anything that we can really understand. For the concept of matter, he thought, makes no sense. They are like the person who says his skiing trip was venerable, repeating words as if they understood them. And this is Berkeley's ghost, the idea he started that haunts later philosophers. How do we know when we are making sense? How do we know when we talk about things that are a long way from our everyday experience, for example, things far away in space such as quasars and black holes, or things unimaginably small, like viruses or quarks, that we are not just deluding ourselves that what we are saying makes sense?

To answer questions like this we need a theory of content. That is, we need a theory that explains what the range of things that people can believe is, and how these beliefs can come to be true or false. There is one way of giving a theory of content that has been very influential in the twentieth century. It is *verificationism.* Consider an example. Someone says "There are apples at the very top of the tree." What does this mean? (What would be the content of the belief of someone who said it?) Well, one thing it would mean is that if you climb to the top of the tree you will find apples. If you climbed to the top of the tree and didn't find any you would think that they were not speaking the truth. So in this case the meaning of the sentence can be explained, in part, by saying how you might find out whether it was true or false. According to verificationism, this is the basic fact about meaning: *the meaning of a sentence is the evidence which would confirm or disconfirm it.* And, what is really the same idea, the content of a belief is the evidence that would strengthen or weaken it, make the person more or less convinced that their belief was true.

If verificationism is true then when we can neither confirm nor refute a sentence it is neither true nor false. It is meaningless. Verificationism is therefore close to the spirit of Berkeley's philosophy. For if someone claims that something exists, but claims also that it cannot be observed, then their claim is very hard to show to be either true or false. If the claim was that something exists but there can be no evidence of its existence, then according to verificationism the claim would definitely be meaningless. (Berkeley's philosophy suggests the claim that the meaning of a sentence is the perceptual evidence which definitively proves or refutes it. And this is much stronger than verificationism, as defined above.)

Is verificationism true? Taken literally, almost certainly not. Powerful arguments against it were produced by the American philosopher W. V. Quine.

Quine's arguments appeal to a fact about the relation between beliefs and the evidence for or against them: evidence is never for or against a belief in isolation, but always for or against a belief as part of a body of beliefs. For example, suppose someone believes that the earth is flat. There are various bits of evidence that can be cited against her. Ships sailing over the horizon slowly disappear until only their masts are visible; ships and planes traveling due west for long enough eventually return to their starting point. And so on. But each one of these bits of evidence would be harmless if the flat-earther does not believe

---

Box 28 Logical Positivism

One particular version of verificationism has a very special place in the history of philosophy. Logical positivism arose in the 1920s from the work of the "Vienna Circle" of philosophers, psychologists, and mathematicians. (Prominent among them were Otto Neurath, Mauritz Schlick, and Rudolf Carnap. A book arising out of their tradition that is still widely read is A. J. Ayer's *Language, Truth, and Logic*.) The most striking claim of logical positivism was that much of what had been previously thought of as deep and important philosophy, theology, or even science was really nonsense. That is, we often waste our time thinking hard about things that could not really be either true or false, as they do not have any definite meaning at all. To show this, logical positivists combined the recently invented symbolic logic – an artificial language in which ambiguities like the scope ambiguities of Section 15.5 cannot occur – with a verificationist attitude to meaning. This results in the logical positivist *criterion of significance*: a proposition is meaningful only if it can be either established or refuted.

Claims that could not ever be established or refuted are not worth thinking about, according to logical positivism. Most religious claims could never be established or refuted, so both religious belief and atheism are nonsense. Atheism is as nonsensical as religious belief, according to logical positivism, because it says that religious beliefs are false. But they are not false; they are nonsense. Positivism thus creates a more troubling and more subversive enemy for religion than traditional atheism. (A horrifying consequence for Bishop Berkeley, who started the whole thing to head off a danger to religion.) For traditional atheism engages religion with deep and serious debate; positivism refuses to take it seriously.

Logical positivism is no longer a live doctrine, mainly because arguments such as those of Quine have undermined the verificationism on which it depends. But its effects are permanent. Many contemporary philosophers, especially those influenced by Ludwig Wittgenstein, are haunted by the thought that much of what they say may be neither true nor false but nonsense, verbal junk. The fear of nonsense is no doubt a healthy thing, but it may not be the philosophers as much as the critics of art and literature, the advertisers, and the politicians, who ought to be haunted by it.

a large number of other things, for example, that light travels in straight lines or that one end of a compass needle always points north and the other south. (Note that these beliefs as I have stated them are not precisely true: a clever flat-earther can find lots of room for quibbling. See Chapter 1, Section 7.) So if we want to define the meaning of "the earth is flat" in the way suggested by verificationism we run into problems. Verificationism assumes that "the earth is flat" predicts things like: any part of a distant object (such as a ship on the horizon) will be as visible as any other part, ships traveling due west will reach the end of the earth, and so on. And these predictions, or others even nearer to bare observation, will then be the meaning of the sentence (and the content of the belief). But in fact none of these consequences does follow from "the earth is flat" taken in isolation. They only follow from it when it is joined to a complex of other beliefs. So verificationism is trying to explain the meaning of sentences and the content of beliefs in terms of something that individual sentences and beliefs do not have.

Assume, with most contemporary philosophers, that simple crude verificationism is wrong. That does not mean that Berkeley's ghost is fully exorcized. For there is still a troubling question in the air. How can we have complicated beliefs about things that cannot be observed, and whose truth would be very hard to establish? How can we tell which of these beliefs really might be meaningful and which are just empty words? Those are very fundamental and difficult questions.

15.7 Instrumentalism versus Realism

Suppose that you are depressed and have a choice of three therapists who may help you with your difficulties. The first therapist believes that psychological difficulties are caused by traumatic events in early childhood. Her therapy is based on recovering memories from childhood and creating fantasies of childhood and discovering ways the patient can tell the story of their life so as to evoke healing emotions. The second therapist believes that psychological difficulties are caused by the words and pictures in which people present problems in their adult lives. So his therapy is based on creating a new set of pictures and a new set of descriptions which the patient can use in order to think differently about the present. The third therapist believes that psychological difficulties are caused by disorders in brain chemistry, and his therapy is based on prescribing medicines to his patients. Each therapist describes the other therapists' beliefs as rubbish.

How should you decide which therapist to choose? One question you might ask is: "Which therapist's beliefs are true?" This may be a hard question to answer, but you might get advice from experts in the field. Another question you might ask is: "Which therapist gets good results? Which one helps patients with their difficulties in living?" Suppose that the answer to this last question is "All of them." Then you may feel much less interested in knowing which one's therapy is based on true beliefs.

In fact, if you know that different theories about what causes psychological difficulties, and how to alleviate them, all work, you may find yourself wondering if the question "Which one is true?" makes sense. Although the therapists say each other's theories are wrong, what is to decide whether they are right or wrong besides the test of whether they get the desired results? To think this is to take an instrumental attitude to beliefs about therapy.

Instrumentalism is the result of applying verificationism to science. Instrumentalism says that scientific theories are devices for explaining and predicting observable data. We should judge them only by how well they do this job. Truth, plausibility, and consistency with other theories do not matter.

> Instrumentalism says that scientific theories are data-predicting devices. Realism says that they are literally true or false, and could be false however well they predict data.

Instrumentalism can be supported with subtle arguments about meaning. But a simple reason for it comes from asking: why do we want scientific theories? Part of the answer must be that we want them for their practical applications. We want to know what medicines are effective against what diseases, how electronic devices will behave under various conditions, what therapies will help us with our difficulties, and so on. But all these practical matters turn on what observable phenomena will occur under what conditions. So the truth of a whole scientific theory is not in itself practically relevant: all that matters is the truth of its observable consequences.

Practical applications are not everything. We also want simply to have our curiosity satisfied. We want to know why things happen. But what is it for a theory to explain why things happen? One answer is that it is for it to fit them into intellectually satisfying patterns, to make sense of a variety of phenomena by grouping them together into a simple unity. If a theory does this why should we ask further that it is true? Don't we in fact call a theory "true" precisely when it does explain and predict data in an intellectually satisfying way? The world does not have to have any deep resemblance to the theory's description of it – there don't actually have to be any viruses or quarks – as long as it works.

That is an extreme view. The extreme opposite view is *scientific realism.* It says that some theories really are literally and objectively true and others literally and objectively false. Moreover, a theory could turn out to be false even though it was a very good predicting and explaining device. Perhaps our current theories are false even though they predict and explain very well.

One problem scientific realism immediately faces is that of intelligibility: does it make sense? What is this "really are literally and objectively" business? The standard reply is "something more than explanatory and predictive success." That is, scientific realists point out how we usually want more of a theory than that it be a good prediction-giving device. For example, we want different theories that we accept to be consistent with one another. Suppose that theory A gives good predictions and so does theory B, but A is inconsistent with B. (The inconsistency would have to be in what they say about things that are not observable.) Scientists would take this to be a worrying situation: both theories cannot be true, so we should try to find out whether one or both of them is false. But if predictions are all that matter, we should shrug our shoulders and say: so what?

The contrast between instrumentalism and scientific realism can be brought out by considering how they treat three rather wild possibilities about science.

Two equally good theories   There might be two completely different theories of some basic science, for example, fundamental physics, both of which explained all the evidence we have and were not refuted by any counterevidence. They might be so different that if either one was true the other would have to be false, but we might never be able to find any evidence to decide between them.

All our theories might be false   Although we may find better and better scientific theories and although they may seem to be getting nearer and nearer to the truth, it may be that in fact the truth is completely different from any theory human beings will ever have.

Different ways of seeing the world   Some other culture might have a completely different way of perceiving and thinking. The way they see the world around them and the way they explain what they see might work in terms of concepts so different from those used in science that there is no way of translating what they think into scientific terms. And yet their concepts and beliefs might allow them to understand things that scientists never will grasp.

Instrumentalism and scientific realism have very different attitudes to these three possibilities. These can be represented in a chart.

	According to instrumentalism	According to scientific realism
Two equally good theories	Impossible	Possible
All our theories might be false	Impossible	Possible
Different ways of seeing	Possible	Impossible

(You may find it surprising that instrumentalism denies *equally good theories*. But notice that the full description of it says that if the one theory is true the other has to be false, and instrumentalism does not agree with this.)

Return now to the example at the beginning of this section, of the opposing but effective therapies for depression. Here are some points that realists and instrumentalists about therapy could use against one another.

(i)   If all these theories are good theories then we ought to believe all of them. But that would be absurd.

(ii) The only evidence that is relevant is about what helps troubled people, and so there is no way of discovering a "truth" here.

(iii) In the scientific picture of the world there may be only one truth, but theory may require a different picture of the world.

(iv) Although the theories may be equally good as guides to therapy, they may say different things outside the topic of therapy. For example, we may be able to use them to make different predictions about what films people will be depressed or comforted by. We should try to find such predictions so we can think out which ones to believe.

In a group, each person could indicate which of (i)–(iv) he or she finds plausible. Then other people could classify that person as an instrumentalist or a realist about psychotherapy. Do you accept your classification?

Consider the following claims about theories and what they explain.

(a) A belief doesn't really explain unless it is true.

(b) Concepts are just tools and we can use very different tools.

(c) The theories we actually have do successfully predict many things.

(d) Theories making the same predictions will mean the same thing.

(e) Truth is prediction.

(f) Different concepts can explain different things.

(g) If two theories have the same meaning then either both are true or both are false.

(h) The beliefs in a nonscientific culture will not be true.

Which of these points could be used by an instrumentalist and which by a scientific realist? Which ones could be used to justify which of the possible/impossible conclusions in the table above?

If the theories in question are theories about basic physics, which of (a)–(h) do you agree with? Does this make you a realist or an instrumentalist about basic physics? Is this the same as your position about psychotherapy? What does it suggest if it is not the same?

15.8 First Case Study: Crystal Spheres

From the time of the Greek astronomer Ptolemy in the second century, astronomers believed in a theory of the universe in which the earth occupied a central place and was surrounded by a number of spheres. These were often described as "crystal spheres," as they had to be transparent for light from the sun and stars to shine through them. The sun and the planets were located on the inner spheres and as the spheres turned they rotated around the earth. The outermost sphere contained the stars; it also rotated. By setting the right speeds for the spheres to rotate Ptolemy and later astronomers into the late Middle Ages could predict fairly well the positions of the stars and planets in the sky. Their theories were useful to sailors who needed to be able to tell the time and locate themselves far from home. The fit between what the theory could predict and what astronomers observed in the sky was not perfect. In particular, the way in which planets move in the sky was very hard to explain. To get more precise predictions astronomers invented "epicycles," smaller spheres located on the crystal spheres. If a planet was located on an epicycle and it turned on the larger sphere while the larger sphere turned around the earth, then the predicted motions would be much more like the actual movements of planets.

The first scientist to doubt this theory was Copernicus in the sixteenth century. He wrote a book in which he explained that if the sun rather than the earth was put in the center of the universe, and the earth revolved around it, then fewer epicycles would be needed to get predictions which match the observed motions of the planets. A preface to the book, not by Copernicus, pointed out that in order to get these simpler predictions we do not have to believe that the sun is at the center of the universe, just that the observations are *as if* the sun were at the center. This was one of the very first explicit contrasts between realist and instrumentalist philosophies of science.

Astronomers over the next couple of centuries came to accept Copernicus' suggestion that the earth and planets revolve around the sun. One important factor was their increasing power to make observations. Galileo was the first astronomer to use a telescope to observe the planets, and he discovered that planets had moons revolving around them. If the planets had been attached to crystal spheres the moons would have crashed into them. Astronomers had no answer to the problem of how the planets and moons stay in their orbits if there are no crystal spheres, until Newton's theory of gravitation explained the motion of the planets as a balance between their momentum (which would tend to make them move away from the sun) and the gravitational attraction of the sun (which would tend to make them move toward it).

When we think of the history of astronomy we usually think of a primitive belief in an earth-centered universe with planets on a crystal sphere being replaced with a much truer belief in a moving earth and planets controlled by gravity. This is a way of seeing scientific history that makes us inclined to accept scientific realism. So it is good mental exercise to try to see things differently and give the crystal spheres some credit. Here are three ways in which we might take crystal spheres more seriously:

(a) We still believe in crystal spheres. We just have a new name for them. Crystal spheres are what keeps the planets in their orbits. And that is gravity. So "crystal sphere" is simply a more poetic name for the balance between a planet's momentum and the gravitational attraction between it and the sun.

(b) Crystal spheres were a pretty good device for predicting the motions of the planets. And the fact that they did not predict perfectly is not due to their being crystal spheres but to the arrangements of orbits around the earth. If we put the earth and all the other planets on crystal spheres going around the sun we get even better predictions. (The planets will have to roll on grooves on elliptical spheres, actually.)

(c) Gravity is just as mysterious as crystal spheres. Both are simply names for what we do not understand.

Which of these seems to you the strongest defense of crystal spheres? The opposing view is that modern astronomy shows that there are no crystal spheres. What could be said from that position to oppose whichever one seems to you the strongest defense of them?

The preface to Copernicus' book argued that in order to get these simpler predictions we do not have to believe that the sun *is* at the center of the universe, just that the observations are *as if* the sun were at the center. Does this distinction make sense to you? If you find this a worrying distinction is it because (a) you do not see how the observations could be as if the sun were at the center unless it was, or (b) you do not see any difference between it being as if the sun were at the center and the sun actually being there?

When working at the previous section did you classify yourself as an instrumentalist or a realist? If you are an instrumentalist but your response to the *as if/is* distinction is (a), you should think again. Why? If you are a realist but your response is (b), you should think again. Why?

The responses (a)–(c) suggest that crystal spheres were not such a stupid idea. But they do so in different ways. Different ways in which we could take crystal spheres seriously are:

(i) Crystal spheres exist in the crystal sphere world, which is as real as the world of modern astronomy.

(ii) Crystal spheres exist in the only real world.

(iii) Crystal spheres exist in our minds, as do all scientific concepts.

The three ways (i)–(iii) are not consequences of (a)–(c), but there are similarities between them. Which of (i)–(iii) are *consistent* with which of (a)–(c): that is, which of (i)–(iii) could be believed by someone who held each of (a)–(c)?

One of (a)–(c) describes a realist position, one describes an instrumentalist position, and one describes a position which while against realism is not instrumentalist. Which is which?

15.9 Second Case Study: Phlogiston

In the eighteenth century chemistry was just beginning. Early chemists wanted to understand what happens when some substances are combined, which leads to a reaction, which leads to some quite different substances. For example, wood is combined with air, heat is applied, and the result is ash and smoke. An obvious idea to use in explaining such things was that the substances at the beginning and end were combinations of simpler substances, which got recombined during the reaction. And that is basically what modern chemists think. But early chemists did not have the modern list of chemical elements, the basic substances which get recombined in reactions. It took a lot of careful experimentation and daring theorizing to get to our present list of chemical elements. In the early days of chemistry they did not even have the words "oxygen," "hydrogen," "helium." These words, and the idea that they name simple substances, have come into common sense from chemistry during the past two hundred years.

One big stumbling block to understanding chemical reactions was the fact that many of them involved burning, or combustion. When wood burns or iron rusts, heat is emitted and some of the products of the reaction are gases. Gases are hard to identify and study, and flames and burning are hard to think of in terms of material elements. Some early chemists tried to understand combustion in terms of a substance called *phlogiston* (sometimes called the "food of fire"). Substances like charcoal, sulphur, or phosphorus, which burn readily, were considered to be rich in phlogiston. When these or other substances burned or rusted they were thought to emit phlogiston. One reason for thinking that charcoal and phosphorus were rich in phlogiston was that in combustion they were totally or almost totally consumed: when the phlogiston was released very little else was left. When eighteenth-century chemists described reactions in terms of the gain or loss of phlogiston the reactions began to fall into simple and intelligible patterns.

The phlogiston theory began to collapse in the late eighteenth century when the French chemist Lavoisier (who was executed by guillotine during the French revolution) discovered oxygen. Lavoisier's way of thinking about combustion became our modern way. When wood burns, modern chemists think of the carbon in the wood as combining with the oxygen in the air to form the gas carbon dioxide. So instead of releasing phlogiston the wood absorbs oxygen, but the resulting compound escapes as a gas. Very often where modern chemistry sees a gain of oxygen, the phlogiston theory saw a loss of phlogiston; and where modern chemistry sees a loss of oxygen the phlogiston theory sees a gain of phlogiston. Lavoisier's experiments suggested that after combustion the nongaseous products sometimes weigh more than before combustion. (For example, rusted iron weighs more than the iron before it rusted.) Lavoisier explained this by supposing that oxygen has weight, so that when it combines with a substance the result is a heavier compound. He challenged the phlogiston theory to explain how combustion could result in a weight gain. Some defenders of phlogiston replied that phlogiston must have negative weight, so that when it was released by a substance the result was an increase in the substance's weight. (So iron might be rust plus phlogiston, and the weight of this before rusting is the weight of the rust plus the negative weight of the phlogiston, which is less than the weight of the rust alone, which is left after burning.)

Here are three attitudes we might now have to the phlogiston theory:

(A) On the way to discovering the truth we have to go through many false theories. The phlogiston theory suggests many things which we now know to be false, such as that there are substances with negative weight, or that burning is the release of a special substance. So it is simply an example of a plausible theory which we now know to be false.

(B) The phlogiston theory is true, or at any rate as true as modern chemistry. For phlogiston is just lack of oxygen. So it is true that when something burns it releases phlogiston – that is, it combines with oxygen. And phlogiston does have negative weight, for that is exactly the same as saying that oxygen has weight.

(C) The phlogiston theory is one way of explaining the facts of chemistry. It doesn't explain all the facts. Neither does contemporary chemistry. Contemporary chemistry can explain many facts that the phlogiston theory cannot, and to that extent we might call it "true-er." Perhaps there are some facts that the phlogiston theory can explain that contemporary chemistry cannot. If so, there is a small way in which the phlogiston theory is "true-er" too.

Two of these can be supported with arguments drawn from an instrumentalist philosophy of science, and one of these three can be supported with arguments drawn from a realist philosophy of science. Which ones? And what arguments? As a first step toward answering these you might consider the following points. (Some of the points might be wrong. That does not matter; the important question is which ones could be used by which philosophies.) Which ones might be made from a realist perspective and which from an instrumentalist one? Which ones would support which of the attitudes (A)–(C) above?

(i)   Our scientific equipment is much better than it was a couple of centuries ago, so we can make much more accurate tests of theories.
(ii)   There's no such substance as phlogiston.
(iii)   Phlogiston and oxygen are both useful ideas for explaining chemical reactions.
(iv)   Oxygen enters into other theories besides chemistry.
(v)   Anything we can say in terms of oxygen we can translate into a statement in terms of phlogiston.
(vi)   If scientists had stuck with the phlogiston theory they would have found other kinds of evidence for it.
(vii)   We now know how oxygen is made up of neutrons and protons, but nothing like this could be true for phlogiston.
(viii) When you believe a theory you look for facts it could explain; if we had believed different theories we would have looked for facts they might explain.

15.10 Arguments for Realism and Instrumentalism

The scientific picture of reality is very different from the commonsense picture. And as science develops it gets even more different. This suggests many hard questions. Can the world really be that way? If we accept modern physics do we have to think of our ordinary ways of thinking as simply a mistake? Are the everyday concepts of space, time, cause, and object – and perhaps free will and personal identity as well – outmoded ways of thinking, that we should abandon if we can? Scientists and philosophers both very often respond to the difficulty of these questions by looking for a very general attitude to science which will guide them through the labyrinth. (Sometimes it seems that they are looking for a simple comprehensive view as protection from the disturbing quality of the questions.)

Instrumentalism can provide straightforward answers to these questions. If scientific theories are simply data-predicting devices then their success does not show that common sense is false. Common sense is another instrument, useful for other purposes, of which the prediction of everyday nonscientific data is only one. Scientific realism can also give straightforward answers here. If scientific theories are literally true and if they contradict commonsense beliefs, then those commonsense beliefs are literally false. This is a dogmatic application of a very crude scientific realism, as dogmatic and crude as the instrumentalism just considered. But it may help to show the appeal of both realistic and instrumentalist views.

Feeling the appeal of a position is one thing, finding a convincing argument for it is another. Here is one argument for scientific realism, followed by one argument against it.

The consistency argument   Very often it happens that we have two good theories, each of which predicts data adequately in its own field, which we find conflict with each other. For example, late in the nineteenth century there was a conflict between geology and astronomy. Geologists had theories about the age of the earth, based on ideas about how mountains and other physical features are formed, and based on the evidence of fossils. At the same time astronomers were trying to understand how stars work. They were beginning to be able to estimate the size and chemical composition of stars such as the sun. They thought that the heat and light produced by a star must be the result of chemical processes such as combustion. But their calculations based on this assumption led them to believe that the sun must burn itself out in less time than the geologists estimated the age of the earth. So either the earth is older than the sun, which was hard to believe on other grounds, or the theories of how stars work must be wrong. Something had to give.

But why should anything have to give if instrumentalism is true? If you have two data-predicting devices and each works well enough to predict its own kind of data, why should you worry if they embody incompatible assumptions? Truth was not supposed to be the aim of the game; adequate prediction was to be everything. So to the extent that we do try not to hold incompatible theories we are committed to thinking of our theories as more than data-predicting devices.

To make the argument more explicit, summarize it in skeleton form. Thus the *consistency argument* FOR scientific realism:

We insist that the theories we accept be consistent with one another.
This would not be necessary if theories were simply predictive devices.
Therefore theories are more than predictive devices.

One thing that the consistency argument brings out is the motivational power of realism in science. Scientists often take themselves to be discovering new areas of reality. When they make theories they try to be able to picture what the reality the theory is about is like. (So applications of laws of nature are usually accompanied by what in the Introduction to Part III were called constitutive principles.) And these depictions of areas of reality often guide the formation of new theories. So whether or not theories are true, or even have any chance of being true, thinking of the enterprise as a search for truth seems often to pay off. (Why should this be? Instrumentalists will say: "That's a quirk of the psychology of scientists. They work best thinking of themselves as discoverers." Realists will say: "It pays off because there is something they are discovering.")

The fragility argument   If science is a quest for truth then it must be truth about the hidden structure of things. The molecular basis of heredity, the structure of space–time, the structure of the human nervous system: things like this are what science discovers. But suppose that we tried to abandon commonsense concepts like "thing," "part," "cause," leaving them behind us as prescientific relics. Then we would find that we could no longer describe the quest. For we could not say that its object is the hidden *parts of things*, and we could not talk about discovering *structure*, because "part," "things," "structure," are all concepts that come from common sense and that scientific theory makes us doubt as it unravels the ideas of space and time. Similarly, scientific realism makes us think that scientific theories are about the reality that causes the observations. But "cause" is another of the concepts that modern science makes us unsure about. So scientific realism makes us worship physics, and physics eats up realism. In skeleton form, the *fragility argument* AGAINST scientific realism runs as follows:

Realism requires that real parts of things cause observable phenomena.
But the notions of part and cause are undermined by physical theory.
Therefore the basic idea of realism cannot be taken literally.

The fragility argument is in a way the ghost of one of Berkeley's arguments against Locke. Locke had said that some ideas in the mind resemble things outside the mind. But no idea can resemble a thing (at any rate, not as science conceives of physical things). An idea of "space" or of "molecule" is only an idea, after all, and objective space or an objective molecule will always be essentially different from it. And in the same way, physics reminds us that reality is very different from the concepts that common sense and human evolution have given us. But the more alien to our way of thinking we take it to be, the less easy it is to describe our relation to it in terms of these ordinary concepts.

This last way of putting the point suggests another argument. Human evolution has equipped us to think in certain ways, which adapt us for life in a particular environment on the surface of a small planet near a medium-sized star. Those are pretty specialized conditions, and it would be very surprising if creatures adapted to that specialized life, and with only a few million years of evolution behind them, were able to think accurately about the whole wide and complex universe. So it is extremely unlikely that any of our concepts or theories, including scientific ones, are accurate depictions of reality. This line is both realist and instrumentalist. It suggests that our theories are about a world which is really there, and richer than our feeble attempts to catch it in concepts. But it also suggests that it is naive to treat our theories as literally true. So the safe way to appreciate science is as an instrument, and when we suggest that some parts of science may be near the truth we are making a bold and risky guess.

15.11 The Last Word

Two immortals, Athena and Zeus, have temporarily taken the bodies of human surfers on a beach in Hawaii. They talk.

Athena: They amuse me, these humans, they can have so much fun, and yet they're so unhappy. Poor short-lived small-brained things.

Zeus: I must admit they annoy me, though these bodies are good for riding waves. It's the way they think they understand things that makes me despise them. I'll enjoy it in six minutes and thirty-two seconds when that one just north of us, the confident one, is wiped out by a freak wave.

Athena: Don't be so hard on the poor dears; they have no way of knowing. For all they know their silly science could be the truth. By the way, can you see that pink cloud eight minutes ago to the southwest against that girl's green bikini two minutes from now: what a combination!

Zeus: Don't make me have to defend them. Some of their science is true. Trivial, but true. If only their physicists could talk to their mystics, they'd be onto some almost middle-sized truth. By the way, that girl in the green bikini is going to meet those two boys who never know where the waves are going to break. They'll find that they were all at the same party five years ago in Miami, though none of them has been there before or since. That's the kind of thing that really puzzles them.

Athena: And they'll waste their feeble powers marveling that they should all now be on the same beach, without even thinking to ask why they should ever have discovered that they were all at the party. Why do they never notice anything?

Zeus: You know perfectly well why. It's because they want to fit everything into their little sciences, and find causes. And they think that if something doesn't fit in it cannot be real. Its like a picture you can turn upside down and get another picture. Both pictures are there, but you have to have the sense to turn the frame.

Athena: Easy for us to see that; we're not stuck in one moment at a time like them. Ah, look at the purple mountain with your left eye, twelve minutes from now, and hear the color of that seagull's cry, 63 seconds ago: great harmony. If they could see combinations like that they'd begin to understand about coincidence and randomness and fate.

Zeus: Let's hope they never do. It could be a real nuisance. Remember the trouble we had with Prometheus. Nothing to worry about, though. They wouldn't understand a word of what we're saying.

Conclusions of This Chapter

◆ Berkeley argued that nothing can exist unless it is connected with some mind. His arguments were based on the fact that whenever we have evidence that something exists, or whenever we think of something, we are connecting it with our minds. It is hard to accept Berkeley's arguments as they stand, but they have suggested similar arguments to many later philosophers.

◆ Verificationism claims that the meaning of a statement is the evidence that would confirm or refute it. This is a development of Berkeley's ideas in that it suggests that a claim that something exists is meaningless unless we have evidence for it. And verificationism suggests that two theories will have the same meaning if we cannot think of any evidence that would support one and not the other.

◆ Scientific realism claims that scientific theories are about things which are as real as the familiar objects around us. It is opposed by instrumentalism, which claims that scientific theories are just devices for making predictions about the things around us, and the objects mentioned in the theory may just be useful myths. One way of investigating the dispute between the two is to see which one makes more sense of the way scientists do science, and the successes and failures they have.

◆ If, unlike Berkeley, we think that the world is independent of our perceptions of it, then we will suspect that many of our theories about it might be false. In fact, many of our ways of thinking may be inadequate to describe the world accurately, even though they give useful predictions about what we will experience. So scientific realism can be used to argue that we should sometimes think of scientific theories as predictive devices.

Further Reading

Berkeley

Selection from Berkeley in Part II of John Cottingham (ed.), *Western Philosophy: An Anthology*. Blackwell, 1996.

George Berkeley, *Dialogues between Hylas and Philonous*, edited by Colin M. Turbayne. Bobbs-Merrill, 1954.

Jonathan Dancy, *Berkeley: An Introduction*. Blackwell, 1987.

A. C. Grayling, *Berkeley: The Central Arguments*. Duckworth, 1985.

Howard Robinson, "Berkeley," in *The Blackwell Companion to Philosophy*.

On logical positivism

Chapter 1 of Robert M. Martin, *There Are Two Errors in the the Title of this Book*. Broadview Press, 1992.

A. J. Ayer, *Language, Truth, and Logic*, second edition. Gollancz, 1946.

On realism versus instrumentalism in science

Chapter 1 of Paul Churchland, *Scientific Realism and the Plasticity of Mind.* Cambridge University Press, 1979.
J. J. C. Smart, *Philosophy and Scientific Realism.* Routledge, 1963.
*Bas van Fraassen, *The Scientific Image.* Oxford University Press, 1980.

On the history of science

A. R. Hall, *The Scientific Revolution 1300–1800.* Longman, 1962.
Arthur Koestler, *The Sleepwalkers.* Hutchinson, 1968.

On coincidences

Chapter 2 of John Paulos, *Innumeracy.* Penguin, 1990.

On the wider issues

*Ian Hacking, *Representing and Intervening.* Cambridge University Press, 1983.
*Thomas Nagel, *The View from Nowhere.* Oxford University Press, 1986.

Electronic resources

Routledge Encyclopedia of Philosophy (available online at many universities): articles on Berkeley, George; Idealism; Logical Positivism; Scientific realism and antirealism.
Stanford Encyclopedia of Philosophy (http://plato.stanford.edu/): *Berkeley, George.*

Postcard History of Philosophy III

Plato believed that the physical world was unreal and that the true reality was the world of "forms," abstract patterns whose imperfect instances we experience. *Aristotle* argued that forms are not separate from the world but part of it. In trying to explain this Aristotle invented the concept of matter. Later ancient philosophers, such as Democritus, *Epicurus*, and *Lucretius*, argued that the world is entirely made up of atoms of matter. For Epicurus and Lucretius this was part of an argument for a way of life in which the greatest aim of human beings is a sustainable pleasure, using an acknowledgement of our mortality as a cure for the fear of death.

With *Descartes* in the seventeenth century a contrast between mind and matter became central to philosophy. Matter was subject to the laws of physics while mind was entirely different. *Hobbes* disagreed. For him everything was material, and he constructed a system of ethics which did not need any nonmaterial element. Among the empiricist philosophers *Berkeley*, writing in the eighteenth century, argued that the ideas which are fundamental to thought are also fundamental to reality. For Berkeley everything is ideas, either in a human or a divine mind. Berkeley thus invented idealism, the claim that everything is mental. In the nineteenth century *Hegel*, building on ideas of *Kant*, worked out another form of idealism in which human history is the source of the fundamental elements of reality.

In the twentieth century two influential strands of thought were logical positivism and scientific realism. Both of these are unfriendly to metaphysics, but for very different reasons. Positivism argues that assertions which cannot be proved or disproved empirically are meaningless. In some ways it is a descendant of Berkeley's idealism. Positivism was influenced by *Russell's* work in logic and *Wittgenstein's* early philosophy of language. Many of the positivists were members of a group called the Vienna Circle; the most influential of these was *Carnap*. Positivism was criticised by *Popper*, *Quine*, and the later work of Wittgenstein. Scientific realism argues that our best understanding of what the world is like is got by taking physical science seriously and literally. Although positivism is hostile to metaphysics, it does not insist that the scientific picture of reality is the only one, and later antirealist views, such as those of Hilary Putnam and Michael Dummett, also resist the claim of science to give us our only understanding of reality.

Definitions

Below is a list of philosophical terms used in this book, with definitions. The index to the book will say where in the book the words are used. When a word used in a definition is written in *italics* that means that it is either defined in another definition or discussed somewhere in the book. Note that some of these words have different meanings outside philosophy, or in different parts of philosophy.

accuracy: a way of getting beliefs is accurate if it minimizes the risk of getting false beliefs. Accuracy is not the same as *informativeness*.

altruism: acting for the benefit of other people without any consideration of benefits to yourself.

argument: a way of giving a reason for believing something by starting with some assumptions and showing step by step how the conclusion you want to be believed follows from them.

authority for belief: a trustworthy source of beliefs. For example, a good textbook might be an authority for beliefs about chemistry.

background beliefs: beliefs which have to be assumed if evidence is to support a belief. For example, the belief that Mars has two moons is supported by the evidence that when we look through a telescope at Mars we can see what look like two satellites orbiting it, but this evidence assumes as background beliefs that what telescopes show is really there.

belief: thinking that something is true. Most of us believe that $2 + 2 = 4$, that cats give birth to kittens, that the flu is caused by a virus. So there is a great range and variety of our beliefs.

Cartesian doubt: temporarily acting as if you did not believe things which seem obvious, in order to find out if you can discover good reasons for believing them, and in order to discover whether some of them are not true. It is the method of *Descartes*.

categorical imperative: the moral principle that you should always act in accordance with some general rule which could apply to everyone's actions all the time. It is the main principle of *Kant's* ethics. Kant also described it in quite different ways. See also *deontology*, *impartiality principle*.

certainty assumption: the assumption that in order to show that a belief is not mistaken you have to show that it could not possibly be wrong.

compatibilism: the claim that people's actions can be freely chosen and also at the same time determined by physical laws. See *determinism*.

concept: You have a concept when you have a way of thinking about a kind of thing. For example, you have the concept of a cat if you understand the word "cat" or if you have some other way of thinking "that's a cat" when you see one. Concepts are needed for *beliefs*, because in order to believe, for example, that cats eat mice, you have to have the concept of a cat, the concept of a mouse, and the concept of eating.

consequentialism: a way of judging the moral value of actions by weighing up their good and bad consequences. An action is more morally valuable if it leads to more good and fewer bad effects. Different kinds of consequentialism use different concepts of good and bad consequence.

counterexample: a counterexample to a general claim is a single case that shows that the claim is false. For example, if someone says "all cats eat mice" then a vegetarian cat would be a counterexample. A counterexample to an *argument* is a single case which shows that the assumptions of the argument could be true while the conclusion was false. Suppose, for example, that someone argues "all daughters have mothers, therefore all mothers have daughters." A counterexample to this argument would be a family in which there are two sisters, one of whom has three girls and the other two boys. Then in this family all the daughters have mothers but it is not true that all the mothers have daughters.

deduction: a kind of reasoning in which you begin with assumptions and show that conclusions follow logically from them, so that the conclusions have to be true if the premises are. A deduction often goes from a general assumption to a particular instance, as when someone reasons "everyone can be bribed, so there must be some way I can bribe this person."

deductively valid argument: a kind of argument in which if the assumptions are true then it is impossible for the conclusion to be false. We usually think of a deductively valid argument as proceeding step by step so that it is obvious why each step follows from the ones before.

demon possibility: a possible situation which if it were true would mean that you do not know a lot of what you think you know. For example, if everyone had been lying to you all your life, or if your whole life had been spent in a virtual reality machine, then you would not know even that you are living in the town you think you are, or that you have a family.

deontology: a moral theory which classifies some actions as forbidden or permissible however good or bad their consequences. Most deontological theories, for example, will hold that it is forbidden to kill an innocent person even if killing them is the only way to prevent other people dying.

determinism: the theory that everything that happens is caused to happen in a way that makes it impossible for it to happen any other way. According to determinism, if you scratch your nose then given the state of the universe at an earlier time you could not have scratched your chin instead, or scratched your nose a moment later.

dogmatism: the view that some beliefs can be taken for granted and should not be challenged. For example, a religious dogmatist might think that it was obvious that the beliefs of his or her religion were true, and react with anger to anyone who doubted them.

dualism: the view that there are two basic kinds of thing in the universe, usually minds and physical objects.

eliminative materialism: the view that there are no minds, and that we should learn to think of ourselves entirely in terms of the operations of our brains. Eliminative materialists think that *folk psychology* is false.

empirical evidence: evidence drawn from experience to support a theory or belief. For example, empirical evidence for the theory of gravity includes evidence of how fast objects fall downwards near the earth. Note that empirical evidence never proves a theory beyond a doubt; it can only give good reasons for believing it.

empiricism: the view that our thought is (or should be) based on experience. Empiricism can be about the reasons for our beliefs, when it holds that our reasons should always depend on *empirical evidence*. Or it can be about our concepts, when it holds that the concepts we think with must always be based on *ideas* that are found in experience.

epicureanism: an ancient Greek philosophy of life which holds that the best life is based on a sensible and moderate pursuit of pleasure.

existentialism: the view that people face basic choices in life about what kinds of people they are to be, and what they are to consider right and wrong, and that there is no way of being guided through these choices. You just have to face the possibilities, make your choice of who you are to be, and then live with it.

fallibilism: the view that any belief could turn out to be false. This does not mean that there is not a difference between beliefs which we have good reasons to hold and beliefs which we hold just because of, for example, superstition or laziness. But even if you have the best reasons for believing something you may later discover that it is false.

falsifiable: A theory is falsifiable if we can see what kinds of evidence would show that it is wrong.

falsificational strategy: the strategy for testing scientific theories by thinking of interesting ideas which would explain the available evidence, and then trying hard to show that they are false. If a theory survives our attempts to refute it, then we have good reasons to believe it.

fatalism: the view that everything that happens had to happen. Fatalism is not the same as *determinism* because determinism says that everything is determined by earlier events, so the past changes the future. But fatalism says that whatever had happened in the past then what happens in the present is fated to be the way it is. So there is no way of changing the future.

fideism: the view that religious beliefs cannot be established by reason alone, so faith is necessary for religion.

folk psychology: the beliefs about human minds, and why people do what they do, that we normally use to understand ourselves and others. For example, folk psychology holds that people normally act in order to satisfy their desires, choosing acts in accordance with their beliefs. *Eliminative materialism* holds that folk psychology is mostly false.

ground clearing: the ground-clearing assumption is that in order to get beliefs which we can be sure are not false we must first abandon all the beliefs which come from our societies and our traditions, which we cannot be sure are true. *Empiricist* and *rationalist* philosophers both often make ground-clearing assumptions.

harm principle: John Stuart *Mill* stated that no act should be forbidden unless it causes harm to some person besides the person performing the act.

hypothetico-deductive method: a way of getting sound scientific beliefs by first making hypotheses to explain available evidence and then deducing predictions from them. If the predictions are true then we have evidence for the hypothesis and if they are false we have evidence against it.

idea: according to *British Empiricism*, the basic building blocks of our thought are sensations we get when we experience the world through our senses. These are simple ideas (or "impressions"), and they get joined together to make the complex ideas which make up our thoughts.

idealism: the view that everything that exists depends on a mind. So mind is more basic than matter.

identity theory: the identity theory of mind and body holds that what happens in our minds is part of what happens in our brains. So a person's thought or imagination is really something happening in their brain.

impartiality principle: the rule that it is wrong to treat people differently unless there is some good reason for doing so.

implicit contract: a bargain or promise between people that they have not expressed in words, but assume by acting the way they do.

incoherence: a belief or a statement is incoherent when you can show from what it itself says that it cannot be true. For example, if someone says "we are getting richer and richer in this country; soon everyone will have above average wealth" what they say is incoherent because if everyone gets richer the average increases with their wealth.

incoherent desire: a desire which could not possibly be satisfied. For example, if someone wants to be loved by someone so wonderful that they could not possibly love him, his desire is incoherent. If anyone loves him he will conclude that they are not wonderful enough.

incompatibilism: the view that if *determinism* is true then our actions are not free. It is opposed to *compatibilism*.

individualism: the view that a single person can get a substantial body of trustworthy beliefs without having to trust what other people believe.

induction-friendliness: the world is induction-friendly if beliefs we form by *simple induction* are likely to be true. It is induction-unfriendly if they are likely to be false.

inductive reasoning: reasoning which goes from particular instances of a pattern to the general pattern. It is contrasted with *deductive* reasoning.

informativeness: a way of getting beliefs is informative if it maximizes the chance of getting true beliefs (particularly true beliefs on a given topic). Informativeness is not the same as *accuracy*.

instrumentalism: instrumentalism about scientific theories is the view that they are devices (instruments) for predicting observations. If two theories are just as good as each other at predicting what will be observed then neither is a better theory than the other.

libertarianism: the view that since many human actions are freely chosen *determinism* is false.

logic: the study of good and bad reasoning. See *deduction, deductively valid, simple induction*.

logical positivism: the view that much of religion, metaphysics, and philosophy is meaningless nonsense.

materialism: the view that everything that exists consists of matter.

metaphysics: the study of what exists, especially in terms of how the human mind can know it.

moral hedonism: the view that people ought to do what will bring them the most pleasure. Compare with Epicureanism. Not the same as *psychological hedonism*.

moral relativism: the view that right and wrong are relative to a society. What is right in one society may be wrong in another, and there is no way to judge a society itself.

moral status: the classification of a thing in terms of its relation to morality. For example, adult human beings have rights and are responsible for their actions; they are full moral agents. Physical objects like stones and clouds have no rights and are not responsible for their actions. Animals are somewhere in between: they are not responsible for their actions but – according to some philosophies – they have some rights.

naturalism: the view that everything that exists is part of nature. You can be a naturalist without believing in *materialism*.

paradox: a very hard to believe conclusion based on assumptions which it is hard not to believe.

philosophical doubt: a doubt that our reasons for believing something are as good as we might think.

primary quality: a basic physical property of things, such as mass or location or shape. Contrast with *secondary quality*.

prisoner's dilemma: a situation in which two or more people can choose between a cooperative and an uncooperative action. If they both choose the cooperative action they both do quite well, but not as well as each person will if they choose the uncooperative action and the other chooses the cooperative one.

proof: an argument which shows that its conclusion must be true.

psychological hedonism: the view that people always act so as to get as much pleasure as possible. Not the same as *moral hedonism*.

Pyrrhonism: an ancient Greek philosophy, defended by *Sextus Empiricus*. According to pyrrhonism we should stick with the simple appearances of things, which are certain, and not try to make conjectures about why things are the way they are. As a result we should not feel disturbed or uncertain about moral or religious matters.

realism: realism about science is the view that scientific theories can be true or false of real objects and real aspects of the world. So, unlike *instrumentalism*, scientific realism holds that a theory that makes accurate predictions may still not be a perfect theory, because it may be false.

reason: the capacity to think and decide, using evidence, memory, and logic to discover what is true and what we should do.

reflective equilibrium: if our general beliefs about right and wrong and our reactions to particular moral problems could ever be changed so that there were no conflicts between them, they would be in reflective equilibrium. It is discussed by John *Rawls*.

relativism: the view that "humanity is the measure of all things," that anything you believe is true for you.

secondary quality: properties things have in our experience which are not basic physical properties, for example, colors and smells.

simple induction: suppose that all observed things of one kind have been of some other kind, then simple induction suggests believing that all things of the first kind are of the other kind. For example, all cats that we have seen have whiskers, so we believe that all cats that there will ever be will have whiskers.

skepticism: the view that we can know very little.

state of nature: the imaginary situation in which people have no social rules and each person struggles against each other for survival and gain. It is discussed by Thomas *Hobbes*.

syllogism: a pattern of deductive reasoning in which the words "all" and "some" are central. For example, the syllogism "all cats have whiskers; anything with whiskers has a nose; therefore all cats have noses."

traditionalism: the philosophy of accepting beliefs which people in your society normally believe.

utilitarianism: the view that an action is right when it produces the greatest balance of pleasure over pain among all people it affects. See *consequentialism, deontology*.

utility: the balance of good over bad effects of an action. See *utilitarianism, consequentialism*.

verificationism: the theory that the meaning of a sentence is the evidence which might show that it was true.

vitalism: the view that living things are fundamentally different from non-living things, so that physics and chemistry alone cannot explain life.

Index

Abraham and Isaac problem, 338–40
accomplishment, value of, 383, 391, 392, 393–4
accuracy versus informativeness, 247–9, 252, 274, 281
actions
  and emotion, 150, 151–2, 156
  free will, 373–82
  harm principle, 163–5
  reasons for, 328
  rightness of, 3, 4
  see also behavior; folk psychology; Kantian ethics; utilitarianism
alternative belief systems, 8, 9
alternative medicine, 219–20
altruism, 179–80, 186, 189, 391
animals, 290, 304, 360
anomalies, 272–3
Anselm of Canterbury, 54
antidepressants, 326–7
Aquinas *see* Thomas Aquinas
argument from analogy, 250–3, 255–6
argument from explanation *see* folk psychology
arguments, 41, 42–7, 57, 60
  existence of God, 49–54
  hidden premises, 85–6
  ontological, 54, 57
  paradoxes, 54–5
  reasons for belief, 406–7, 409–12
  skeleton form of, 43–5, 51
  sub-arguments, 48–9
  tree form, 43
  validity, 45, 49, 131–3, 134–7, 138–40
  see also inductive reasoning
Aristotle, 37, 63–4, 139, 170, 222–3, 305, 429
astrology, 261–2

atheism, 414
Austrian economic school, 196
authority for belief, 36–9, 57, 60
  and Descartes, 66
  and Kant, 201
  and sacred books, 36, 38, 41, 78, 117
awful cultures, 106, 109–10
Ayer, A. J., 414

background beliefs, 281–2, 285–6, 301–2, 308
  inference to the best explanation, 257, 262
  moral status, 286–90
  probability theory, 282–4
Bacon, Francis, 305
Bayes' theorem, 286
Beauvoir, Simone de, 114–15, 170
beliefs, 230–3
  alternative systems, 8, 9
  content of, 412–14
  conventionalism, 7–9
  cultural, 36, 47, 60
  eliminative materialism, 332–3
  and perception, 264–7, 281
  philosophical sense of, 11
  religious, 39–40, 78, 201, 222, 414
  scientific, 19, 246
  suspension of, 67
  see also background beliefs; closed-belief trap; commonsense beliefs
benevolence, 91, 92, 152
Bentham, Jeremy, 182–3, 184–5, 186, 305
Berkeley, George
  idealism, 224, 305, 369, 404–12, 414, 425, 429
  on matter, 404–5, 408, 412–13
  verificationism, 413